Ido Baum

Professional Testimonial Privileges

GABLER EDITION WISSENSCHAFT

Ökonomische Analyse des Rechts

Herausgegeben von
Professor Dr. Peter Behrens
Professor Dr. Thomas Eger
Professor Dr. Manfred Holler
Professor Dr. Claus Ott
Professor Dr. Hans-Bernd Schäfer (schriftführend)
Universität Hamburg, Fakultät für Rechtswissenschaft und Fakultät für Wirtschafts- und Sozialwissenschaft

Die ökonomische Analyse des Rechts untersucht Rechtsnormen auf ihre gesellschaftlichen Folgewirkungen und bedient sich dabei des methodischen Instrumentariums der Wirtschaftswissenschaften, insbesondere der Mikroökonomie, der Neuen Institutionen- und Konstitutionenökonomie. Sie ist ein interdisziplinäres Forschungsgebiet, in dem sowohl Rechtswissenschaftler als auch Wirtschaftswissenschaftler tätig sind und das zu wesentlichen neuen Erkenntnissen über Funktion und Wirkungen von Rechtsnormen geführt hat.

Die Schriftenreihe enthält Monographien zu verschiedenen Rechtsgebieten und Rechtsentwicklungen. Sie behandelt Fragestellungen aus den Bereichen Wirtschaftsrecht, Vertragsrecht, Haftungsrecht, Sachenrecht und verwaltungsrechtliche Regulierung.

Ido Baum

Professional Testimonial Privileges

A Law and Economics Perspective

With a Foreword by Prof. Dr. Hans-Bernd Schäfer

GABLER EDITION WISSENSCHAFT

Bibliographic information published by the Deutsche Nationalbibliothek
The Deutsche Nationalbibliothek lists this publication in the Deutsche Nationalbibliografie; detailed bibliographic data are available in the Internet at http://dnb.d-nb.de.

Dissertation Universität Hamburg, 2008

1st Edition 2008

Editorial Office: Frauke Schindler / Anita Wilke

Gabler is part of the specialist publishing group Springer Science+Business Media.
www.gabler.de

Cover design: Regine Zimmer, Dipl.-Designerin, Frankfurt/Main
Printed on acid-free paper
Printed in Germany

ISBN 978-3-8349-1341-8

Foreword

This work contributes to a field in the literature of law & economics in which little research has been done thus far namely the relationship between corporate law and procedural law such as the rules of evidence and of civil procedure.

As the reader will discover in the following pages, attorneys, accountants, and journalists, each play an important role in promoting corporate compliance with the law as gatekeepers and monitors against wrongdoing. Ido Baum evaluates the importance of the professional testimonial privilege - a rule that allows the professional to refrain from testifying with regard to information received from his client - in promoting this objective. He does so by looking at the efficient performance of the professional privilege in the United States, England, and Germany while taking into account systemic differences such as the starkly different civil procedure regimes and the structural differences in corporate ownership and control in the capital markets of the compared jurisdictions.

Focusing on the relationship between the corporate counsel and the corporation, this book provides new insights into the internal effects of the corporate lawyer-client privilege on corporate decision-making. For example, it is shown that the narrow application of the privilege in some US states creates an inefficient incentive to inflate corporate boards in order to reduce the exposure to sanctions for corporate malfeasance.

As accounting standards are converging around the world, the author provides some warnings with respect to situations in which accountants and lawyers choose to work together. Especially interesting to German legislators is the conclusion presented here that granting a professional privilege to combined accountancy and lawyer firms would not be a desirable move when accountancy firms tend to present pro-active consulting behaviour that stretches the boundaries of the law.

Finally, in a chapter on the reporter's privilege, this work offers the first model-based comparison of the American and English rules with regard to compelling the revelation of confidential media sources and shows that the American rule is somewhat superior to the English one in maximizing the amount of truthful information available to the capital market.

The following pages make a valuable contribution to the intensive and ongoing discussion both in the United States and in Europe regarding the efficiency of corporate governance mechanisms and the importance of regulating professional groups. The book is a valuable and highly readable contribution to law and economics and it provides new and important insights. It also shows that it is impossible to understand the consequences of different substantive norms without taking into account the underpinning procedural rules. The book is interesting for all scholars in law and economics, as it provides a thorough economic analysis of the consequences of legal norms regulating professional testimonial privileges. It is especially recommended to those who are interested in institutions designed to improve corporate governance.

Prof. Dr. Hans-Bernd Schäfer

Acknowledgements

This dissertation would not have been written without the support and advice of Professor Hans-Bernd Schäfer, who introduced me to the field of Law and Economics and insisted on fortifying my knowledge of formal methods. I especially appreciate his ongoing personal and unique support of Israeli-German academic exchanges, without which I would not have had the opportunity to become part of this unusual academic bridge.

Additionally, my gratitude goes to Thomas Eger, Eberhard Feess, Jesse Fried, Oren Gazal-Eyal, Mark Grady, Avery Katz, Francesco Parisi, Eli Salzberger, and Ansgar Wohlschlegel, for their helpful support, advice, and insights during my research process.

I cherish three vibrant years of intensive academic discourse in the wonderful atmosphere of the Graduate College Law & Economics at Hamburg University. This time shall remain forever vivid in my memory thanks to each and every member of the college, with special regard to my dearest friend and office-partner, Thorben Rein. In addition, I had the pleasure of conducting research as a visiting scholar at Boalt Hall School of Law at the University of California (Berkeley) and my gratitude goes to Robert Cooter for making this possible.

The decision of an Israeli scholar to conduct his doctoral studies in Germany is unusual. Without the initial support of Stephan Vopel and the strong ongoing friendship of the members of the German-Israeli Young Leaders Exchange Programme of the Bertelsmann Foundation – it would never have happened. For that I am sincerely grateful.

My passion for legal studies and the stamina to pursue them I owe my parents and my grandparents and I shall forever be in their debt.

This book is dedicated to Lena, with love.

Ido Baum

Content

List of Abbreviations

ABA	American Bar Association
AICPA	American Institute of Certified Public Accountants
AktG	AktienGesetz
AO	AbgabeOrdnung
BGB	Bürgerliches GesetzBuch
BGH	BundesGerichtsHof
BOE	Bank of England
BRAO	BundesRechtsAnwaltOrdnung
BVerfG	BundesVerfassungsGericht
CCBE	Council of Bars and Law Societies of Europe
ECHR	European Court of Human Rights
ECJ	European Court of Justice
EU	European Union
FASB	Financial Accounting Standards Board
GG	GrundGesetz
HGB	HandelsGesetzBuch
IASB	International Accounting Standards Board
IASC	International Accounting Standards Committee
IRS	Internal Revenue service
MDP	Multi Disciplinary Practice
PCAOB	The Public Company Accounting Oversight Board
PubG	PublikationsGesetz
SEC	Securities Exchange Commission
SOX	Sarbanes Oxley

StGB	StrafGesetzBuch
StPO	StrafProzessOrdnung
SW	Social Welfare
UK	England
US	United States
UWG	Unlauteren Wettbewerb Gesetz
WiPrO	WirtschaftsPrüferOrdnung
WpHG	WertpapierHandelsGesetz
ZPO	ZivilProzessOrdnung

List of Figures

List of Tables

Introduction

I. Overview

When should society protect secrets? This question will come up in various forms throughout the course of this dissertation, which focuses on the professional testimonial privileges of lawyers, accountants (auditors) and reporters in the corporate setting. The professional testimonial privilege is a legal mechanism that allows the holders of the privilege to refuse to testify about information that they receive in the course of their work. In the case of lawyers and accountants, the protected information originates from their clients. In the case of reporters, the protected information concerns the identity of confidential sources.

Motivation

When courts are deprived of information that is relevant for the adjudication of a specific dispute, the accuracy of adjudication is hindered. Consequently, one party gains an unjustified surplus and the opposing party loses a justified award. However, the effects of inaccurate adjudication are not purely distributional. Courts hand out precedents - norms - which influence the behavior of their subjects. Inaccurate norms create inefficient behavior. It therefore follows that inaccurate adjudication is detrimental to social welfare. Nevertheless, all the legal systems surveyed in this dissertation acknowledge the need to grant professional testimonial privileges. Furthermore, courts themselves respect the privilege and endorse it. One of the reasons often cited for upholding the privilege of professionals is that it promotes compliance with the law. In the corporate setting, it is said to promote corporate compliance with the law. The fundamental assumption of this dissertation will be that the laws and regulations of a jurisdiction reflect the socially desirable behavior. Desirable behavior is behavior that enhances social welfare. It follows that by ensuring the highest level of adherence to the law, society maximizes social welfare.

Lawyers, accountants and reporters claim (or are expected) to have a role in corporate compliance. In a discussion of the preconditions for a strong securities markets, ***Black*** (2001) counts, among other components, lawyers, accountants and the media as fundamental elements of a healthy market. Lawyers and accountants enhance compliance through their role as relational gatekeepers whereas the media uncovers corporate wrongdoing and acts as a deterrent. Indeed, a survey conducted by ***Dyck, Morse & Zingales*** (2007) indicates that the media is responsible for uncovering approximately 14% of corporate fraud cases. Auditors are responsible for uncovering exactly the same proportion of fraud cases[1].

Professional interest groups assert that the professional testimonial privilege is crucial for the efficient performance of their role. As noted, privileges cause inaccurate adjudication that hinders social welfare. It is therefore important to examine whether privileges do promote the ability of the aforementioned professionals to ensure corporate compliance and if so, are the privileges structured in the most efficient way to achieve this purpose. Here lies the motivation for the research that follows.

The law of professional testimonial privileges has received little attention in Law & Economics literature as a field of its own. One reason may be that this field positions itself in

1 The authors found that the no market actor dominates in uncovering wrongdoing. The SEC uncovered 6% of frauds, financial analysts uncovered 14% and most frauds were uncovered by whistleblowers (19%). The role of relational lawyers was not examined.

the nexus between corporate law, the law of civil procedure and the law of evidence. The multitude of laws and doctrines make the analysis difficult. In some of these fields of law there are stark differences between Anglo-American law systems and continental law systems. Yet in both systems the testimonial privileges are recognized. However, there are differences between the legal systems that must be attended to in the course of analyzing the privileges (the clearest example is that Germany recognizes a strong privilege for accountants and auditors whilst Anglo-American systems do not). Therefore, comparative law shall be a central component of this dissertation. I explore the privilege of the three professions in three jurisdictions: United States, England and Germany. These jurisdictions represent starkly different approaches to civil procedure, to corporate ownership and control and oftentimes to other relevant issues such as the conflict between the interests of freedom of speech and reputation.

Key Issues

The key questions raised by the role of professional privileges in corporate compliance can be summarized as follows:

1. Does the testimonial privilege of each of the professions really promote corporate compliance?
2. Do the legal mechanisms through which the privilege is applied serve the goal of enhancing corporate compliance in a socially efficient way?
3. Do the systemic differences between the legal jurisdictions justify the different characteristics of the privileges in each of the jurisdictions? And if not – which of the jurisdictions applies the privilege in the most efficient way?

The following discussion will demonstrate that some of these questions have been answered, at least for some of the privileges, yet many remain open.

Structure

I proceed in three chapters preceded by an introductory note that outlines those systemic differences between the Anglo-American jurisdictions and the German jurisdiction which are relevant for the ensuing analysis.

The following chapters are each dedicated to one issue. Chapter 1 concerns the corporate lawyer client privilege. Chapter 2 discusses the effects of the privilege on professional collaborations between lawyers and accountants or auditors (also known as Multi Disciplinary Practices) in corporate consulting. Chapter 3 discusses the reporter's privilege with an emphasis on civil defamation lawsuits filed by corporations against the media. The last chapter summarizes the conclusions and comments on the relationship between the privileges.

The discussion in each of the three main chapters contains the following components: first, a theoretical explanation of the issue; a comparative legal survey of the issue in the US, England and Germany; a theoretical economic analysis of the issue which includes, where relevant, contrasting different rules from different jurisdictions; and finally, an application of the findings to the surveyed jurisdictions, where such an application is relevant.

The Corporate Lawyer Client Privilege

The first chapter focuses on the lawyer client privilege in the corporate setting. Existing economic models already cast a doubt on the traditional legal justifications for the individual lawyer client privilege. Hence, the first of the three key questions has already been analyzed in Law & Economics literature. This chapter provides a comparative law survey of the privilege and also a discussion of the justifications of the lawyer-client privilege and the critiques of these justifications by traditional and Law & Economics scholars. I then discuss three main issues:

- The first issue is whether the existing Law & Economics analysis of the individual lawyer-client privilege changes when it is extended to corporate clients. I claim that it does. My observation is that due to the unique traits of the corporate lawyer-client privilege, the alignment of interests between the principals (shareholders) and the agents (management) is distorted by the privilege. The potential implications of this distortion on the choice of actions by corporate managements are then discussed. This chapter proposes that each of the legal systems solves the problem created by the privilege differently and I exemplify the proposition by looking at the application of corporate lawyer-client privilege in the area of competition law.
- The second section discusses a previously overlooked privilege mechanism – the rules used by courts to determine which agent of the firm can communicate with the lawyer under the protection of the privilege. Different rules are applied in each of the surveyed jurisdictions and the rules even vary within the US state jurisdictions. Using a simple model I demonstrate that restrictive rules do not yield the supposed efficient results.
- The final section analyzes another mechanism that has not received attention in the Law & Economics literature: the inadvertent waiver doctrine. According to this rule, if privileged information is accidentally disclosed by the lawyer or the client, the privilege is lost and the lawyer can no longer refuse to testify. The doctrine is analyzed through the lenses of economic analysis of accidents. The importance of the doctrine for corporate clients is discussed, followed by a comparative law analysis. I find that in the corporate setting, the more information that is shared with the lawyer, the higher the risk of inadvertent waiver. It follows that waiver liability and harm rules influence the amount of information exchanged between the corporate client and the lawyer. Hence, the quality of legal advice depends on the toughness of the inadvertent waiver doctrine. One finding is that corporate clients can circumvent harsh inadvertent waiver regimes by changing the type of precautions they use, thereby reducing corporate compliance.

Multi-Disciplinary Practices (MDPs)

There is a global trend toward formal collaboration between lawyers, accountants and auditors, known as MDPs. The trend is accompanied by a debate on the risks that MDPs pose for ethical obligations towards confidentiality, but little has been said on whether MDPs enhance or discourage corporate compliance.

The comparative law analysis suggests that systemic differences like the behaviour of professionals and the institutional setting influence the results. I survey and analyze three systemic differences: (1) pro-activity versus passivity, (2) creativity versus conservatism and (3) the rules versus standards debate. This chapter analyzes the performance of MDPs with and without a professional privilege as compared to the performance of unprivileged non-

MDP (informal) collaboration between professional consultants. This is done by modelling a sequential interaction of the regulator, the consultants and the clients.

My conclusions indicate that regulators should be mindful of the compliance implications of MDPs when they decide on granting a privilege to a professional group. The components that regulators should take into account are the proportions of legal and illegal avenues of action available to firms, the firms' knowledge of the law and the conservatism or pro-activity of professional consultants. The striking observation is that when consultants only advise about the legality of the contemplated action chosen by the firm and do not direct the firm to the most profitable action, the higher the proportion of legal avenues the more socially desirable it is to grant a privilege to MDPs. In contrast, granting a privilege to MDPs would not be socially desirable in a system dominated by pro-active consultants.

The model fortifies the institutional approach of the surveyed legal jurisdictions. However, in view of the invasion of American-style pro-active legal consulting to Europe, policy recommendations regarding which professional group should be in charge of German MDPs are drawn.

The Reporter's Privilege

The reporter's privilege facilitates the flow of information from corporate insiders to the media. Insiders hold valuable information that enables the market to monitor firms and punish them for wrongdoing. Some sources leak false information. However, firms may try to deter the publication of negative information by filing defamation lawsuits, regardless of whether the leaks are true or false.

There are two contrasting mechanisms of trial by which the conflict between reputation and freedom of information is solved. In the English Rule, the burden of proof in a defamation lawsuit is on the reporter to show that the information that he published was true (or that he had taken due care to ensure that it is true). In contrast, the American Rule puts the burden on the firm to show that the story was false. The objective of both legal rules is to maximize the flow of *truthful* information about corporate wrongdoing to the public and to maximize the suppression of *false* information. Since both rules aim to achieve the same objective, in this chapter, a model is developed in order to determine which of the rules is superior.

As will be shown, the American Rule is weakly superior to the English Rule in achieving the objective of maximizing true stories and minimizing false stories regardless of whether sources leak more true stories or more false stories, provided that the source's utility from leaking is small. The English Rule is optimal when sources expect high gains and small sanctions from leaking.

In addition to the corporate arena, the model is also extended to political defamation. Finally, this chapter analyzes the German rule, which is an amalgam of the English and the American Rules and I point to the advantages and the disadvantages of this approach.

In the final conclusion I will comment on the complementarity of the professional privileges: lawyers, accountants and auditors only monitor compliance with legal norms whereas the reporter's privilege enables the media to enhance the corporate adherence to softer norms. The substitutive nature of the privileges is also discussed, namely, the need to bolster the flow of information to external monitoring agents like reporters when relational gatekeepers like lawyers and accountants perform sub-optimally.

In the concluding remarks the question of secrets surfaces again. When should a regulator protect the secrets of a party that has divulged information to a professional? The Law & Economics analysis of professional testimonial privileges indicates that the answer to this question can be found by contrasting ex-ante and ex-post efficiencies. Namely, privileges are desirable when the social welfare gain from the confidential communications outweighs the social welfare loss from inaccurate adjudication.

II Introductory Note: Systemic Differences

This dissertation examines the implementation of professional testimonial privileges in the corporate settings of the United States (US), England and Germany. Where applicable, I also take into account additional legal jurisdictions such as the overarching European Union (EU) law in Germany and England, and internal differences in state jurisdictions in the US. In order to understand the Law & Economics implications of the privilege in the legal systems surveyed here, we must resort to some degree of abstraction in the description and analysis of these legal systems as we strive to identify the efficiency advantages of each system and determine which is superior. Having noted that, one cannot discuss professional privileges without understanding the context within which they are applied. This introductory part outlines some of the fundamental systemic differences identified in the legal and economic literature with regards to those legal jurisdictions which are the subject of our attention. First, the different objectives of civil procedure are surveyed followed by an overview of the differences concerning pre-trial discovery and burden of proof. The second part of this introductory note discusses the corporate setting, namely, the differences in ownership and control regimes, investor protection mechanisms and, in conclusion, the tendency toward convergence in this field.

1. Civil Procedure and Pre-Trial Discovery

1.1 Objectives of Civil Procedure

The differences between common law and civil law often motivate comparative legal research, yet often receive only short explanatory shrift[2]. These differences have a significant bearing on the efficient consequences of legal rules. Continental and common law civil procedures differ in three main areas: (1) court organization, (2) temporal organization of fact finding, and (3) different distribution of the fact finding process between the court and the parties[3].

The first two differences are less relevant to our discussion. The first difference focuses on the structure of courts and juries. The second difference concerns the procedural stages of the trial – which are stricter in common law and laxer in continental law systems[4]. The third difference is often described in terms of "adversarial" versus "inquisitorial" fact-finding. The German judge is "managerial-inquisitorial" whereas, in the Anglo-American system the judge is more of an umpire reacting to the expositions conducted by the parties. In fact, US, English and German civil fact-finding mechanisms are all adversarial in one sense: the parties collect the evidence and the courts must conduct the proceedings with whatever the parties provide. In Germany, each party produces evidence to prove its assertions[5], then the court evaluates the evidence and points to lacking evidence which the parties may then produce or not[6]. If they choose not to produce the evidence or are unable to produce it, the result is likely to be a

---

2 For further characteristics of the Common Law see Simpson, Brian A.W., "English Common Law" in **The New Palgrave Dictionary of Economics and the Law**, Peter Newman, ed. (UK, 1998) Vol. II, 57.

3 Damaska, 840.

4 Kötz, 68; Kaplan et al., 1233. The order of proof-taking in continental law is determined by the court on the basis of efficiency.

5 Freckman & Wegerich, 160-161.

6 Freckman & Wegerich, 142.

judgement to their detriment. Naturally, a party's refusal to follow a direction from the court is not without effect[7].

The traditional view of the civil procedure in Germany, since the conception of the ZPO (ZivilProzessOrdnung) in 1877, has been that the objective of civil litigation is to solve disputes between individual parties[8] which have no impact outside the courtroom. Given this view, the efficiency of the procedure – meaning a swift procedure with minimal costs to the court and the parties - has achieved supremacy over accuracy of adjudication. Since according to §1 BRAO, the lawyer is obliged to act as an "organ of law keeping", this view has also affected the role of the lawyer in civil procedure[9]. In this respect, the primary role of the lawyer is to promote an efficient resolution of the case. Accurate decisions are secondary. In the early twentieth century, awareness of the social role of civil justice grew, and consequently the need to promote accuracy in civil litigation gained some standing. This notion has since infiltrated the ZPO and its interpretation[10]. Still, the continental system shows considerable tolerance to the incompleteness of evidence in civil procedures. This situation is explained by the idea that when coercing parties to provide information against their right to privacy and personal dignity, the state should use its power carefully and sparingly[11]. Yet still, the common view is that German civil law is willing to accept decisions that reflect the "judicial truth" rather than an "objective truth" to a much larger extent than what is found in Anglo-American jurisdictions[12]. According to ***Damaska,*** this accounts for the strong formulation of testimonial privileges in continental systems and for the fact that testimonial privileges are seldom invoked. ***Damaska*** attributes these observations to the fact that lawyers seldom interact with the witnesses in a competitive way[13].

There is a long controversy over the comparative accuracy of the German and Anglo-American civil procedures. Conventional wisdom suggests the German system is more efficient while the Anglo-American is more accurate[14]. This discussion has received ample attention in the Law & Economics literature. To briefly mention just a few contributions: ***Milgrom & Roberts*** (1986) show that a decision-maker that intends to promote the welfare of the litigating parties can effectively rely on the information produced by two interested and conflicting yet competing parties, even when he is unsophisticated and not informed of the decision variables. Otherwise, competition among the litigating parties is insufficient and the decision maker must employ sophisticated strategic scepticism. Results along similar lines are obtained by ***Dewatripont & Tirole*** (1999). ***Demougin & Fluet*** (2002) show that a German-style shifting of the burden of proof can produce optimal results with imperfect evidence, if a 'preponderance of evidence' standard of proof is used.

The following simplifying observations will be employed here: Civil procedure in continental law systems traditionally prefers an efficient procedure at the expense of accurate adjudication. Anglo-American civil procedure, on the other hand, strives to find the "objective truth" underlying the dispute, even at the cost of a lengthy and expensive process.

---

7 Kötz, 66-67; Kaplan et al., 1225.

8 See generally Zöller, **ZivilProzessOrdnung Kommentar**, Einleitung.

9 Lindenberg, 54-55.

10 Zöller, Einleitung. For example, the obligation to substantiate claims and to testify truthfully was only added in §138 ZPO in 1933. See Lindenberg, 62.

11 Damaska, 842.

12 See Kötz, 67; and generally in Kaplan et al., 1233 and Rühl (2005).

13 Damaska, 848. At the same time this can be economically explained by the fact that the cost of trying to overcome the privilege is high and the probability of success is very small.

14 Reitz, 990.

1.2 Pre-Trial Discovery

The use of a pre-trial discovery mechanism is a strict difference between the Anglo-American and the German systems. The Anglo-American system is characterized by a partisan method of collecting evidence through a discovery process that precedes trial. Pre-trial discovery is a competitive framework for gathering the evidence substantiating the claims of the litigating parties. Each party may pose questions and require the opposing party to produce any evidence that may be relevant to the dispute. ***Kötz*** claims that American pre-trial discovery is more extreme than the mechanism used in England. It tends to be overbroad, costly and misused for the purposes of fishing, and imposes excess costs on the opponent[15]. However despite these criticisms, US pre-trial discovery is also said to give both parties equal weapons to collect from the opponent the required evidence. Law & Economics literature has shown that pre-trial discovery can be a mechanism which reduces litigation by reducing the asymmetric information between parties. However, some parties hold unequally distributed evidence or have other methods of imposing high discovery costs on the opponent which decrease the welfare enhancing qualities of pre-trial discovery[16].

In the Anglo-American system, a party opposing a discovery demand bears the burden of proving why discovery should not be allowed in the specific case, while in Germany, the party seeking information must show - and this tends to be difficult - why the court should compel disclosure or draw the relevant conclusions from a refusal to disclose.

The provision for pre-trial discovery is almost non-existent in German law[17]. Some limited pre-trial disclosure procedures focus on documents that a party will rely on, yet they lack the competitive and intrusive nature of the Anglo-American process. The German law allows only very limited means of obtaining documents that are held by the opponent or third parties. Parties are in charge of collecting information to establish their own claims and when the information is in possession of the opponent or a third party, the requesting party could either file a separate claim for information (Informationsanspruchklage) or direct the judge to the fact that the information should be in possession of the opponent. The obligation to produce documents is very restricted[18]. The duty to furnish the court and the opponent with documents arises when a party relies on the document in his evidence or pleadings, and the document is in his possession (§420 ZPO) or in the opponent's possession (§423 ZPO). A party has a duty to surrender documents according to §422 ZPO when the document was drawn up in the requesting party's interest, the document records an agreement or negotiations between the parties, business letters or books of account (§258 HGB). The same rules apply to the obligations of third parties to furnish evidence (§429 ZPO).

Pre-trial discovery is said to be yet another manifestation of the polarized balancing of truth-seeking and privacy, which in the Anglo-American system is struck in favour of the former interest, and in Germany, in favour of the latter[19]. ***Kötz*** notes that the extreme balance in the US can be justified by the heavy American reliance on private rather than government enforcement. Private litigants require robust tools of gathering evidence to exercise their rights[20].

---

15 Kötz, 72.
16 See Cooter & Rubinfeld (1994)
17 Kötz, 72.
18 Based on the Lex Mundi Survey.
19 Kötz, 74; Reitz, 1001-1003.
20 Kötz, 75.

Comparative law scholars tend to reject proposals to introduce competitive proof-taking to the German civil procedure. ***Damaska*** claims such a legal transplant will require expanded fact-finding by lawyers[21], which runs contrary to the legal tradition in continental systems where the lawyer is barred from contacting the opponent's witnesses before trial and is also free of disclosure obligations.

1.3 Burden of Proof

The German civil procedures are laxer than the Anglo-American civil procedures with regard to shifting the burden of proof between the plaintiff and the defendant. In continental law systems, the burden of proof normally lies with the party aiming to upset an existing situation. Whilst the opponent has the burden of proving affirmative defence claims[22]. Furthermore the civil standard of proof in Germany is higher than the balance of probabilities[23], with some scholars even considering the burden in Germany to be "conviction beyond reasonable doubt"[24].

When the evidence required for substantiating a claim is deliberately withheld by the opponent, German law finds it sufficient if a litigant shows that this is the *prima facie* situation in order to shift the burden of proof[25]. When the burden of proof is shifted to a party that holds privileged evidence, without which he is unable to substantiate his case, the privilege is rendered worthless.

2. Corporate Ownership and Control

Since much of the discussion regarding professional testimonial privilege in the corporate setting concerns corporate compliance, it is important to distinguish corporate compliance from corporate governance. Corporate governance and corporate compliance are not necessarily one and the same, yet some of the mechanisms that serve to promote the former are also used to promote the latter. Corporate governance employs a myriad of mechanisms to ensure that the agent in the corporation (the management) runs the firm to the benefit of the defined principles (shareholders, creditors etc.). These mechanisms include the market for corporate control (take-overs), monitoring by shareholders and creditors, internal monitoring

---

21 Damaska, 847.

22 Clermont & Sherwin, 248.

23 Kaplan et al., 1245.

24 Clermont & Sherwin, 245.

25 §138 ZPO; BGH NJW 1996, 1826. In this case the plaintiff (the seller) sold a shipment of shoes to the buyer and claimed that the buyer did not transfer all the payment. The defendant (the buyer) claimed in defence that the plaintiff did not provide all the required shoelaces. Since the defence claim was not made immediately pursuant to the delivery of the goods, the defendant could only prevail - according to German law - if the seller was fraudulent. The defendant therefore claimed fraud. The defendant did not substantiate the claim but indicated - by name - an employee of the plaintiff company that was witness to the packaging process and the lack of shoelaces. The BGH held that this is enough to meet the substantiation requirement under §138 ZPO. Thus the opponent could only prevail by presenting the employee and having him testify that the shoelaces were in fact delivered (or by producing other convincing evidence to that effect).

through boards of directors and other institutions, gatekeepers such as auditors, etc[26]. Different governance regimes fit different corporate ownership and control structures.

Corporate compliance however, is concerned with the furtherance of corporate adherence to laws, regulations and contractually imposed obligations or precaution levels. Compliance of this sort may be to the benefit of principals in the firm, but this is not necessarily the case. Hence, mechanisms that increase corporate governance are always desired by corporate principals. However, mechanisms that promote corporate compliance will be desired by corporate principals only in so much as, corporate compliance increases the private benefits of the corporate principals.

Corporate principals in the jurisdictions surveyed here face different structures of corporate governance. This fact influences their ability to exert control over managers in furtherance of compliant or prevention of noncompliant behaviour. These main differences concern ownership structures and levels of investor protection. I therefore briefly survey these differences below, in turn.

2.1 Ownership

The most notable difference in the corporate setting is the dispersed ownership in the American and English capital markets, compared to the high concentration of ownership and control - by families, banks or other blockholders - in Germany.

Becht & Boehmer (2003) show that in most German companies, voting power is concentrated, usually in one block, with voting blocks clustered around important voting thresholds, thus indicating that the blocks are held for control purposes[27]. The degree of concentration is remarkable[28]. Clearly, owners must be extracting a premium for block control in Germany[29].

Even though the German economy is significantly larger than that in England, its market capitalization and the number of listed corporations are significantly smaller[30]. The reason for the slow development of the German financial market is often attributed to a variety of determinants: a lack of sufficient minority protection, ineffective monitoring by banks, the inefficiency of co-determination in large boards etc[31].

---

26 Goergen et al., 1.

27 Becht & Boehmer, 7.

28 Gordon, 10.

29 Goergen et al., 9.

30 Goergen & Renneboog, 15 citing data according to which German economy is 1.8 times larger than UK economy in GDP terms but the number of listed German companies is only a third of the number in the UK.

31 Gordon, 7-9. Additionally, to state broadly, Germany is characterized by a path dependent development of a banking-based capital system as opposed to a market-based capital system in the US and England. One powerful example for the implications of this path dependence is the pension system in the US, which relies on market investments. In Germany, it is not.

2.2 Investor Protection

Conventional wisdom is that in dispersed ownership regimes the main problem is shareholder oversight of management. Meanwhile, in concentrated ownership regimes, the main problem is that firms are controlled by one major shareholder which closely oversees management but which may abuse minority shareholder rights. Thus, regulation in America and England is focused on overcoming the problem of exercising control over management, given that shareholders are dispersed, unorganized and uninterested in exercising direct control[32]. Efficient control by capital markets is reliant on the accurate and timely flow of information to shareholders who then exercise their buy or "exit" rights, which reflect management performance in the price of shares. Controlling for management misconduct, and deterring it, is a crucial goal in dispersed ownership markets[33]. One major concern targeted by regulation is the misleading of shareholders by management, through the dissemination of incorrect or inaccurate information.

La Porta et al.[34] claim that investor protection is generally better in common law countries than in continental law countries, and that inferior shareholder protection is related to higher concentration of ownership in the corporate capital market. They show that common law countries have both, better rights-based protection for minority shareholders and better enforcement of these rights compared to the Germanic and French legal systems. It is important to note that ***La Porta et al.*** do not include security exchange regulation or disclosure rules in their survey (with the exception of accounting standards as a proxy for disclosure rules)[35]. Such disclosure rules are extremely important for private enforcement through efficient markets. There are indications that Germany's disclosure regimes are underdeveloped when compared to American and English disclosure regulation[36].

Historically, Germany had a tendency to regulate the corporate market through state regulatory mechanisms rather than through market mechanisms[37]. The historic introduction of the German welfare state dating back to the Bismarck era in the 19th century - shifting the responsibility for social welfare from society at large to the state - also meant an increase in restrictive corporate regulation[38]. German corporate law gives the shareholders wide power to exercise control over management[39]. This control empowers majority shareholders, but at the expense of minority shareholders who may be abused[40]. The monitoring problem in concentrated ownership markets is not the provision of truthful and timely information to owners. The latter is readily and easily available for a controlling blockholder. Instead, the

---

32 Shareholders do have the option of disciplining management through derivative or representative actions. In the derivative action in the US, the privilege is pierced since the claimant is perceived to be acting on behalf of the corporation. ***Garner v. Wolfinberger***, 430 F.2d 1093 (5th Cir. 1970) Cert. denied 401 US 974 (1971). This tool is further supported by the ability to use representative claims. German law allows for derivative actions and might generally accept that privilege should not be given to the corporation in this case. But German law also contains various procedural barriers (such as a minimum amount of shares that must be held by the claimant) which make such claims very rare. In addition, German law does not allow representative actions.

33 On the incentives of managers that lead to accounting scandals see Coffee, John C., "What Caused Enron? A Capsule Social and Economic History of the 1990's" (2003), at 14 and 24.

34 La Porta et al. (1998).

35 La Porta et al. (1998), 1120.

36 See Möllers (2005).

37 Baum, 4.

38 Baum, 11.

39 Gordon, 22-24; Franks & Mayer, 953.

40 Goergen & Renneboog, 6.

concern is the legal and illegal "tunnelling" of wealth by the controlling shareholders away from the firm[41].

The German market for corporate control is significantly weaker than the American and English markets[42]. Hostile takeovers are not common in Germany. The turnover of German management boards is primarily related to poor stock performance and earnings losses, but less to growth in sales and earnings[43]. Managers in Germany are generally paid less than their US counterparts[44]. Stock options which tie manager compensation to the performance of the firm have been allowed in Germany only since 1998[45]. However, as yet, a clear impact of stock options on the managers' tendency to inflate earnings has not been documented.

The major role played by German banks as controlling shareholders in many corporations is unique[46]. However, the reliance on banks as providers of capital is perceived to be less effective than the market financing approach[47]. Banks are also perceived to have lost credibility as monitoring agents of business enterprises[48]. The main banks are often both the largest lenders (as Hausbanken) and significant shareholders in the same firm. These positions may cause conflicts for the bank when the firm is in financial trouble[49].

Finally, Co-determination which is widespread (and statutory) in large German firms means that corporations are required to have employee representatives on the supervisory board. Nonetheless, the supervisory board is perceived to be inefficient as a monitor. One of the impediments created by co-determination concerns the flow of information. Managements attempts to restrict the flow of information to the supervisory board due to the presence of employee representatives who might use the information in distributional ways[50].

2.3 Convergence

In recent years Germany has been undergoing a shift from state to market control of the capital market[51]. German policy makers are attempting to promote shareholder culture in the German market in order to develop broader stock market channels for equity finance[52]. Consequently, the German government introduced a plan to increase investor protection. One

---

41 Goergen et al., 6. A simple example for "tunnelling" and minority abuse: 51% of the shares of firm A are owned by a shareholder who also owns and is the 100% of firm B. Firm A is the supplier of firm B. The owner can reduce the supply price that firm A charges from firm B in order to maximize his private profits in firm B. The owner will be pocketing the entire surplus in firm B, but he will bear only 51% of the cost of the reduction given by firm A. The rest will be borne by minority shareholders.

42 Franks & Mayer (1998).

43 Goergen et al., 14.

44 Gordon, 26.

45 Shareholder approval is required. §192(1)(3) AktG; Gordon, 27.

46 See La Porta et al. (1999); see also Baums & Scott (2003); Franks & Mayer (2001) at 944, 947.

47 Gordon, 5.

48 Gordon, 5-6.

49 Goergen et al., 19. An example for the impediments for efficient monitoring through banks in Germany is the failed 1997 hostile takeover attempt initiated by Krupp AG against Thyssen AG. Deutsche Bank was consulting Krupp but a representative of the bank was also on the supervisory board of Thyssen. See Gordon, 32, based on newspaper reports.

50 Gordon, 21-22.

51 Baum, 12.

52 Gordon, 4; Goergen et al., 2.

initiative was introducing personal liability for providing false information[53]. Regulation of information is indeed growing, but with less vigour than in the Anglo-American systems[54]. The legal structure required in order to ensure that the market is accurately informed about listed corporations is still developing. For example, in the law on securities trading, §37c WpHG does not create individual director liability for misrepresentation. The common scholarly view is that it would also be hard to establish such liability through §823(2) BGB which concerns injuries to another person's lawfully protected right[55].

Another measure aimed at enhancing market control is that in §161 AktG, German listed companies are obliged to report whether they comply with the German Corporate Governance Code 2002, or explain why they do not. There are views according to which German companies have not fared very well with regard to voluntary self-regulation[56].

In 2004 the government introduced yet another piece of legislation aimed at empowering investors which for the first time will enable exemplary investor lawsuits[57]. Yet in order to be able to act, investors must have information about the wrongdoing in the firm. The means of encouraging the flow of such information from within the firm to the public is at the heart of our discussion in this work.

3. Summary and Abstraction

The objective of this work is to evaluate the role of professional testimonial privileges of attorneys, accountants and journalists in promoting corporate compliance with the law. The need for such an evaluation stems from the fact that these professionals often assert that the privilege is a crucial element in the performance of the functions. Specifically, they refer to the role they play in fostering corporate compliance.

The law of professional testimonial privilege does not operate in a vacuum. In this introductory note I have briefly outlined the backdrop against which the privileges are set in the legal systems discussed below.

The discussion of privileges in the corporate setting combines corporate law and procedural law. With respect to the latter, I have shown that civil procedure in continental law systems traditionally prefers a swift legal process at the expense of accurate adjudication whereas, Anglo-American civil procedure strives to find the "objective truth" underlying the legal dispute, with less emphasis being placed on the swiftness and cost of the process.

Continental law systems (e.g. German law) place a high level of importance on the protection of the privacy of litigants. Consequently, continental law systems discourage compelling the production of evidence which was not voluntarily offered, or evidence which is protected for

53 Entwurf eines Gesetzes zur Verbesserung der Haftung für Falsche Kapitalmarktinformation, 7.10.2004. See also Baum, 24.

54 See generally Möllers (2005).

55 Ryan, 452. The imposition of corporate – rather than individual – liability for misrepresentations may or may not be efficient, depending on other factors. This is further discussed *infra* in chapter 1, section III.1.3.

56 See Hopt (2002).

57 Baum, 14.

privacy reasons. On the other hand, Anglo-American courts interpret evidentiary privileges restrictively since they are perceived to be detrimental to accurate adjudication.

In the Anglo-American system parties are encouraged to collect and explore evidence from the opponent prior to the trial. Continental law systems have almost no procedure for such explorations. Consequently, Anglo-American courts often compel the disclosure of relevant evidence whilst Continental law courts do not. Instead, Continental law courts are more willing to shift the burden of proof from a party that shows that the opponent is better suited to prove a disputed issue.

With regards to corporate law, several fundamental observations were noted. First, that those mechanisms that promote corporate compliance will be desired by corporate principals only in as much as corporate compliance increases the private benefits of the corporate principals. This is true regardless of which corporate ownership and control regime is in force.

Corporate ownership tends to be dispersed among many shareholders in the Anglo-American legal system, and concentrated in blockholders in the German system.

Dispersed ownership has its implication. Anglo-American capital markets face problems regarding the monitoring and control of management, presumably due to this characteristic. Consequently, Anglo-American law contains developed mechanisms for the provision of information to the market and for takeovers.

On the other side of the scale, German law is said to provide weak protection for minority investors in corporations. However, there are attempts to enhance a shareholder culture in Germany that are aimed to increase the participation in the capital market. Some of these legislative actions, primarily in financial reporting and the regulation of corporate transparency, indicate a trend of convergence towards Anglo-American concepts.

Chapter 1: The Lawyer-Client Privilege

This chapter focuses on the corporate lawyer-client privilege. Much has already been written on the lawyer-client privilege in traditional legal scholarship. However, the extension of the privilege to the corporate setting is still a matter of debate.

This chapter proceeds as follows. Part I deals with the justifications for the lawyer-client privilege. Section 1 is a brief expositional outline of the privilege mechanism. Section 2 then surveys the rationales for the privilege in the traditional legal scholarship and in the Law & Economics literature. Section 3 goes on to survey the extension of the privilege to the corporate lawyer-client setting.

In part II the comparative legal situation is surveyed with respect to three jurisdictions: US, England and Germany. The survey focuses on the historical development of the privilege (section 1), the duty of confidentiality and its relationship with the privilege (section 2), the formulation of the rule itself (section 3), the issue of who represents the firm in its communications with the lawyer (section 4), the exceptions to the privilege (section 5), and finally, the concept of waiver (section 6).

Part III analyzes three topics from a comparative Law & Economic perspective. Section 1 extends the existing models of the privilege to the corporate setting. In this section I conclude that the corporate lawyer-client privilege might have an adverse effect of the principal agent problem of the firm. Under certain conditions, the privilege may induce decision makers in firms to choose illegal actions or actions that have a social welfare reducing effect. The structure of the corporate lawyer-client privilege influences the kind of actions chosen by managers, depending on whether the sanctions for the said actions are borne by the firm, the managers or both. The conclusions are then exemplified by the different sanction structure for violations of competition law in the US and the EU.

Section 2 deals with the different rules used in order to determine who represents the firm in its communications with the corporate lawyer. The section focuses on the restrictive "control group" test according to which the corporate lawyer-client privilege applies only when the top managers communicate with the corporate lawyer. The privilege does not attach itself to any communication by other employees. This section produces two main conclusions. The first is that the restrictive rule causes a hidden social loss since firms have a tendency to inflate their management circle beyond the efficient size. The second conclusion is that in jurisdictions that apply the restrictive "control group" test, firms may have an incentive to falsely assert a privilege because mimicking the behavior of truly privileged firms can deter claimants from pursuing their claims. Both conclusions are supported by case law examples and the hiring patterns of in-house counsel in US corporations.

Finally, in section 3, the doctrine of inadvertent waiver is analyzed. According to the doctrine, if privileged material is accidentally disclosed by the client or his lawyer, the privilege may be lost and the court might admit some or all of the privileged material into evidence. The topic is especially crucial for corporations since they tend, on the whole, to transmit large amounts of information to lawyers and therefore face substantial risk in cases of inadvertent waiver. This section applies the economic analysis of accidents to the waiver doctrine. One observation is that the choice of liability and harm rules can influence the amount of information exchanged between firms and their lawyers. Another observation concerns the incentives of lawyers to take efficient precautions against inadvertent waiver. Since only the client bears the harm from inadvertent waiver, incentive schemes must be structured in order to induce lawyers to take care. This section concludes by describing how harsher harm rules imposed by the courts strengthen the ability of clients to enforce the taking of efficient precautions by their lawyers.

Part IV concludes and summarizes this chapter.

I The Rule and its Justifications

1. A Brief Outline of the Rule

1.1 The Privilege

Generally, all competent individuals may be compelled by a court to testify about evidence in their knowledge or possession. The lawyer-client testimonial privilege means that lawyers may not be compelled to testify about, or produce evidence that has been the subject of, confidential communications between themselves and their clients.

1.2 The Characteristics of the Privilege

A testimonial privilege has two characteristics: its strength, and its scope. The *strength* of a privilege is measured by whether it is "qualified" or "absolute". This refers to the power of courts to remove the privilege and compel the professional that asserted the privilege to reveal the information[58]. An absolute privilege cannot be revoked regardless of the interests opposing it. Meanwhile, a qualified privilege can be abrogated by the court when the judge finds sufficient grounds to do so. A weak privilege is a qualified privilege that can be easily abrogated. The lawyer-client privilege is traditionally absolute, or at least close to the absolute end of the strength spectrum.

The second characteristic of the testimonial privilege is its *scope* (or *breadth*). This term refers to which type of information will be included within the privileged material and which will fall outside the scope of the privilege or into the unprotected exceptions to the scope of the privilege[59].

1.3 Who Controls the Privilege?

The professional privilege usually belongs to the client. The client is the "master of the secret". When a lawyer is called upon to testify on confidential information that has been communicated to him by his client, he should assert the testimonial privilege and refuse to testify, unless the client has released him from the privilege.

---

58 For example: the priest-penitent privilege in most US state laws is absolute. The court has no discretion to compel a priest to reveal information that was communicated to him by the penitent in a confession. The journalist's privilege is a qualified privilege in all Anglo-American systems and courts may compel a journalist to reveal information when more important interests outweigh the privilege.

59 To exemplify scope: the doctor-patient privilege covers only information required for the medical service and not consulting one's doctor on preparing tax returns, for instance. The scope of privileges often has exceptions. For example, whilst consultation with respect to the legality of contemplated actions falls within the scope of attorney -client privilege, the most famous exception to the privilege - the "crime-fraud exception" - states that consulting the attorney about how to commit contemplated crimes is outside the scope of the privilege

1.4 The Duty of Confidentiality

The privilege is linked to the professional and ethical duty of confidentiality. Most professions have ethical rules concerning confidentiality that impose a duty on members not to reveal information confidentially communicated from clients[60].

The confidentiality between lawyer and client is a result of both the agency relationship,[61] as well as an implied contractual term in the relationship[62]. It is a duty not to disclose communications that transpired in confidence between the lawyer and the client. The rule of confidentiality is also part of the professional and ethical rules of the lawyer's conduct.

2. Rationales for the Lawyer-Client Privilege

In this section I discuss the rationales for the lawyer-client privilege. As shown below, even traditional legal scholarship takes into account some cost-benefit analysis at the basis of professional privileges. According to this approach the privilege trades-off accuracy of adjudication for more candid communications between lawyers and clients. It seems the trade-off should flexible since the two social values being traded may change from case to case. In subsection 2.1 I propose explanations for the inflexible nature of the lawyer-client privilege. Subsection 2.2 surveys the utilitarian rationale and its weaknesses. The following subsection 2.3 discusses the Law & Economics literature with respect to the utilitarian rationale. Subsection 2.4 briefly outlines the non-utilitarian rationale (further elaboration is provided in subsection 3.2 regarding the application of this rationale in the corporate setting). In subsection 2.5 I discuss the attempt to describe the privilege as a property right, the interaction of the property right with the contractual obligation to confidentiality and the weaknesses of this approach. I conclude with an outline of the "work product" privilege which is strongly linked to the lawyer-client privilege.

2.1 Cost Benefit Approach (Wigmore)

In his treatise on evidence, ***J. H. Wigmore*** developed a four-pronged test for deciding whether professionals should be granted a privilege: "(1) the communication must originate in a confidence that they will not be disclosed; (2) this element of confidentiality must be essential for the full and satisfactory maintenance of the relation between the parties; (3) the relation must be one which in the opinion of the community ought to be sedulously fostered; and (4) the injury that would inure to the relation by the disclosure of the communications must be greater than the benefit thereby gained for the current disposal of litigation"[63].

Wigmore's test embodies a cost-benefit analysis. The third condition requires that the professional relationship promote social welfare. The fourth condition requires in order for the privilege to be justified, that the loss in social welfare caused to the relationship be greater

---

60 Usually this obligation is broader in scope than the professional privilege. For lawyers in the US see Rotunda, 44 .

61 Rotunda, 44-54.

62 Auburn, 58.

63 Wigmore, Vol. VIII, §2285.

than the benefit in the specific case. This formulation calls for a qualified privilege rather than an absolute privilege since it does not overrule the possibility that the social value of the privilege may be outweighed by its value to a specific matter under adjudication.

In contrast to ***Wigmore***'s general view, lawyer-client privilege is absolute. Why is that so? One answer may be that the privilege is so socially valuable that it always outweighs the value of an accurate result in an individual underlying litigation. This is the answer lawyers would have us believe. However it is more probable that the value of accurate adjudication varies and may in some cases be extremely high. It may also be reasonably assumed that abrogating the privilege in a very small number of cases would have only a small probabilistic effect on the certainty of the privilege. Given these assumptions, judicial discretion, i.e., letting the courts decide whether to withhold the privilege where its social value is outweighed by the specific case, sounds acceptable, but there are some considerations that may weigh against such an approach. First, clients may be risk-averse and perceive the privilege to be less certain than it actually is[64]. Secondly, judges may err in their estimation of the value of the case. Thirdly, judges may be biased against the privilege. There are reasons to believe that judges would tend to err in favour of removing the privilege. Judges, specifically in Anglo-American jurisdictions, do not conceal the fact that they dislike privileges in general. Judges have an interest in handing down accurate decisions and may overestimate the present value of the privileged information to the litigation at hand compared to the very vague value of the privilege to society in the future.

Indeed, if we accept the premise that judges as a group promote their own interests, then an explanation for the difference in the formulation of the privilege in Anglo-American and Continental systems emerges. The German lawyer-client privilege has a very strong absolute formulation in the law. In the US and England, the privilege was initially judge-made law. US and English judges are often former trial lawyers and their appointment, election or promotion may be influenced by the trial lawyer community. As such, although they have an interest in accurate adjudication, they are also affected by the interests of their milieu, the group of litigation lawyers. The latter perceive the privilege to be very important for their professional welfare. Hence, Anglo-American lawyers will not lightly discard the privilege even if it is formulated in weaker language in the law or in court decisions applying it. If judges are influenced by the lawyer-group, they will tend to treat the privilege carefully in spite of their inclination to abrogate it. German judges are career judges whose professional path is separate from that of litigating attorneys. Therefore they are less likely to give up the opportunity to increase the accuracy of adjudication. Since their inclination to abrogate the privilege is not balanced by a reliance on a professional group for their promotion, a regulator that is interested in preserving a privilege should - and does - enact a tougher formulation of the privilege that leaves the courts less manoeuvrability.

Another assumption that can account for the absoluteness of the lawyer-client privilege relates to the cost of privilege fights – the procedure of deciding whether an assertion of the privilege by a party in litigation is justified. If the social value of the privilege is only rarely outweighed by the need to reach a more accurate decision in a specific case, then an absolute privilege can save the large cost of frequent privilege fights.

---

64 At the moment, clients seem to hold the opposite belief. Since the privilege is absolute and is celebrated as such, many clients believe that the privilege has a wider application than it actually does. See: "Attorney Client Privilege: Perceptions and Implications in the Corporate Setting", A Survey of Personnel, Evidence Project, American University, April 1998.

In contrast, exceptions to the scope of the privilege represent the mirror situation, where the value of the individual cases systematically outweighs the value of the privilege or where the privilege has systematically negative social value.

2.2 Utilitarian Approach (and Bentham's Critique)

The theoretical rationales for the lawyer-client privilege have changed over the course of legal history. It is customary to assume that the initial (and outdated) rationale for the privilege was the honour rationale, postulating that lawyers are gentlemen and as such they should not be compelled to breach their word of honour. By granting the privilege, the gentleman would be freed of the "lawyer's trilemma" consisting of three actions that a gentleman should avoid: breach the confidence of a client, lie on behalf of a client or remain silent and be accused of contempt of court. Alternatively, the honour rationale can be considered to rest on the claim that the nobility had a right against compelled testimony[65].

In modern times, justifications of the privilege can be divided into the utilitarian and the non-utilitarian approaches. Non-utilitarian rationales include right-based justifications[66], personal autonomy[67], human dignity and privacy[68]. The utilitarian approach has, however, in one form or another, been the prevalent justification for the privilege in Common Law in the 19th and 20th centuries[69]. The utilitarian rationale argues that professionals can optimally perform their professional service only if they are able to receive all the relevant information from their client. It is a three-step argument, applied to lawyers in the following way:[70]

1. For the adversary system to operate people must use lawyers to resolve disputes and lawyers must be able to represent clients effectively.
2. Lawyers can be effective only if they have all the relevant information.
3. Clients will not employ lawyers, or at least not provide them with all the relevant information, unless the information communicated in this relationship can be kept secret.

More recent scholarly work has challenged all of these arguments. First, the stated contribution of lawyers to an efficient functioning of the adversary system is a controversial issue especially in Law & Economics literature[71]. Secondly, the lawyer's need for complete information in order to be effective is a problematic claim: perfect information is impossible to obtain unless one has infinite time and resources. Additionally, clients may not know how to separate relevant from irrelevant information. Hence, lawyers will never obtain all the relevant information but only a certain amount of relevant information depending on the sophistication of the client, the lawyer, and resource constraints. Finally, the claim that clients

---

65 Auburn, 2-7, rejects this proposition.

66 The privilege as a human right. See Auburn, 16-55.

67 Auburn, *id.* Viewing the consultation of the client with the lawyer as an extension of the client's "self" and thus claiming that penetrating this confidentiality is intruding one's autonomy.

68 Auburn, *id.* Human dignity and privacy seem to be related rationales defending individuals' right to protect the information that one is most likely to wish to be kept in secret.

69 Auburn, 14.

70 Zacharias (1989). The same principal is applied to other professions as well. For example, in the context of journalists, the discussion revolves around the fear of "chilling the sources" in the absence of the privilege. If the flow of information from sources is dried - the freedom of information and the freedom of expression are hindered.

71 See Kaplow & Shavell (1989); for a different view see Bundy & Elhauge (1991) and Croson (1997).

will not use lawyers without confidentiality assurances is contradicted by the mere fact that individuals retain other professionals (like accountants) and share confidential information with them even without the existence of a privilege. Benefits that can be associated with the work of lawyers such as their economies of scale and expertise in the legal procedure motivate the use of lawyers regardless of the operation of the testimonial privilege.

The Law & Economics opposition to the lawyer-client privilege dates back to the beginning of the 19th century. During this time, the English scholar and philosopher Jeremy ***Bentham*** applied notions that later became the fundamentals of the Law & Economics approach in evaluating the privilege. ***Bentham*** claimed that the privilege is only valuable to guilty clients since they have an interest in hiding information from the court[72]. In his opinion, an innocent party would be completely candid with the lawyer, since the party has an interest to empower the lawyer with as much exonerating information as possible.

2.3 Law & Economics Literature

Steven ***Shavell*** and Louis ***Kaplow*** have devoted several Law & Economics papers to analyzing the functions that lawyers perform on behalf of their clients, the social welfare consequences of these services, and the effect of the privilege in this context. They observe a weakness in ***Bentham***'s argument, in that ***Bentham*** did not take into account the possibility of client mistakes. A defendant may possess damaging information that he mistakes to be supportive to his case. Conversely, the defendant may possess information beneficial to his case, but perceive this information to be damaging. Both mistakes are a result of the defendant's ignorance of the law[73]. Therefore, in ***Bentham's*** world (absent the lawyer-client privilege) an innocent but ignorant defendant might suffer adverse consequences if he mistakenly communicates to his lawyer damaging facts, and withholds other exonerating information that he mistakes to be harmful.

Many modern traditional scholars accept ***Wigmore***'s position that there is social value in promoting lawyer-client consultation[74]. However, there is no empirical evidence to justify this claim. In fact, given that legal advice and its consequences are, and often remain privileged, it will be hard to empirically support the theory. Aware of this difficulty, traditional legal scholars attempt to dissuade objection to the privilege by claiming that even if the benefits are vague, the cost side of the equation is clear: costs are zero. The reason for that is that the privilege withholds from the court only information that would have been withheld from the court anyway. Thus, accuracy of adjudication is not harmed as a result of the privilege. This conclusion is founded on the incorrect assumption that absent the privilege, clients will withhold damaging information from both their lawyer and the court. In the presence of the privilege however, the client will reveal the damaging information to the lawyer, but the lawyer will prevent the client from revealing the incriminating information to the court. As ***Kaplow & Shavell*** find, in the absence of the privilege the court might still receive damaging information from a defendant that mistakenly believes the information to be supportive to his case. With a privilege intact, a lawyer will prevent the client from volunteering this information in court. It can be concluded, that the more ignorant the client is of the evidential value of his information, the higher the impact of the privilege on the

---

72 Bentham, Vol. IX, 304.

73 Kaplow & Shavell (1989), 605.

74 For a brief survey see Auburn, 61-69.

accuracy of adjudication. Whether the impact is positive or negative depends on the type of the client's mistake. If clients tend to mistake positive evidence for negative then the privilege will increase the flow of information to the court and thereby increase accurate adjudication. If the converse is true, the privilege may harm accurate adjudication since lawyers will be able to prevent negative information from reaching the court.

Perhaps the most problematic facet of the traditional utilitarian justifications for the privilege is their failure to analyze the social value underlying the objectives that the privilege aims to promote. ***Kaplow & Shavell*** criticize the failure of traditional legal scholarship to examine whether the objectives of the legal system are served by the privilege[75]. This raises the question: Even if the privilege does promote client-lawyer consultation, is that socially desirable? ***Kaplow & Shavell***'s reply to this question is not as unequivocal as the reply of the legal profession. Lawyers would like us to believe that their advice enhances social welfare, but it is in the interest of lawyers to foster demand for their advice[76].

A group of Northwestern University professors have confronted ***Kaplow & Shavell***'s arguments. ***Allen et al.*** have developed "the contingent claim" theory along the following reasoning: the privilege increases the costs for opponents in litigation by making it more difficult to obtain evidence. Only if the privilege increases the cost for opponents in discovering information from a party's lawyer will there be any increase in the flow of information from the client to the lawyer. That is exactly the object of the privilege[77]. The privilege affects the amount of negative information that clients will communicate, and the amount of potentially negative information that the lawyer will produce on his own[78]. The Northwestern group parts ways from ***Bentham*** and ***Kaplow & Shavell*** by considering "contingent claims" that is, defence claims that can be developed only after admitting to the initial liability. For example, only after a client has admitted negligence to his lawyer can the lawyer develop a defence claim of contributory negligence. If a legitimate contingent claim exists, in the absence of a privilege it might not be discovered). The Northwestern group suggests that when the privilege does not further the opportunity to develop or raise a contingent claim there is no reason to protect it[79].

2.4 Neo-Utilitarian Approach

The "neo-utilitarian" rationale is founded on the idea that lawyer-client privilege can advance compliance with the law. This rationale was initially developed in the corporate lawyer-client setting by the late US Supreme Court Justice, William Rehnquist, in his opinion in the highly influential ***Upjohn*** decision[80]. ***Rehnquist***'s argument was that the law is complex (especially for corporations) and not necessarily intuitive to comply with[81]. Therefore, clients should be encouraged to share information with lawyers who will direct them to legally compliant behaviour[82]. As will be discussed below, the main problem with this rationale is the

---

75 Kaplow & Shavell (1989), 608-610.

76 Kaplow & Shavell (1989), 599.

77 Allen et al., 360.

78 Allen et al., 361.

79 Allen et al., 365-372.

80 ***Upjohn v. U.S.***, 449 US 383 (1981), 389 (hereinafter – ***Upjohn*** or the ***Upjohn*** ruling).

81 ***Upjohn***, 392.

82 The approach of the court has been severely criticized by Fischel, 14: "The court got it exactly backwards. Confidentiality rules either have no effect or decrease the level of legal compliance".

assumption that once a lawyer instructs the client about the legal avenues of action, the client will indeed follow these desirable actions. No such guarantee exists.

2.5 Property Rights Approach (Easterbrook)

2.5.1 The Economics of the Privilege as a Property Right

As ***Easterbrook*** observed in the wake of the ***Upjohn*** ruling[83], the privilege can be considered a property right in the information it protects. Furthermore, it is a unique property right. This becomes clear if we compare it with a typical intellectual property right: in such cases copyright belongs to the creator of the copyrighted material. He is the master of the right and may dispose of it as he wishes. He may assert the right if he believes it has been infringed. He may also appoint an agent - a lawyer - to assert the right on his behalf. The copyright allows the holder to prevent unauthorized use of the information, and charge a rent for its use. Hence, copyright secures the author's ability to accumulate a monopoly payoff from his creation, and thereby encourages him to create.

The lawyer-client testimonial privilege is however a little different. It was first developed in the context of criminal law. An individual has the right against self-incrimination. This is a right not to share information that the individual believes will support the state's prosecution against him, and lead to his sanctioning. This right does not enable the individual to exclude the state from using incriminating information to prosecute the individual if the state obtained this information through its own efforts[84]. The lawyer-client privilege has often been construed as an extension of the right against self-incrimination. An accused has the right to consult a lawyer in order to develop their defence. If the accused were unable to share information with their lawyers without the fear that the state will be able to extract from the lawyer what it cannot extract from the client, the right to counsel would be rendered meaningless. Therefore, the analogy to copyright is that without monopoly over the information, the owner of the information (the defendant) would not produce the required legal defence. The lawyer is merely a vehicle through which legal defence is produced.

Nevertheless, it would be wrong to characterize the lawyer-client privilege as a property right in the asset (information), granted as a result of labour invested in the creation of the asset. Instead the privilege is granted when the information is communicated by the client to the lawyer. The assumption is that it is this communication that is both privately and socially valuable. Hence, the privilege does not directly promote productivity. Rather, it promotes asset creation insofar as the client that produces the asset believes that he can communicate the asset (the information) to the lawyer and obtain a positive benefit as a result of the reciprocated advice.

This peculiarity of the privilege is particularly evident in civil litigation. A litigant does not have a property right in the information in the form of a right to remain silent - when a civil litigant is called to testify, he may not refuse to answer questions posed to him. However,

---

83 Easterbrook (1981).

84 Stein & Seidman (2000) show that the right against self-incrimination has a signalling value in adversarial prosecutorial legal systems. In such a system, the right to remain silent can ensure that innocent defendants are not wrongfully convicted. However, this is achieved at the cost of releasing some guilty defendants.

when the lawyer of the very same client is asked to testify about information that the client had communicated to him, the lawyer can assert the privilege and refuse to supply the tribunal with this information.

The reasoning that attributes a property right only to communicated information that has both private welfare and social welfare enhancing consequences has important consequences for the type of information that should be privileged. For example, information that is likely to have negative social effects should not be privileged. This explains why most countries have exceptions that revoke the privilege when the client seeks advice about prospective crimes. However the exception assumes that the advice of the lawyer is more likely to facilitate the planned crime than to dissuade the client from undertaking it. It assumes that the lawyer's advice would reveal to the client that the expected sanction is low enough to make the crime worthwhile, or that the advice will increase the probability that the client will be able to escape the sanction. Conversely, however the opposite may also be true. Clients may also be dissuaded from criminal activity after communicating with their lawyer. In such cases, social welfare is promoted by legal consultation and by the privilege that encouraged it. The welfare-enhancing value of the privilege thus depends on the accuracy of sanctions (criminal or civil), on the effective detection and enforcement (either private or public) of breach of laws or obligations, and on the accurate knowledge of the expected sanctions by the clients and the lawyers.

2.5.2 The Economics of Confidentiality as a Contractual Right

Lawyers may claim that the privilege is required to protect the ethical promise of confidentiality which is explicitly or implicitly assured to the client at the outset of the communication with the lawyer. This is a dubious claim.

Confidentiality - unlike the privilege - is a contractual obligation between the lawyer and the client. The lawyer promises to the client that the information conveyed to him and also the content of the advice rendered on the basis of this information will be kept in confidence. The price of the professional legal service also encapsulates the professional's costs of maintaining the secrets of the client. This is in contrast to the legal privilege, which as I have shown above, confers a property right on the holder of the privilege to refrain from surrendering the information he holds to any authority that demands it. A property right, as a monopoly, produces a negative externality on third parties. When a property right such as the privilege is attached to the contractual obligation of confidentiality, the cost of maintaining confidentiality decreases, and third parties, such as the court and opponents, bear the negative externality. This is supposedly done to generate a social benefit. This leads to the questions: Are promises of confidentiality likely to be breached? Are they difficult to enforce?

Enforcement difficulties may arise since the interaction between the lawyer and the client occurs in the present while the promise of confidentiality is to be executed in the future. This gives the lawyer the opportunity to accumulate the rents from the legal service, and then turn his back on the client. Alternatively, the lawyer can extort the client for additional rents to ensure his silence. None of this is unforeseeable from the client's point of view. This being the case, clients will therefore refrain from sharing damaging information with their lawyers. As this would decrease the ex-ante incentives for clients to seek legal advice, lawyers therefore have an incentive to commit to confidentiality. The way this is done is through their ethical rules of conduct. The legal profession is often able to maintain a high level of obedience to its ethical canons. This is made possible since the legal profession, like most other free professions, is often a self-regulated monopoly by a mandate from the state[85]. Thus, lawyers' guilds are reputedly strong enforcers of their ethical rules.

Lawyers also have private incentives to adhere to promises of confidentiality regardless of the threat of ethical sanctions. Lawyers want to encourage clients to use their services; therefore they want to provide services their clients perceive as valuable. First, the more informed the lawyer is, the more accurate his advice will be and the more valuable it will be for the client. Hence, the more information the client can communicate to the lawyer without the risk of exposure, the higher the value the client attributes to the legal advice and the higher the likelihood that advice will actually be sought. Secondly, reputation matters. A lawyer that reveals his client's secrets will suffer reputational consequence – clients will perceive the expected benefits from consulting with him to be lower and his profits will decrease. Finally, but hardly the least important, ongoing relationships affect the parties. The higher the future rents expected from a client are, the lower the willingness of the lawyer to breach the contract and lose the client. This latter argument is extremely important in the context of corporate lawyers. Corporations supply their lawyers with a stream of legal work, often with generous remuneration. If a lawyer believes that breaching the confidence of the corporate client will put a stop to the stream of work and the ensuing rents, he will be reluctant to breach the contractual duty to confidentiality.

In light of these arguments, the need for court enforcement of the contractual obligation to secrecy (as well as enforcement by ethical tribunals) should be minimal. The existence of possible court enforcement of the contract (or ethical sanctions) only further decreases the likelihood that a lawyer will breach his obligation. Of course, courts may refuse to remedy certain contractual breaches, such as a breach of confidentiality by a lawyer that revealed his client's intentions to commit a crime. Such an action would deter clients from consulting with their lawyers about how to commit future crimes, depending on the probability that the lawyer will volunteer, or be required, to disclose the incriminating communication. However, an infinite horizon interaction between the lawyer and the client can solve this difficulty for the client. The lawyer's income from supplying further legal advice in the future need simply be higher than the immediate one-shot gain from turning the client in. In the criminal setting this is exemplified in the extreme case of the mafia *consigliore*[86] whose legal advice regularly includes issues that are not protected under ethical obligations of confidentiality (and thus breaching the confidence of the client would not create contractual liability), but whose confidentiality is bought "contractually" through a sharing of the ongoing benefits of the criminal proceeds, which in the long term tend to exceed the one-time benefit of "ratting" on the mafia-client. One should also add to the lawyer's cost side the looming almost certainly fatal sanction for breaching the trust of the "family".

---

85 Taupitz, 63-67. According to Taupitz, the individuals in the "free professions" were supposed to be "altruistic" in the sense that they had to identify with and promote the most personal interests of their clients. As such, they claimed they needed a mandate to regulate the profession themselves and not be subject to regulation by the state. Posner (1996) adds to this that professional groups may be better suited to regulate themselves then the state. However, as Gilson (1990) notes, various factors may drive quality regulation downwards.

86 The word "Consigliore" comes from renaissance Italy and describes a trusted advisor that took a solemn oath of total confidentiality, loyalty, and discretion.

In sum, concern over lawyers breaching confidentiality as a justification for the privilege seems exaggerated. In many aspects lawyers are amenable to capture by their clients. Insofar as this is true, the law should be more concerned with overcoming confidentiality when the lawyer-client relationship turns into an engine of wrongdoing.

2.6 Supplement: The Work Product Privilege

When referring to the information protected by the lawyer-client privilege I mean the information that the client communicates to the lawyer and also the information that the lawyer then communicates back to the client. The latter is the product of the lawyer's work, based on the initial information received from the client. The privilege in Continental legal systems makes no distinction between the two types of communicated information. In common law systems, the product of lawyer's work is protected under a separate privilege termed the "work product privilege" in the US (or "litigation privilege" in England). In common law systems, the work-product privilege has developed closely but separately from lawyer-client privilege. It is intended to ensure fair play in adversarial proceedings.

Easterbrook suggested that economic analysis of intellectual property rights can be used to understand the reason for the development of the work-product privilege[87]. The concern in adversarial proceedings is that after investing effort in collecting evidence, analyzing the law, and developing legal theories and litigation strategies, all this information will be costlessly appropriated by the opponent's lawyer who will build his case at a marginal cost based on the work that has already been done. Therefore, the lawyer's products - documents, thoughts and theories - should be privileged. Otherwise the incentive to produce innovative theories that will develop legal thought through litigation will be diluted by the inability to appropriate the full value of the original legal theory[88], much like the incentives to produce original literature or music.

Shavell & Kaplow note that the work-product privilege applies to a specific type of legal advice which they define as advice about how to present evidence in court. They contend that in this case the privilege only serves to lower expected sanctions but does not affect behaviour because it is only available after the fact[89]. This claim is especially true when the privilege applies to one side of the litigation while the other side is under an obligation to expose its strategy. This is often the rule in criminal proceedings, where the state has the main burden of proof and is often obliged to share its prosecutorial evidence with the defendant prior to trial. The argument is weaker in the civil setting where both parties to litigation may enjoy

---

87 Easterbrook (1981).

88 Assume that the plaintiff and the defendant, i = [P, D], have equally convincing legal claims. The strength of the claims shall be denoted by x_j. Hence, $x_P = x_D$. Assume the parties are represented by equally talented lawyers. Thus the probability of prevailing in court depends solely on the investment of the lawyers in developing the strategy of how to present the evidence and the claims in a convincing manner. The cost of developing the case is denoted by c_D and c_P and the probability of prevailing is a function, F_i, increasing in c_i and in x_j. If the lawyers have the ability to privilege their work, the parties have an incentive to invest in c_i up to the marginal increase in probability of prevailing in court. If, however, the plaintiff's lawyer can appropriate the strategy developed by the defence lawyer, this party will have better chances to prevail in court since its probability of prevailing will now be $f_P(c_P+c_D, x_P) > f_D(c_D, x_D)$. Since the defendant lawyer can also appropriate the work of his opponent, neither party has an incentive to invest in c_j at all, in the absence of the privilege.

89 For a critique of this view, stressing the value created by the use of lawyers in an adversarial system see Bundy & Elhauge (1991).

the privilege and the benefits for each party from withholding information from the opponent are likely to offset each other. Of course, when parties are not equal, or when one type of opponents has systematically more information hidden under the veil of the privilege, benefits accrue to this party.

In their work, the Northwestern group rejected, at least partially, ***Easterbrook***'s idea that work-product privilege serves as a sort of copyright. In their view the copyright effect is a mere by-product of the privilege. They postulate that when lawyers produce evidence, theory and strategy, the result may be both harmful and useful for the client. Absent a privilege, all the information that the lawyer produces will be available to opponents. Since the client does not know which information will be produced by the lawyer's work, the expected total private benefit of this information to the client is zero, since the gain from any beneficial strategy that is developed by the lawyer is offset by the losses from any harmful strategy. In such cases, the client would prefer not hire a lawyer at all. By privileging the lawyer's work-product and allowing the lawyer to present only the beneficial information that he generated in court, the client is induced to hire the lawyer and promote truth-seeking through the adversarial legal system. However there is a welfare loss due to duplication of work. This arises because both parties hire lawyers who gather the same information and develop the same strategies, but each presents only the results favourable to his case. But then, this is what the adversarial system is all about – promoting truth through deliberation[90].

3. Extending the Lawyer-Client Privilege to Corporate Clients

To date, the extension of the lawyer-client privilege to corporate client has received only limited analysis in the case law[91]. This is surprising, since the justifications for the individual privilege may not fit the corporate client, nor do they take into consideration the unique attributes of corporations as clients or as litigants, and the unique functions of corporate lawyers. This part shall survey the rationales that can support the extension of the privilege to the corporate setting. Note that legal systems that predicate the privilege on non-utilitarian arguments may face rationale problems, such as difficulty in the application of human dignity, human rights, and autonomy rationales to a corporate entity. Privacy argumentation applies only when the corporate property ownership rights in information are stretched to new dimensions. Therefore I shall focus on the utilitarian and neo-utilitarian rationales. I first examine the literature concerning the rationales for the extension of the privilege.

3.1 The Utilitarian Rationale

The objections raised with respect to the extension of the utilitarian rationale of the lawyer-client privilege to corporate lawyer-client relationship are primarily related to economies of scale. Corporations use lawyers more than individuals do and they are repeat litigants. Hence, if there are social welfare losses from the privilege they will be larger in the corporate

90 Allen et al., 383-391; See Fischel (1998) for criticism of the concept. On the other hand, see Dewatripont & Tirole (1999) for a model supporting this perception of adjudication.

91 Indeed, most jurisdictions with the exception of the US have not discussed whether the privilege should apply in the corporate setting at all. In the US, the privilege was assumed to apply to corporations and this seems to have turned into an ongoing working assumption. See ***Upjohn***, 390.

setting. Additionally, if corporations and individuals litigate, the initial imbalance between the parties will only be exacerbated by the privilege. Little analysis has been given to the organizational perspective which will be discussed below.

One convincing and frequently raised objection to the corporate lawyer-client testimonial privilege is that the costs of the privilege are unevenly distributed in favour of corporate repeat litigants, and to the detriment of smaller, often individual, non-repeat litigants[92]. The one-shot litigant expects only a single payoff from litigation. The probability of encountering a privilege which either increases litigation costs or decreases the probability of prevailing in court will discourage this litigant. On the other hand, the repeat litigant, often a corporation, although likely facing the initial higher cost of proving the validity of an asserted privilege, expects a multi-period gain, since prevailing in the first litigation will increase significantly the chances of prevailing in identical repeat lawsuits (or simply deter them by setting a desirable precedent). In practice, this concern can be resolved. Many legal systems have recognized the systematic disadvantage borne by one-shot litigants. To correct the imbalance, legislation often shifts the burden of proof to repeat defendants in many of the typical cases that raise this concern. One typical example is the law governing producer liability for product defects[93]. The resulting effect is that the privilege is no longer a relevant consideration for the party initiating the litigation, since this party no longer needs to seek evidence from the opponent to prove his case. In fact, the defendant might now be concerned about the plaintiff's use of a privilege. For example, if the law allows a defendant to escape liability by proving contributory negligence by the plaintiff, the possibility that a justified defence claim will fail because the plaintiff can privilege the evidence of his contributory negligence means an increase in the defendant's expected damages. The decision to shift the burden of proof is therefore predicated on the assumption that the social welfare loss resulting from increased liability payments of producers is smaller than the social loss which would have occurred had producers been able to avoid liability by using the privilege. In the latter case, any social loss will have been the result of cheaper but more dangerous products, and the consumers would have borne the social costs of the damage. In the former case, producers would over-invest in care, raising the cost of the product. Social loss then results from under-consumption of the product, due to higher pricing. Still, since corporations are better suited to hiding information under the privilege, this seems to be a superior solution. Hence, shifting the burden of proof is the optimal of the two second best solutions in the presence of a privilege, especially since the individual plaintiffs can only rarely use the privilege to actually increase the expected liability incurred by the producers.

Elisabeth ***Thornburg***, an outright opponent of the corporate lawyer-client privilege, suggests that by making information costlier for the opponent in litigation, the corporate privilege amounts to unjustified concealment[94]. In her view, the privilege is especially useful for corporations due to their organizational legal structure[95]. ***Thornburg*** claims that the social welfare costs generated by the privilege are much higher than the benefits of the lawyer-

---

92 Fischel, 4.

93 For example, according to the EU Directive 85/374/EEC of 25 July 1985 (on the approximation of the laws, regulations and administrative provisions of the Member States concerning liability for defective products (OJ L 210, 7.8.1985, p. 29–33)) after the injured proves that the product is defective and that the defect has caused the damage for which the injured is suing, liability is presumed. Hence, the injured does not have to prove knowledge of the defect or any other level of negligence which requires information about the producer's state of mind. The producer needs to prove a defence in order to escape liability.

94 Thornburg, 192-3.

95 Thornburg, 195-6.

individual client privilege. The costs includes, in her view, (1) increased efforts of litigants to discover what information is concealed, (2) more privilege litigation fights[96], (3) excessive use of lawyers to hide information under the privilege, and (4) inefficient application of norms due to settlements, which are the result of litigation being too costly to pursue due to the privilege.

These are valid comments. However in some cases, ***Thornburg***'s arguments are not entirely accurate, especially with regard to her depiction of the cost side. For example, litigants against corporations expect the additional cost of obtaining evidence and the additional costs of privilege fights. To counteract this the social welfare loss caused by these additional costs may be offset by a decrease in lawsuits and by earlier settlements, both of which reduce social litigation costs rather than increase them as ***Thornburg*** claims. This offsetting occurs because litigants are uncertain about the availability of privilege claims to their opponents. When an opponent does raise a privilege claim, the litigant can re-evaluate the costs and decide whether to incur the additional cost of the privilege fight or not. The privilege thus turns every trial, at an initial stage, into a bifurcated trial. The litigant must now weigh the probability of prevailing in the first stage - the privilege fight. In addition the initiator of the litigation must also weigh the ex-ante probability that a trial will be bifurcated (that a claim of privilege will be raised), and the relevant costs it will impose on him, before initiating the litigation. Bifurcated cases can be a litigation costs saving mechanism. The problem with the corporate lawyer-client privilege is that the costs saved by firms are apparently much higher than the costs saved by the opposing individual litigants, which in turn may cause legal precedents to shift in favour of firms, as ***Thornburg*** correctly observes. ***Thornburg*** is also critical of the contingent claim theory. She argues that when there is no contingent claim the privilege only adds costs to opponents, and when there is a contingent claim, trained lawyers should be able to identify it even without any privilege[97].

There is another reason to believe that contingent claim theory is weaker in the corporate setting. The theory claims that the privilege is valuable when the client shares damaging information with the lawyer that enables the lawyer to develop a contingent claim that the client was not aware of[98]. However in the corporate setting the privilege belongs to the corporation and the managers and employees cannot be certain that their communications with the lawyer will not be disclosed as the result of a waiver by the corporation. Rational utility maximising managers will be disinclined to share personally-damaging information with the corporate lawyer if they suspect that this information may be used to shift the liability from the corporation back to them. Surprisingly, managers and corporate employees do not always understand this. In at least one survey, a significant percentage of respondents declared that they would cooperate with the corporate lawyer even when this seemed to be contrary to their interest[99]. The reasons given for this ranged from a misunderstanding of the privilege, to a belief that corporate interests are aligned with the agent's interests.

---

96 Privilege fights are ancillary litigation for the purpose of determining whether certain evidence is protected by the lawyer-client privilege or not. These fights will often be part of the pre-trial civil discovery process in common law systems, increasing the cost of pre-trial for both parties. However, the increase in costs due to the privilege fight is not necessarily equal. It is the party that asserts the privilege that has to prove all the elements of the privilege in order to prevail.

97 Thornburg, 215-6.

98 For example, once the client admits to negligence, the lawyer can develop a contingent mitigating claim of contributory negligence by a third party.

99 The survey was a written questionnaire submitted to employees of "Fortune 100" corporations. The astonishing finding was that 50% of the corporate actors claimed that they would be candid with the corporate lawyer even if their personal liability was at stake. After they were explained the

3.2 The Neo-Utilitarian Rationale

The neo-utilitarian rationale was initially developed in a corporate context in the ***Upjohn*** ruling. In order to evaluate the rationale, I briefly review the facts of the case.

Upjohn was a pharmaceutical corporation selling products in and outside the US (it was later assimilated into the Pfizer Corporation). In 1976, independent auditors working for Upjohn detected suspicious payments by managers of Upjohn subsidiaries abroad to foreign government officials in order to secure deals. The information was relayed by the auditors to the corporation's in-house counsel, and through him to the management. The management decided to initiate an internal investigation, which was conducted by its in-house counsel, to determine whether wrongdoing had occurred. The in-house counsel's report unravelled details of illegal bribes by the corporation's foreign subsidiaries. The report was subsequently submitted to the SEC and the Internal Revenue Service (IRS). The IRS suspected that the illegal payments may have tax implications and ordered Upjohn to produce all the evidence collected by the in-house counsel in the process of the internal investigation. Upjohn declined and claimed that the information was privileged under the "work-product" doctrine, as information collected in prospect of litigation. The IRS and Upjohn litigated over the issue. Finally, the US Supreme Court decided in favour of Upjohn. Justice ***Rehnquist***, writing for the court, determined:

> "The narrow scope given the attorney-client privilege by the court below not only makes it difficult for corporate attorneys to formulate sound advice when their client is faced with a specific legal problem but also threatens to limit the valuable efforts of corporate counsel to ensure their client's compliance with the law"[100].

The rhetoric of the ***Upjohn*** ruling is compliance-oriented: the flow of information to the lawyer may be hindered if the privilege is not extended; in Justice ***Rehnquist***'s opinion, if the flow of information to the lawyer is hindered, his valuable efforts in ensuring the corporation's compliance with the law will be jeopardized. The following example will demonstrate why at least two of the underlying assumptions of the ***Upjohn*** court are invalid.

> Firm A needs to dump waste. The firm's truck driver prefers to avoid driving 6 hours to the legal waste dumping site and instead dumps the waste in a river near the firm's factory. Each truckload of waste contains 10 gallons of toxins. Near the river there is a clear sign: "Waste dumping is illegal and subject to a fine of $100 per gallon of toxic waste". Since dumping the waste in the river takes only one hour, the driver can take an additional side-job that pays $15 an hour. When the manager of the firm learns that waste has been dumped to the nearby river he appoints the corporate counsel to investigate the issue (assume the manager does not know whether the dumping is done by his own firm or by others, hence the internal investigation). The corporate counsel detects the culpable driver. The corporate counsel adheres to the conditions of the privilege when he

---

inapplicability of the privilege for their own protection, 25% still maintained they would be candid with the corporate lawyer. "Attorney Client Privilege: Perceptions and Implications in the Corporate Setting", A Survey of Personnel, Evidence Project, American University (April 1998).

100 ***Upjohn***, 392.

communicates with the driver for the purpose of collecting information about the frequency and the magnitude of the illegal dumping. After collecting this information, the counsel also advises the manager that, due to understaffing, the environmental authority only checks the river once a month and given the relatively small amounts of toxic waste in each truck, the detection probability is 5%. Thus the expected fine is $50 per truck (10 gallons * $100 * 5%). The manager fines the driver $50 per truck. Since the driver's benefit from breaking the law is ($15 * 5) - $50 = $25, he continues to break the law. The subsequent month, environmental authority inspectors detect the illegal dumping. In order to calculate the fine the authority demands from the firm data about the aggregate amount of toxic waste dumped by the driver. The firm refuses to reveal this information, which was collected under the **Upjohn** privilege. The authority is unable to prove the amount of dumped toxic waste.

In this example, we assume that enforcement authorities are required to produce proof (evidence or information) which they can only obtain from the suspected violator of the law[101]. This can be the case when there are multiple tortfeasors with different and unobservable levels of liability and the court is expected to assign the correct sanction to each liable party. This can also be the case - as in our example - when the sanction is a function of the magnitude, or the frequency of the violation (or both) and these are unobservable or difficult to measure post-factum.

The example clarifies that in cases where optimal enforcement depends, partially or entirely, on information that needs to be collected from the violator himself, the application of the privilege can hinder such enforcement. By assigning the task of internal information collection to the corporate counsel, the firm secures the privilege with respect to the information collected by the lawyer. This refers not only to the total amount of toxins dumped (which will be privileged) but also to the identity of the driver. Therefore the privilege according to ***Upjohn*** will force the authority to incur significantly higher costs and investigate the entire firm's drivers (and possibly other employees) in an effort to discover the information independently[102].

One underlying assumption in the ***Upjohn*** ruling is that legal advice necessarily directs the client to the legal and socially desirable course of action. As the example shows, the more sophisticated the client (and the lawyer) the more they can use the legal advice to find profitable illegal, as well as legal avenues of action, which may or may not be desirable from a social welfare perspective.

---

101 Assume that dumping in this case does not fall into the definition of the "crime-fraud exception" of the privilege (indeed it is unlikely to fall into this definition – see *infra* section II.5). Alternatively, we can assume that the fine in such violations is a civil or administrative sanction (hence, again, the crime-fraud exception to the privilege is not applicable). This assumption is needed in order to ensure that the privilege would apply.

102 It would perhaps be more socially efficient in this case to design a sanction for illegal dumping according to the environmental damage caused to the river, thereby causing the tortfeasor to internalize the social harm of the dumping action. However, measuring such damage is not always possible, nor is it accurate. Additionally, it does not solve the need to collect evidence that identify the correct tortfeasor.

The second assumption implicit in the court's decision in ***Upjohn*** is that lawyers have the power to "ensure their client's compliance". If Justice ***Rehnquist*** meant that lawyers can force their clients to comply with the law, he was sadly mistaken. Lawyers can do no more than ensure that the client is aware of the law.

What then, is the ***Upjohn*** case really about? One possibility is that it is about a situation unique to the corporate setting (and exemplified in the waste dumping story), where an organ of the corporate entity can commit an illegal action without the knowledge of the entity itself (as embodied by the management or the owner). Both ***Upjohn*** and the dumping example deal with lawyer-client communications that occurred ex-post the illegal action. The wrongdoing has already taken place. The purpose of the internal investigation conducted by the lawyer was an assessment by the management of whether an illegal act had been actually committed and hence, whether the corporation is potentially liable, and what can be done to minimise the consequential liability. The evidentiary products of such investigations are privileged under the ***Upjohn*** ruling. Are these lawyer's efforts valuable in increasing corporate compliance as claimed in ***Upjohn***?

If the corporation concludes that the wrongdoing is likely to be detected and sanctioned by the relevant enforcement agency, only then would the corporation have an incentive to report the findings of the internal investigation in hope of reducing the sanction through voluntary cooperation. Hence, the privilege can enhance internal monitoring in firms only when sanctions are optimally set and imposed to induce corporations to both internally monitor in a way that deters violations and to voluntarily report internal findings in order to save the cost spent by authorities in litigating against firms. As ***Arlen*** suggests, sanctions cannot be too high otherwise firms will be discouraged from internal monitoring altogether[103]. Nor should sanctions be too low or else firms will continue breaking the law. At any rate, the ability of the firm to shift the liability to the corporate agent responsible for the culpable behaviour lies at the foundation of this privilege. Thus, the situation is best suited to criminal or administrative fines, but not civil liability in which plaintiffs are mostly seeking deep corporate pockets rather than individual agents with limited resources.

In spite of the critique on the ***Upjohn*** decision mentioned here, when sanctions are correctly set to deter socially undesirable behaviour, legal advice rendered ex-ante should induce corporations to avoid socially undesirable illegal actions. Nonetheless, if the corporate privilege has social costs and thus should be minimized, at least one refinement to the ***Upjohn*** rule can be suggested. An underlying assumption of ***Upjohn*** is that the law is so complicated that corporations need lawyers in order to comply with it. This is not always true. Some laws are clear and simple. Some managers are familiar with the law. Yet ***Upjohn*** does not exclude simple laws from the scope of the privilege. In the Law & Economics literature it is conventional wisdom that rules are easier to comply with than standards[104]. Since courts often require the party raising a privilege to prove that the privileged material concerns legal advice, a welfare increasing refinement to the ***Upjohn*** rule would be for the courts to examine whether the legal advice concerned an issue governed by rules or by standards. Such a rule should decrease the use of the ***Upjohn*** privilege. When the court observes that the firm consulted a lawyer regarding a matter governed by a rule rather than standard, it is less likely that the underlying communication with the lawyer was for the purpose of discovering what the legal course of action is. Notably though, some legal issues are governed by a very complex forest of rules where it could reasonably be assumed that managers are not aware of

103 Arlen (1994).

104 The "Rules versus Standards" debate is addressed in chapter II *infra*, at section 2.2.3.

each and every regulation. The SEC securities regulation is such an example[105]. Under these circumstances, the justification for applying the ***Upjohn*** privilege increases again - provided as mentioned earlier, that expected sanctions are optimally set to deter illegal actions.

4. Summary

In this part I surveyed the justifications for the professional lawyer-client privilege. The privilege allows lawyers to refuse to testify about information communicated between themselves and their clients in their professional capacity. The privilege is a unique property right that enhances the implied contractual confidentiality between the parties. Confidentiality promotes candour between the client and the lawyer, which in turn, improves the accuracy of the legal advice provided by the lawyer.

The lawyer-client privilege is absolute. It cannot be removed in a balance of interests in favour of a competing interest. In comparing the formulation of the privilege in the surveyed jurisdictions, I have noted that the German law contains a far stronger absolute wording than its Anglo-American counterparts. Since judges are generally opposed to the privilege, I proposed that the reason for the emphasis on the privilege in the German law lies in the allegiance of judges to their interest group. German judges are less dependent on the professional group of lawyers for their career progression whilst Anglo-American judges are more so. Hence, Anglo-American judges are more likely to protect the interests of lawyers in the privilege even without an explicit strong law whereas German judges would be less inclined to do so.

In the Anglo American law, the prevalent justifications for the privilege are the utilitarian and neo-utilitarian rationales. In Germany, in addition to the latter two justifications, the privacy of clients per-se is a vital justification.

The utilitarian rationale is based on the premise that the privilege promotes social welfare in spite of the fact that depriving the court of some evidence may result in less accurate adjudication. The neo-utilitarian rationale relies on the theory that social compliance is the primary social good that is gained from the privilege.

Law & Economics literature has shown that the benefits of the lawyer-client privilege depend on the optimality of enforcement and the accuracy of sanctions. It has criticized the utilitarian rationale for overlooking the objective of the consultation between the lawyer and the client, namely, in most cases, promoting compliance with the law. It has also criticized the neo-utilitarian rational for misconceptualising the social outcomes of the consultation between the lawyer and the client. The neo-utilitarians did not envision that consultation could lead to socially undesirable behaviour when sanctions are set at a sub-optimal level.

I have also touched on the analysis of the privilege as a quasi-intellectual property right and how it serves to lower the costs of the lawyers' contractual obligation to confidentiality. I suggested that the property right is unique because it is designed to encourage the communication of the privileged information and not the creation of the information per-se. However, we are interested in the way this information is subsequently used by the client.

105 Bratton (2003).

Therefore the insights from analysing the privilege as a property right are of little consequence in the ensuing discussion.

Both Law & Economics and traditional legal scholarship suggest that the lawyer-client privilege in the corporate setting is problematic due to the extensive use of lawyers by firms, their sophistication as litigants and their role as repeat players.

Focusing on the neo-utilitarian rationale, I have shown that the assertion that lawyer-client privilege promotes corporate compliance with the law is based on two fundamental assumptions: (1) that lawyers always advise the firm on the legitimate course of actions, and (2) that firms always follow the legal course of action advised by the lawyer or that lawyers have the ability to ensure such compliance. As demonstrated, neither one of these assumptions is necessarily true.

II Comparative Legal Survey

In this part I survey the operating mechanism of the corporate lawyer-client testimonial privilege in each of the jurisdictions considered here. The aim is to give an account of the treatment of the privilege in each jurisdiction. In order to enhance the comparative analysis, the survey has been broken down into the main components of the privilege and each is reviewed with respect to the relevant jurisdictions. Section 1 surveys the historical background of the privilege. In section 2, the duty of confidentiality and its legal anchors are surveyed. Section 3 describes the fundamental privilege rule. Section 4 compares the legal rules determining who represents the firm in communications with the lawyer. This issue is the subject of further economic analysis in part III. Sections 6 and 7 concern situation in which the privilege is denied: exceptions (in section 6) and waiver (in section 7). The latter is also the subject of analysis in part III.

1. The Historical Development of the Corporate Lawyer-Client Privilege

The privilege of lawyers[106] emerged in Common Law in the 16th century. There has been recent debate as to the exact time at which it was born and the initial rationale for its introduction. However, it is the oldest professional privilege known[107] (with the exception of clergy, perhaps).

1.1 United States

There is no doubt that a corporation, although a mere creature of law, can be a client[108], but should the corporation, as a client, enjoy the lawyer-client privilege? Decisions in US Court cases have not discussed the normative desirability of the lawyer-client privilege in the corporate context in a convincing way. In two rulings, revolving around the same case, ***Radiant Burners v. American Gas***[109], the federal district court held that a corporation should not enjoy the privilege, because the court found no precedent on the issue. This is the only case to have doubted the applicability of the privilege in the corporate setting. The initial decision is consistent with the legal approach advocating that privileges should be interpreted restrictively, so as not to hinder the judicial fact finding process. But in fact, the court was misguided, in taking this approach. There is ample case law where a corporation has received the privilege without the courts ever considering or averting themselves to the issue[110]. In these cases the privilege was considered so self-evident that no court found any reason to discuss the matter. On these grounds, the federal appeal court immediately reversed the ***Radiant Burners*** ruling[111].

---

106 I refer to the privilege as the "privilege of lawyers", "lawyer's privilege" or "attorney-client privilege" interchangeably although the privilege in fact belongs to the client and is only exercised by the lawyer.

107 Auburn, 2-8.

108 Gergacz, 1-11.

109 ***Radiant Burners v. American Gas***, 207 F.supp. 771 and 209 F.supp. 321 (N.D. Ill. 1962).

110 Gergacz, 1-14.

111 ***Radiant Burners v. American Gas***, 320 F.2d 314 (7th Cir. 1963).

Indeed, precedent - and to a significant extent, path dependence - is a strong justification for the privilege in the case law[112]. Other justifications put forward for the privilege are encouraging corporate client candour[113] and promoting compliance with the law[114].

1.2 England

The English legal profession has an ingrained differentiation between barristers and solicitors. The latter are significantly limited in their ability to represent clients in court. Historically, the barrister enjoyed the professional privilege, possibly as a result of the "Gentlemen's code" whereas the solicitor was not considered a gentleman for this purpose but an agent-servant of the master. Ancient Roman law also prevented servants from testifying against their masters, thereby providing a basis for extending the privilege to solicitors as well[115].

As in the US, there is no significant discussion on the extension of the lawyer-client privilege to corporations in the English case law. As far back as the 19th century there are cases that simply assume the privilege applies to corporations[116]. England has been significantly slower than the US in creating separate rules applying to the corporate lawyer-client privilege, and the relevant body of case law is small compared to the massive body of law in the US[117].

1.3 Germany

Prior to the 19th century, German law only disqualified testimonies on the basis of unreliability. Professional privileges as we are familiar with them today, developed only after liberalism introduced the consideration of personality interests. Lawyer's privilege was first recognized in Württemberg and Hamburg in the second half of the 19th century[118]. The BGH has noted that the privilege existed as early as the 16th century[119]. This observation is, however, not entirely accurate. It refers to the obligation of the lawyer to confidentiality, which can indeed be found already in the Oath of Lawyers in 1555[120]. However, in German law, privilege and confidentiality are often treated as one and the same. As in Anglo-American jurisdictions, the extension of the privilege to corporate clients is trivially assumed in German law.

---

112 Gergacz, 1-13-14
113 Gergacz,, 1-15.
114 Gergacz, 1-16.
115 Gergacz, 1-5.
116 Gergacz, 1-18 at footnote 46.
117 Gergacz, 1-19.
118 Wichmann, 61.
119 BGHZ NJW 1990, 510, 512.
120 Henssler, 1819.

2. The Duty of Confidentiality

Confidentiality between lawyer and client is part of the agency relationship,[121] as well as an implied contractual term in the relationship[122]. It is an obligation not to disclose communications that transpired in confidence between the lawyer and the client. The obligation to confidentiality is part of the lawyer's professional rules of conduct.

2.1 United States

In the US, the obligation to confidentiality is promulgated in Model Rule 1.6 "Confidentiality of Information" of the American Bar Association (ABA) Model Rules of Professional Conduct. The broad obligation contains several exceptions. Model Rule 1.6 reads as follows:

> "(a) A lawyer shall not reveal information relating to the representation of a client unless the client gives informed consent, the disclosure is impliedly authorized in order to carry out the representation or the disclosure is permitted by paragraph (b).
>
> (b) A lawyer may reveal information relating to the representation of a client to the extent the lawyer reasonably believes necessary:
>
>> (1) to prevent reasonably certain death or substantial bodily harm;
>>
>> (2) to prevent the client from committing a crime or fraud that is reasonably certain to result in substantial injury to the financial interests or property of another and in furtherance of which the client has used or is using the lawyer's services;
>>
>> (3) to prevent, mitigate or rectify substantial injury to the financial interests or property of another that is reasonably certain to result or has resulted from the client's commission of a crime or fraud in furtherance of which the client has used the lawyer's services;
>>
>> (4) to secure legal advice about the lawyer's compliance with these Rules;
>>
>> (5) to establish a claim or defence on behalf of the lawyer in a controversy between the lawyer and the client, to establish a defence to a criminal charge or civil claim against the lawyer based upon conduct in which the client was involved, or to respond to allegations in any proceeding concerning the lawyer's representation of the client; or
>>
>> (6) to comply with other law or a court order".

121 Rotunda, 44 and 54.
122 Auburn, 58.

The current text of Model Rule 1.6 as given above is an amended version from 2002. Compared to earlier versions it contains a significant amendment to the lawyer's discretion to voluntarily disclose information about client's wrongdoing. The preceding version of the Model Rules did not allow the lawyer any discretionary disclosure[123] whereas the new formulation of sub-paragraph 1.6(b), reads "a lawyer ***may*** reveal...".

The Model Rules have no formally binding power. They are used by the states as a basis for the development of their own rules of conduct. There is no uniformity between the States regarding the extent to which the model rules are incorporated in the individual jurisdictions. So far, 36 states have adopted the Model Rules of Professional Conduct[124], but the vast majority of states had not adopted the restrictive pre-2002 version which forbade disclosure. By now 41 states have adopted rules of conduct that permit a lawyer to disclose confidential information to prevent criminal fraud. Four states have gone even further and *oblige* the lawyer to report crime or fraud committed by the client. Nine states and the District of Columbia, have opted for the restrictive approach that completely forbids the lawyer from breaching the confidence of the client[125].

2.2 England

The UK Law Society Rules of Conduct for Solicitors state in rule 16.01 "General duty of confidentiality" that "a solicitor is under a duty to keep confidential to his or her firm the affairs of clients and to ensure that the staff do the same". Rule 16.02 provides: "The duty to keep a client's confidences can be overridden in certain exceptional circumstances". The exceptions are identical to the American rules.

An additional, non-binding, yet influential, source of the duty of confidentiality in EU member-states can also be found in the Code of Conduct for Lawyers in the European Union (2002), published by the Council of the Bars and Law Societies of Europe (CCBE). The code is relevant to English as well as German lawyers. The code refers to the justifications underlying confidentiality, and to the importance of ensuring these justifications by protective state legislation. The relevant section of the code reads:

> "2.3.1 It is of the essence of a lawyer's function that he should be told by his client things which the client would not tell to others, and that he should be the recipient of other information on a basis of confidence. Without the certainty of confidentiality there cannot be trust. Confidentiality is therefore a primary right and duty of the lawyer.

123 Brown, 705-6; Cramton, 157-8; in securities cases, historically, the SEC and the ABA have debated what should the obligations of lawyers be when they discover that a wrongdoing is taking place in the client firm. The SEC held the position that a lawyer is committing an ethical offence if he did not take immediate steps to correct the wrong and otherwise stopped participating in it by resigning. The ABA held that Rule 1.6 in its pre-2002 version applies to such a case. Until 2002 the ABA seemed to have prevailed. However, post Enron, winds of change may have tilted the balance towards the position of the SEC, that seeks to improve the function of lawyers as relational gatekeepers.

124 Brown, 656.

125 Cramton, 157.

> The lawyer's obligation of confidentiality serves the interest of the administration of justice as well as the interest of the client. It is therefore entitled to special protection by the state.
>
> 2.3.2 A lawyer shall respect the confidentiality of all information that becomes known to him in the course of his professional activity
>
> 2.3.3 The obligation of confidentiality is not limited in time.
>
> 2.3.4 A lawyer shall require his associates and staff and anyone engaged by him in the course of providing professional services to observe the same obligation of confidentiality.
>
> ..."

In these rules, confidentiality is given very high regard and described as serving the interests of the client as well as the interests of the legal system. While confidentiality is not described as serving the interest of the lawyer himself, it is established as a "primary right and duty of the lawyer". The concise formulation does not, however, explain how the lawyer should resolve potential conflicts between this right (or is it a duty) and contradicting interests of the legal system, of administration of justice or of the client.

2.3 Germany

In 1994, the German Federal Lawyers Act (BRAO) was amended to include the duty of confidentiality. The text of §43b(2) BRAO, as translated to English, reads:

> "The lawyer is bound by professional secrecy obligations. This duty refers to information that the lawyer became aware of in the course of the exercise of his profession. This does not apply to facts which are public or do not require secrecy according to their significance"[126].

The duty of confidentiality is therefore statutory[127], but it is also founded on the contractual relationship between the lawyer and the client. Although the lawyer's ethical obligation to confidentiality - in the Lawyers' professional guidelines, §42 RichtlinieRA - is not binding law, the BVerfG reads this ethical obligation together with the BRAO to create a legally enforceable obligation[128]. This duality enables both criminal enforcement of the duty - a breach of the duty of confidentiality would constitute a criminal offence punishable by up to one year imprisonment, according to §203(1)(3) StGB - as well as the right of civil enforcement for breach of confidence which may result in civil liability[129]. The BVerfG has also held that some professions cannot perform their social service to the citizen-client

126 The translation is taken from the comment letter of Dr. Dombek, President of the German Federal Bar dated 12.17.2002 to the SEC on the proposed rules regarding the implementation of standards of professional conduct for attorneys.

127 The 1994 revision of the BRAO clearly stresses the obligation of the lawyer to confidentiality through §43a II BRAO. See Kleine-Cosack, 2251.

128 BVerfG NJW 1988, 191; Henssler, 1818.

129 Alfes, 100.

without the trust relationship and therefore must have the right to confidentiality (protected by criminal liability) whereas some professions do not require a privilege[130].

The purpose of the obligation to maintain professional secrecy has always been (since its first mention in 1555) the protection of the client's confidences. The client is "the master of the secret"[131]. The professional secrecy of the lawyer is a founding principle of the German "Rechtsstaat"[132]. Scholarly work sketches the duty of confidentiality as an important foundation for the trust relationship between the lawyer and the client[133]. This relationship can only develop when the client knows that his personality rights are protected. These rights, along with the right to informational self-determination, have been constitutionally protected by the German constitutional court[134]. This seems to reinforce the justification for protecting communications between the lawyer and the client.

In Germany, as in other continental law systems, there is an attempt to create perfect symmetry between the ethical duty of confidentiality and the lawyer's testimonial privilege. The duty of confidentiality is very wide in scope and encompasses all information that the lawyer receives in the course of exercising his profession[135]. Given the strong symmetry between the scope of the duty of confidentiality and the scope of the privilege, they are often treated in the literature as one, especially when discussing their justifiability.

3. The Privilege Rule: Legislation or Judge Made Law

3.1 United States

Federal Rule of Evidence 501 reads: "Except as otherwise required by the Constitution of the United States or provided by Act of Congress or in rules prescribed by the Supreme Court pursuant to statutory authority, the privilege of a witness, person, government, state, or political subdivision thereof shall be governed by the principles of the common law as they may be interpreted by the courts of the United States in the light of reason and experience. However, in civil actions and proceedings, with respect to an element of a claim or defence as to which state law supplies the rule of decision, the privilege of a witness, person, government, state, or political subdivision thereof shall be determined in accordance with state law". Hence, the privilege is governed by both common law and state law.

As summarized in ***Upjohn***, for the corporate privilege to apply, the following must hold: (1) the communication by the employee to the lawyer must be made in order to secure advice to the corporation, (2) be within the scope of the employees official duties, (3) the employee must be aware that the communications are made for the purpose of securing advice for the corporation and (4) the communication is confidential and is kept so[136].

When the requirements are met, the privilege is absolute.

---

130 BverfG 33, 377; BVerfG 38, 325. Social workers and veterinary-doctors have no privilege.

131 BGHZ NJW 1990, 510, 512.

132 Alfes, 112; Henssler, 1820.

133 Alfes, 112.

134 BVerfG 65, 1 (Volkszählungsurteil, The "Census decision"); confidentiality can also be theoretically defended through freedom of occupation and rights to privacy. See Henssler, 1819.

135 Ben Basat, 253.

136 ***Upjohn***, 394.

3.2 England

The English lawyer-client privilege is judge made law[137]. The legal advice privilege in England is absolute[138]. It belongs to the client. The lawyer is not entitled to withhold information or documents which the client himself would not be entitled to withhold[139]. In the ***Three Rivers*** (UK, 2004) case, the House of Lords held that the legal advice privilege is not confined to advice about litigation but also extends to advice concerning what a client should do in a relevant legal context[140]. This can be interpreted as an acceptance of the compliance rationale.

3.3 Germany

Professional privileges were developed to enable those professionals who require their clients to share secret information or to form a trust relationship with them to perform their social functions[141]. Other theoretical explanations motivating the development of privileges in Germany include the claims that privileges contribute to a smoother legal process, prevent unreliable evidence from reaching the court, protect personality rights of witnesses and safeguard the professional interests of witnesses[142]. The last justification should not be interpreted as a professional "status symbol" but rather, "professional" as in an instrument to advance trust relationships that further the interests of society[143].

The privilege is promulgated in section §203 of the Criminal Code (StGB)[144] which provides that a lawyer who reveals secrets regarding personal or professional matters of the client is committing a criminal offence punishable by up to one year imprisonment or a monetary fine. The offence can only be indicted upon a formal complaint by the client[145].

In matters of civil litigation, §383(1)(6) ZPO allows lawyers (as well as other professionals) to refuse to testify on matters they have learned in the process of their professional work[146].

---

137 "The Professional Secret, Confidentiality and Legal Professional secret in Europe" (The Edward's Report Update 2003) CCBE Council of the Bars and Law Societies of the European Union. Available from: www.ccbe.org/doc/En/update_edwards_report_en.pdf (last visited 14.7.2005); Ede, at 18. This data seems to refer particularly to lawyers.

138 ***Three Rivers District Council and Others (respondents) v. Bank of England (appellants)***, [2004] UKHL 48 (hereinafter – ***Three Rivers***). Opinion of Lord Scott, §§25-28.

139 ***R. v. Peterborough Justice, ex p. Hicks*** [1977] 1 W.L.R. 1371, DC.

140 ***Three Rivers***, opinion of Lord Scott, §38. Lord Rodger, §58.

141 Wichmann, 183-185.

142 Wichmann, 186-194.

143 Wichmann, 193.

144 The German text reads: "Wer unbefugt ein fremdes Geheimnis, namentlich ein zum persönlichen Lebensbereich gehörendes Geheimnis oder ein Betriebs- oder Geschäftsgeheimnis, offenbart, das ihm als... 3. Rechtsanwalt, Patentanwalt, Notar, Verteidiger in einem gesetzlich geordneten Verfahren, Wirtschaftsprüfer, vereidigtem Buchprüfer, Steuerberater, Steuerbevollmächtigten oder Organ oder Mitglied eines Organs einer Rechtsanwalts-, Patentanwalts-, Wirtschaftsprüfungs-, Buchprüfungs- oder Steuerberatungsgesellschaft, ... anvertraut worden oder sonst bekanntgeworden ist, wird mit Freiheitsstrafe bis zu einem Jahr oder mit Geldstrafe bestraft".

145 StGB §205 and StPO §172.

146 The German text reads: "Zur Verweigerung des Zeugnisses sind berechtigt: ... (6) Personen, denen kraft ihres Amtes, Standes oder Gewerbes Tatsachen anvertraut sind, deren Geheimhaltung durch ihre Natur oder durch gesetzliche Vorschrift geboten ist, in Betreff der Tatsachen, auf welche die Verpflichtung zur Verschwiegenheit sich bezieht".

4. Who Represents the Corporation?

In the relationship between a lawyer and a corporate client, the corporation is the client and not the individuals within the corporation. Not every member in the corporation that communicates with the layer necessarily "represents" the corporation. By "representation" I refer to the situation where an individual member of the corporation communicates with the corporate lawyer and privilege attaches to such communications because this member is authorized to speak on behalf of the corporation. There are several possible criteria that may be applied in order to determine who is authorized to represent the corporation. In this subsection I outline the legal background on this issue. Further economic analysis of this issue is given in depth in part III.

4.1 United States

The privilege belongs to the client, the corporate entity. It survives through changes of the individuals in the corporation, it is controlled by the acting, never the former, management and it also survives in receivership[147].

Since the client is the corporate entity as a whole and not its individual constituents, the duties of lawyers are owed to the corporate client as a whole[148]. The privilege does not belong to the agent communicating on behalf of the corporation[149]. The representatives of the corporation do not directly enjoy the privilege. However, they may enjoy the privilege indirectly if the corporation has an interest in protecting the communications. ABA Model Rule 1.13 indicates to the lawyer that notifying the employee of this fact may be suitable when conducting internal investigations on behalf of the corporation[150]. Thus agents may not be forthcoming if personal liability is at stake. At least in theory, this might reduce the willingness of employees to be forthcoming with the lawyer.

Two rules have emerged with regards to the question as to who in the corporation is entitled to communicate with the lawyer on behalf of the corporation under the umbrella of the privilege. These are: (1) the "control group test"[151] and (2) the "subject matter" doctrine[152]. Although the prevailing rule in most US state courts seems to be the "subject matter" doctrine[153]. I discuss both tests in turn.

147 Gergacz, 2-5 citing ***CFTC v. Weintraub***, 471 US 343 (1985).

148 Rotunda, 65; Auburn, 32-33; In the US, see also Model Rule 1.13(a).

149 Gergacz, 2-5-7.

150 Model Rule 1.13(f) states: "In dealing with an organization's directors, officers, employees, members, shareholders or other constituents, a lawyer shall explain the identity of the client when the lawyer knows or reasonably should know that the organization's interests are adverse to those of the constituents with whom the lawyer is dealing".

151 ***City of Philadelphia v. Westinghouse Electric Corp.***, 210 F.supp 438 (E.D. Pa. 1962).

152 ***Harper & Row Publishers v. Decjer***, 423 F.2d 487 (7th Cir. 1970).

153 State courts that adhere to the "control group" test are, for example, Illinois, Texas and Alaska.

4.1.1 The Control Group Test

The "control group test" has been formulated as follows: "If the employee making the communication, of whatever rank he may be, is in a position to control or even take a substantial part in a decision about any action which the corporation may take upon the advice of the attorney, or if he is an authorized member of a body or group which has that authority, then, in effect, he is (or personifies) the corporation when he makes his disclosure to the lawyer and the privilege would apply"[154]. The test certainly includes top managers but may also apply to lower ranks. The benefits of the test are its narrowness and predictability[155]. In practice, the privilege has protected mostly upper-echelon management[156].

4.1.2 The Subject Matter Doctrine

Dissatisfaction with the limited scope of protection provided by the "control group" test prompted several judicial attempts to form a different test. This judicial activity resulted in the subject-matter doctrine, even before the Supreme Court weighed in on the issue in ***Upjohn***[157]. The ***Upjohn*** case is a unanimous decision (written by Justice ***Rehnquist*** with a concurring opinion by Justice ***Burger***). This is significant with regards to the rejection of the control group test[158]. However the court in ***Upjohn*** did not mention the subject-matter test by name and specifically declined "to make a broad rule"[159] thereby advocating a case-by-case approach[160]. Nevertheless, ***Upjohn*** can be dismantled into components that do comprise a rule.

The court asks the first step questions regarding the privilege[161]: (1) was the communication made to the corporate counsel, (2) was the purpose of the communication receiving legal advice from the counsel, and (3) was the communication made and kept in confidence. The court in ***Upjohn*** then goes on to consider the following factors[162]: (1) was the communication made by a corporate employee[163], (2) did the employee communicate upon an order of his superior, (3) was the information sought by the counsel not available from upper rank employees, (4) was the information communicated within the employee's corporate duties[164], (5) was the employee aware that the purpose of the communication was the production of legal advice for the corporation[165] and (6) the burden on the resources of the opposing party.

154 ***Philadelphia v. Westinghouse***, 210 F.supp 483, 485 (E.D. Pa. 1962).
155 Gergacz, 3-62.
156 Gergacz, 3-63.
157 Gergacz, 3-64-69.
158 Gergacz, 3-73.
159 ***Upjohn***, 386.
160 Gergacz, 3-74.
161 Gergacz, 3-78.
162 Gergacz, 3-79.
163 Case law indicates that also communications from former employees will be protected. Gergacz, 3-81.
164 For example, in ***Leer v. Chicago, Milwaukee, St. Paul and Pacific Railroad***, 308 N.W.2d 305 (Minn. 1981) a railroad employee suing the corporation asked to receive the testimony of another employee that witnessed the accident and described it to a company investigator. The court held that the witnessing of the accident was not part of the employee's scope of duties (the employee was a switching line worker) and a privilege was denied.
165 This factor is consistent with Model Rule 1.13, which requires that the lawyer informs the employee that his obligation of confidentiality is to the firm and not to the employee. Of course, this decreases the chances that the employee would cooperate if his personal liability is at stake.

Many courts have since interpreted these factors as an acceptance of the subject-matter doctrine[166]. The doctrine allows the lawyer to delve deeper into the lower echelons of the corporate structure in order to retrieve information required for the formation of his legal advice without losing of the privilege.

4.2 England

Until recently, English courts did not set a clear standard regarding which employees were eligible to communicate with the lawyer under the protection of the privilege[167]. A fairly recent decision by the House of Lords in the case of ***Three Rivers*** (UK, 2004) laid down an important ruling on corporate lawyer-client privilege with implications on the definition of the corporate client. The ruling can be interpreted as setting the test for the identity of the corporate representative in lawyer-corporation communications. The application seems to be very restrictive, akin to the US control group test, but perhaps even more stringent.

Three Rivers concerned the July 1991 collapse of BCCI bank. At the time of its collapse its liabilities exceeded assets and its depositors stood to lose most of their money. According to the UK Banking Acts of 1979 and 1987, the Bank of England (BOE) had statutory supervisory duties over BCCI. The government formed an independent inquiry into the supervision of the BOE, headed by Lord Justice Bingham (the "Bingham inquiry"). The BOE established an internal unit, whose duties were to prepare and communicate information to the Bingham Inquiry. The BOE retained the legal counsel of the law firm Freshfields for the purpose of advising the BOE on the preparation and communication of information to the Bingham inquiry. Following the publication of the Bingham inquiry report, 6231 BCCI depositors and also the liquidators of BCCI sued the BOE for the losses they sustained from the BCCI collapse. However before successfully lodging such a claim, the claimants were faced with a high hurdle. Namely that the Banking Act section 1(4) relieves the BOE from liability unless it is shown that the supervision failed due to an act or omission conducted in "bad faith". The claimants sought wide discovery of documents in order to overcome this hurdle. Their request for discovery included documents prepared by the internal unit of the BOE and communicated to Freshfields in the course of preparing for the Bingham inquiry.

Already in the earlier stage of the trial, in the lower courts, the parties agreed that only the unit within the BOE that was authorized to communicate with the bank's attorneys shall be viewed as the client. The court noted that even higher echelons than the specified unit would not be privileged in their communications with the lawyers[168].

In an appeal on other issues of the attorney-client privilege in this ruling, the Court of Appeals made no comment on this point. Further leave to appeal to the House of Lords was refused.

In a different appeal in the same case, the House of Lords first addressed the difference between privilege for legal advice and litigation privilege. Litigation privilege covers all documents that come into being for the purpose of litigation. The litigation privilege has been previously held to be a "creature of adversarial proceedings" and therefore unavailable in non-

---

166 26 A.L.R. 5th 628 §17; Gergacz, 3-79-87.

167 Gergacz, 1-22.

168 ***Three Rivers District Council v. Governor and Company of the Bank of England*** **(No.5)** [2003] QB 1556.

adversarial proceedings[169]. Indeed the BOE did not assert the litigation privilege since the Bingham inquiry was not an adversarial proceeding[170]. The BOE asserted the legal advice privilege. The House of Lords then noted the restrictive definition of the client as agreed by the parties and accepted by the lower court - but made no further comment on the matter. As pointed out by the court, even the Governor of the BOE does not fall into the restrictive definition[171]. As it is, the matter is still open for discussion at the higher courts in England but the approach that has been adopted in practice and silently approved by the court is similar to the "control group" test.

4.3 Germany

The German corporate law contains specific instructions regarding who may represent the firm. For instance, the most common form of German firm, the GmbH (limited liability company), may only be represented by its managing director[172]. However, the laws regarding the representation of the firm hardly affect the relationship with the lawyer. Unlike the US, the privilege is not lost when the lawyer communicates with lower echelon employees, so long as this communication is required for the professional execution of the employee's work[173].

Clear separation between the firm as a client and the individual representatives of the firm is promulgated. The fact that a lawyer has advised individuals acting as organs of the corporate entity does not mean that a legal relationship has existed between the lawyer and the individuals, if the lawyer was advising on matters of the corporation. Only if there was a specific personal legal relationship with the lawyer and the individuals - separately formed - would they have a protected relationship. Since such a personal relationship may produce a conflict of interest with the firm, a high burden of proof must be required from a party that asserts that such a double relationship existed[174].

In bankruptcy, as in US case law, the receivers take over the person of the client and become the "master of the secret"[175]. The receiver may waive the privilege with respect to communications of former management.

5. Exceptions

Overlooking the exceptions to the privilege would give an incomplete picture of the privilege. However, it should be noted that the exceptions are not the main focus of this work. Recall, that in the "Wigmorian" cost-benefit view of the privilege, exceptions reflect cases where the privilege has social detrimental consequences that strictly outweigh the benefits from candid

---

169 ***Three Rivers***, opinion of Lord Scott, §10 and §29. Lord Scott notes this with regards to the justification for the litigation privilege for material exchanged between the litigant and third parties. Lord Carswell, §§101-102.

170 ***Three Rivers***, opinion of Lord Carswell, §83.

171 ***Three Rivers***, opinion of Lord Scott, §§12-14.

172 GmbHG §35.

173 Alfes, 110.

174 BGHZ NJW 1990, 510, 512.

175 See §6 KonkursOrdnung and BGHZ NJW 1990, 510, 512.

lawyer-client consultation. I therefore briefly outline the exceptions and propose some insights into the way they are applied. Note that, given this level of abstraction, exceptions in the US and in England are fairly similar and therefore I shall focus on the former jurisdiction and not elaborate on the latter.

5.1 United States

The veil of the privilege is pierced by exceptions. Under common law, the exceptions to the privilege and to the equivalent rules of ethical confidentiality may differ slightly. Three groups of exceptions have been developed on both the ethical and the legal levels.

- The crime-fraud exception.
- Self defence.
- Disputes between the lawyer and the client.

Later another exception was developed by the courts, namely, the "good cause" exception, which is not part of the regular exception promulgated also by the ethical rules in the US.

5.1.1 The Crime-Fraud Exception

When the client knowingly consulted the lawyer in "bad faith" trying to further a future or ongoing crime or fraud, the lawyer is often not obliged to confidentiality[176]. The lawyer-privilege certainly does not apply[177]. This is true both when the lawyer knows about the fraudulent purpose of the consultation at the time the advice is sought, as well as when the lawyer learns of the purpose *post-factum*[178]. For example, asking a lawyer for advice regarding the destruction of evidence in order to decrease the risk of expected sanctions for already committed offences would not be protected[179].

There are several causes for uncertainty concerning the application of the crime-fraud exception. The formulation of the exception seems strictly limited to criminal and civil frauds and to actions defined as "crimes" rather than lower types of criminal acts such as felonies or misdemeanours. However, courts have in some occasions applied the exception in additional circumstances. For example, in one case the court held that the exception should also apply when a fiduciary duty has been breached[180]. This creates uncertainty in the wrongdoer's

---

176 Subin, 1113; whether the lawyer is obliged to inform third parties who might be harmed by the actions of the client is a matter of different approaches.

177 Rotunda (1984), 475.

178 Rotunda (1984), 475. See ***State v. Phelps***, 545 P.2d 901, 904 (1976).

179 Gergacz, 4-3.

180 ***Radiac Abrasives, Inc. v. Diamond Technology, Inc.***, 177 Ill.App.3d 628, at 638 (Ill.App. 2 Dist.,1988) cited in Gergacz, 4-10. An employee that left a company to establish a competing business may have sold the employer's machinery to a third party in order to buy it later for his new firm. The court held this to be a possible breach of fiduciary duty and noted that the crime-fraud exception would apply. The case has a strong scent of fraud in it. The lawsuit concerned an employee who, if the facts of the claim were to be found correct, abused the trust of his employer to start a competing business using unfair methods. Denying the privilege would require the employee to exert higher cost to monitor his employees against such breaches of confidence, causing an increase of the employer's production costs. Intuitively, the social costs of creating increased deterrence through the exception seem cheaper

expected cost of the equation when deciding to pursue actions that are not crimes or frauds. This also creates uncertainty for the victim with regards to the level of ex-ante prevention investments that he should undertake to deter such actions. If one assumes that removing the privilege increases the probability that a defendant will be found liable and thus increases the expected sanction for committing an illegal act, there is no reason to limit the exception to illegal actions of a certain level. Therefore, the restriction of the exception only to "crime" and "fraud" makes no sense.

The party seeking to remove the privilege in accordance with a crime-fraud exception bears the burden of proving that a crime or a fraud was advanced through the communications. Courts demand a *prima-facie* showing before they are willing to apply the exception[181]. Since it is not clear what level of proof will be required from the party claiming the crime-fraud exception, uncertainty as to the probability of successful claims arises in addition to the uncertainty already mentioned with respect to the application of the privilege.

5.1.2 Self-Defence

When the lawyer is innocent of wrongdoing, he might nevertheless face liability simply because he is unable to defend himself by presenting confidential evidence[182]. The self-defence exception allows the lawyer to protect himself without bearing liability for breaching confidentiality. The exception itself seems to serve the professional at the expense of the client. It adds to the client's uncertainty since the client has little influence on the probability that a legal proceeding against his lawyer will succeed.

Since third party claims against lawyers are not common, this exception is not widely used. One can only speculate as to the reason why so little use of this exception is known. Lawyers seem to believe that clients will have a higher tendency to retain legal services the stronger and the wider the privilege they are offered. Rational individual lawyers will thus have an incentive to offer the strongest and widest possible privilege. The self-defence exception can be invoked by a lawyer when he is facing criminal charges, ethical violation charges, or sued by a third party (not his client) for civil liability. In all of these cases, when the lawyer invokes the exception and reveals confidential information, it is done because the lawyer believes this will increase his chances of a successful defence. The exception enables the defendant-lawyer to mount a defence that is as strong as one mountable by a non-lawyer. Obviously, the plaintiffs that initiate proceedings against lawyers are often represented by lawyers or use lawyers to conduct the proceedings. Regardless of whether the final result of the litigation is favourable to the plaintiff or not, the case will have a negative externality on the entire legal profession, shared, albeit insignificantly, by the plaintiff's lawyer, if he expects that the defendant will invoke the self-defence exception. The negative externality is the result of increased client uncertainty in the confidentiality of their lawyers and the perceived reduction in demand for legal advice. Although the loss for one specific lawyer is minuscule, he should still rationally prefer to litigate against non-lawyer defendants, all other things being equal.

---

than the aggregate social costs of firms monitoring every contract of their employee for breach of confidence.

181 Gergacz, 4-13.

182 Subin, 1136; See also the critique in Fischel, 4.

5.1.3 Disputes between Lawyer and Client

In litigation between lawyers and their clients, lawyers are not bound to confidentiality. This is clearly a self-serving exception. It deters clients from suing their lawyers by increasing the expected cost of such litigation to include also the cost of the revealed information.

Consequently, one might expect that the lawyers' incentives to take optimal care when advising their clients will be decreased. The reason for this is that the expected cost of reckless advice is diminished by the lower probability of being sued. This proposition is discussed further in part III section 3.5.

5.1.4 The "Good Cause" Exception

The "good cause" exception is unique to the US. The exception was first developed in ***Garner v. Wolfinberger***[183] to deal with derivative shareholder lawsuits. In these lawsuits, the privilege can be used by the corporate management as a shield against legal actions that are for the benefit of the corporation.

The ***Garner*** case concerned a derivative lawsuit by shareholders who claimed a fraud took place in the offering of corporate securities. The court noted that in such a situation, abolishing the privilege would result in costs for the corporation and its management. On the other hand, an absolute privilege would harm shareholders' interests. The court then developed the "good cause" exception according to which plaintiffs must show good cause to remove the privilege, based on the following factors: (1) the number of plaintiff-shareholders and the percentage of stock they represent, (2) the bona-fide of the shareholders, (3) the nature of the shareholders' claim and whether it is obviously colourable, (4) the apparent necessity or desirability of the shareholders having the information and the availability of it from other sources, (5) whether, if the shareholders' claim is of wrongful action by the corporation, it is of action criminal, or illegal but not criminal, or of doubtful legality, (6) whether the communication related to past or to prospective actions, (7) whether the communication is of advice concerning the litigation itself, (8) the extent to which the communication is identified versus the extent to which the shareholders are blindly fishing for evidence, (9) the risk of revelation of trade secrets or other information in whose confidentiality the corporation has an interest for independent reasons[184].

The list creates a rather vague standard. In order to make sense of it, the components of the norm must be weighed together. For example, all other things being equal, why should a minority shareholder holding one percent of the shares not have the same advantage as a minority shareholder holding 20% (as suggested in factor 1)? One answer could be that since a derivative lawsuit is supposed to be for the benefit of the corporation, a large proportion of the minority shareholders should support it. If the plaintiff wants to convince the court that he is entitled to the privileged information he would then invest in signalling his "good cause" by overcoming the collective action problem, approaching other shareholders and creating a larger group of plaintiffs.

---

183 ***Garner v. Wolfinberger***, 430 F.2d 1093 (5th Cir. 1970).

184 ***Garner v. Wolfinberger***, 1104.

A prerequisite of the exception is the existence of a fiduciary relationship between the corporation asserting the privilege and the plaintiff attacking it[185]. This typically involves lawsuits by shareholders against managers or directors of the firm[186], lawsuits by minority shareholders against controlling majority shareholders[187], lawsuits by investors who claim they purchased company securities due to misrepresentations prior to their becoming shareholders[188], lawsuits by debenture holders[189], as well as lawsuits by principals against their agents[190]. ***Gergacz*** notes that the applicability of this exception depends on the party asserting it (a fiduciary) and not on the circumstances of the communication (furtherance of crime or lack of secrecy), thus making the privilege less certain since it is not in the control of the lawyer or the client[191].

To the extent that the Anglo-American capital markets rely on private enforcement to monitor the management of firms, this exception to the privilege makes sense. If management (for itself or for controlling owners) can design actions to usurp shareholders' interests while mounting privilege barriers in a way that deflects private enforcement efforts, such an exception is valuable. The complex application of the exception may be justified by the need to prevent excessive litigation by shareholders which would exhaust corporate resources in legal fights.

The crime fraud exception is recognized in England, as are the other common law exceptions discussed above[192]. Since the exceptions do not go the heart of my subsequent analysis, a detailed discussion of the English exceptions is not required.

5.2 Germany

Since the legal discussion of the privilege in German law is scant compared to Anglo-American jurisdictions, the issue of exceptions to the rule is discussed quite thinly. Furthermore, the classic exceptions familiar from the Anglo-American jurisdictions can be found in German law in their familiar form. The main observation here is that the exceptions to the duty of confidentiality and to the privilege are almost symmetrical, in accordance with the general attempt to minimize the discrepancies between the ethical and the legal obligations to secrecy.

5.2.1 Crime Exception

A lawyer that becomes aware that the client is using his advice to further criminal activities must withdraw from service[193]. The lawyer is also obliged, as is any other citizen, to report

185 Gergacz, 6-17.
186 For example, in cases of management opposition to tender offers.
187 For example, in cases of abuse minority rights; Gergacz, 6-21 citing ***Neusteter v. District Court***, 675 P.2d 1 (Colo. 1984) – an accountant privilege case.
188 Gergacz, 6-22 citing ***In re LTV***, 89 F.R.D. 595 (N.D. Tex. 1981).
189 Gergacz, 6-23.
190 Gergacz, 6-24.
191 Gergacz, 6-3.
192 Gergacz, 1-21.
193 StPO §261.

certain ongoing or future crimes that he becomes aware of[194]. The privilege would not be extended when a lawyer himself is an abettor to the crime.

5.2.2 Self Defense and Litigation between the Lawyer and the Client

Legal actions by the client against the lawyer and actions by the lawyer against the client concerning fees are an exception from the duty of confidentiality as well as from the privilege[195]. The exception in the case of a lawyer suing the client is traditionally justified by the lawyer's need to substantiate the factual basis for his claim.

The lawyer is also freed from the obligation when sued by the client, when the client injures the lawyer's honour, or when the lawyer himself faces criminal proceedings and needs the privileged evidence in order to mount a defence[196].

6. Waiver

This section outlines the comparative legal differences with respect to the doctrine of inadvertent waiver. The doctrine is then further analyzed in part III using insights from the economic analysis of accidents. Indeed, inadvertent waiver deals with, as the name of the doctrine suggests, accidental disclosure of privileged material. The issue is of unique importance for corporations since they transmit higher volumes of information to their lawyers compared to individuals and they do so more frequently. Therefore, they are potentially exposed to higher harm when privileged information is accidentally disclosed.

6.1 United States

A client may voluntarily waive the lawyer-client privilege at any time. However, waiver can also occur unintentionally. Courts have viewed a variety of actions and omissions by clients and lawyers as constituting waiver of the privilege. Most notably, when the communications between the client and the lawyer take place in the presence of a third person who does not belong to the privilege-circle, the waiver doctrine applies. The same is true when the privileged communication is accidentally disclosed to a third party. For instance, if a privileged email is sent to a person that does not belong to the privilege-circle[197].

The waiver doctrine is a good example for the difficulties in applying a rule initially designed for individuals in the corporate setting. The doctrine had to be adapted to fit the fact that corporations often dismantle some of their activities and transfer them into fully controlled subsidiaries. Normally the privilege is lost when the communication between the client and

---

194 StGB §138; Alfes, 101. The section contains a list of criminal violations that must be reported, by any citizen, as well as lawyers. For example: Treason, murder, money forgery etc.

195 Alfes, 102.

196 Henssler, 1822.

197 See generally on email confidentiality: Foote, Rebecca J., "Email, Privilege, Confidential Information and Inadvertent Disclosures" (2003) at: http://www.fmew.com/archive/EmailSecurity/index.html (last visited 10.5.2006).

the lawyer occurs in the presence of a third party, since the presence of another indicates that confidentiality is less important. However, when the client is a subsidiary-firm and its managers consult a lawyer with the representatives of the parent-firm being the third party present in the communications, the privilege is not lost[198]. This rule can have implications when the subsidiary-firm is sold. If a dispute later arises between the buyer and the former parent-firm, then the buyer now controls the subsidiary and its privilege. He can waive the privilege with respect to those communications that transpired between the lawyer and the managers of the parent-firm in the presence of the managers of the subsidiary.

6.2 England

English law recognizes the doctrine of inadvertent waiver as well. As in the US, the privilege may be lost as a result of accidental disclosure, either by the client or by his lawyer.

The waiver can happen during the trial, or the pre-trial discovery process. For example, it could happen by mistakenly disclosing in court a document that should have been privileged[199]. The waiver can also be inferred from the client or the lawyer's indiscretion with respect to privileged communications on contemplated actions not within the scope of a specific trial (before a trial actually materialized)[200], as in the mistaken email example in the US. As will be discussed in part III, the time and place in which the inadvertent waiver occurred has implications on the magnitude of the harm in English law. English courts may be exceptionally severe compared to US courts. Only in England do we observe that courts order the disclosure of all privileged material on all matters exchanged between a lawyer and a client as a result of inadvertent waiver[201].

6.3 Germany

There is no danger of involuntary waiver of the privilege in Germany. The client may intentionally waive the privilege which will then force the lawyer to testify[202], both in civil and in criminal procedures[203]. This is the rule in §385(2) ZPO and §53(2) StPO. When the

---

198 Gergacz, 3-55 citing ***Insurance Co. of North America v. Superior Court***, 108 Cal. App. 3d. 758 (1980). The court observed that two additional participants in the meeting between the legal adviser and the subsidiary's agents were not connected to the subsidiary but only to the parent firm. The court seems to have made an effort to define the two as a "temporary employee" and as an additional "legal adviser".

199 Matthews & Malek, 231-232, citing ***Great Atlantic Insurance v. Home Insurance*** [1981] 1 W.L.R. 529.

200 Matthews & Malek, 223.

201 ***George Doland Ltd v. Blackburn Robson Coates and Co.*** [1972] 1 W.L.R. 1338, though in this case it was held that a waiver with regard to conversations did not entail a waiver with regard to physical documents. See also generally on this matter: **Cross On Evidence**, 346 and Matthews & Malek, 223 and on.

202 French law is significantly different than other civil law systems in this matter. French law allows the lawyer to refuse to testify even after the client's waiver. The reasoning: the obligation of the lawyer stems from professional secrecy which is a duty conferred and administered by the lawyer and not by the client. Therefore the lawyer has the final word on waiver. Buhart, Jacques, „Confidentiality of Advice Given by In-House Legal Counsel Practicing in the European Union", 2 (available from www.acca.com. Last viewed: 25.11.2005)

203 Alfes, 101-103.

client is a legal entity, waiver can be made by the person or persons representing the legally authorised organ of the entity, regardless of whether this person was the one that transmitted the information to the lawyer, or not. When the waiving person is not the one that originally communicated the information, the fact that the original communicator may have his own interests in keeping the information secret has no effect on the lawyer's obligation. The lawyer's obligation is to the client that hired him ("Auftraggeber")[204].

A waiver of confidentiality by the client does not necessarily remove the constitutional private sphere of the lawyer (protected in §12 GG) which protects communications with third parties and personal impressions[205].

7. Summary

This part outlined the development and application of the privilege in the US, England and Germany. It focused on the emergence of the rule, whether in courts or in legislation; on the complimentary obligation to confidentiality; on the exceptions and on some unique traits of the corporate lawyer-client privilege. If one should try to paint, roughly, the differences between the Anglo-American and the German legal systems, then the color of privacy will emerge as the most dominant difference of all. The German sanctification of the privacy interests of the client, be it an individual or a corporation, yield in many cases applications that are starkly different than the Anglo-American applications - for the same rules or concepts. These are the highlights of the topics outlined above:

- In all jurisdictions the privilege emerged from the individual lawyer-client setting. I observed that all jurisdictions extended the privilege to the corporate lawyer-client setting without giving substantial weight to the different nature of the corporate client as compared to the individual client. The extension of the privilege occurred in some spontaneous process. The process seems to have nourished itself and the corporate lawyer-client privilege became so widespread that path-dependence has evolved. By that I mean that the courts feel obliged to go on recognizing the corporate lawyer-client privilege since revoking it now would presumably have dramatic consequences for corporate structures and for the provision of legal services.
- Confidentiality is part of the lawyer-client agency relationship. In the US and in England the lawyer's obligation to confidentiality is primarily ethical. Therefore, it is enforced by the professional associations' enforcement mechanisms (professional tribunals) or by the clients. The latter can sue for the breach of an implicit or explicit obligation to confidentiality. I observe that the obligation to confidentiality often contains exceptions that allow the lawyer to disclose confidential information. Some exceptions serve a social interest (such as reporting contemplated crimes) but others serve the lawyers themselves (such as the ability to disclose privileged information in a legal dispute with the client). Contrary to the Anglo-American systems, the obligation to confidentiality in Germany is statutory and enforceable by civil as well as criminal law. The reason is that protection of confidentiality in Germany is motivated by a strong, constitutional, protection of privacy rights. Nevertheless, in all jurisdictions one can detect the effort to create congruence between the scope of the privilege and the scope of the confidentiality obligation. This produces contradicting

204 BGHZ 109, 260, NJW 1990, 510.
205 BGHZ NJW 1990, 510, 512.

results. In Germany, the obligation is very strong since the privilege is also formulated in a very determined language whereas in Anglo-American law the privilege is at the mercy of the courts. Courts narrow the privilege by introducing wider interpretations for the exceptions to the privilege. As a result, more restrictions are then added to the obligation to confidentiality.

- The privilege in all jurisdictions is absolute. Hence, no matter how valuable the information held by the lawyer may be to the case at hand, the courts cannot revoke the privilege for the sake of a more accurate decision in a given case. In the US and in England, the privilege is primarily judge-made law whereas in Germany it is statutory and can also be enforced through criminal sanctions. Therefore, if a systematic situation is detected wherein the privilege needs to be limited – courts are generally able to react faster than legislators and generate a judge-made exception to the rule.
- There are four tests that can be used to determine which individuals in the corporation represent the corporation when communicating with the corporate lawyer. Most US states use a complicated "subject matter" test that requires observing the position of the communicating individual, his authority and the content of the communication. A few states opt for the restrictive "control group" test that focuses on the rank and the function of the agent. This test has been recently used also in English law. In Germany, as privacy matters most, all agents of the firm can communicate with the lawyer under the umbrella of the privilege.
- The three most notable exceptions to the privilege in all jurisdictions are: (1) the crime-fraud exception, (2) the lawyer's self-defense exception and (3) disputes between the lawyer and the client. The crime-fraud exception enables the lawyer to report or testify about future crimes contemplated by the client and thus deters clients from using the lawyer to obtain legal advice about how to reduce the expected sanction for a contemplated crime or fraud[206]. The other two exceptions cannot be said to have such a desirable social objective. They seem to serve the interests of lawyers and thus reflect, perhaps, the monopoly power that lawyers have, as an interest group, over the provision of legal services and their influence on the pertinent legislation. The ability of Anglo-American courts to produce judge-made exceptions led to the creation of an exception in cases of derivative lawsuits - a concept that cannot be found in Germany. The exception increases the ability of shareholders to police rampant managers that do not act for the benefit of the firm.
- If due care is not taken in order to safeguard the secrecy of privileged information and consequently privileged material is inadvertently disclosed, Anglo-American courts may declare that the privilege on some or all of the lawyer-client communications will be lost. In Germany, the doctrine of inadvertent waiver does not exist. This reflects once again the emphasis on privacy interests, also in the corporate arena.

206 As will be discussed below, this only holds if the sanctions are set correctly to deter the crime.

III Comparative Law & Economics Perspectives

In this part Law & Economics will be used to evaluate three issues in the application of the corporate lawyer-client privilege in the researched jurisdictions. First, the control of the privilege and the implications of the control on the behaviour of the firm is discussed, given different ownership and control regimes. In section 2, I analyze the control group test in comparison with other rules that determine who may represent the firm when communicating with the lawyer. Finally, I discuss involuntary waiver in the context of the economic analysis of accidents.

1. The Separation of Ownership and Control of the Privilege

We have observed that in all of the surveyed countries, the privilege is owned by the client, which means it belongs to the corporation and not to the individual agents of the corporate entity. In this section I shall analyze the implication of this fact on the behavior of firms in the surveyed jurisdictions, given that there are underlying systemic differences, as mentioned in the introductory note. Subsection 1.1 outlines the functions performed by lawyers in the corporate lawyer-client context. In subsection 1.2 I focus on the corporate lawyer's most central role: providing legal advice regarding contemplated actions. The existing model for individual lawyer-client privilege is then extended to the corporate setting. As will be shown, the most significant implication is the distortion of the alignment of interests between the principal and the agent in the firm. In subsection 1.3 the implications of these findings are exemplified in the context of compliance with competition laws in the US and Europe.

1.1 Functions Performed by Lawyers

"Legal services" is a general term that is used (and perhaps misused) as an umbrella term for the various functions that lawyers perform. Some of the functions are traditional. Some are relatively new. Not all functions are voluntarily provided by legal professionals – some are imposed on them.

The functions lawyers perform can be broken down into four categories. The first two categories are legal advice (before taking actions and after them) and gate-keeping. Two additional functions that lawyers perform will not be discussed here: the provision of business advice[207] and negotiating on behalf of clients[208]. The latter two categories are not directly linked to the legal aspect of the lawyer's role and therefore are normally not privileged.

The first category is "legal advice". Economic analysis has observed that legal advising itself should be broken down into two sub-categories: (1) Advice about contemplated acts (ex-ante advice), and (2) Litigation advice about acts already committed (ex-post advice).

---

207 Lawyers in their capacity as business advisors will not be discussed here since courts have consistently held that only legal advice (and not business advice) shall be protected by the professional privilege.

208 This aspect of the lawyer's role will be neglected here since it has relatively small implication in the context of the privilege discussion.

The provision of the first type of legal advice is part and parcel of the decision making process of a client that wishes to take into consideration the cost of expected sanctions in the event of choosing illegal or actionable avenues of action. This legal advice pertains to the legality or illegality of optional actions, the magnitude of the sanction for illegal actions, and the probability of enforcement (which is comprised of the enforcer's detection efforts, the sanctioning mechanism etc.). This type of legal advice is given ex-ante to the choice of the action and thus has an influence on the client's chosen action.

The second type of legal advice occurs ex-post the action, after enforcement procedures have materialized (regardless of whether the action chosen was legal or not). At this stage the role of the legal advice, the litigation advice, is to assist the client in presenting his case to the court in the optimal way, that is, the way which will minimize the probability of being found liable and decrease the expected magnitude of a sanction. This advice concerns the strategy of the client's defence claims in court, which evidence should be presented to the court and which should not be offered (as far as the client is able to control this factor), how to respond to evidence and strategies of the opposing party, etc.

The second category of functions that lawyers perform is increasingly central to the corporate setting. Gate-keeping and whistle-blowing functions have been extended to lawyers through legislation and case law. Lawyers seem to accept these roles with discomfort. They may also be limited in their capacity to optimally perform these functions. Gate-keeping and whistle-blowing roles stand in direct contrast with confidentiality and the privilege[209].

1.2 Ex-Ante Legal Advice in the Corporate Setting

Existing models analysing the lawyer-client privilege reflect the behaviour of human clients. I use the model developed by ***Shavell***[210] and extend the analysis to include the peculiarities of the corporate lawyer-client privilege. ***Shavell*** analyzed the effect of confidentiality on the seeking of ex-ante legal advice[211]. The analysis path is, first, to determine whether and when the obtaining of legal advice is socially desirable. Then, to determine whether confidentiality induces clients to seek legal advice and finally, to determine whether it does so when the legal advice is socially desirable or not.

In order to extend the analysis to corporations we must first account for the principal-agent problem in the corporate setting[212]. We assume the corporation is supposed to maximise the interests of the shareholders, and that within the corporation the principal-agent relationship is such that the interests of the corporation and those of the managers of the corporation are perfectly aligned. This means that the managers are induced to choose acts that increase the value of the shares of the corporation. For simplicity, we assume one corporation and one manager.

By assumption, the privilege decreases the probability of being sanctioned or found liable when a client chooses to pursue an act that is sanctionable. Without the privilege, the

---

209 See generally Langevoort (1993), Kraakman (1986).

210 Shavell (1988), 130. For a more informal analysis see also Kaplow & Shavell (1992).

211 Whether Shavell meant the analysis to apply also to privilege seems very plausible. Though the cost of confidentiality to the lawyer is not part of Shavell's model, I assume this to be his intention, since privilege simply ensures confidentiality at no cost to the lawyer.

212 Jensen, & Meckling (1976).

probability of being detected and sanctioned increases since the incriminating information can be obtained from an additional source - the lawyer. The use of the term "sanction" in this context will broadly apply both, to criminal or administrative sanctions, and to civil liability that is imposed by the court when an act is tortious or in violation of contractual obligations[213]. We assume that sanctionable acts are socially undesirable (since they reduce social welfare) so that the purpose of the sanction is to reduce the incentives to choose them.

In ***Shavell***'s model, the client might or might not be sanctioned, depending on his choice of act and the probability of enforcement. In the suggested corporate-client extension of the case, sanctions can be imposed on the corporation, or on its agents (manager or employee), or on both. The analysis of the effect of the privilege should therefore be extended to look at the choice of acts by the manager given the different sanction schemes[214]. As in ***Shavell***'s model, the manager faces the choice between engaging in sanctionable or non-sanctionable acts. The manager consults the lawyer in order to decide which act should be undertaken by the corporation.

The lawyer's advice is given both with respect to the corporation's liability, and the manager's personal liability. Note that although the lawyer's advice concerns the manager's personal liability, the manager is not the client. The client is the firm. We examine a situation in which the sanctionable action is privately beneficial for the firm but socially harmful. The extension of ***Shavell***'s model to the corporate setting is provided by enlarging the choice of sanctionable acts to three types:

Act	Manager	Corporation
Type 1	Sanction	Sanction
Type 2	Sanction	No sanction
Type 3	No sanction	Sanction

Table 1: Division of Sanctions

In acts of type 1, both the corporation and the manager can be sanctioned. In type 2 acts only the manager faces a sanction and in type 3 acts only the corporation faces a sanction[215].

213 Continental law traditionally does not recognize the possibility of criminal liability for corporations, unlike common law. Nevertheless, administrative monetary sanctions and equivalent monetary civil liability on corporations can accompany the personal liability of managers and have the same effect.

214 We assume that expected benefits and sanctions are the same for the corporation and for the manager for a given act, such that incentives are aligned.

215 The situation in which a manager is sanctioned and the corporation is not can happen when the manager acted *ultra-vires*. It is also possible in many criminal cases in civil law systems where corporations do not have criminal liability. In such cases privilege is unlikely to apply, or is likely to be waived by the corporation. The possibility of liability only for the firm is common. For example, under German law the corporation, rather than the managers, will be the most likely bearer of liability for incorrect statements made by the managers in the IPO prospectus as well as in *ad-hoc* statements. See BörsenGesetz §44 and WertpapierhandelsGesetz §37(b) and (c). This is also the case for competition law violations in the EU. In contrast, US antitrust laws contain criminal sanctions applicable both to the firm and to its managers. Corporate civil liability would also often fall under type 3 acts since collective action problems or high litigation costs reduce the probability of private enforcement through litigation. Corporations are the typical targets for multi-plaintiff claims, thus they are most likely to reap benefits from a privilege in this case. For example, managers might decide to take too little precaution in product safety testing if they believe they will not bear personal liability for damages from

The analysis below follows the footsteps of ***Shavell*** (1988).

A. 1. Advice is sought regarding the sanctionability of the act. Advice is definitive (rather than probabilistic) and sanctions correctly reflect social harm.

Assume that a privilege is not available. An individual client is contemplating an act but does not know whether the act is legal or sanctionable. The client wishes to avoid the illegal act. In the absence of the privilege, ***Shavell*** concludes that the individual client would only consult the lawyer when he believes that the act he is contemplating might be sanctionable. If the client believes the act is legal he would proceed to carry it out without consultation. Since legal advice is definitive and sanctions are set correctly, the legal advice will cause the client to avoid the sanctionable act and choose the socially desirable behaviour (since the sanction is set correctly to deter the act).

The effect of the privilege is to reduce the expected sanction in case a sanctionable act is chosen. Since the client will only consult the lawyer when he intends to avoid the sanctionable act, privilege has no relevance in promoting lawyer-client consultation.

This result would not change in the corporate setting. When the client, individual or corporate, is law abiding, the privilege does not increase the probability that a client will consult a lawyer prior to choosing an action.

A. 2. Advice is sought regarding the sanctionability of the act. Advice is probabilistic.

At this stage I also dispense with the restrictive assumption of obedience to the law. ***Shavell*** concludes[216] that if the expected probability of sanctions is set correctly, to reflect the expected social harm from the act, then legal advice will lead the client to choose the socially desirable act (as in case A.1).

The probabilistic nature of the lawyer's advice may induce the client to seek it. The privilege further decreases the probability of being sanctioned. ***Shavell*** then concludes that the privilege is socially desirable if the eventual expected sanction reflects the true social harm of the chosen act. This is because the client is induced to seek legal advice, but then restrained from the pursuing the illegal action. However, if the expected sanction is too low, the individual client might find it optimal to choose to engage in the socially undesirable act. In this case, the privilege decreases the probability of being sanctioned. Thus, it only reinforces the choice of the socially undesirable act. This might not occur if the client's private gains from engaging in the sactionable act are not high enough to offset and exceed the expected sanction, even post the privileged-advice. Thus, when sanctions are too low, privilege might or might not be socially desirable, depending on whether the client would seek legal advice with or without privilege in the first place[217].

---

defective products. Then, claimants that will have to prove that the firm did not abide by the standard of care will be discouraged since they will have no access to privileged information about the firm's decisions. Therefore, the choice of such acts will be desired by managers since they themselves are at no risk and the risk of the firm from liability is reduced by the privilege.

216 Shavell (1988), 133-4.

217 A numerical example can clarify the point. Assume the client wishes to choose between legal action A which yields a profit of 20 and another action B with yield a profit of 40. The client does not know whether action B is legal and consults a lawyer. The lawyer informs the client that action B is illegal and entails a fine of 30. If advice is definitive, the client would choose action A. Now assume the

In cases where a client would seek advice also without the application of the privilege, then the privilege has only adverse effects because it will increase the probability that the client will choose sanctionable acts. If the client only consults the lawyer when there is privilege, the choice of his act depends on his private gains and therefore might or might not have socially desirable results. Notably, as ***Shavell*** points out, the extent to which a privilege would induce a client to seek legal advice depends on how likely he believes it is that he will engage in the sanctionable act after being provided with the advice.

Assuming the advice is probabilistic with regard to both the manager and the corporation then extending the analysis to the corporate setting does not change the results. If expected sanctions reflect social harm, the privilege is socially desirable. If sanctions are too low, legal advice may or may not be desirable, as in the single client case. However, since the privilege belongs to the corporation, managers cannot be certain that the information that they communicate to the lawyer will remain privileged. Future events may lead the corporate entity to waive the privilege and expose the managers. In the corporate extension of ***Shavell***'s model, this can be expressed by the assumption that the privilege reduces the expected sanction for the corporation and for the managers, but the reduction is not identical. The reduction in the manager's probability of being sanctioned is smaller than the reduction in probability for the corporation. Hence, privilege distorts the alignment of principal-agent interests in the firm.

As explained, if sanctions are not set optimally, the existence of the privilege could induce the choice of undesirable actions. The structure of the corporate privilege would create a hierarchy amongst the types of sanctionable acts. If managers view the application of the privilege with respect to their own liability as less certain than the application of the privilege to the corporation, then managers should be induced to prefer the choice of type 3 acts. This will occur when expected sanctions are low for the corporations and managers face no liability. Type 2 acts will be least preferred by managers since the corporation might choose to waive the privilege and expose them. Acts where both the manager and the corporation face sanctions would be the second best choice: the corporation is likely to refrain from waiving the privilege to avoid exposing itself. However, *ceteris paribus*, managers still face a higher expected liability relative to the firm.

B. The client knows the act is sanctionable and seeks advice only with regard to the probability or the magnitude of the sanction.

Shavell's conclusions[218] are parallel to those outlined in A.2. The extension of the results to the corporate setting also remains the same.

C. Advice is sought only to find out how the magnitude or the probability of the sanction can be reduced.

---

privilege is not available and the lawyer's advice is probabilistic. For example, that the probability of enforcement on action B is 70%. In that case the expected fine is 30*70% = 21 and the expected profit from choosing B is 40 – 21 = 19. The client would then prefer choosing the legal action A with profit 20. The availability of the privilege would decrease the probability of enforcement since it will be harder for the authorities to prove the case against the client without the evidence collected from the lawyer. Assume the privilege reduces enforcement probability to 60%. Now the expected fine from choosing action B is 30*60% = 18 and the expected profit from action B is 40 – 18 = 22, which is superior to action A. Thus, privileged legal advice induces the client to choose an illegal action.

218 Shavell (1988), 136.

According to ***Shavell***, the privilege in this context is strictly undesirable because it encourages advice that will enable the choice of socially undesirable acts[219]. The result does not change in the corporate setting. However, as before, managers prefer type 3 acts if they believe that the certainty of their own privilege is lower than that of the corporation.

1.3 Application: Competition Law

EU competition law does not impose sanctions on individuals. Only undertakings are subject to monetary fines. This stands in stark contrast to the US antitrust laws which allow the imposition of monetary sanctions on corporate managers and may even impose incarceration[220]. In terms of our analysis, for US managers a decision to violate competition law would constitute a type 1 act, whereas such a decision in the EU would constitute a type 3 act. We would therefore expect, *ceteris paribus*, managers in the EU to lead their firms to violate competition laws with a higher frequency than their US counterparts. If the latter hypothesis were true, the legal system would have reacted by introducing a more complex liability scheme.

There is no clear evidence that such a difference in corporate compliance with competition laws actually exists. The following proposition may explain why.

Kornhauser (1982) shows that in many situations, making the corporation liable in tort is likely to produce greater care than putting the liability on the individual manager. This analysis applies to competition law as well. Several costs cause different levels of care in corporate/individual liability regimes[221]: (1) imperfect work contracts due to the inability of the corporation to perfectly write and enforce wage contracts on the level of care taken by the agent, (2) agent might be judgement-proof, (3) principals may not screen hired agents on the basis of carefulness, (4) principals may not have incentives to create a work environment that induces care, (5) inability to detect the exact agent that was liable, (6) the conflict of interests between agents that prefer less care and principals that care about maximising profit, and (7) inability of the principal, for whatever reason, to communicate the incentives to the agent.

Kornhauser's basic model assumes that the interests of the corporation and the manager diverge, and that the corporation cannot condition the wage of the manager on optimal care. Under these conditions, corporate liability is likely to induce the same level of care as personal liability[222]. However, if there is limited liability of agents this complicates the result. Judgement-proof agents may take less care, and since corporations may be better positioned to identify the responsible actors and deter or punish careless behaviour, then it might be more efficient to choose corporate liability over personal liability[223]. Court or corporate difficulty in assigning or enforcing liability to the correct agent also affects the efficient liability target, which may depend on which institution monitors or enforces better[224].

---

219 Shavell (1988), 136-7.
220 See for example section 2 of the most the Sherman Act 1890, 15 U.S.C. 1-7
221 Kornhauser, 1349-1351.
222 Kornhauser, 1351.
223 Kornhauser, 1351.
224 Kornhauser, 1351 and 1370-1371.

1.3.1 Effects of Systemic Differences

The influential systemic difference between the compared jurisdictions in this case is the different structures of ownership and control. Combined with the conclusions drawn from ***Kornhauser***'s analysis, this difference can explain the lack of disparity between US and EU corporate compliance with competition laws.

1.3.1.1 United States

In the US, ownership is dispersed amongst many shareholders who are presumed to be indifferent to controlling the management as a result of the collective action problem. Accordingly, managers have an incentive to seek higher rents by choosing actions that put the corporation at risk of liability, but not themselves (i.e. type 3 acts). In the absence of individual liability for violations of antitrust regulations, managers whose compensation is performance-related will have an incentive to violate antitrust laws in order to increase the corporate earnings. Even if the corporation will eventually be sanctioned, the managers would be able to abandon ship with a sizable rent in their pockets. The additional effect of the corporate lawyer-client privilege will only act to increase the incentive to engage in such actions, if we operate under the assumption that antitrust sanctions are imperfect. Since the privilege decreases the probability of the corporation being sanctioned - managers have the option to pursue even more harmful strategies, or alternatively pursue the illegal acts for longer periods.

This problem is partially solved by introducing individual liability for managers, which - assuming it is set correctly - aligns the interests of the managers with those of the corporation. Since managers face liability for antitrust violations and the lawyer-client privilege may be waived by the firm, under this rule the expected liability faced by managers is higher than the corresponding expected liability of the firm for the same violation. Therefore, socially detrimental behaviour should be deterred by personal liability in order for corporate compliance to function properly given the existence of the corporate privilege in the dispersed ownership regime.

1.3.1.2 England

The structure of ownership and control in the capital market in England is rather similar to the US. The English market presents a high level of dispersed ownership yet the level of potential remuneration from performance-based managerial compensation schemes is lower than the American average. This can explain why despite the absence of individual manager liability in English competition law, a significant excess of competition law violations is not observed in England.

Another explanation may be the absence of corporate lawyer-client privilege for in-house lawyers in EU competition enforcement procedures. This is the result of European Court of Justice (ECJ) case law spawned specifically by competition cases emerging from England. This is analyses in section 1.3.1.4 below.

1.3.1.3 Germany

In Germany, manager compensation is less dependent on the firm's performance. Hence, managers have a lower incentive to engage in inflating earnings, compared to their US counterparts. Additionally, concentrated ownership ensures that blockholders do not suffer from the same collective action problem in exerting control over management. German blockholders make sure that managers avoid taking actions with negative impact on the firm. The absence of individual liability is thus substituted by stronger principal control. Since violations of EU competition laws are type 2 acts, they will only be chosen when they are profitable for the corporation (or the principal). Under these circumstances the effect of the lawyer-client privilege is equivalent to the one discussed in ***Shavell***'s original model. This means the effect of the privilege on the behaviour of the firm is identical to the effect of the privilege on the behaviour of the controlling blockholder.

The effort to converge the regulation of the German market with that of the US market is aimed at reducing concentrated ownership and promoting a "shareholder culture" along with introducing performance-related managerial compensations schemes. The convergence trend in the German capital market should. Nevertheless, be a matter of concern. Under these circumstances, the German lawyer-client privilege poses a special danger. Since the German privilege is very strong, in the absence of individual liability for competition law violations, managers of German companies would have a higher incentive to engage in illegal anti-competitive actions. If the current trends continue, it would be wise to consider the introduction of individual liability.

1.3.1.4 EU Competition Law: Corporate In-House Counsel Privilege

The ECJ first recognized the corporate lawyer-client privilege in ***AM&S v. Commission***[225] more than 25 years ago. The case was referred to the ECJ from the English courts. It concerned an investigation by the competition authorities regarding suspected breaches of competition laws by AM&S. In its judgement, the court accepted that the privilege is generally recognized in most EC countries. However, in the context of investigations by the EC competition authority, the court only recognized the privilege under the conditions that: "On the one hand, such communications are made for the purpose and in the interests of the client's rights of defence, and on the other hand, they emanate from independent lawyers, that is to say, lawyers who are not bound to the client by a relationship of employment"[226].

Thus, through the ruling in this decision, in-house counsel were excluded from attracting the privilege in EU competition law. The legal reasoning was that in-house counsel are less independent than outside lawyers in their advice. Therefore, they are more likely to be compliant to their client rather than to observe the client's compliance.

As ***Buhart***[227] reports, the European parliament has twice considered a legislative extension of the privilege to in-house counsel. In the first time, in 1999, the Competition Commissioner Mario Monti was able to dissuade the parliament from pursuing this action by promising not to treat evidence of in-house counsel warning management about noncompliant behaviour

225 155/79 ***AM&S v. Commission*** [1982] ECR 1575, [1983] 1 QB 878 ECJ (hereinafter - ***AM&S***).
226 ***AM&S***, §21.
227 Buhart, 9.

with competition law as aggravating circumstances. This promise has never been formalised. In 2004 the European Commission and the European Parliament rejected a second attempt to extend the privilege to in-house counsel - this time in Council Regulation 139/2004 on the Control of Concentrations between Undertakings, (the EC Merger Regulation).

Proponents of expanding the privilege also to in-house counsel claim that the powers of the European Competition Commission are so strong that it does not need to intrude on the relationship between in-house counsel and their clients. Regulation (EC) 1/2003 of the European Council of 16.12.2002 concerning the application of articles 81 and 82 of the EEC Treaty (regarding competition rules)[228] empowered the EU competition authority with significant investigative powers and with effective immunity and leniency measures, which increase its effective enforcement of anti-competition law violations. The regulation did away with the obligation to submit agreements for prior approval by the commission, and instead it now relies on the parties own legal evaluation of the situation. It is therefore claimed that the EC competition authority's need for information held by in-house lawyers has decreased significantly, while there is an increased value in promoting the candid discussion between corporate clients and their in-house competition law advisors[229].

In ***Hilti v. Commission***[230], the European Court of First Instance extended an in-house lawyer-client privilege to communication in which the lawyer reported and summarized the advice of outside lawyers. This has not been a significant improvement from the in-house counsel's point of view.

Indeed, in some EU countries, in-house counsel are not admitted to the bar. They are perceived to be dependent on their employer, while independence is a pre-condition for recognition as a lawyer. Therefore they do not enjoy the privilege[231]. In Germany, in-house lawyers may be registered as lawyers, if their employment terms comply with certain requirements, such as occupying a high level position in the firm, in which case they are referred to as Syndicusanwälte. The question of whether the Syndicusanwalt is entitled to the privilege was never formally decided by the courts. Nevertheless, in practice this is the case[232]. As for documents prepared by the Syndicusanwalt, when they are in the possession of the lawyer they are protected from seizure. Whereas, documents in the possession of the corporation are not protected[233].

The issue has once again come for consideration before the European Court of First Instance, in the recent case of ***Akzo-Nobel v. Commission*** - which called on the court to reconsider broadening the corporate lawyer-client privilege to include in-house counsel[234]. The case concerns documents seized in a search conducted by the EU competition authority in the offices of the complaining corporations - again, in the United Kingdom. The seized documents contained, among others, notes that documented correspondence between management and the in-house counsel in charge of compliance with competition law. The corporation claimed in preliminary hearings that the privilege should be extended to cover the documents. The court decided the matter merited serious consideration and postponed it to

228 The EU competition authority can impose financial sanctions on companies in administrative procedures that in many respects resemble criminal procedures against companies.

229 Buhart, 10.

230 Case T-30/89, ***Hilti v. Commission*** (1990), §18.

231 Buhart, 4-5. For example: Belgium, Italy, Austria, Slovenia.

232 Buhart, 6.

233 §97 StPO.

234 Case T-125/03 ***Akzo Nobel v. Commission***, order from 30.10.2003 (hereinafter – ***Akzo-Nobel***).

the main proceeding. Proponents of the in-house counsel privilege are hopeful, since the court pointed out the existence of effective rules of conduct in EU member states that bind and restrict in-house counsel and ensure the independence of their actions, in spite of their employment by the corporation[235].

Reconsidering the ***AM&S*** argument of independence, the claim that in-house counsel are less independent than outside lawyers is no longer convincing. Independence seems to have been used by the court as a proxy for ensuring compliance by the client. This assumption obviously does not hold, and there is no reason to assume that the form of contractual relationship between the corporate client and the lawyer would in itself change the decision of the management with regards to following, or ignoring, the lawyer's legal advice.

A different answer lies in the nature of the firm. Firms retain in-house counsel because producing the legal advice "in-house" is more efficient than acquiring it from outsiders[236]. One advantage of the in-house counsel is the specialized intimate knowledge of the firm they are able to acquire. Another benefit is his immediate and total availability to the firm. The fact that European corporations have retained in-house lawyers for the last 25 years, in spite of the lack of privilege, is evidence that these lawyers provide the corporation with benefits regardless of the privilege[237]. Of course, an in-house counsel privilege might have encouraged firms to retain even more in-house counsel[238].

There is reason to suspect that in competition law cases the privilege creates private benefits for corporations and - if sanctions are imperfectly aligned - social costs that exceed the private benefits. Both the ***AM&S*** and ***Akzo-Nobel*** cases demonstrate the willingness of corporations to invest in high litigation costs in order to obtain a privilege. The ***Upjohn*** decision in the US specifically singled out competition law as a field of law that is not intuitive to comply with. Hence, legal advice is valuable here. In fact, the increased uncertainty with regards to the application of the law, resulting from the reform of European competition regulation, makes legal advice even more valuable. This leads to the question: to whom is the value created by the advice flowing? When the ***AM&S*** court considered the dependence of the in-house lawyer on the corporation, it did not consider whom within the corporate entity the lawyer is dependent upon. In the German concentrated control structure, the in-house lawyer, like the rest of the management, is likely to serve the interests of the owner. In England, the in-house lawyer is retained by the management, which is controlled by dispersed shareholders. Thus the lawyer will tend to serve management interests, which may not be aligned with those of the shareholders.

The effects of the ***AM&S*** rule in England are to induce a reduction in managerial decisions violating competition law which fall under the definition of type 3 acts. This reduction is likely to be countervailed by the shift of some corporations from internal to external lawyers,

---

235 ***Akzo-Nobel***, §126.

236 Coase (1937).

237 The website of the European Company Lawyer Association (www.ecla.org) which represents European in-house counsel reports 31,000 in-house counsel members in 16 European states. ECLA was established in 1983, exactly one year after ***AM&S***, and has been an adamant proponent of extending the privilege to its members. See also Buhart, 12.

238 The ***Akzo-Nobel*** case, be it in the initial phase as it is, offers a clear reply to those who claim that lack of privilege hinders candid exchange of information between the client and the lawyer. In this case, the investigators had the opportunity to look at the documents as they were seized and found them - prima facie – valuable to their case against the corporation. This shows that the manager in this case relayed damaging information to the lawyer in spite of the absence of the privilege. The court held that if privilege will be extended, the authority will not be allowed to use the documents as evidence.

who still enjoy a privilege. The ***AM&S*** rule induces corporations to seek *external* competition law advice regardless of whether their ownership is concentrated or dispersed. The ***AM&S*** rule is socially desirable in that it reduces social harm by increasing the deterrence of type 3 acts in firms with in-house counsel (in the absence of a privilege). This reduction is dampened by the decision of some firms that relied on in-house legal advice to shift to external legal advice and continue to enjoy the shield of the privilege. Not all firms would choose to shift (as the case of ***Akzo-Nobel*** shows) since disintegration of legal advice from the corporation has costs which may make it inefficient. Furthermore, the post-***AM&S*** disintegration of legal advice may be privately desirable for firms, but is socially welfare reducing (assuming that the socially efficient firm structure is to have in-house legal advice). Hence, the ***AM&S*** rule is only efficient if the reduction in harm outweighs the efficiency loss caused by the related corporate disintegration of legal advice services.

In Germany, managers have a-priori lesser incentives to engage in type 3 violations, since their personal benefits are lower, and tighter control by owners ensures that they only engage in illegal acts that have a positive payoff for the corporate owners. Thus the ***AM&S*** rule does not change the managerial choice of type 3 acts. However, it does reduce the incentive of owners to violate competition law. Therefore - as in England - the rule induces the countervailing inefficient shift to external legal advice, but without the associated benefit of reducing the managerial harm.

Before concluding, the underlying assumptions should be recalled. We assumed sub-optimal competition law enforcement wherein after consulting the lawyer, a client is more likely to engage in an illegal act than to be deterred from such an act. We also assumed that overall the damage of the illegal acts undertaken as a result of legal advice is higher than the damage prevented by illegal acts that were deterred by the provision of legal advice. If the opposite is true, then the ***AM&S*** rule would have an opposite effect. The lack of privilege would eventually increase violations of the law. However, violations would decrease if corporations shift to external legal advice, with a corresponding social efficiency loss.

1.4 Summary

In this part I focused on how the structure of the corporate lawyer-client privilege influences the choice of actions by managers under different ownership and control regimes, building on the existing Law & Economics models of legal advice regarding contemplated actions.

In the corporate setting, sanctions or damages can be imposed either on the firm, or on the manager or on both. However, the structure of the corporate lawyer-client privilege is such that the privilege reduces the probability that the firm will be sanctioned but the probability that the managers will be sanctioned is not reduced quite to the same degree. Hence, the starkest conclusion of this part is that the corporate lawyer-client privilege distorts the alignment of interests between the principals and the agents in the firm. It follows that managers would prefer to choose sanctionable actions that put the firm at risk of sanction (or liability) but not themselves. This implies that in the presence of the corporate lawyer-client privilege, deterring socially detrimental actions by imposing sanctions or liability strictly on the corporate entity is less effective.

Considering the differences in corporate ownership and control between the Anglo-American and the German systems, I conclude that the German block-holder culture enables the firm to better monitor the management thereby realigning the interests of principals and agents as compared to systems with dispersed ownership.

This difference does not necessarily mean that German managers will avoid taking sanctionable actions. It means that they will choose such actions only when these actions serve the benefit of the principals. Indeed, this is the outcome of applying the conclusions to competition laws in Europe and in the US. Competition law sanctions in Europe are usually directed at the corporation whilst in the US they are aimed at both the corporation and the managers. However, there is no known significant difference in competition law violations between the jurisdictions.

Finally, still within the framework of competition law, I discussed the deliberation in the European court system on whether to grant a corporate lawyer-client privilege to in-house counsel. The matter has been debated since the European Court refused to acknowledge such a privilege in competition law investigations. I conclude that the European rule may have induced firms to shift from efficient in-house legal services to less efficient (in this case) external legal services. I propose that in the German system this shift is not welfare enhancing whilst in England it may have enhanced social welfare since the loss from shifting to less efficient legal services can be outweighed by some decrease in violations of competition law.

2. Who Represents the Corporation?

The rules determining which agents can represent the client in their communications with the lawyer are crucial. The corporate entity must communicate with the lawyer through individual agents. Only communications conducted by agents recognized for the purpose of the privilege are protected by the privilege. I focus here on the rules used by courts to determine which agents trigger the privilege when communicating with the corporate lawyer on behalf of the corporation.

In the United States, the prevailing rule until the last decades of the 20th century was the restrictive "control group test"[239] which is still in force in jurisdictions such as Illinois, Texas and Alaska. In most other states and in the federal courts it has been replaced by various versions of the "subject matter" test[240]. However, in a recent decision in England a vague test similar to the control group test, or even more restrictive, was used[241], raising the relevance of the issue once again. German courts grant a privilege to all employees communicating on behalf of the firm regardless of rank[242].

---

239 Developed in ***City of Philadelphia v. Westinghouse Electric Corp.***, 210 F.supp 438 (E.D. Pa. 1962)..

240 Developed initially in ***Harper & Row Publishers v. Decker***, 423 F.2d 487 (7th Cir. 1970).

241 In ***Three Rivers***, the parties agreed that only the unit in the defendant (the bank) that was authorized to communicate with the lawyers and decide on the actions pursuant to the communications will enjoy the privilege. The court noted that even higher echelons than the specified unit will not be privileged in their communications with the lawyers. This approach is more restrictive than the control group test since the control group loses the privilege if it delegates authority to lower echelons. The House of Lords did not comment on this application and therefore the matter is open for further interpretation.

242 See *supra* in section II.4.3.

The rule that will be chosen to determine who represents the corporation can have dramatic implications on adjudication costs. In the following subsection I explain why this is so and give some examples from US case law. Subsection 2.2 then summarizes the four rules, also referred to as "tests", which will be analyzed. In subsection 2.3 I present the hypothesis that restrictive tests cause hidden social losses as a result of inefficient restructuring of management echelons in firms. Furthermore, I claim that restrictive tests induce firms to assert the privilege without merit in order to deter potential litigation. These claims are based on the two main observations in the case law, which are summarized in subsection 2.4. These observations indicate two irregularities in the consequences of the application of the restrictive control group test compared to the supposed expectations of the framers of this test. Subsection 2.5 provides a general example which is then used in order to formalize the economic analysis of hidden restructuring. Case law supporting the analysis is then discussed. Subsection 2.6 explains the second irregularity by a simple game theoretic model. Case law analysis follows. Subsection 2.7 addresses the hiring patterns for in-house counsel in US firms in relation to the previous observations. Subsection 2.8 concludes and discusses the comparative legal implications of the results.

2.1 Adjudication Costs

The magnitude of judicial resources invested in adjudicating corporate privilege assertions is huge. The courts must inspect the content of each document for which the privilege has been asserted in order to ascertain whether it contains information communicated for the purpose of seeking legal advice.

Courts in all systems assume that the lawyer-client privilege has some social benefit. All courts also assume that this benefit is limited to situations in which the privilege is used for the purpose of procuring legal advice. The court and the party claiming the privilege exert costs in the process of verifying that the communication took place for the purpose of seeking legal advice. Courts are wary of losing or precluding factual evidence that does not serve this purpose. This motivates courts to examine the purpose of the communication[243]. The underlying assumption is that while communication for the purpose of seeking legal advice is likely to produce more social benefits than social harm, an all-encompassing privilege is more likely to be abused and be socially adverse.

An assertion of the privilege in litigation creates a bifurcated case. The first stage of the litigation involves determining whether the privilege assertion holds. Although bifurcated cases may save litigation costs, since some cases will not continue to the second phase after the privilege issue has been decided, the bifurcation of the case creates an additional cost in itself. Courts must invest a considerable effort in deciding the privilege claim. Privilege fights may become very costly.

---

243 For example, in ***Spectrum Systems v. Chemical Bank***, 157 A.D.2d 444, 447-448 (1990) the plaintiff requested internal report prepared by external lawyers for the defendant bank. The lawyers were hired to investigate possible fraud on the part of the employees of the bank and to suggest future corruption prevention measures. The court noted that the burden of proving the elements of the privilege lie with the party asserting the privilege because of the strong public policy consideration in favour of full disclosure. The court held that there was no legal advice involved in this case and that the investigation also did not refer to any imminent litigation. The role of the lawyers was to investigate and develop facts rather than to render legal opinion, in the view of the court. Therefore privilege was not extended.

The "control group" test is essentially a rule of thumb. It assumes that communications for the sake of securing legal advice are conducted by the individuals who are authorized to make decisions on the basis of the legal advice - the corporate control group. Therefore the court can save the cost of inspecting communications by other agents and automatically reject the privilege assertion and admit them. The control group test thus has tremendous judicial cost saving consequences.

The effect that the control group test has on adjudication costs can be seen in the following two cases. In ***Duplan***[244], a case involving 22 parties in which pre-trial discovery lasted five years and encompassed one million documents, privilege was asserted with respect to 4500 documents, all of which had been submitted to the court for *in-camera* inspection. The court described the process as "painstaking". It took ten days and this was no exceptional case. In comparison: in ***In re E.I. DuPont de Nemours***[245], an asbestos damage claim by more than 100 plaintiffs, the defendant voluntarily discovered 55000 pages and claimed privilege with respect to another 607 documents. The trial court rejected the privilege without examining the content of the 607 documents. On appeal, the Texas Supreme Court held that the global rejection of documents that the "privilege log"[246] indicated were written by lawyers was unjustified and these documents must be individually examined. As for the other documents, they considered that here the privilege would not apply since the defendant did not show any relationship between them and the control group. The latter decision creates a pure saving in judicial time which would not have been possible in non-control group jurisdictions.

Despite the clear savings in adjudication time and effort, most US jurisdictions have departed from the control group test and instead opted for a more work-intensive inspection of privilege assertions. One court said: "...Obviously, as a corporation needs legal advice, it cannot deal solely through the chairman of the board of directors. ... If only one, two, three, or four persons within a corporate structure could be the corporation when it must seek legal advice, then, for all practical purposes, any corporation would not have an effective attorney-client privilege. The chairman of the board and other top executives necessarily have more important matters to attend to than gathering information for either outside or inside counsel"[247]. In ***Upjohn*** the US Supreme Court rejected the control group test and adopted a case-by-case approach normally referred to as the "subject matter test". The test can be generalized in the following stages:

(1) Court examines whether the corporate representative was

(a) A member of the control group ***or***,

(b) An authorized lower echelon agent,

(2) Court examines whether the subject matter of the communications was seeking legal advice ***and*** if the representative was an agent authorized by a member of the control group - whether the advice concerned a matter within his corporate duties.

---

244 ***Duplan Corp. v. Deering Milliken***, 397 F.supp 1146 (D.C.S.C., 1975).

245 ***In re E.I. DuPont de Nemours and Co.***, 47 Tex. Sup. Ct. J. 583 (Tex., 2004).

246 A privilege log is the documentation of the circumstances of the lawyer-client communications, which supposedly describes the justification for the privilege assertion.

247 ***Duplan Corp. v. Deering Milliken***, 397 F.supp 1146, 1164.

The two tests should be considered along with two polar tests: (1) an all inclusive rule – where all corporate agents can trigger the privilege regardless of their echelon, and (2) an all exclusive rule – where no employee can trigger the privilege.

2.2 The Tests

As indicated, four tests can be applied by courts in order to determine which corporate agent triggers the protective "umbrella" of the privilege when communicating with the corporate lawyer.

1. **No Privilege**. The firm is a separate entity from the employees for the purpose of the privilege and none of the agents trigger the privilege when communicating with the lawyer on behalf of the corporation. To clarify: in this admittedly purely theoretical case, a corporate lawyer-client privilege may still exist, but it is never granted since none of the individuals in the corporate entity can trigger its activation.
2. **The Control Group Test**. Only the top management that has decision-making authority represents the firm. Any other communicating employees, even when authorized by a manager, will not be privileged.
3. **The Subject Matter Test**. The privilege protects communicating with lower echelon employees when acting within the scope of their function and specifically authorized to communicate with the lawyer by the management.
4. **All Privileged**. All employees may communicate with the lawyer and the privilege extends to all communications.

The following graphic display represents the tests. The firm is represented as an organizational pyramid with several echelons. Echelons are separated by dotted lines. The top echelon is the management group, which contains a smaller number of employees, but is in charge of the decision-making which influences the corporation as whole. The lower echelons contain more employees. As one slides down the corporate ladder, employees perform specific tasks rather than make decisions that influence the corporation a whole.

The agents whose communications are privileged are represented by the dark areas.

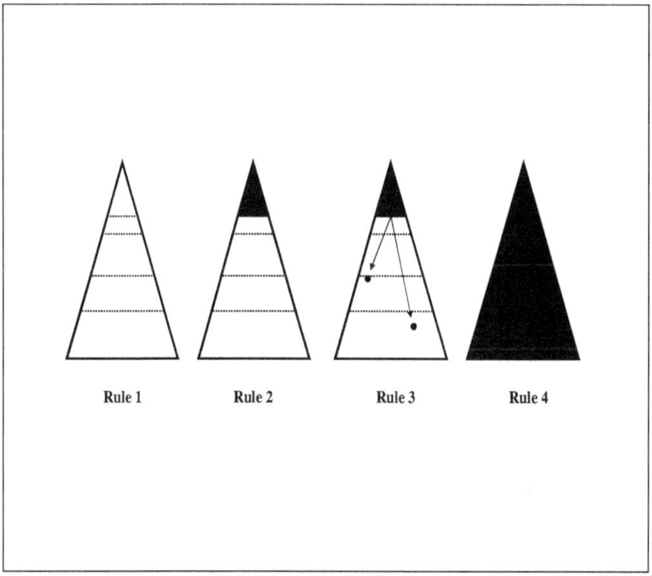

Figure 1: Graphic Depiction of the Tests

Under the first rule, the communications of a corporate entity as a client will never be privileged. In fact, there is no such jurisdiction. The second rule, the control group test, applies the privilege to communications made by the authorized top management.

The third rule enables the management to authorize privileged communications between lower echelons agents and the lawyer. The black dots in Rule 3 represent individual employees in lower echelons that were authorized by the control group to communicate with the lawyer and will therefore also trigger the protection of the privilege. Note that the management can only authorize specific employees to communicate with the lawyer (described by the black dots in the graphic example) and not an entire echelon of employees. Finally, according to the fourth rule - which exists in Germany, for example - all agents of the firm may communicate with the lawyer under the privilege so long as the communications are for the purpose of seeking legal advice.

2.3 Hidden Costs – The Hypothesis

The corporate lawyer-client privilege gained notoriety in the United States when tobacco corporations used it to conceal research and evidence their lawyers perceived to be detrimental to a defence assertion that there is only a weak causal link between smoking and lung cancer. Tobacco corporations structured communications on such research activities through external attorneys in order to secure the privilege, which also applies to communications between lawyers and third-party professionals[248]. Courts later had to sift through endless documents in numerous lawsuits to determine which of the documents legitimately attracted the protection. Often the privilege was denied because communications were not in furtherance of legal advice but for public relations or business purpose (one example of many, ***Burton v. R.J. Reynolds***[249]). Courts have done away with this "outsourcing" of corporate activity by holding that the communications of in-house lawyers with third party professionals will only be privileged when the professional acts as an "interpreter" for the lawyer[250].

The tobacco litigation exposed how the presence of the privilege induced corporations to disintegrate some of their activities - in this case research activities - and structure them differently in order to secure the protection of the privilege in potential litigation. These are observable structural changes that shift activities from the firm - outside.

The tests for determining who communicates on behalf of the firm also have an affect on the structure of firms. The Courts seem to overlook the hidden corporate structural changes caused by the operation of the more restrictive of those tests. I hypothesize that restrictive tests adopted in order to restrict the privilege or in order to save adjudication costs are likely to have an inefficient hidden effect on the structure of corporate decision making. The tests used by courts to determine which agent triggers the privilege induce firms to structure their communications with their lawyers in such a way that would decrease the availability of evidence for potential opponents. Managers have an incentive to do so. This re-structuring is inefficient and may have detrimental social welfare effects.

I further assert that when courts adopt restrictive tests in order to decrease the privilege's misuse, for example to avoid sanctions for socially undesirable actions, firms that do not normally enjoy a privilege may consequently also be induced to engage in sanctionable actions.

2.4 The Control Group Test: US Case Law Observations

The number of US states that still adhere to the control group test is, as mentioned, very small. The main producers of case law in the area are Illinois and Texas, and the extent of the relevant case law is small. However, there are two significant observations that do emerge from the case law[251]:

(1) Some firms assert the control group privilege for lawyer-client communications that were conducted by individuals that appear to be (or are asserted to be) in control positions, but whom after closer inspection by the court, are found not to meet the control group test requirements.

(2) Some firms assert the privilege for communications that were conducted by employees that were *not* control group members, and could not have possibly been mistaken as such.

248 See generally, Savage & Luster (2005).

249 ***Burton v. R.J. Reynolds***, 200 F.R.D. 661, Kansas, 2001).

250 Courts started to curtail this cooperation between lawyers an third-party professionals in 1961 in ***United States v. Kovel***, 296 F.2d 918, 922 (2d Cir., 1961). However, the application of this rule depends on the each court's interpretation.

251 The case law is surveyed in section 2.5.2, *infra*.

Law & Economics can provide an explanation for both peculiarities. With respect to the first observation, the hypothesis is that firms alter their internal structure in order to fulfil the criteria of the control group test. This hypothesis is supported by case law, although such cases are rare, since when firms successfully alter their internal structure they are then able to fend off potential plaintiffs by successful privilege assertions.

The second observation is explained by the hypothesis that even firms that cannot "squeeze" into the control group test may be able to discourage potential plaintiffs by mimicking the behavior of firms that have a valid control group privilege.

2.5 Law & Economics Analysis: Hidden Inefficient Restructuring

2.5.1 Why and How Do Firms Restructure

As I have observed in section III.1.2, corporations perceive the lawyer-client privilege to be privately desirable when they believe that after learning the legal advice they may decide to engage in a profitable, yet illegal (sanctionable) action. If the lawyer can be a source through which enforcement authorities, or opposing parties in litigation, can obtain evidence regarding prior corporate knowledge of the illegal nature of the action - the expected sanction increases and the illegal action could be deterred. If litigating opponents are denied access to damning information due to the existence of the lawyer-client privilege, then illegal or sanctionable actions can be chosen. Assuming of course, that corporations have imperfect knowledge about the law; that they believe illegal actions maybe sub-optimally sanctioned; and that after consulting the lawyer they might opt for an illegal action.

Factual information is the basis for both corporate managerial decisions and the provision of legal advice. Often, factual information is collected by lower echelon employees and must, in turn, be obtained from these echelons. Rational managers and lawyers should be privilege-minded. They will try to structure the lawyer-client consultation process in a manner that will maximise the probability the privilege will be granted by the court. The following scenario, reminiscent of many US fraudulent misrepresentation cases, may help clarify the interactions.

> Soft-corp is a firm that produces business software. The software contains an internal problem detecting routine. When the software detects a problem it generates a problem report and asks the user whether he wishes the problem report to be sent to the online problem center (OPC). In the OPC a software engineer (employee E) analyzes the nature of the problem. The firm can then fix the problem by developing software updates.
>
> The OPC recently received a report from a single user indicating that the software malfunctioned as a result of a clash with another program. Employee E analyzed the problem and found that it can be repaired at a low cost by developing a repair software. However, he also noticed that the same problem can cause anti-virus malfunctions and expose users to viruses and hackers. The modifications to the software required to solve this problem are significant and costly. Employee E reports both observations to the manager.

The manager of the firm (manager M) consults the corporate lawyer on possible avenues of action. The lawyer needs to evaluate the liability risks faced by the firm and therefore requires information about the exposure to litigation expected as a result of the second problem. The information needs to be collected from employee E. If asked, employee E suggests that the likelihood of the problem actually occurring is low, however the magnitude of the potential damage is high. Employee E would suggest warning all users and disabling the software until a solution is developed since users may be exposed to immediate loss of all their saved files. On the basis of this information, the firm's lawyer would advise to immediately develop repair updates since the firm will be liable for any defect which it was aware of and did not fix. The lawyer would also advise that reporting the problem to the stock market is obligatory since this is material information for investors. Omitting the material is fraud and the manager will be liable for it personally if proven to have knowingly withheld the information.

Any information about the second problem would have a dramatic effect on the firm's share price. Manager M instructs employee E to "develop the required solutions to any problem that may arise from the recently discovered problem". He then informs the stock market that Soft-corp has recently become aware of a problem in the software as a result of a user report, that the problem is being solved and that repair updates will be distributed within one week. After one week the firm distributes the repair update for the first problem but does not mention that it is working to solve the second problem as well.

In this situation Soft-corp is exposed to product liability. However in addition to this, the manager's concern is also reporting the information to the market as legally required. Under US securities law a plaintiff against Soft-corp for fraudulent misrepresentation can only succeed if he is able to prove "scienter" on the part of the manager, which translates to knowledge of the fraudulent nature of the misrepresentation. In this example, the lawyer's testimony is the cheapest evidence of the manager's scienter.

Let the value of the final decision to the firm be denoted by v_L. The cost of each internal or external communication shall be denoted by c. The firm is interested in minimizing the cost of the decision-making process. Hence, it is interested in the most efficient information-flow structure. The firm's payoff function is: $\Pi = v_L - n \cdot c$. Let n^* denote the number of communication steps required in the most efficient state of events. We can generalize the steps leading to decision-making in a stylized way using the Soft-corp example. In the most efficient state, the following stages transpire:

1. Employee E reports the problem to manager M.
2. M directs E to communicate all relevant information to the corporate lawyer, along with the relevant optional actions.
3. The corporate lawyer collects the relevant information from E.
4. The corporate lawyer renders the legal advice to M on the basis of the information collected from E and the contemplated actions.
5. M chooses an action and instructs E to implement the action.

In the most efficient structure, $n^* = 5$.

We now apply the privilege tests that determine who is authorized to communicate on behalf of the firm. Under the first and fourth tests, firms have no incentive to alter the efficient n^*-step structure, since re-structuring would not alter the results.

Results differ however under the control group test. Since employee E is not a member of the corporate control group, any communication between him and the lawyer will not be privileged. A privilege-minded corporation will have an incentive to alter the information flow process. In some firms, the process may take the following form:

1. Employee E reports the problem to manager M.
2. M reports the problem to the corporate lawyer.
3. The corporate lawyer directs M which information is required in order to render legal advice.
4. M collects the informational from E
5. M communicates the information to the lawyer.
6. The corporate lawyer renders the legal advice to M.
7. M chooses an action and instructs employee E to implement it.

In this structure, the manager, who is a member of the control group, is the only representative of the firm that interacts with the lawyer, thereby ensuring that a privilege based on the control group test will not be lost. The result is $n = n^*+2 = 7$ stages.

Since the privilege-minded n^*+2 steps process is costlier than the more efficient n^*-step process, it will only be used by the firm if it expects that privileged communications will allow it to choose a sanctionable action (denote the value of a sanctionable action for the firm by v_H). We assume that sanctionable actions are privately desirable by corporations since they produce a higher expected profit, yet they are socially harmful. The condition,

$$v_H - (n^*+2)\cdot c > v_L - n^*\cdot c$$

must hold for the corporation to choose a sanctionable action, or to alter its structure in the first place.

The last test we examine is the "subject matter test". It is applied by US courts on a case-by-case basis and therefore is highly uncertain. Under this test, communications between the control group and the lawyer are privileged as in the control group test. In addition, authorized lower echelon employees may also trigger the privilege, but sometimes courts may deny granting the privilege to lower echelon employees. In the Soft-corp example, the employee was specifically authorized to communicate with the lawyer and the privilege would normally be triggered. However, some courts may rule that the employee's function in the firm was related to repairing software and not to representations in the stock-market. Hence, if the lawyer and employee exchanged information on this matter - it might not be privileged. The uncertainty of the test is captured by the probability of the privilege being triggered under the subject matter test, β. The incentive of a firm to restructure its information flow process increases with any decrease in β, as long as the condition

$$v_H - (n^*+2)\cdot c > \beta v_H - n^*\cdot c,$$

is satisfied.

Some firms fit "naturally" into the control group test. By "naturally" I mean that the efficient structure of the firm is such that the managers in the control group already hold all the required information for consultation with the lawyer as part of the efficient operation of the firm. When this is not the case, a firm interested in ensuring the privilege would have to add an information-collecting task to its manager's roster. The additional steps in the (n^*+2)-step process are necessarily performed by the manager of the firm or by a member of the control group. As noted in the case law survey in the next section below, courts that apply the control group test make a point of verifying that the member of the control group performing the communications is *de-facto* involved in the process of deciding the action pursuant to the legal advice[252].

Managers and control group members are arguably the individuals with the highest opportunity cost in the firm. The manager must divert a cost c from efficient managerial work to the information collection task. Managers are constrained in their decision-making resources, such as the time used to collect the underlying information and to assess the advantages and disadvantages of the decision. In large corporations, it may be inefficient for top managers to collect legally-relevant background information about contemplated acts. This activity can be more efficiently carried out by the lawyer communicating directly with lower echelons. Managers divert their attention from managerial work to the information and legal-communications role (as embodied in the additional steps of our example) only when the gain from the possibility of choosing a sanctionable action is higher than the loss from unperformed efficient managerial work. This shift of managerial attention is less likely (1) as corporations grow larger, (2) as corporations face frequent litigation which requires individual attention, and (3) when intensive collection of factual information is necessary for decisions. Under these circumstances communicating with lawyers becomes an intensive, time-consuming activity which is too costly for managers to attend to.

There is an alternative course of action which is often exploited by corporations, but which also produces a hidden efficiency loss. In privilege-minded corporations subject to restrictive tests, the costlier it is for management to collect information for the purpose of legal advice, the more privately profitable it is to enlarge the circle of decision-makers. However, unless managers are entirely homogeneous (which is not a realistic prospect), the larger the size of the decision-making group - the higher the cost of reaching a decision. Let x denote the number of managers in the control group. Management contemplation of the proposed actions occurs in the final decision stage (step n^*+2). The cost of this stage for the firm will now be denoted by $k(x) \geq c$, with $k'(x) > 0$, $k''(x) > 0$[253]. There is an optimal size for the decision making group in an efficient structure, x^*, and for simplicity $k(x^*) = c$. Hence, in the socially optimal structure, the cost of the last decision step is equal to the cost of all prior decision steps. As a consequence of the control group test, corporations have an incentive to increase the size of the control group. By adding managers to the control group the firm can ensure that these additional managers will be available to collect information internally and communicate it to the corporate lawyers. However, recall that for the privilege to be in force these managers must take an active part in the decision process. Denote the number of

252 See ***Claxton v. Thackston*** (1st Dist., 1990, 201 Ill. App 3d 232, 559 N.E.2d 82, 147 Ill.Dec. 82, 1992) (hereinafter – ***Claxton***).

253 The more members in the group, the costlier it is to reach a decision and the longer the deliberation. Although there are mechanisms to speed up decision-making (like voting), courts examine the process of deliberation and observe whether all the members of the group are being consulted. If a member is not consulted (for example, if the protocol of a board of directors' meeting does not reflect that the opinion of a director was asked for and heard) then the court can rule that this member is not a member of the control group, either generally or for the purpose of the decision in question.

members in the enlarged control group by $\tilde{x}$. Since our starting point was the optimal size of the control group, we know that $\tilde{x} > x^*$. The cost of the decision stage increases accordingly to $k(\tilde{x}) > k(x^*)$. Firms have an incentive to enlarge the control group as long as the privilege is privately beneficial and opportunity costs discourage managers from shifting their attention from regular managerial activities.

Corporations will restructure under the control group test when:

$$v_H - (n^*+1)c - k(\tilde{x}) > v_L - n^* \cdot c$$

Which translates to the condition:

$$v_H - v_L > (n^*+1)c + k(\tilde{x})$$

Under the subject matter test, the following condition must hold:

$$(1 - \beta)v_H > (n^*+1)c + k(\tilde{x})$$

The conditions tell the following story: the restrictive control group test (and to a lesser extent also the subject matter test) creates an incentive for corporations to increase the size of the control group beyond the socially efficient x^* when the managers have high opportunity costs and cannot divert their resources to collecting information for the lawyers themselves. However, the inflation of the control group is limited by the increasing costs of decision making by large groups. Hence, some firms will find it inefficient to increase the control group beyond a certain size. This will result in the deterrence of some sanctionable actions by firms that will not always be able to "squeeze" into the control group test.

2.5.2 Relevant Case Law

The courts of the state of Illinois are the most ardent supporters of the control group test and produce the most relevant case law on the implementation of the control group test. While corporate presidents and vice presidents are always acknowledged as part of the control group[254], decisions become interesting when lower echelons are involved. Not every "manager" is necessarily a member of the control group.

In ***Dietz v. United States***[255] the defendant corporation tried to privilege an accident report communicated prepared by a building manager. The plaintiff slipped on a patch of ice in front of a building owned by the Federal Deposit Insurance Corporation (FDIC), a government corporation. The plaintiff sued for negligent care. The accident was documented by Susan Kent, the manager of the building. The report was communicated to the FDIC's insurer (who was protected by the lawyer-client privilege through an extension of the privilege to co-defendants). Although the case was tried before a federal court, the substantial issue was a matter of tort law, governed by the laws of Illinois. Thus, the court held that the

---

254 26 A.L.R. 5th 628 §13 and §14.

255 ***Dietz v. United States*** (N.D. Illinois, 1992, Westlaw 26712, affirmed 989 F2d 502, 1993) (hereinafter – ***Dietz***).

relevant privilege test was the Illinois control group test. The defendant was concerned about the detrimental evidentiary value of the accident report. Although Susan Kent was an external contractor and not an FDIC employee, the FDIC nevertheless attempted to incorporate Kent into the control group *a-postriori* by admitting that Kent was an employee and not a contractor. The court decided to accept this claim, although no proof was presented, because this was a "statement against interest"[256]. Indeed, by making this admission, the FDIC risked liability for any negligence that Kent may have been responsible for. This is what happened when the court then determined that the FDIC had not proved that as an employee, Kent was a member of the control group and therefore the burden of substantiating the privilege had not been met and the plaintiff subsequently prevailed.

The ***Dietz*** case represents a post-factum attempt of the corporation to incorporate the manager Susan Kent into the control group. An act which would have decreased the FDIC's expected liability. The necessity for such a move raises the question: why wasn't Kent part of the control group ex-ante? One can assume that damages caused by negligent building managers are probably too random and rare compared to the cost of changing the employment status of all building managers from contractors to permanent employees. Since the FDIC did not spend the *a-priori* cost of re-structuring its information flow process and incorporating Kent into the control group, it had no proof that Kent was a member of the decision circle. The court was therefore correct in its ruling.

In this case there was another factor to consider: the FDIC was not a corporation based in a control group test jurisdiction like Illinois. It was a federal corporation. Under federal law the applicable test would have been the subject matter test. Therefore, the probability of facing the control group test would have been very small, and the cost of restructuring would have been large compared to the expected benefits - since only three states use the control group test. Hence, the FDIC had no overall incentive to re-structure[257].

In ***Claxton v. Thackston*** a storage corporation appointed a member of the board of directors in charge of investigating production accidents. The plaintiff Claxton was an employee injured in the course of his work. By chance, the director was also an eye-witness to the accident. He wrote an eye-witness report, within the scope of his duties, to the insurance company. The corporation asserted that the report was privileged. The court held that the defendant had not proved that the director "had an advisory role in top management, whether a decision in this area would normally not be made without his advice, or whether his opinion would in fact form the basis for any decision by others with authority in the company"[258]. Therefore privilege was denied. Essentially, the court observed that in spite of the managerial title, the director was not a decision-maker.

---

256 A "statement against interest" is a procedural norm that allows the court to accept that a certain statement is true in spite of the fact that no evidence is provided to prove this statement. The idea behind this norm is that a statement against interest exposes the party that made the statement to liability. Hence, this party would normally avoid making such a statement and the court can safely assume that if the party made the statement fully knowing that liability might ensue, then the statement is true. In ***Dietz***, the FDIC knew well that by stating that the house manager was an employee of the firm regardless of the fact that there was no evidence to such an employment relationship, the firm will have to bear the liability for the actions of the manager.

257 The FDIC, as a federal corporation, should have generally expected that most of its litigation would be governed by the federal test, which is the subject matter test. It thus had a low incentive to change its structure to accommodate a stricter test.

258 ***Claxton v. Thackston*** (1st Dist., 1990, 201 Ill. App 3d 232, 559 N.E.2d 82, 147 Ill.Dec. 82, 1992).

In contrast to ***Dietz***, the corporation in ***Claxton v. Thackston*** was an Illinois based firm. Although the firm appointed a member of the board of directors to be in charge of collecting the information, which shows it was mindful to the control group test, it failed to obtain the privilege since the director did not have any influence on the decisions made by the firm with respect to the information he collected. One possible explanation can be the fact that the firm was family-held. The director was the only non-family member on the board. One can speculate that a decision circle comprised of family members may be relatively homogeneous (in this case). Incorporating a non-family member into the decision group would increase the friction in the decision process significantly. Therefore the marginal increase in the cost of decision making $k'(x)$ would be higher in such a case, reducing the incentive to enlarge the decision-circle *de-facto*, and not merely by title.

In many cases corporations assign fact collection and communications to high ranking employees in the hope that the title will be a sufficient signal to secure the privilege. This often fails. In ***Consolidation Coal Co. v. Bucyrus-Erie Co.***[259] the defendant was a company that produced machinery for coal mining. Following the collapse of an excavator wheel it was sued. It attempted to avoid liability by claiming privilege with respect to a detrimental report by its metallurgical engineer who had examined the damaged wheel. The company had to concede that the engineer was not a member of the control group test, but still tried to convince the court that he regularly advised the management on such issues. The court examined the exact role of the engineer and found that he supplied factual information and had no influence on decision-making. The privilege was denied. A similar situation occurred in ***Archer Daniels Midland Co. v. Koppers Co., Inc.***[260]. The case concerned the collapse of a construction structure. The defendant claimed privilege regarding a report prepared by its "senior engineer". The court held that the engineer (in spite of his "seniority") was only in charge of collecting factual information and had no decision making capacities. Privilege was denied. Similarly, when a store "safety director" in ***Shere v. Marshall Field & Co.***[261] wrote a report about an accident that caused bodily harm to the claimant, the court declined to privilege the report since the "director" had no actual authority.

These cases can be contrasted with that of a successful privilege assertion. In ***Hayes v. Burlington Northern and Santa Fe Ry. Co.*** [262] the widow of a switchman who died in a train accident sued his employer, the railroad company. The plaintiff requested the disclosure of reports prepared by the corporation's regional director of claims. The court found that the director of claims was solely responsible for such claims and that he had decision making authority regarding some of the claims up to a certain magnitude, and thus belonged to the control group for that purpose. The privilege was affirmed.

In this case, the management had delegated some decision making authority to the regional manager. While this de-centralized structure may have complicated the application of centralized policies in the firm, it had increased the corporation's ability to deprive opponents from damning evidence.

---

259 ***Consolidation Coal Co. v. Bucyrus-Erie Co.*** (89 Ill.2d 103, 59 Ill.Dec. 666 Ill., 1982).

260 ***Archer Daniels Midland Co. v. Koppers Co., Inc.*** (485 N.E.2d 1301 Ill.App. 1 Dist.,1985).

261 ***Shere v. Marshall Field & Co.*** (327 N.E.2d 92 Ill.App. 1 Dist., 1974).

262 ***Hayes v. Burlington Northern and Santa Fe Ry. Co.*** (752 N.E.2d 470 Ill.App.1.Dist., 2001).

2.6 *Law & Economics Analysis: Mimicking by Unprivileged Firms*

2.6.1 *The Mimicking Game*

Law & Economics can explain the observation in the case law of firms asserting a control group privilege, not only when it is clearly appropriate, but also when the communicating individual clearly did not belong to the control group. The explanation seems to be that mimicking privileged firms pays off.

The existence of the privilege does not mean that the plaintiff will always fail in an attempt to obtain discovery of lawyer-client communications, but privilege does decrease the expected probability of prevailing in court. Consequently, some meritorious claimants are deterred from suing. Under the first test, no such deterrence occurs whereas the fourth test is the strongest deterrence for meritorious claimants.

To understand the effects of the control group test, assume a litigation sequence where an upheld privilege is a strict barrier for plaintiffs. Hence, in the following game, if the privilege is granted - plaintiffs lose, regardless of whether their claim has merit or not. Plaintiffs do not know whether a specific defendant corporation fulfils the requirements of the test or not. The internal structure of the defendant corporation is strictly the private knowledge of the corporation. However, the proportion of firms in the market with a naturally efficient structure which allows them to meritoriously assert a control group privilege is exogenously given, and denoted by (α). Assume α is common knowledge.

The firm (F) faces a choice between a legal and an illegal action. Illegal actions are socially harmful but under-deterred. Hence, privileged firms expect a positive benefit (r) from engaging in the illegal action. The payoff from the legal alternative is 0. When a firm takes an illegal action, the plaintiff (P) suffers damage (*d*). Assume launching a law suit is costless. Therefore plaintiffs always sue when they are harmed. In order to prevail, plaintiffs need evidence which is part of the corporate lawyer-client communications. The firm can refuse to provide the evidence by asserting a privilege. The assertion is costless. Hence, the firm would always assert the privilege when it is truly a privileged firm, but also firms that do not have the required privilege structure ($1-\alpha$) have an incentive to assert a privilege, if they can successfully mimic privileged firms.

The plaintiff must then decide whether to fight the privilege claim or fold. Fighting requires expending a cost (*k*). In our simplified model, the privilege is a strict barrier for claimants. Hence, if the firm is privileged, the plaintiff's fight always fails since he is unable to obtain the required evidence to support his claim and prevail in court. If the firm is bluffing, the plaintiff is always successful and a sanction (s) is imposed on the firm[263]. The stages of the game unfold in the following order:

1. Nature decides the probability with which a firm efficiently fulfils the requirements of the control group test (α).

---

263 While we assume that fighting the privilege is costly for the plaintiff we do not account in this model for the cost of proving the privilege that is borne by the defendant. This cost has no significant effect on our results. In the case that the firm does not have a privilege it will fold immediately after the plaintiff fights and expends the cost k, so it will only bear the cost of the sanction S. In the case of firms that have the privilege - the more plaintiffs fight, the more often litigation costs will be spent to prove that the firm is entitled to the privilege, but we can assume that even after expending this cost the return from illegal actions, R, is profitable.

2. Privileged firms choose illegal actions; unprivileged firms choose illegal action with probability (y) and legal actions with probability (1–y). If a legal action is chosen the game ends.

3. When illegal actions are chosen, in our model, this implies that the plaintiff files a lawsuit and that the firm then asserts a privilege regardless of its real type.

4. The plaintiff decides whether to fight the privilege (x) or fold (1–x), after which the game ends and payoffs are distributed.

The extended form of the game is displayed below.

The payoffs are displayed in the order (plaintiff, firm).

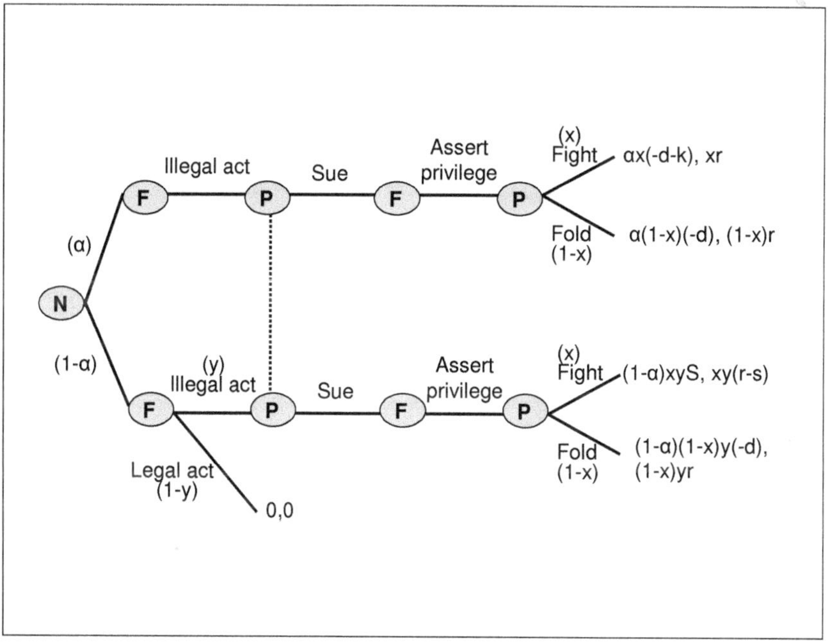

Figure 2: Extensive Form of the Mimicking Game

We solve by backwards induction. Clearly, the plaintiff's problem is that an assertion of the privilege is not a credible signal of the firm's true type. Hence, after observing an illegal act, the plaintiff does not know which type of firm he is facing in court. Calling the bluff of type (1–α) firms by fighting them is costly. The plaintiff then decides to fight only if

$$(1-\alpha)xys - \alpha x(d+k) > \alpha(1-x)(-d) + (1-\alpha)(1-x)y(-d).$$

Re-arranging yields:

$$y > \frac{\alpha}{(1-\alpha)} \cdot \frac{x(2d+k) - d}{x(s-d) + d}.$$

Since privileged firms always choose illegal actions, I focus on unprivileged firms. The firm knows its type and knows α. It should therefore be able to anticipate the plaintiff's behaviour. The firm will choose an illegal action whenever:

$$xy(r-s) + y(1-x)r > 0$$

which simplifies to: $y(r-xs) > 0$.

Hence, whenever the probability that the plaintiff will fight is smaller than the profit/sanction ratio, $x < (r/s)$, unprivileged firms will find it desirable to mimic the behaviour of privileged firms (by setting $y = 1$). When $x = (r/s)$, firms are indifferent. When $x > (r/s)$, unprivileged firms face a negative expected return from choosing the illegal action and would therefore be deterred from choosing it.

For the plaintiff to be indifferent, the following must hold:

$$y = \frac{\alpha}{(1-\alpha)} \cdot \frac{(r/s)(2d+k) - d}{(r/s)(S-d) + d}.$$

Recall that α represents the proportion of firms that fit "naturally" into the control group test. In other words, α represents the proportion of firms that the framers of the control group test, in their respective jurisdictions, expected to use (or abuse) the privilege. Now assume, as I have observed earlier, that firms find it profitable to restructure their internal organization in order to secure the privilege. Let β denote the probability that a firm fits the requirements of the control group privilege in such a reality. Of course, $\beta/(1-\beta) > \alpha/(1-\alpha)$. This implies that with β, *ceteris paribus*, the probability that an unprivileged firm will mimic the behaviour of a privileged firm will increase compared to α. And the probability of a plaintiff fighting a privilege assertion decreases. The intuition is as follows: when more firms fulfil the requirements of the privilege, the signal of an asserted privilege becomes more credible and more plaintiffs prefer to fold, which means that for the few firms that falsely assert the privilege, the likelihood of getting away with bluffing increases.

2.6.2 Relevant Case Law

There is ample US case law to support the hypothesis that corporations assert the existence of a privilege even when they clearly cannot expect that it will be recognized by the court under the control group test.

In several cases, hospitals have asserted the privilege for communications conducted by nurses - clearly not "control group" personnel. In such cases one could not seriously presume these assertions would hold. ***Buckman v. Columbus-Cabrini Medical Center*** (651 N.E.2d 767 Ill.App. 1 Dist., 1995), ***Mlynarski v. Rush Presbyterian-St. Luke's Medical Center***

(572 N.E.2d 1025 Ill.App. 1 Dist., 1991) and ***Chicago Trust Co. v. Cook County Hosp.*** (698 N.E.2d 641 Ill.App.1.Dist., 1998) all involve failed attempts by hospitals to claim a control group privilege for reports made by nurses in negligence cases. In the latter case the assertion attributed the report - on the accidental disconnection of a patient's ventilator - to the "head-nurse" that was in charge of patient care.

Similar failed attempts to privilege evidence prepared by lower echelon employees can be found in ***Day v. Illinois Power Co.*** (199 N.E.2d 802 Ill.App.,1964), which concerns Gas company employees that investigated a pipe explosion, and in Texas state cases such as ***Cigna Corp. v. Spears*** (838 S.W.2d 561 Tex. App.-San Antonio,´1992), ***National Tank Co. v. Brotherton*** (851 S.W.2d 193 Tex., 1993), ***Boring & Tunneling Co. of America, Inc. v. Salazar*** (782 S.W.2d 284 Tex.App.-Hous. 1 Dist. ,1989). In ***Boring & Tunneling***, the control group privilege was claimed with respect to an interview with a truck driver in the company that caused a deadly accident. These cases strengthen the assertion that once they are sued, even firms that clearly do not fulfil the requirements of the control group test attempt to deter claimants by mimicking the privileged firms.

2.7 Further Evidence: US Hiring Patterns for In-House Counsel

Our hypothesis can be further strengthened by observing the pattern of development for the hiring of in-house general counsel in US corporations. ***DeMott*** (2005) and ***Daly*** (1997) report that in-house general counsel were first hired by US corporations as early as the 19th century. Between 1940 and the 1970's, the role of general counsel diminished and external law firms grew stronger. This period corresponds to the prevalence of the control group test. General counsel turned into "contractors" of external legal services. To understand why, note that even when the lawyer was integral to the corporation, under the control group test he could not communicate with lower echelon employees without losing the privilege. Managers would have to collect the information themselves and transmit it to the in-house counsel if they wanted to secure the privilege (the n*+2 step process). Therefore the full benefits of integrating legal counsel into the corporation could not be exploited.

From the 1970s, the role of general counsel again increased in prominence. It reached a peak in 1982 when in-house attorneys gained such strength that they formed an independent political organization to further their agendas by leaving the American Bar Association (ABA) and establishing the American Corporate Counsel Association (ACCA). ***DeMott*** (2005) and ***Daly*** (1997) recount many reasons for the empowerment of in-house counsel during this period. One they do not mention however, is that this period corresponds to the emergence of subject matter tests in various US jurisdictions (although they note that some legal services became cheaper to produce inside the corporation). Under the subject matter test, in-house counsel were able to communicate with lower echelon employees with significantly smaller risk of losing the privilege. This was exactly the case in the Supreme Court ruling in ***Upjohn*** (1981), the hallmark case for the subject matter test, only one year prior to the establishment of the ACCA. This indicates - as demonstrated here earlier - that after the acceptance of the less restrictive subject-matter test, firms found it more valuable to integrate the legal consulting into the firm, by retaining in-house counsel.

2.8 Conclusions and Implications

2.8.1 Conclusions

In control group jurisdictions, corporations have an incentive to assert the privilege not only when it is warranted, but also when the assertion is false. The reasons for this are twofold: first, it is costly for plaintiffs to challenge the assertion. Second, since the assertion might be true, a positive payoff for the plaintiff is not certain. In fact, the expected payoff is diminishing as more corporations fulfil the requirements of the control group test. Hence, under the control group test corporations that would not be granted a privilege also have an incentive to pursue sanctionable actions and subsequently assert a false privilege. In equilibrium, all corporations that fulfil the requirements of the control group test engage in sanctionable actions and some of the corporations that do not fulfil the requirements of the test successfully engage in sanctionable actions as well.

As discussed previously, by altering the internal information collection process, a corporation can secure the privilege and its expected benefit. Corporations will pursue this avenue when the certain profit from a sanctionable action, less the cost of re-structuring, outweighs the expected gains under false privilege assertions, or the gain from legal actions.

One can then compare two static equilibria. The first equilibrium represents the perception of the framers of the control group test, where only a restricted share of corporations naturally fit the control group test. Under the second equilibrium, more corporations squeeze within the test's requirements. With the shift to the second equilibrium, unprivileged corporations find it increasingly profitable to assert a false privilege. The consequence should be an increase in social welfare losses due to sanctionable actions, although some adjudication costs may be saved due to a decrease in the frequency of privilege fights.

The mechanism described here also characterizes the subject matter test. When the test is applied perfectly, corporations will be privileged regardless of the internal structure and claimants will be deterred. When uncertainty about the application of the test arises, some corporations find it privately efficient to alter their control group in order to secure the privilege. Some corporations however, will not alter their structure but assert a privilege even when they expect that it would be denied upon closer inspection by the court, since they also expect that the false assertion will deter the plaintiff from pursuing the claim. The bottom line is, that the benefits of the control group test are smaller than courts in the relevant US jurisdictions would have us believe. Furthermore, if firms can determine where they will be sued (for example by choosing their state of incorporation), firms that cannot enjoy the privilege under the control group test will tend to self-select out of control group jurisdictions. As a result, the proportion of protected corporations will increase, causing an additional decrease in the screening benefits of the test.

2.8.2 England

In England, the courts had not addressed the issue of who represents the corporation for the purpose of the privilege until the recent case of ***Three Rivers***, which was discussed here above[264]. Recall that in this case, the parties had mutually agreed to use a very restrictive

[264] See section II.4.2, *supra*.

version of the control group test. The lower court accepted the choice of the parties and the House of Lords made no further comment, thereby leaving the issue open for further consideration in future cases.

To the extent that English courts are considering the adoption of the control group test as a tool for restricting the use of the privilege, one should bear in mind the hidden social costs described here. As privilege claims in English courts are much less frequent than in the US, it might be more efficient to avoid these costs by adopting broader tests like the "subject matter" test or the protect-all German rule, in spite of the high judicial cost.

2.8.3 Germany

German courts apply a broad test, protecting all communicating employees, regardless of their echelon[265]. The broad approach means courts should be expending high efforts to determine whether the content of communications emanating from a variety of echelons were in furtherance of legal advice. The willingness of courts to adopt a protect-all test for corporations, which is the costliest test from the point of view of adjudication efforts, can be explained by two factors: first, a strong privilege deters claimants and therefore produces less adjudication on the whole; secondly, pre-trial discovery is minimal. German civil procedure does have some discovery measures[266], however, when the evidence is in the hands of an opposing litigant, German courts are very likely to shift the burden of proof (§138 ZPO and, for example, BGH NJW 1996, 1826). This renders a privilege irrelevant from the outset.

German courts are confronted with an assertion of privilege at a considerably lower frequency than Anglo-American courts. Thus, they can afford to invest the effort of verifying the purpose of the communication in each case.

Privilege assertions are more valuable in German *criminal* cases where shifting the burden of proof is rare. Since corporate entities are not subject to criminal liability in continental law, they often have an incentive to waive the privilege in order to expose their managers to liability and avoid corporate sanctions. In cases where the privilege has not been waived, as in the ***Panzergeschäft*** case[267], the court indeed does seem to labour to determine the accurate nature of the communication, and does not apply any preliminary screening tests. Although the case concerned the corporate auditor-client privilege, the similarity between the auditor and lawyer privilege in German law makes the decision applicable to lawyers as well.

In the case at hand, the BVerfG discussed a petition submitted by an auditing firm, after the State Attorney had conducted a search and seizure of documents in its offices as part of an investigation into suspected tax evasion by a client corporation, apparently through "shelf corporate entities" in the Virgin Islands. The auditing firm asserted that the search was a disproportionate breach of the privilege against search provided in §97 I StPO; was in breach of the constitutional right to fair process (Article 2 I GG and 20 III GG); and in breach of freedom of occupation.

265 Alfes, 180.

266 See in the introductory chapter.

267 BVerfG, 2 BvR 2211/00, from 27.10.2003 www.bverfg.de/entscheidungen/rk20031027_2bvr221100 .html (Panzergeschäft).

In its ruling, the BVerfG stressed that the privilege (and its extension to searches) inhibits the public prosecution in carrying out its socially valuable function of clearing up criminal suspicions and offences, and therefore should be interpreted restrictively[268]. By that the court meant, that only communications that were made truly for the purpose of professional consultation should be privileged. In this case, the organs of the corporate client were the accused in the underlying criminal procedure (firms have no criminal liability in German law). The BVerfG reiterated that the "bond of trust" between a corporate legal entity and the "privilege carrier" exists only between the professional (in this case an auditing firm) and the client corporation - not its organs[269]. The court further noted that the interests of the firm and of the individual organs may be in coalition, but may also be diametrically opposed to each other[270]. Having said all that, the BVerfG rested the crux of its ruling on the purpose of the underlying communication. The identity, position or authority of the communicating officers was not a matter of discussion at all. The BVerfG relied on the findings of the lower court that regarded the relationship between the firm and the auditing firm as an "Innenrevision" (which can be translated as internal controlling), and ruled that the seized documents regarding the tax evasion were only transferred to the auditing firm for "asylum" purposes[271].

Although ***Panzergeschäft*** deals with the physical transfer of documents for the purpose of concealment, the rule that emerges fits all lawyer (or auditor) and client communications. The BVerfG hence instructed courts to look into both the nature of the privileged relationship between the professional and the client, and whether the communicated information serves the purpose of the privilege. As noted, these are work-intensive issues of adjudication. The court did not devise rules of thumb regarding the identity of the communicating agents.

The ***Panzergeschäft*** scenario is impossible to apply to a civil dispute in Germany. Note that privilege was claimed after the prosecution had already seized the disputed documents in a search. Civil litigants rarely have the ability or opportunity to intrude on their opponents with such force.

3. Inadvertent Waiver

A client or a lawyer may waive the privilege and allow the disclosure of privileged lawyer-client communications. Waiver can be made voluntarily, or occur inadvertently (involuntarily). Inadvertent waiver means that the privilege is lost as a result of a negligent or mistaken disclosure of confidential communications. The inadvertent waiver can occur as a result of the client's independent behavior, or as the result of the lawyer's independent behavior. Therefore it fits within the scheme of the familiar economic analysis of accidents[272].

The issue of inadvertent waiver is of unique importance in the corporate setting. The reason for this is related to economics of scale. Corporations communicate with lawyers more frequently than individual clients; they transmit to their lawyers a significantly higher

268 BVerfG, 2 BvR 2211/00, from 27.10.2003 (Panzergeschäft), at 13.

269 BVerfG, 2 BvR 2211/00 at 11; see also **Karlsruher Kommentar zur StPO**, 5. Aufl., §97 Rn. 6.

270 However, as this was a criminal case and the corporate entity itself was at no risk of facing sanctions, it did not waive the privilege. Had this been a civil liability case, the corporation may have been able to deflect its own liability by shifting it to the managers.

271 BVerfG, 2 BvR 2211/00, at 8.

272 The analysis that follows is based on Schaefer & Schoenenberger (1999) and on Brown (1973).

magnitude of information; and they often interact with their lawyers on a larger variety of legal matters than those of an individual client. Hence, for corporate clients, the magnitude of the harm caused by the accidental loss of the privilege (as a result of an involuntary waiver) can be proportionally higher than it is to an individual client.

In the following subsection inadvertent waiver is compared to an accident. I then discuss the unique traits of inadvertent waiver that make it different from the conventional economic analysis of accidents. Then, the liability rules and the harm rules used in case law for accidental waiver are summarized. Subsection 3.2 analyzes the optimal investment in care for individual and for corporate clients. I also discuss the type of precautions that would be preferred by corporate clients. The incentives of lawyers to take care are also discussed.

Subsection 3.3 concerns the implications on two components of social welfare: (1) accuracy of adjudication and (2) frequency and volume of communications between lawyers and clients. The following subsection surveys the pertinent case law. In subsection 3.5 I comment on the difficulties in enforcing the lawyer's optimal investment in care due to the exceptions to the privilege. Subsection 3.6 concludes.

3.1 Inadvertent Waiver as an Accident

The courts grudgingly grant privilege because they are interested in maximizing the information available to them when deciding cases. Courts assume that inadvertent waiver by the client is a signal of the client's disinterest in observing the confidentiality of the privileged information. Consequently, courts that observe an accidental disclosure of privileged material will often conclude that an "inadvertent waiver" has occurred, meaning that the privilege should be removed.

The disclosure of privileged information may cause harm to the client when privileged evidence, adverse to his case, is exposed to the opponent in litigation. The harm that the client may suffer as a result of the accidental disclosure of privileged evidence is the expected increase in the loss (or the expected decrease in the gain) that the client will have to bear in the litigation outcome as a consequence of the fact that the opponent can now submit this previously-privileged information to the court. Since this harm manifests itself as more information available to the court, it increases the probability of courts reaching accurate decisions. Hence, if we assume that corporations use the privilege in order undertake more socially undesirable (sanctionable) actions, then the private harm to the corporation as a result of accidental disclosure is a social gain in terms of accurate adjudication.

The nature of the "accident" is in this case similar to the classic unilateral accident known from textbook Law & Economics literature. In the classic unilateral accident, the injurer's activity causes the harm and the victim is entirely passive and cannot prevent the harm in any way. In the bilateral accident case, both the victim and the injurer may prevent the harm by taking care. In the case of inadvertent waiver, harm can be caused independently by either party. The client may be his own victim if he is careless and accidentally discloses privileged information to a third party or fails to maintain some required standard of confidentiality. The client can also be the victim of careless disclosure by his lawyer. The first case, where the client is his own victim, is essentially a unilateral accident. The second case is more unique since the lawyer is the injurer, and the client cannot take precautions that will reduce the probability of an injury. However, the client can avoid the activity altogether, thereby preventing the accident. This means that the concept of inadvertent waiver has turned the activity of consulting with a lawyer into a risky activity. A rational risk-neutral actor would only engage in a risky activity when the private utility from this activity (denoted u) is higher than private costs.

The harm resulting from accidental waiver is always borne by the client, regardless of whether the accidental disclosure occurred as a consequence of his own negligence or that of the lawyer. One should note carefully that the harm in this "accident" is quite unusual. It is a harm that is court-created. In the classic economic analysis of accidents, harm is exogenous. However in this case, the court can decide whether it is desirable that accidental disclosure would lead to harm, and also what magnitude this harm should have. Consequently, courts can determine whether consulting a lawyer will be a risky activity in the first place, and how risky shall it be.

In the economics of tort law, courts deal with determining liability for the harm caused in an accident, and then the compensating of victims by determining damages. Accidental waiver is different. There is no issue of compensation (except in lawyer malpractice, which will be discussed later), since the matter concerns evidence law and not tort law. Since the harm in accidental waiver is court-created, the issue is whether to create harm or not, and what magnitude this harm should have.

3.1.1 Liability Rules

The classic economics of tort law offers the social planner a choice between negligence and strict liability regimes for the purpose of determining the distribution of compensatory damages for a given harm. In inadvertent waiver, as we shall observe, courts use these regimes as a mechanism to determine whether harm occurred or not. Under a strict liability standard, any accidental disclosure is considered a waiver of the privilege, whereas under a negligence regime, some standard of confidentiality is defined, and waiver occurs only when the client or the lawyer do not invest sufficiently in securing confidentiality.

In the case law[273], three liability rules can be discerned that are applied by courts in order to determine whether an accidental disclosure of privileged material (by either lawyers or clients) should be deemed a waiver of the privilege:

I. ***No liability*** – accidental and unintentional disclosure of privileged information is not deemed to be a waiver of the privilege and the court will prevent the opponent from using the inadvertently disclosed evidence.
II. ***Negligence*** – inadvertent disclosure of privileged material will only be considered a waiver of the privilege if the injurer (the client or the lawyer) did not take sufficient precautions to prevent the inadvertent disclosure from occurring.
III. ***Strict liability*** – any inadvertent disclosure of privileged material will be considered as a waiver of the privilege (regardless of whether precautions were taken or not).

273 Surveyed in section 3.4, *infra*.

3.1.2 Defining Harm

As previously explained, the magnitude of the harm resulting from accidental waiver is defined by the court. An analysis of the case law reveals three levels of harm that courts may inflict upon a litigant that accidentally disclosed privileged information. These levels can be generalized into the following harm rules:

A. **No waiver** (no harm) – inadvertent disclosure is not a waiver and the court will prevent any use of the disclosed privileged material by an opponent. Hence, it is an accident that causes no harm. None of the legal systems surveyed here apply this rule.
B. "**Limited waiver**" (intermediate harm) – at this level of harm, when inadvertent disclosure of privileged material occurs the courts admit into evidence only the specific information that was accidentally revealed. Other privileged information that was not disclosed remains confidential and is not entered into evidence.

C. "**Complete waiver**" (high harm) – there are three versions of this rule:

(1) Any inadvertent disclosure results in the loss of the privilege with regards to all communications between the same client and the same lawyer *pertaining to the relevant legal proceeding.* To clarify: when any unit of privileged information exchanged between the client and the lawyer is accidentally disclosed, the court will order the disclosure of *all* privileged information that is relevant to the specific litigation at hand. However, this information will only be available *in this specific trial* (other litigants against the corporation in separate trials will not be able to use this privileged information).
(2) Any inadvertent disclosure entails the loss of the privilege with regards to all communications between the same client and the same lawyer *on the same subject-matter.* The magnitude of this harm is higher than C.1 since the disclosed material is available to litigants in other trials on the same matter.
(3) Any inadvertent disclosure entails the loss of the privilege with regards to all communications between the same client and the same lawyer *covered by the same type of privilege.* The magnitude of this harm is highest of all since it determines that all the privileged information that transpired between the client and the lawyer on any issue will now be disclosed and be available to all other litigants in all other cases.
(4)

3.2 Cost of Care

3.2.1 The Client

In this part I analyze the client's optimal investment in preventing inadvertent waiver. The analysis applies to individuals as well as corporations. The main difference between individuals and corporations is that the latter presumably communicate larger volumes of information to their lawyers and do so more frequently. This is considered below.

Assume the client does not know the probative value of the evidence that he holds. In other words, the client does not know whether each unit of information (evidence) is positive from his point of view (i.e., supports his claim) or negative (i.e., adverse to the client's claim and in support of the opponent's claim). Let (n) denote the number of units of evidence that are communicated between the client and the lawyer on the specific matter in trial. The client may be either a defendant or plaintiff in the case at hand.

Only the lawyer can inform the client whether the evidence is positive or negative. In order for that to happen, the client must communicate the information about the evidence to the lawyer. After the client learns which units of evidence are positive and which are negative, he will only present in court the positive evidence. Additionally, the client will attempt to conceal the negative evidence in the pre-trial discovery procedure. If the opposing party tries to obtain the negative evidence from the lawyer, the client's lawyer will assert the privilege in order to prevent this disclosure.

Each unit of evidence has a value, denoted by (ν), that can be positive or negative. This value represents the monetary increase or decrease in the final sum that would be awarded (or demanded as compensation) to the client. Let $v = |\nu|$. For simplicity, it is assumed that (v) is the same for all (n) units of evidence and that $\nu \neq 0$.

The standard of care for the client will be denoted by (x). Let c(x) denote the cost of care required to avoid inadvertent waiver during the communication with the lawyer, $c'(x) > 0$ and for tractability $c''(x) = 0$. The probability of inadvertent waiver by the client shall be p(x), $p'(x) < 0$, $p''(x) < 0$.

A number of different precautions may be available to both clients and lawyers. Precautions in this case – for both clients and lawyers - can take, for example, the form of encryption software that ensures that electronic mail communications between the client and the lawyer cannot be obtained by a third party, or a safe-box to prevent theft of privileged documents etc. These are durable precautions. Precautions may also be non-durable[274], such as costs that must be incurred for each and every unit of information when it is communicated. For example, documents may have to be delivered by a trustworthy messenger to avoid the risk of wire-tapping on fax-lines. Since durable precautions are essentially sunk costs, in the analysis below I focus on nondurable precautions[275].

Recall, that neither the client nor the lawyer knows the value of the information underlying the lawyer-client communication *prior* to their communications. The inability of the client to distinguish between positive and negative evidence is crucial to prompt the investment in precaution that must be taken in order to prevent accidental disclosure of privileged communications. Since positive evidence will be presented by the client in court anyway, he should not be concerned if such evidence is accidentally disclosed. However, since the client does not know whether the evidence he is communicating is positive or adverse to his case, he must invest in precautions to prevent *any* accidental disclosure.

First, let us ignore the lawyer and observe the behavior of the client.

Liability rule I (no liability). Under liability rule I (no liability) the client has no incentive to take care, $c(x) = 0$, since no information will be admitted into the court even if privileged information is inadvertently disclosed. The client's total costs are zero ($TC_{\text{no liability}} = 0$).

274 The difference between durable and nondurable precautions has been initially observed by Grady (1988).

275 This assumption will be relaxed later on.

Liability Rule II (negligence). Under liability rule II (negligence), we assume x* is the efficient standard of care and $\tilde{x}$ is the standard chosen by the court. The client's strategy is then to minimize harm (denoted by *h*) by choosing his precaution level as follows:

$$
\begin{array}{ll}
x = \tilde{x} & \text{if } \tilde{x} \leq x^* \\
x = \tilde{x} & \text{if } \tilde{x} > x^* \text{ and } c(\tilde{x}) \leq c(x^*)+p(x^*)h \\
x = x^* & \text{if } \tilde{x} > x^* \text{ and } c(\tilde{x}) > c(x^*)+p(x^*)h
\end{array}
$$

In the first strategy, the client can avoid harm by choosing the court's standard of care, which is lower than the efficient standard of care. Therefore it makes no sense for the client to choose any higher level of care. In the second strategy, although the court-determined standard of care is higher than the efficient standard of care, the client's total costs (precaution cost plus expected harm) at the efficient care level are higher than the cost of care under the court-determined standard. Therefore, the client chooses the court's standard.

Finally, if the cost of care under the court-determined standard of care is higher than the sum of the cost of socially efficient care and expected harm, then the client's best strategy would be to disregard the court's standard and opt for the socially efficient level of care, as shown in the third strategy[276].

The total costs faced by the client are then:

$$
\begin{array}{lcll}
TC_{neg.} & = & c(\tilde{x}) & \text{if } \tilde{x} < x^* \\
TC_{neg./full\ liability} & = & c(\tilde{x})+p(\tilde{x})h & \text{if } \tilde{x} \geq x^* \\
TC_{neg./part.\ liability} & = & c(x^*)+[p(\tilde{x})-p(x^*)]h & \text{if } \tilde{x} \geq x^*
\end{array}
$$

Liability Rule III (strict liability). Under liability rule III (strict liability) the client always chooses the efficient standard of care and exerts the cost c(x*). This is because under strict

276 This can happen under the so called "partial liability" rule. See Schaefer & Schoenenberger (1999), at 601. Under the partial liability rule, as described by Schaefer & Ott (1986) the injurer only bears the damages in the amount of additional harm that would have been prevented if the injurer had taken the legally required level of care. A numerical example will serve to clarify this point. Assume that a corporate lawyer must review 100 documents for the purpose of a pretrial disclosure request made by an opponent in litigation and that 30 of the documents satisfy the criteria of the corporate lawyer-client privilege and therefore should not be disclosed. Now assume that if the lawyer satisfies the standard of care required by the court he would overlook 10% of the privileged documents. Hence, 3 privileged documents will be handed over to the opponents in the course of pretrial disclosure. When the opponent lawyer discovers the privileged documents and decides to serve them in court in order to prove the liability of the corporate client – the court will have to rule whether inadvertent waiver occurred and what are its consequences. Under strict liability, the court will admit the privileged material. If the harm rule chosen by the court is tough (like rule C.3.) rule, then the court will force the corporation to produce all the 30 privileged documents whereas under the least harsh harm rule (C.1.) then only the 3 documents that were accidentally disclosed will be accepted by the court. If a negligence regime is applied then the court will examine whether the lawyer took due care to verify that privileged material will not be disclosed. If the lawyer did meet the standard of care then the court would refuse to accept the 3 documents that were accidentally disclosed. Assume now that the lawyer applied the socially efficient level of care, but that this level of care was was below the standard required by the court, and that consequently 10 privileged documents were accidentally disclosed. In a regime of negligence with partial liability, the additional harm resulting from the lawyer's choice of the efficient standard of care (but not the court standard of care is 10 – 3 = 7. Hence, under such a regime only 7 privileged documents will be disclosed in fact and accepted by the court.

liability the client bears all the harm caused by inadvertent waiver. By adhering to the efficient standard of care, the client exerts care up to the marginal point where every additional 1$ of care reduces the expected harm by 1$. The client's total costs in this case will amount to: $TC_{st.\ liabilty} = c(x^*) + p(x^*)h$.

Consider now the magnitude of the harm.

Harm Rule (B) Limited Waiver. Under rule (B), the intermediate harm rule, if the inadvertently disclosed evidence is not adverse evidence, the client will suffer no harm as a result of the accidental disclosure. The reason for this is that unlike the complete waiver rules (C), the court will not use this accidental disclosure to unveil the entire bulk of privileged communications. Under rule (B) only the single unit of evidence that was accidentally disclosed is revealed in court. Hence, if we assume that the information communicated between the lawyer and the client is equally likely to be positive or negative, then in half of all accidents there will be no harm to the client.

In formal terms, the harm equals the value of the unit of information that is accidentally disclosed (v), thus the expected harm is: $\frac{1}{2}p(x)v$.

Harm Rule (C) Complete Waiver. Under the complete waiver (rule C), there are three levels of anticipated harm in the case of an accidental waiver.

- Under rule C.1., all the units of information that were communicated between the client and the lawyer are unveiled. Since we assume that 50% of the units are positive and would have been revealed in court anyway, then harm is caused only by $\frac{1}{2}n$ of the units. Expected harm is then: $\frac{1}{2}p(x)nv$.
- Under rule C.2., the accidental disclosure of the evidence means that the waiver takes affect in all the litigation that the client is involved with on the same matter. Denote the additional loss to the client as a result of that by (L) and accordingly, the expected harm is: $\frac{1}{2}p(x)nv+L$.
- Under rule C.3. the privilege is removed from all the information that the client exchanged with the lawyer including information that is not relevant to the litigation at hand. Denote this additional harm by (H) and accordingly, the expected harm is: $\frac{1}{2}p(x)nv+H$. Assume $H > L$.

The ranking of the harm rules is then: C3 > C2 > C1 > B. The following table presents the client's total costs for harm rules B and C.1. given the different liability rules. The no liability/no harm rules are disregarded since both of these rules result in zero total costs.

Harm rule:	B	C.1
$TC_{negligence}$ $(\tilde{x} < x^*)$	$nc(\tilde{x})$	$nc(\tilde{x})$
$TC_{neg./full\ liability}$ $(\tilde{x} \geq x^*)$	$nc(\tilde{x}) + \frac{1}{2}p(\tilde{x})v$	$nc(\tilde{x}) + \frac{1}{2}p(\tilde{x})nv$
$TC_{neg./part.\ liability}$ $(\tilde{x} \geq x^*)$	$nc(x^*)+\frac{1}{2}[p(\tilde{x})-p(x^*)]v$	$nc(x^*)+\frac{1}{2}[p(\tilde{x})-p(x^*)]nv$
$TC_{strict\ liability}$	$nc(x^*)+\frac{1}{2}[p(x)-p(x^*)]v$	$nc(x^*)+\frac{1}{2}[p(x)-p(x^*)]nv$

Table 2: Client's Total Costs under Harm Rules B and C.1

In each of the liability rules, total costs under harm rule (B) are superior to rule (C) whenever more than one unit of information is transmitted to the lawyer (since then $v < nv$ holds). As for the ranking of the liability rules, from the client's private point of view, simple negligence with a socially efficient standard of care imposes the lowest total costs ($nc(\tilde{x})$), while strict liability (in the last row of this table) imposes the highest. In between lie both cases of negligence with an inefficiently high standard of care.

The client's profit from legal advice is a crucial factor in deciding how much information to transmit to the lawyer. The client's benefit (denoted by *b*) increases with the amount of information that he communicates to the lawyer. The reason for this being that a better-informed lawyer can provide more accurate and more valuable advice. Hence $b(n)$ is an increasing function of (n). This means that the client will continue to transmit information to the lawyer as long as the marginal increase in the benefit derived from legal advice outweighs the marginal cost of care. For example, under strict liability with the operation of the limited waiver harm rule (B), the condition is:

$$b'(n) = c(x^*).$$

Under strict liability with the complete waiver harm rule (C.1.), the condition is:

$$b'(n) = c(x^*) + \tfrac{1}{2}[p(x) - p(x^*)]v.$$

Implications on the Behavior of Firms. The implications of the marginal conditions depend on the assumptions about the behavior of the functions $b(n)$ and $c(x)$. A plausible assumption about the behavior of the function $b(n)$ is that it is increasing, since the accuracy of legal advice increases with increasing information. Therefore, $b'(n) > 0$. However, as the amount of information provided to the lawyer increases, the additional information might slightly improve the accuracy of the advice but not change it fundamentally, hence $b''(n) < 0$.

If we assume $c(x)$ is an increasing linear function, then under harm rule (B), we observe that while there is no unique equilibrium, there are many possible equilibria. This is depicted in the following graph.

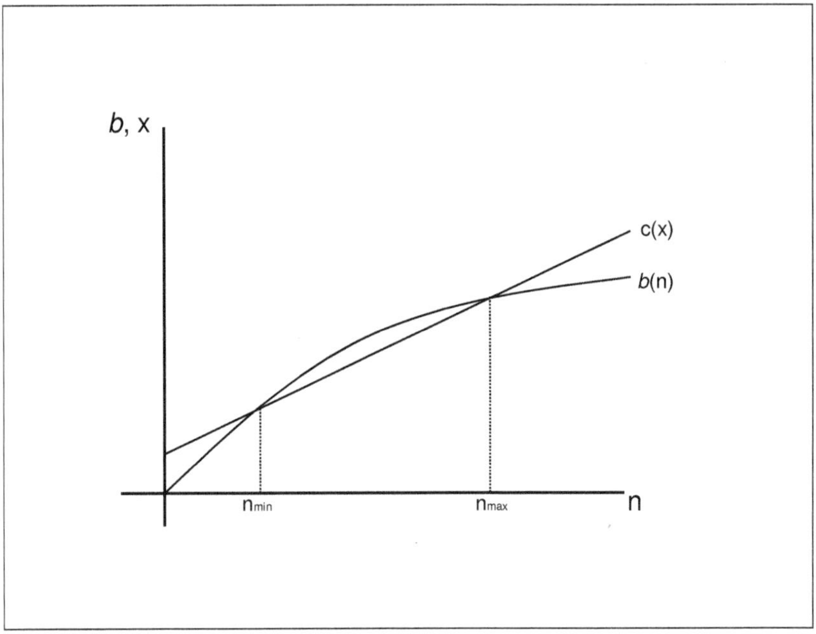

Figure 3: Firm's Benefits and Cost of Care with Non-Durable Precautions

Assuming that the lawyer can only render advice on the basis of factual information and given the assumptions about the behavior of $b(n)$ and $c(x)$, there is a minimal amount of information (n_{min}) that the firm will transmit since below that amount the advice is expected to be so inaccurate that its value is lower than the cost of securing the privilege against inadvertent waiver. There is also a maximal amount of information that the firm will be willing to transmit to the lawyer (n_{max}). After this point, the marginal benefit from any additional unit of information communicated to the lawyer is smaller than the additional cost of care required for preventing inadvertent disclosure.

However, in some cases firms may be obliged by law to consult with their lawyers before taking certain actions. In such cases, if lawyers require a certain amount of information in order to render the legal advice and that amount is higher than n_{max} - then any increase of the standard of care can potentially increase the amount of evidence that reaches the court as a result of inadvertent waiver. The condition is, though, that the firm will choose an illegal course of action after obtaining the advice, in spite of the risk of inadvertent waiver.

This can be understood through the following numerical example: a firm is obliged to obtain a legal opinion from a lawyer prior to an Initial Public Offering (IPO) in the stock exchange. The firm expects to raise $100 in this IPO. The firm has 100 documents that need to be evaluated by the lawyer and the cost of securing the confidentiality of each document is $1. The firm suspects that 20 documents will have a detrimental effect on investors and would like to avoid disclosing them. If the firm can transmit only these 20 documents to the lawyer, then the lawyer could advise the firm that misrepresenting the content of 10 out of 20 documents will probably not be noticed by the securities enforcement authority. This advice will increase the value of the IPO to the firm from $100 to $140. The sanction for misrepresentation is $50 but the probability of being found liable given the existence of a privilege is only 20%. Hence, the net value of the investment in securing confidential legal advice is positive: $40 – (20*$1) – ($50*20%) = $10. However, if the lawyer requires the firm to transmit all the documents prior to rendering his opinion, the cost of confidentiality is $100. The lawyer now finds 15 documents which, he hints, could be suppressed from the public at a relatively low risk of detection. This advice increases the value of the IPO by $60. The firm should not be willing to invest more than $60 in precautions against inadvertent waiver. However, this means only 60 documents will be protected, whereas 40 documents will not be protected. If the harm rule is such that any inadvertently disclosed document will lead to the disclosure of all the content of the communications, then the probability of being found liable increases. If the expected sanction is then sufficiently high, the firm's optimal strategy will be to pursue a legal course of action.

To sum, when firms are obliged to seek legal advice on contemplated actions and this advice requires the transmission of confidential information, increasing the standard of care would deter firms from pursuing sanctionable actions. Only if firms choose to take the risk and pursue sanctionable actions, then the increased standard of care would mean result in more evidence being revealed in court.

Mostly though, firms can choose whether to consult or not. In such cases, the court's decision to increase the standard of care (x), thereby driving the equilibrium boundary point n_{max} down, will decrease the number of cases in which the firm will find it beneficial to consult with the lawyer. The firm will only consult when the expected value of the advice outweighs the total cost of care. Conversely, if the court decreases the standard of care, the firm will consult more often. Either way, the change in the standard of care will not change the amount of evidence that will be accidentally disclosed in court.

Earlier we assumed that precautions are primarily nondurable. That is, that care must be exerted for each and every unit of information transmitted to the lawyer. However, large corporate clients may find it desirable to invest in more durable precautions. For example, setting up an encrypted phone/fax line between the corporation and the lawyer could save the cost of sending a messenger for each unit of information. If this is done, then the cost of care would take the form of an almost linear horizontal function, thereby enabling corporations to transmit very large amounts of information to their lawyers, as shown in the graph below.

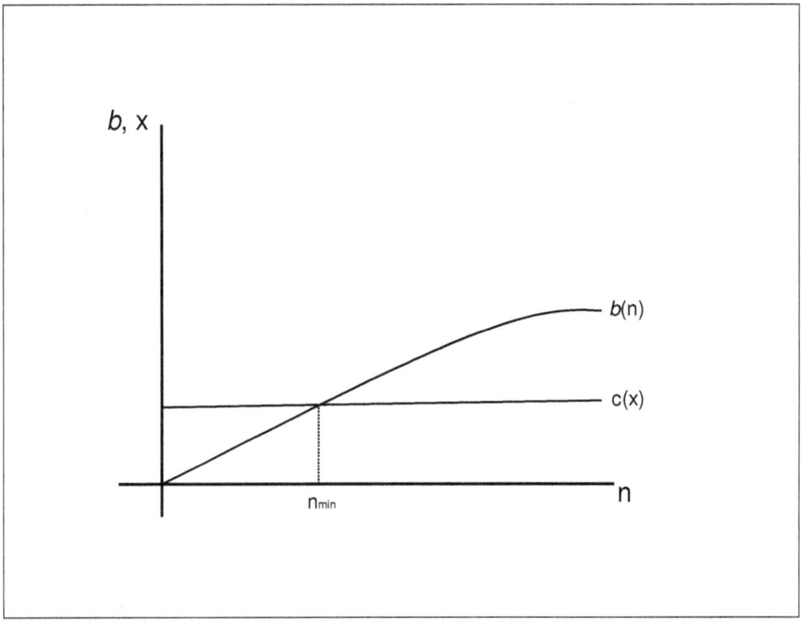

Figure 4: Firm's Benefits and Cost of Care with Durable Precautions

In the case of durable precautions, the cost of care remains almost constant. The shift to durable precautions thus enables firms to communicate very high, if not unlimited, amounts of information to their lawyers, since any amount (n) above n_{min} is a possible equilibrium.

As the first graph shows, privilege is only valuable for an intermediate range of (n). That means that clients will not invest in privileged legal advice (though they might invest in *un*privileged advice) when a very small amount of information, or a very high amount of information is involved. It also means that courts can decrease or increase (or even completely erase) the extent of this intermediate range by increasing or decreasing the requisite standard of care. However, as the second graph indicates, it is possible for clients that require legal advice based on high amounts of information to shift from nondurable precautions to durable precautions, thereby ensuring privileged communications.

3.2.2 The Lawyer

When a lawyer accidentally discloses confidential information, the court may view this as a waiver and impose harm on the client that provided the information. This harm is described earlier in the case of accidental waiver by the client. As discussed above, courts determine whether harm will have occurred by choosing either a strict liability or a negligence regime.

The efficient standard of care for the lawyer can be denoted by (y*). This is the standard of care for inadvertent waiver. The harm caused by accidental waiver is borne by the client and not by the lawyer, since the client is the party affected by the revelation of the privileged information in court. However, when a lawyer is responsible for accidental disclosure, a client may sue the lawyer for malpractice. For simplicity, assume that the same standard of care (y*) is used by the court for deciding whether the lawyer is liable for malpractice when a client sues the lawyer. A Lawyer's liability for malpractice is always governed by a negligence regime.

Regardless of the threat of malpractice lawsuits, lawyers have an incentive to commit to a certain level of care. If they do not do so, the additional expected harm borne by the client as a result of the lawyer taking no care will reduce the willingness of clients to consult with lawyers. It is therefore in the lawyers' interests to have an explicit pre-contractual obligation to maintain confidentiality in their ethical canons. Consequently, an accidental disclosure of confidential information can be viewed as a negligent breach of contract.

The possibility of suing the lawyer for negligent loss of confidentiality causes the lawyer to internalize the harm that he would have otherwise shifted to the client. Consequently, given the same liability regimes and harm rules, the lawyer will choose the same precaution level that the client will have taken.

A special case arises if the court uses a strict liability regime to determine whether a lawyer accidentally disclosed privileged information, but applies a negligence regime to determine liability in lawyer malpractice lawsuits. In such a case, as long as the lawyer maintains the efficient standard of care (y*), he will be able to avoid liability for malpractice. However, since strict liability is applied in the case of accidental waiver, then some residual harm will be caused. This residual harm, formally described by $\frac{1}{2}[p(y) - p(y^*)]h$, will be borne by the client. Hence, when a court chooses to apply the strict liability regime to a lawyer's accidental waiver, it increases the cost of privileged legal advice for clients, thereby decreasing the client's incentive to engage in such activity. Strict liability is therefore the least desirable regime from both the lawyer's and the client's point of view.

3.3 Social Welfare

Two components of social welfare, both of which are affected by the choices of the liability regime and the harm rule, are at the center of the discussion. These are the accuracy of the adjudication and the frequency and magnitude of communication with lawyers. Each of these factors will be discussed in turn below.

3.3.1 Accuracy of Adjudication

Courts improve their accuracy of adjudication when more information is available to them. The privilege adversely affects this process. Under the negligence regime with an efficient standard of care, both the client and the lawyer are induced to take the socially-optimal standard of care. If they do so, then the court will not let into evidence any information that is inadvertently disclosed. This result depends on the ability of the court to determine the accurate standard of care, which is difficult. It is also the least best result for the court in terms of increasing accuracy. If the court sets a standard of care that is significantly higher than the socially efficient standard, $\tilde{x} > x^*$, the client may prefer to disregard the court's standard and maintain the socially efficient standard of care. In that case, a residual harm will occur, $[p(\tilde{x}) - p(x^*)]h$. This "harm" is evidence that the client has accidentally disclosed. These units of evidence will be admitted in trial and increase the accuracy of adjudication. The same analysis holds true when the imposed liability regime is strict liability. The difference is that under strict liability the court does not have to exert any costs in developing a standard of care. Under strict liability, the amount of evidence that will be admitted as a result of "efficient" harm is the highest: $[p(x) - p(x^*)]h$.

3.3.2 Frequency and Volume of Communications with Corporate Lawyers

It is hard to dispute the fact that corporations consult with lawyers more frequently than individuals do. If this consultation, under the veil of the privilege, is used in order to promote sanctionable, socially adverse actions, then the strict liability regime - more than any other - causes the corporate client to internalize this social harm. As the magnitude of information transmitted between the client and the lawyer increases, the expected harm is increasing. Hence, under strict liability, the units of evidence communicated to the lawyer will be fewer than the number expected under other liability regimes. The effect of the strict liability regime will be even more powerful in discouraging lawyer-client consultation when the harm rule imposes a heavier magnitude of harm on the client seeking the advice.

In essence, courts turn privileged legal consultation into a risky activity. Whether this approach is socially desirable or not depends on the presumed effect of the lawyer-client privilege. If lawyer-client privilege reduces corporate compliance with the law, then the strict liability regime reduces privileged consultation and therefore has socially desirable effects. If the converse is true, and the privilege rather encourages compliance with the law, then the strict liability regime is the most inferior option. Nevertheless, a better option should only be adopted if the social welfare benefits from more compliance are higher than the welfare loss resulting from less accuracy in litigation.

3.4 Case Law Analysis

3.4.1 United States Relevant Case Law

There is no settled liability rule for inadvertent waiver by lawyers in the US, though negligence seems to be used more often than strict liability. With regards to the standard of care, in many cases – at least with regards to the care of lawyers - it seems that the courts conclude whether the standard was adhered to by observing the ratio of inadvertently disclosed documents to the overall amount of pre-trial discovery documents that the lawyers had to review. It therefore follows that the lawyers are free to choose the cheapest precautions as long as they can guarantee to minimize the quantity of accidental disclosures.

Choice of Liability Rule

In ***International Business Machines Corp.***[277] the lawyers for the plaintiff, IBM, mistakenly disclosed four privileged documents during expedited discovery in a tax related proceedings against the Internal Revenue authorities. The court held that a protective order re-instating the privilege would only be issued if the lawyers could prove which precautions they had taken to pre-screen the material in order to avoid such mistakes. Thus the court acknowledged a negligence regime for accidental waiver by lawyers.

The court in ***In re Standard Financial Management Corp***[278] also supported a negligence rule, stating in *obiter dictum* without further elaboration, that in the real world inadvertence is, after all, merely a "euphemism for negligence". In its decision the court referred to the case of ***Mendenhall v. Barber-Greene Co.***[279], which is perhaps the most noted for adopting an approach in which the negligence of the lawyer (or any other third party confidant) will *not be attributed* to the client. Thus according to this case, the privilege will not be lost and the court should issue a protective order barring the material from being used. In essence this means a no liability rule for accidental disclosure by lawyers. This led to the privilege being retained with respect to four letters which the lawyer inadvertently handed over as part of a discovery encompassing 28 files.

In ***F.D.I.C. v. Singh***[280], the plaintiff intended for a certain memo to be privileged. The plaintiff's lawyer took the memo out of the material prepared for disclosure and then invited the defendant's lawyer to review the documents in her law offices. The defendant's lawyer noticed the privileged memo inadvertently, and requested its disclosure. The court held that the privilege was lost. In this case, the lawyer had taken what may be considered apparently adequate precaution, yet the court ruled for waiver. The case can be interpreted as adopting a strict liability regime. The residual damage was shifted to the client.

To summarize, in US case law the negligence regime is applied to the behaviour of clients. In the case of the behaviour of lawyers, whilst negligence is the most commonly used regime, we find also cases that apply a no-liability regime on the one hand or a strict liability regime on the other hand.

Standard of Care - lawyers

With regards to the standard of care, there is a variety of possible precautions and this indicates that courts apply a case-by-case approach. In ***Ciba-Geigy Corp. v. Sandoz Ltd***[281] the plaintiff claimed that the defendant should participate in the costs of cleaning up a hazardous waste site previously owned by a joint venture of the parties. The lawyers of the defendant submitted many documents for discovery but one of the batches of documents was not screened for privilege. The batch included four privileged documents which the defendant then asked the court to suppress. The court applied a multifactor test. The court considered relevant factors to be: the reasonableness of the precautions to prevent inadvertent disclosure, the number of inadvertent disclosures (some of the documents were disclosed several times), the extent of the disclosure, any delay and measures taken to rectify the

277 ***International Business Machines Corp. v. U.S.***, 37 Fed. Cl. 599, 79 (1997).
278 ***In re Standard Financial Management Corp.***, 77 B.R. 324 (Bankr. D. Mass. 1987).
279 ***Mendenhall v. Barber-Greene Co.***, 531 F.Supp. 951, 954 (D.C.Ill.1982).
280 ***F.D.I.C. v. Singh***, 140 F.R.D. 252 (D. Me. 1992).
281 ***Ciba-Geigy Corp. v. Sandoz Ltd.***, 916 F. Supp. 404 (D.N.J. 1995).

disclosure, and whether the overriding interest of fairness and justice would be served by relieving the party of its error. The court noted that the disclosed documents were in German (disclosed twice) but then they were disclosed without screening again after a translation had been made. The court held that this was carelessness by the lawyers and the privilege was waived.

In ***re Natural Gas Commodity Litigation***[282] it was held that a party that inadvertently disclosed three privileged pages in the course of producing 65,000 pages of documents in response to pre-trial request for production did not thereby waive the work product privilege. The court found that the party took reasonable precautions by conducting page-by-page reviews of all documents before production, asserting privilege immediately upon discovery of inadvertent disclosure, that the number of pages inadvertently disclosed was very small, and that the opposing party was not prejudiced by restoration of privilege since it had not used or relied upon privileged pages. The small number of inadvertently disclosed pages seems to have been used as an indication of the level of care.

It seems that oftentimes, when courts find it hard to determine whether the precautions taken by the lawyers were sufficient, the ratio of accidentally disclosed material compared to the entire amount of exchanged evidence is used to by the court as an indication of the level of care. Hence, if thousands of documents were scanned by the lawyers and out of those only a few single privileged documents were overlooked and disclosed, then the standard of care is presumed to have been adhered to. This method proves mainly how difficult it is to develop a reasonable and observable standard of care.

Standard of Care – client

Also in regards to client behavior, courts employ different liability rules. There is case law authority supporting the placement of strict liability on the client for the loss of privilege, even if the loss is due to circumstances not entirely in the client's direct control such as theft of the documents or wire-tapping[283].

In ***Suburban Sew & Sweep v. Swiss-Bernina***[284], the court held that the client was negligent for not destroying a draft document that was retrieved by the opponent from a trash-bin. Hence, liability is the result of not adhering to a standard of care. ***Gergacz*** opines that the ruling is too harsh, as it is not the behaviour of a "reasonable client" to destroy every draft[285]. This critique overlooks the fact that unless confidential material is discarded differently than regular non-privileged material, an essential screening mechanism that allows the court to filter out intentional waiver (material discarded to trash) from accidental waiver (material obtained elsewhere, for example, by theft) would not exist. Once the standard of care has been set, a client that produces a high volume of privileged documents and places sufficient value on the privilege will probably increase his investment in care by, for example, buying a shredding machine and setting up internal procedures for the destruction of drafts.

---

282 ***In re Natural Gas Commodity Litigation***, 229 F.R.D. 82 (S.D.N.Y. 2005).

283 ***Gergacz*** argues that this approach is too harsh and the client should be allowed to prove that reasonable measures to maintain confidentiality have been taken. Gergacz, 5-44.

284 ***Suburban Sew & Sweep v. Swiss-Bernina***, 91 F.R.D. 254 (N.D. Ill. 1981).

285 Gergacz, 5-44.

In another negligence case, ***U.S. v. Betinsky***[286], the court inferred the client's accidental waiver from sub-optimal control over the material. The case concerned criminal charges against the defendant Betinsky for using his own firm (which later went into bankruptcy) as a vehicle for fraud. The state requested documents that were prepared by the firm's lawyers. The documents were kept in boxes which Betinsky stored in the basement of his neighbour's house. The court held that although the neighbour did not actually look at the documents and "break the seal of confidentiality", nothing would have prevented him from doing so had he wanted to do so (in fact, the neighbour's wife threw away some documents after a flood occurred in the basement). The privilege was denied since the client disregarded the objective of protecting the confidentiality of the documents. Therefore it can be concluded that at least one element of the standard of care required by US courts is that the client must retain full control over the access to the privileged material.

These cases again, as in the standard of care for lawyers, indicate the difficulty of setting an easy to apply and simple to observe standard of care.

Harm Rules

With regard to harm rules, with some exceptions, most US courts apply rule C.2 when an inadvertent waiver occurs, which means they consider that there has been waiver to all documents concerning the same subject-matter.

In ***Duplan***, the court held that inadvertent or voluntary production of one privileged attorney-client communication constitutes a waiver as to all communications between the same attorney and the same client on the same subject-matter[287]. There is ample case law on this point. For example, in ***Texaco Puerto Rico, Inc.***[288], waiver of four documents resulted in the forced disclosure of another 14 documents on the same subject-matter. In ***re Natural Gas Commodity Litigation***[289] the inadvertent disclosure of three documents threatened the exposure of another 65,000 documents on the same matter. However, as discussed above, privilege was eventually not removed.

Nevertheless, at least in one case, inadvertent waiver by a lawyer was deemed to be no waiver at all (hence the use of the no harm rule (A)). In the 2004 case of ***Harold Sampson Children's Trust*** the court held that a lawyer, without the consent or knowledge of a client, cannot voluntarily waive the attorney-client privilege by producing privileged documents, even if the attorney does not recognize that the documents are privileged[290]. In this case, the waiver occurred when, in the process of discovery prior to litigation over a real estate transaction, the lawyer disclosed privileged material, since he was unaware of the client's privilege with respect to the material. In this specific case, the client was not consulted prior to the disclosure. After the lawyer resigned, a new lawyer noticed the disclosure and petitioned the court to undo the disclosure. The court ordered the documents be returned to the client as privileged.

---

286 ***U.S. v. Betinsky***, 1988 WL 97673 (E.D. Pa. 1988), judgment affirmed without published opinion, 877 F.2d 58 (3d Cir. 1989).

287 ***Duplan Corp. v. Deering Milliken***, 397 F.supp 1146 (D.C.S.C., 1975).

288 ***Texaco Puerto Rico, Inc. v. Department of Consumer Affairs***, 60 F.3d 867, 32 Fed. R. Serv. 3d (LCP) 121 (1st Cir. 1995).

289 ***In re Natural Gas Commodity Litigation***, 229 F.R.D. 82 (S.D.N.Y. 2005).

290 ***Harold Sampson Children's Trust v. The Linda Gale Sampson 1979 Trust***, 679 N.W.2d 794 (Wis., 2004).

This decision undermines the incentives of lawyers to investigate whether their clients believe there is a value in maintaining confidentiality for certain material, and thus undercuts the obligation to confidentiality. A more socially desirable incentive would have been the result of denying the privilege and holding the lawyer liable for malpractice. This would have induced lawyers to verify with their client, either when they receive information or before they impart it onwards, whether the client is interested in maintaining the privilege or not.

Additional Tests

Some courts have adopted a unique "significant part" test, according to which, waiver is found only pursuant to a disclosure of a significant portion of the privileged communication[291]. This is the rule in the state of California. Section §912(a) of the California Evidence Code adopted in 1965 provides that a privilege will be "waived with respect to a communication protected by such privilege if any holder of the privilege, without coercion, has disclosed a significant part of the communication or has consented to such disclosure made by anyone". There remains uncertainty regarding the threshold beyond which the waiver occurs. Additionally, from an efficiency point of view, the rule makes sense only if evaluating the precautions taken by clients or lawyers is costlier than reviewing the bulk of the protected material in order to determine how much has been inadvertently disclosed.

3.4.2 England

In England, a more precise distinction is made between inadvertent disclosure of privileged material to an opponent in pre-trial discovery, and inadvertent waiver not within a legal dispute. In the former case, inadvertent disclosure in litigation, the English courts will always find that the privilege has been waived[292] (strict liability). In the latter case, disclosure to a third party, the court will examine the intent leading to the disclosure and whether the person disclosing the material had intended to observe confidentiality, or should have expected wider dissemination of the information[293] (negligence regime).

English courts attribute the lawyer's inadvertent waiver in court to the client. Thus a no-liability rule for lawyer's negligence is rejected. The legal justification is that a lawyer has the power to waive the privilege on behalf of the client and thus may also waive the privilege by mistake. This has been the rationale in cases where lawyers mistakenly read out a privileged document in open court or included a privileged document in a bundle produced to the opponent[294].

One of the prominent English scholars on evidence, ***Cross***, claims that given the huge volumes of disclosure material exchanged between parties, accidents are inevitable[295] and the rule that should be applied by the court is whether the party reading an accidentally-disclosed document would believe that the document had been intentionally disclosed or whether it is

291 ***Thurmond v. Compaq Computer Corp.***, 198 F.R.D. 475 (E.D. Tex. 2000).
292 Matthews & Malek, 223.
293 Matthews & Malek, 223.
294 Matthews & Malek, 231-232, citing ***Great Atlantic Insurance v. Home Insurance*** [1981] 1 W.L.R. 529.
295 **Cross On Evidence**, 349, citing the US case of ***Transamerica Computer Co. v. IBM***, 573 F.2d, 646, where 1.7 million pages were vetted in 3 months resulting in the accidental disclosure of 1338 privileged documents.

obvious that the document was disclosed by error. When a reasonable party would not suspect an error, the privilege would be waived. Only when an obviously erroneous disclosure occurs does the question of waiver merit discussion[296]. This is a problematic proposal for two reasons. First, it is hard to see how the court can determine the beliefs of the opponent at the moment of observing the disclosed document. Secondly, the beliefs of the opponent may be entirely independent of the precaution efforts of the client and the lawyer against inadvertent disclosure. Disregarding these efforts is unlikely to result in an efficient mechanism.

As for the harm, ***Matthews & Malek*** observe indecision in the case law[297]: When the waiver occurs outside litigation, there are conflicting authorities as to whether the waiver applies only to the waived document (limited waiver, rule B)[298] or to all documents concerning the subject matter (rule C.1.). When the waiver occurs at trial, there is a conflict of authorities as to whether the waiver applies to all the material concerning the subject matter in the same case (rule C.1.)[299] or to all the material covered by the lost privilege (either litigation privilege or legal advice privilege) in general (rule C.3.)[300]. There is no mention of rule C.2 (all material regarding the same subject matter but also in other trials). The possibility of using rule C.3. is exceptionally damaging for the client since it seems to lead to disclosure of all the material exchanged with the lawyer on all legal issues, opening the way to many potential claimants. If this is indeed the prevailing harm rule, privilege-minded clients would reduce their expected harm by dividing their legal advice between several lawyers, thereby ensuring that when the privilege is lost by one lawyer, only the portion of protected information handled by that lawyer is revealed.

The high harm rule complicates situations where the client wishes to voluntarily submit favorable privileged material. English courts have treated this as a "fairness" issue: if a litigant is allowed to use waiver to withhold negative material and present only positive material, then the privilege puts the opponent at an unfair disadvantage and courts are also likely to reach inaccurate decisions. However, if the complete waiver rule is combined with a high harm rule, litigants will be disinclined to waive the privilege for affirmative material in fear of the expected costs they may suffer in other cases. A satisfactory solution for this dilemma has not yet been developed by the courts in England.

3.4.3 Germany

In the absence of pre-trial discovery, the issue of inadvertent waiver in Germany is moot. German law espouses a strong privacy and rights based privilege which lends itself to a no-liability rule for accidental waiver. The underlying legal position seems to be that if a party is not entitled to information from the opposing party, inadvertently disclosed information should not create a right where such a right did not exist. Negligence does not diminish one's fundamental right to self-determination over private information. The same is true for corporations.

---

296 **Cross On Evidence**, 346.

297 Matthews & Malek, 235.

298 ***General Accident Corp Ltd. v. Tanter*** [1984] 1 W.L.R. 100.

299 ***Re Konigsberg*** [1989] 1 W.L.R. 1257 at 1264.

300 ***George Doland Ltd v. Blackburn Robson Coates and Co.*** [1972] 1 W.L.R. 1338. In this case it was held that a waiver with regard to conversations did not entail a waiver with regard to physical documents.

In the absence of liability for inadvertent waiver of the privilege, German corporations will only invest in care to the extent that they can profit from confidentiality. For example, a strong reason to invest in confidentiality would be hidden defects in products. If confidentiality is inadvertently lost, clients may discover the defect and sue.

The German approach creates strong social welfare savings in precaution costs and litigation costs. The welfare costs are presumably due to a loss in accuracy of adjudication where information does not reach the court. Some of this loss can be overcome by shifting the burden of proof. However, if a corporation observes that presenting evidence that meets the burden of proof will expose it to liability in future cases, it would rather settle a claim even when it can prevail to avoid the future damage.

3.5 Note: Imperfection in the Enforcement of Lawyer Liability

When the lawyer is responsible for accidental waiver, the harm from the disclosed information is borne by the client. As noted, lawyers might not have an incentive to take care unless some liability is imposed on them. Therefore, loss of confidentiality is a breach of the lawyer's explicit professional obligation and implicit ethical obligations to the client. The lawyer may therefore be liable for malpractice or for negligent breach of contract. In professional malpractice, negligence is the prevailing liability rule[301].

However, enforcement of the lawyer's standard of care is imperfect. Enforcement relies on the client's willingness to sue the lawyer if the lawyer had not taken sufficient precaution to prevent the inadvertent disclosure of confidential communications. The rules are formulated to discourage clients from suing their lawyers for malpractice. A lawyer is allowed to reveal all of the client's secrets, according to the lawyer-client litigation exception, when he is sued by the client[302]. Consequently, policing the lawyer's level of care is related to the court-imposed harm rule.

Assume that after an inadvertent waiver the client threatens to sue the lawyer. The lawyer retaliates by threatening to disclose the client's privileged material in the process of defending himself. When the harm rule is limited waiver, the client stands to lose more from suing his lawyer because the negligent waiver itself does not cause the disclosure of all the privileged material. Under limited waiver the harm amounts to the disclosed unit with value (v). But if the lawyer reveals all of the client's confidential material - the harm could amount to $\frac{1}{2}nv+H$. On the other hand, if the harm rule is initially the higher complete waiver, the client has already lost the privilege with regard to all the material, and he is no longer deterred by the concern of disclosing additional material when suing the lawyer. Hence, only under the complete waiver rule can the client perfectly enforce the lawyer's standard of care.

---

301 There are other methods of motivating lawyers, such as contingency-based fees, which tie the lawyer's payoff to the successful outcome of the litigation thereby inducing the lawyer to take precautions to avoid waiver of evidence that will decrease the probability of success. This aspect will not be discussed here since it has only partial relevance to our analysis. It applies only when the lawyer causes the waiver while representing the client in litigation. However, a lawyer might cause inadvertent waiver while rendering ex-ante legal advice independent of the litigation. He might not represent the client in the pursuant litigation and thus the ability to weave the litigation outcome into the fee-scheme is not always available. In some countries, such as Germany, it is forbidden by law.

302 See section II.5., *supra*.

The criminalization of the duty of confidentiality - as done in Germany - makes sense when private enforcement is imperfect. However, in Germany, another exception allows the lawyer to disclose confidential information when he is mounting a criminal defence in a case where he is the defendant. Since criminal proceedings against lawyers that have breached confidentiality may be opened only after a complaint by the client, the lawyer's defence exception will adversely affect the incentives of a client to complain.

If the prevailing rule in Germany is no liability for inadvertent waiver, the primary concern would be from lawyer's intentional breach of confidentiality, which is in direct contravention with the privacy and personality rights of the clients. In that case, since the harm may sometimes be non-monetary and private enforcement is costly, the enforcement through criminal law can be justified. However, similar results could be obtained through disciplinary sanctions implemented by the lawyers, who as a professional group are interested in maintaining the reputation of the profession, at no cost for the state.

3.6 Conclusion

In this section I discussed inadvertent waiver - the accidental disclosure of privileged communications between the lawyer and the client. The relevance of the issue to corporate lawyer-client privilege relates to two aspects. First, corporations use lawyers more often and transmit larger volumes of information to their lawyers. Hence, they care more about the implications of inadvertent waiver. Secondly, corporations can harness economies of scale to improve their precautions and reduce the risk of inadvertent waiver.

I propose to understand the way inadvertent waiver is treated in the Anglo-American jurisdictions as a unique form of accident. It differs from the regular accident by the fact that the court decides whether to declare that a private harm had materialized when an accidental waiver occurs whilst in a "normal" accident harm is given and the court decides on liability and damages. The private harm is the privileged information that is disclosed. The court can decide whether inadvertent waiver will in fact result in disclosure and what is the extent of information that will no longer be privileged as a consequence of the accidental waiver. The harm rules used by the courts can range from not attaching any harm to accidental disclosure to a decision to order the disclosure of all lawyer-client communications on all matters. Courts apply the familiar liability rules - negligence and strict liability - to determine whether the inadvertent waiver occurred.

The accidental disclosure can be the result of lack of care by each of the parties, the lawyer and the client, independently. The classic analysis of accidents indicates the clients will prefer a liability regime of negligence over strict liability. Naturally, clients would also prefer the least harsh harm rules.

When courts apply inadvertent waiver they turn legal consultation into a risky activity. The more information is shared with the lawyer, the higher the risk of accidental disclosure. I therefore conclude that the waiver liability and harm rules will influence the amount of information exchanged between the client and the lawyer. Since the accuracy of legal advice depends on the amount of information that is provided to the lawyer, it follows that the quality of legal advice depends on the toughness of the inadvertent waiver doctrine. However, as I have shown, firms can overcome tough inadvertent waiver regimes by using their economies of scale in order to shift from non-durable to durable precautions, thereby significantly reducing the marginal cost of care. The harm from accidental disclosure is always borne by the client. Since the lawyer does not directly bear the harm, he does not have a direct incentive to take care. However, care is induced by the interest of lawyers in increasing the incentives of clients to consult them.

If lawyers cause inadvertent waiver, they may also be sued by the client for malpractice. Since in such litigation all jurisdictions recognize the right of the lawyer to disclose all the information exchanged with the client, my analysis concludes that the client's enforcement of the lawyer's optimal care though malpractice litigation is optimal only when the harm rule is the harshest rule.

The scant theoretical analysis of inadvertent waiver in legal literature may serve to explain the lack of uniformity in the case law and the various interpretations taken by the courts. In the US and in England we find a host of liability and harm rules. Uncertainty prevails. In Germany, we find a very clear and settled approach, but the issue is of little importance in the absence of pre-trial discovery.

One final caveat must conclude this part. The optimal inadvertent waiver regime depends on whether the privilege is socially desirable or not. I have conducted the analysis under the assumption that the corporate lawyer-client privilege can be used to choose socially undesirable actions that are sub-optimally enforced. According to this approach the privilege undermines corporate compliance rather than promotes it. However, in regimes where sanctions are set optimally, the privilege can promote compliance and be then socially desirable. If privilege is not socially desirable, a tough regime of inadvertent waiver is desirable. If corporations use the privilege to escape sanctions then strict liability for waiver, which causes the corporate client to internalize the frequency of legal consultation, is advised. However, if privilege is socially desirable, then the converse result should be drawn.

IV Concluding Remarks

This chapter focused on the corporate lawyer-client privilege. The privilege allows lawyers to refuse to disclose confidential lawyer-client communications. This conclusion summarizes the main observations and conclusions.

At the outset I have outlined the legal theoretical justifications for the privilege and the critique offered by current Law & Economics literature. In the Anglo-American law, the prevalent justifications for the privilege are the utilitarian and neo-utilitarian rationales. The utilitarian rationale claims that the privilege promotes social welfare even if it deprives the courts of some evidence. The neo-utilitarian rationale advances social compliance as the primary social good that is gained from the privilege. Law & Economics literature has shown that the social benefits of the lawyer-client privilege are conditioned on the optimality of enforcement and the accuracy of sanctions. When public or private enforcement is sub-optimal, the privilege may induce non-compliant behavior rather than compliance. It should be noted that in Germany, the right to privacy is an important justification for the privilege, but not the only one. The non-utilitarian rationale seems problematic when one considers the extension of the privilege to legal entities. However, German courts recognize that legal entities are entitled to a sphere of privacy.

The lawyer-client privilege is absolute in all jurisdictions. However, the German law contains a far stronger absolute wording than its Anglo-American counterparts. One reason for the emphasis on the privilege in the German law lies in the allegiance of judges to their interest group. Assuming that the privilege serves the lawyers but decreases the accuracy of adjudication, judges should and do treat the privilege restrictively. German judges are less dependent on the professional group of lawyers for their career progression whilst Anglo-American judges are more so. Hence, Anglo-American judges are more likely to protect the interests of lawyers in the privilege even without an explicit strong law, whereas German judges would be less inclined to do so.

The extension of the lawyer-client privilege to corporate clients has been often criticized in academic literature. However, it is entrenched in years of case law precedents. I observed that all the surveyed jurisdictions extended the privilege to the corporate lawyer-client setting without giving substantial weight to the different nature of the corporate client as compared to the individual client. The corporate lawyer-client privilege became so widespread that path-dependence has evolved. Courts seem to believe that turning the wheel back and revoking the corporate privilege is not feasible anymore.

Scholarly work suggests that the corporate lawyer-client privilege is problematic due to the ability of firms to use the privilege in their favour, their sophistication as litigants and their role as repeat players. In the case law, on the other, one can find the assertion that the corporate privilege promotes compliance of corporations with the law. This assertion is based on two fundamental assumptions: (1) that lawyers always advise the firm on the legitimate course of actions, and (2) that lawyers have the ability to ensure compliance. I have shown that both assumptions are dubious.

The lawyer-client privilege is a complicated creature of evidence and procedural law. In order to understand how the privilege works and to enable a comparative study of it, I proceeded to survey the main components of the privilege in the US, England and Germany. Once again, one of the clear distinctions between the Anglo-American and the German systems turned out to be the German reliance on privacy as a foundation for the privilege. For example, in the US and in England the lawyer's obligation to confidentiality is primarily ethical. Therefore, it is enforced by the professional group itself or by civil enforcement initiated by the clients. Contrary to the Anglo-American systems, the obligation to confidentiality in Germany is statutory and enforceable by civil as well as criminal law. The reason is that protection of confidentiality in Germany is motivated by a strong, constitutional, protection of the privacy rights of the client.

The final part of this chapter focused on three aspects that concern the implementation of the corporate lawyer-client privilege and offered a comparative analysis from a Law & Economic perspective.

In the first section I observed that one of the unique traits of the corporate privilege is often overlooked when sanction schemes are devised: the corporate privilege applies to the firm but not to its constituents. This holds in both the Anglo-American and the German legal systems. I concluded that this generates a principal-agent problem. In the Anglo-American systems this problem can oftentimes be solved by imposing direct liability on agents for undesirable corporate actions. However, there are circumstances where it is not possible to efficiently impose such personal liability (for example, when agents are judgment- proof). In Germany, the principal-agent problem is solved by systemic ownership and control structures that ensure strong control of the owners over the management.

The second section concerned the rules that courts devise in order to determine which agents in the firm can communicate with the corporate lawyer under the protection of the privilege. In the US, two main rules are used: (1) the "control group" test, which protects only the high ranking officials that influence corporate decisions or (2) the "subject matter" test, which protects the control group but also whomever they authorize to act in their behalf. Analyzing the rules yields the following conclusions:

- The control group test motivates some corporations to alter their internal structure in order to "squeeze" into the criteria of the test. If the corporation's initial structure was socially efficient, it follows that the new structure would be socially inefficient. It then follows that the altered firm would be able to pursue more sanctionable (welfare reducing) actions as a result of the privilege, thereby further reducing social welfare.
- In control group jurisdictions, corporations have an incentive to assert the privilege not only when it is warranted, but also when the assertion is false. This is because it is costly for plaintiffs to expose mimicking by defendants. Hence, under the control group test, corporations that would not be granted a privilege also have an incentive to pursue sanctionable actions and subsequently assert a false privilege.

In the US, the "control group" test has been losing ground and it can only be found in three states. The majority of state jurisdictions in the US rely on the "subject matter" test. The latter test presents similar yet less pronounced problems compared to the "control group" test. I noted that English law may be heading in the direction of the "control group" test and surveyed the recent case law on the matter. In Germany, in contrast, all agents of the corporation are protected in their communications with the corporate lawyer. In the absence of pre-trial discovery, this approach is less relevant for plaintiffs and less cumbersome in adjudication costs compared to the Anglo-American jurisdictions.

The final section analyzed the doctrine of inadvertent waiver. I examined the doctrine, which deals with the accidental disclosure of privileged communications, through the lenses of the economic analysis of accidents. However, the doctrine differs from the regular accident by the fact that the court decides whether to declare that a private harm had materialized whereas in the regular accident harm is given. The conclusions from an inspection of representative case law in the US and England is that courts apply different and inconsistent standards of care, which they use to determine whether accidental disclosure had occurred. Furthermore, since it is the courts that can determine the magnitude of the harm (i.e., how much of the privileged information will be "outed") the case law on harm has also been reviewed. Here too I found different and inconsistent decisions.

Inadvertent waiver is relevant to corporate lawyer-client privilege for two reasons: (1) corporations transmit high volumes of information to their lawyers, and (2) corporations are repeat players and can also harness economies of scale to improve their precautions and reduce the risk of inadvertent waiver.

Analyzing inadvertent waiver through the economic analysis of accidents shows that the more information is shared with the lawyer, the higher the risk of accidental disclosure. Hence the main conclusion: waiver liability and harm rules influence the amount of information exchanged between the client and the lawyer. Since the accuracy of legal advice depends on the amount of information that is provided to the lawyer, the second conclusion follows: the quality of legal advice depends on the toughness of the inadvertent waiver doctrine. Finally, considering the implications of these conclusions on the behavior of corporations, I suggest that corporations circumvent tough inadvertent waiver regimes by shifting from non-durable to durable precautions. This reduces the marginal cost of care and enables corporate clients to go on transmitting high volumes of information to their lawyers.

Chapter 2: Multi Disciplinary Practices

I Introduction

One of the most controversial issues facing the American and English legal professions in recent years has been the growing pressure to form multi-disciplinary practices (MDPs)[303]. The American Bar Association's (ABA) definition of an MDP is: "a partnership, professional corporation, or other association or entity that includes lawyers and non-lawyers and has as one, but not all, of its purposes the delivery of legal services to a client(s) other than the MDP itself or that holds itself out to the public as providing nonlegal, as well as legal, services... it also includes an arrangement by which a law firm joins with one or more other professional firms to provide services, including legal services, and there is a direct or indirect sharing of profits as part of the arrangement"[304].

MDPs raise a host of ethical problems for both lawyers and for the professionals, such as accountants and auditors, with whom lawyers may be considering forming MDPs.

Arguments against the formation of MDPs include the danger of losing professional independence[305], the rules regarding confidentiality[306] and different professional regulations with potential for conflicts[307].

Arguments in favour of allowing MDPs include: client demand for "one stop shopping", more efficient services (especially as problems become more complex and multi-faceted)[308] and globalization[309]. Market regulation and the complexity of global businesses are often cited as the main driving force behind MDPs[310].

The MDP debate sprang from the concerns raised with respect to auditors providing additional services to clients and thereby jeopardizing their independence. During the 1990's auditing firms expanded with increased vigour into non-auditing services, including legal services, not only in the US, but also in European countries[311]. Since then however, Arthur Andersen's multiple role as tax advisor, consultant and auditor in the Enron scandal has been viewed as an MDP fiasco[312]. Arthur Andersen acted as an MDP of sorts by providing accounting and auditing services along with legal advice to support some questionable financial accounting techniques. One question that often arises in the context of the Enron debate is whether the result would have been different had the lawyers been in control of the MDP. This question assumes that lawyers are bound by stronger ethical rules which would

303 Ourednick, (2003).

304 ABA Committee on Multidisciplinary Practice, Report to the House of Delegates (1999). Available from: www.abanet.org/cpr/mdpreport.html (last visited: February 7, 2006)

305 Ourednick, 169; Hawkins, 499; Lucci, 172. Closely related is the claim that lawyers may be less zealous advocates when the MDP is controlled by the accountants and the latter make the decisions regarding the financial aspect of the MDP. But of course, not all legal work requires zealous advocacy. Lucci, 174.

306 Hawkins, 501.

307 Hawkins, 501-502.

308 Lucci, 162-164.

309 Hawkins, 504-506. Lucci, 166. The claim is that since other countries are allowing MDPs the legal profession in the US must adapt or it will lose in the competition on multinational clients.

310 Daly (2002), 593.

311 Loudenslager, 39-41. The "big five" (now "big four") became literally the largest international employer of corporate lawyers.

312 Ourednick, 170.

have superseded the lax approach of the Arthur Andersen auditors, supposedly driven by an ambition to accumulate consultancy payments[313]. Some MDP supporters propose that MDPs should be allowed only when the lawyers are "in control of the ship". However, as noted by ***Ourednick***, this solution ignores the obligations of auditors. He claims that had the lawyers been in control of Arthur Andersen, Enron's fall would not have been prevented since the auditors would have been bound to the lawyers' confidentiality and this would have prevented them from blowing the whistle[314]. On the other hand, there are claims that incorporating lawyers into auditing processes improves the ability of the auditors to detect corporate wrongdoing[315]. ***Lucci*** claims that liability conscious lawyers partnering with auditors will prevent Enron type failures by pointing out liability risks[316]. This contrasts with ***Ourednick***'s claims that while society may benefit from some MDPs, the lawyer-auditor MDP structure should not be allowed[317]. Finally, in the opinion of ***Loudenslager***, although lawyers may be less prone to capture by management (in itself a debatable claim) - because of the absence of the privilege in MDPs - firms will refrain from fully disclosing information to lawyers, thereby stifling the provision of optimal advice and optimal auditing[318]. Indeed, it is not in every legal system that an MDP would have the benefit of the professional privileges that its individual constituents, be they lawyers or accountants, enjoy when they are acting separately.

Although often mentioned as one of the key problems, the confidentiality aspect of the MDP debate has not been thoroughly analyzed from a Law & Economics perspective[319]. I focus on the role of MDPs as entities that provide ex-ante advice on contemplated corporate actions that have both legal and accounting or auditing implications[320]. The objective is to determine to what extent does the professional privilege affect the social welfare outcome of MDPs under the different regulatory and professional regimes in the US, England and Germany.

The first section in this introductory part surveys the legal situation with respect to the professional privilege of accountants and auditors in the relevant jurisdictions. I show that the privilege in Anglo-American jurisdictions is minimal if not entirely non-existent, whereas in Germany a strong privilege exists. In section 2 I survey the formation of MDPs in the respective jurisdictions either as formal entities or as informal collaborations between professionals. In addition, the position of the EU courts on the matter is discussed. The survey indicates that some forms of MDP exist regardless of whether they are directly encouraged by the governing institutions. However, the institutional endorsement, if it exists, affects the organizational structure of the MDPs.

Part II goes on to explore the effects of systemic differences between the jurisdictions on the social welfare implications of granting a privilege to formal MDPs. Given the conditions of the model, I show that MDPs are least harmful and may also be welfare enhancing, when professional consultants tend to be conservative and not pro-active in the advice that they render to their clients. The findings are then applied in part III to the relevant jurisdictions. Part IV concludes.

---

313 Lucci, 194-195.

314 Ourednick, 192.

315 Lucci, 195-196; see also Kostant (2001), 1219.

316 Lucci, 196.

317 Ourednick, 190-191.

318 Loudenslager, 81-82 citing Painter (2000), 1402-04; Kostant (1999).

319 Loudenslager, (2001).

320 On the increasing nature of such multidisciplinary professional problems see generally in Cunningham (2002) 1454 ("for any business transaction there is an accounting consequence and in turn or simultaneously a disclosure consequence").

1. Privilege for Accountants and Auditors

One commonly heard view is that a jurisdiction that wishes to allow, or even encourage, a lawyer-accountant MDP must enact a professional client-accountant privilege[321]. Before exploring the MDP debate, one should first pause to survey the legal background of the client-accountant privilege in the legal systems discussed here.

1.1 United States

In the US, often the line between the work done by lawyers and accountants can be murky. Lawyers and accountants can perform some tasks with identical levels of expertise. Auditing is just one example of a function that fits both professions. The provision of tax advice is another. Nevertheless, a lawyer employed by an accounting firm cannot formally render legal advice and therefore cannot enjoy the legal privilege. However, if that lawyer renders only business advice, which is not legal, he cannot assert the privilege either[322].

Tax practitioners can give legal tax advice but they find themselves disadvantaged (compared to lawyers) without the privilege. This has developed into a "turf war" between lawyers and accountants in the US since the AICPA started openly lobbying for a privilege statute[323]. The political pressure resulted in a partial statutory victory for accountants, because the accountant-client privilege is merely a shaky "patchwork"[324]: following a long political struggle American accountants were able to persuade US tax authorities to agree to a very limited codified privilege as part of an amendment to the Internal Revenue Code. The federal statute stipulates in §7525:

> "(a) Uniform application to taxpayer communications with federally authorized practitioners.
>
> (1) General rule. With respect to tax advice, the same common law protections of confidentiality which apply to a communication between a taxpayer and an attorney shall also apply to a communication between a taxpayer and any federally authorized tax practitioner to the extent the communication would be considered a privileged communication if it were between a taxpayer and an attorney.
>
> (2) Limitations.
>
> Paragraph (1) may only be asserted in—
>
> (A) any noncriminal tax matter before the Internal Revenue Service; and
>
> (B) any noncriminal tax proceeding in Federal court brought by or against the United States.

321 Loudenslager, 38.
322 Newman, 8
323 Newman, 5-6
324 Loudenslager, 63.

(3) Definitions.

For purposes of this subsection—

(A) Federally authorized tax practitioner. The term "federally authorized tax practitioner" means any individual who is authorized under Federal law to practice before the Internal Revenue Service if such practice is subject to Federal regulation under section 330 of title 31, United States Code.

(B) Tax advice. The term "tax advice" means advice given by an individual with respect to a matter which is within the scope of the individual's authority to practice described in subparagraph (A).

(b) Section not to apply to communications regarding corporate tax shelters. The privilege under subsection (a) shall not apply to any written communication between a federally authorized tax practitioner and a director, shareholder, officer, or employee, agent, or representative of a corporation in connection with the promotion of the direct or indirect participation of such corporation in any tax shelter (as defined in section 6662(d)(2)(C)(iii))."

The privilege is very narrow and qualified, and only applies in strictly defined circumstances. US courts have ruled many times that filing tax returns is not legal work and therefore that information exchanged for that purpose would not be protected by the privilege[325]. The privilege only applies to "tax advice" and therefore would not cover information exchanged for any other service. Furthermore, the privilege applies only to legal tax advice[326], rather than business advice related to tax matters.

Section §7525(b) specifically states that the privilege shall not apply to communications between a tax-practitioner and "director, shareholder, officer or employee, agent or representative of a corporation in connection with the promotion of the direct or indirect participation of such corporation in any tax shelter…".

The privilege applies only in proceedings in which the Internal Revenue Service (IRS) is a party. It does not apply to civil proceedings between private parties. It only applies to civil matters and only when communications would be protected if they were to transpire between a lawyer and a client[327]. The IRS can decide to turn a civil inquiry (where the privilege is applicable) into a criminal one (where the privilege is not applicable), thus it has control over the ability to assert the privilege[328].

Courts have narrowed the field of application of the privilege even further. For example, in the matter of ***KPMG***[329], the court held that tax advice regarding already completed transactions (rather than future transactions) is most likely to be concerned with filing tax returns and therefore should not be protected.

---

325 Oliva, 4.

326 Oliva, 10.

327 ***United States v. Frederick***, 182 F.3d 496, 502 (7th Cir. 1999), cert. denied, 528 U.S. 1154 (2000).

328 §7525(a)(2); Gillet, 43-4.

329 ***US v. KPMG***, 237 F.Supp. 2d, 35 (US, 2002); Oliva, 15

In addition to these federal provisions, some US states have enacted a testimonial privilege for accountants. Fifteen states (and Puerto Rico) have testimonial privilege statutes, and fifteen other states have confidentiality laws that require accountants to keep the communications with the client in confidence, but which do not prevent compelling them to reveal the information in court[330]. Within the states that have enacted a testimonial privilege[331], there are significant variations. For example, six states have included an exception when the client has used the communications to further a crime or fraud. Additionally, nine states have exceptions for quality and disciplinary review of the accountant. Only six states have an exception when disclosure is required according to Generally Accepted Accounting Practices (GAAP). Nine states have an exception when the information is relevant to an issue of breach of duty by the accountant, or by the client to the accountant. At any rate, obligatory disclosures in financial reports do not constitute a waiver of the privilege[332].

A privilege is available however when the client shares information with the accountant (often when he is hired by the lawyer) in order to assist the lawyer in the execution of legal work[333].

Since the legal privilege does not cover advice about tax returns, which is held to be accounting work and not legal work and therefore also unprotected for lawyers, drawing the line in these types of legal consulting is difficult[334].

The US court has made it clear that given the role of the auditor as a "watchdog" on behalf of both shareholders and investors, a privilege for auditors would not make sense[335].

1.2 England

In England the situation is clearer than that in the US, evidently to the disadvantage of accountants. The courts have ruled that advice pertaining to tax matters given by lawyers will be protected under the lawyer client privilege. The courts pointed out that the lawyer client privilege is protected under article 8(2) of the European convention of Human Rights. However, when the same advice is given by an accountant it is not protected[336].

---

330 Loudenslager, 68.

331 Loudenslager, 68. Brodsky et al., 18. The following states have an accountant-client privilege: Arizona, Colorado, Florida, Georgia, Idaho, Illinois, Indiana, Kansas, Louisiana, Maryland, Michigan, Missouri, New Mexico, Pennsylvania, and Tennessee.

332 Loudenslager, 68-69.

333 Loudenslager, 61-62; ***United States v. Kovel***, 296 F.2d 918, 922 (2d Cir., 1961), ***United States v. Schwimmer***, 892 F.2d 237, 243 (2d. Cir. 1989).

334 Loudenslager, 62; ***US v. El Paso Co.***, 682 F.2d 530 (5th Cir. 1982) at 539.

335 ***United States v. Arthur Young & Co.***, 465 U.S. 805, 817 (1984).

336 Held in the ***Three Rivers*** ruling

1.3 Germany

The professional privilege of accountants and tax-advisors in Germany is identical to that of lawyers and is based on the same statutes. It is the auditor's privilege that awakens the attention of legal scholars, especially from the perspective of Anglo-American law, which opposes such a privilege being granted. For German scholars it is obvious: the auditor serves both the private interests of the firm and the public interest, and requires a trust relationship in order to receive information that enables the production of a reliable description of the financial circumstances of the firm[337].

As early as 1900, as the German chambers of commerce (Handelskammer) started regulating auditors (the term used at that time was Bücherrevisor), there is record of the fact that the holder of this position must be a person of trust and must maintain professional confidentiality[338]. By 1931, a new auditor admitted to the professional chambers had to swear to abide by and maintain independence and confidentiality in performance of his professional duties[339].

The auditor's duty to professional confidentiality is now legislated in §57b WiPrO (WirtschaftsPrüferOrdnung). The auditor is a free profession[340] and must maintain its independence. The requirement for confidentiality is justified by the fact that free professions require a trust relationship with clientele and intimate information in order to perform their public service duties. This is the kind of information that would not be given without the development of a strong trust relationship[341]. The German constitutional court has held that some professions cannot perform their social service to the citizen-client without the trust relationship and therefore must have the right to confidentiality (protected by criminal liability), yet some other professions do not require a privilege[342].

The auditor's obligation to secrecy is similar to the lawyer's obligation, although there might be specific cases where they differ[343]. In criminal proceedings, the privilege of auditors is acknowledged in §53 StPO[344] (and §97 StPO with the corresponding protection against search and seizure). Confidentiality is ensured through §203 StGB which imposes up to one year's imprisonment for revealing private or business secrets. When the obligation to secrecy is broken by an auditing firm, the responsible organs in the firm or the persons responsible for the breach are personally criminally liable (through §14 StGB). A similar special criminal

---

337 See for example: Baetzgen (Köln, 1970).

338 Lichtner, 6-7.

339 Lichtner, 8.

340 §1 (2) WiPrO.

341 Lichtner, 11-12.

342 BverfG 33, 377; BVerfG 38, 325. Social workers and veterinary-doctors have no privilege.

343 Lichtner, 29-30. For example, the reporting obligations on auditors in suspicious money laundering cases are wider than those of lawyers.

344 The section reads: "(1) Zur Verweigerung des Zeugnisses sind ferner berechtigt… (3) Rechtsanwälte, Patentanwälte, Notare, Wirtschaftsprüfer, vereidigte Buchprüfer, Steuerberater und Steuerbevollmächtigte, Ärzte, Zahnärzte, Psychologische Psychotherapeuten, Kinder- und Jugendlichenpsychotherapeuten, Apotheker und Hebammen über das, was ihnen in dieser Eigenschaft anvertraut worden oder bekanntgeworden ist, Rechtsanwälten stehen dabei sonstige Mitglieder einer Rechtsanwaltskammer gleich… Die in Satz 1 Nr. 5 genannten Personen dürfen das Zeugnis verweigern über die Person des Verfassers oder Einsenders von Beiträgen und Unterlagen oder des sonstigen Informanten sowie über die ihnen im Hinblick auf ihre Tätigkeit gemachten Mitteilungen, über deren Inhalt sowie über den Inhalt selbst erarbeiteter Materialien und den Gegenstand berufsbezogener Wahrnehmungen. Dies gilt nur, soweit es sich um Beiträge, Unterlagen, Mitteilungen und Materialien für den redaktionellen Teil oder redaktionell aufbereitete Informations- und Kommunikationsdienste handelt".

liability is included in §333 HGB with regards to the auditing of corporations. Additional lex spezialis can be found in §404 AktG, §19 PubG, and additionally §395 AktienGesetz also contains an obligation of secrecy that applies to auditors.

The civil consequences of a confidentiality breach are contractual liability, tort liability through §323 HGB [345] and tort liability through §823 BGB for breach of a personality right.

In civil procedure the privilege is enshrined in §383 1 (6) ZPO,[346] and is similar in context and application to the criminal procedure. The tax code (AbgabenOrdnung) also allows auditors and lawyers to refuse to give information to tax authorities as provided in §102 AO. Refusal may not be considered as evidence against the client[347]. Note however, that this right does not include the material and reports that must legally be served to the tax authorities. This provision reflects a protective approach to privacy in tax procedures which is similar to the approach in criminal procedure. It can be justified by the fact that the defendant faces the state and its strong investigative search powers.

The professional confidentiality of the auditor according to the WiPrO also extends to the employees and members of the auditing firm. The auditing firm as a legal entity carries the same obligations as the single auditor[348]. Much like lawyers, the auditor may breach the obligation to secrecy in legal procedure against the client or to protect himself against criminal proceedings. However he may not breach confidentiality in civil proceedings against a third party without the consent of the client[349]. In fact, it is hard to find a law court or professional tribunal decision concerning an auditor in breach of his duty of confidentiality. Whether this stems from strong adherence of auditors to their obligation, from little demand for such information, or from having little relevant information to reveal is yet unknown.

2. *Formal and Informal MDPs*

This section surveys how MDPs are formed. Evidently, lawyers and other professionals collaborate on a regular basis. When such collaborations are done within one joint entity (for example, a firm comprised of lawyers and accountants) it is referred to as a formal MDP. Other forms of collaboration are informal. Even where MDPs are not formally allowed, lawyers and accountants may work together and form informal MDPs in ways that overcome the ethical hurdles imposed by their professional groups. There are various structures of joint accountant-lawyer services, depending on the degree of integration. The highest separation is in the "contractual side-by-side" structure where the lawyer and the accountant contract to

345 Civil liability for breach of professional confidentiality which applies to injury due to negligent behaviour and is capped at 1 million Euro for a single auditor and 4 Million Euro for an auditing firm.

346 The section reads: "Zur Verweigerung des Zeugnisses sind berechtigt:... (6) Personen, denen kraft ihres Amtes, Standes oder Gewerbes Tatsachen anvertraut sind, deren Geheimhaltung durch ihre Natur oder durch gesetzliche Vorschrift geboten ist, in Betreff der Tatsachen, auf welche die Verpflichtung zur Verschwiegenheit sich bezieht". There are few cases where the privilege of lawyers and auditors in Germany are not symmetrical. One example where the auditor privilege is specifically pierced by legislation and the lawyer privilege is not is the obligation to submit the books of a company car, noting company and private documentation of usage of the car, in an application for appropriate tax deductions. The submission would not be considered the breach of obligation to secrecy by the auditor. See Lichtner, 56-57.

347 Lichtner, 83.

348 Lichtner, 48-49.

349 LIchtner, 100-101.

work together on certain matters but are independent of each other for any other purpose, and also take other separate clients[350].

Under the "cooperation model" the accountant and the lawyer are employed separately but bill the client together and share the payoff. In the US this arrangement has often developed into a model where the lawyer employs the accountant on behalf of the client[351]. This structure was very popular in the US since it enabled the client to interact only with the lawyer and thereby secure the lawyer-client privilege for all communications.

For some time, the perception of the law was that when lawyers needed to consult a third-party professional in order to give the client fully informed advice, then sharing client information with the third party would not cause the loss of the privilege. However, in the sixties the courts moved to curb this artificial extension of the privilege to accountants by holding that the lawyer client privilege shall apply to communications with the accountant only when the accountant acts as an "interpreter" of complex accounting issues for the lawyer, and not when he was hired, through the lawyer, to give additional "legal" or non-legal advice[352]. This structure is also referred to as the "ancillary business" model (when law firms establish a separate business offering related non-legal services). This structure is familiar in the US and in England but less so in continental Europe[353].

In formal MDPs, a "command and control" model is the most common form in Anglo-American discussions. The MDP is essentially a law firm that offers legal services as well as accounting/consulting services while the lawyers control the firm and the ethical rules that guide it[354].

2.1 United States

US lawyers are starting to be left behind as more jurisdictions around the world recognize the possibility of MDPs, including Canada, Australia, South Africa, France, Spain, Switzerland and Germany[355]. The Netherlands allows MDPs but not between lawyers and accountants[356]. Most of the "big four" auditing firms partake and profit from these rules - in Europe[357].

MDPs are prohibited in the US as a result of the self-imposed restraints erected by lawyers. MDPs are prohibited through Model Rule 5.4 (prohibition of fee sharing with non-lawyers). In addition, Model Rule 1.6 (confidentiality) is also a barrier to forming MDPs in the US[358]. Model Rule 1.10 which prohibits a law firm from being engaged by a client if any single lawyer will be in conflict of interest due to the engagement can also be construed as a barrier to forming MDPs.

---

350 Daly, 596-597.
351 Daly, 594.
352 ***US v. Kovel***, 296 F.2d 918 (2nd Cir. 1961).
353 Daly, 595.
354 Daly, 595.
355 Hawkins, 493.
356 Hawkins, 495.
357 Hawkins, 496.
358 Since it is interpreted as a wide obligation which conflicts with narrower professional obligations (or with reporting obligations) such as those of accountants and auditors and since it limits the sharing of information.

2.1.1 Accountant Lawyer MDPs

In 1998 the ABA appointed the Commission for Multidisciplinary Practice to propose changes to the Model Rules that would enable the introduction of MDPs. The commission submitted pro-MDP propositions the following year. The commission recommended that MDPs should be permitted under certain restrictions[359]. The most important with respect to my discussion here was that MDPs should be led by lawyers and that they must ensure that other professionals also adhere to the lawyers' Model Rules of Ethics[360]. As mentioned, Model Rule 1.6 forbids the lawyer to share confidential information with other professionals without the client's consent. The reason for this is that unless the non-lawyer professional is independently privileged, the lawyer-client privilege will be lost as a result of this exchange of information.

In spite of the commission's pro-MDP stand, winds have turned against the MDP supporters and the proposals were rejected by the ABA House of Delegates in 2000[361]. This is the formal position of the ABA to date. But despite this, the "big four" accounting firms remain *de-facto* MDPs[362]. Still, confidentiality differences are described as the biggest problem facing accountant-lawyer MDPs in the US[363].

2.1.2 Auditor Lawyer MDPs

It isn't only that US lawyers do not establish formal MDPs with accountants, but their relationship with auditors is also increasingly tense. An ABA "white paper" concerning company disclosures to auditors warns that waiver of the attorney client privilege as a result of sharing information with auditors at their request is a serious risk to the promotion of corporate compliance through the privilege[364]. This assumes that the corporate lawyer-client privilege promotes compliance and that the loss of the privilege as a result of sharing information with auditors is detrimental to corporate compliance. The essence of the conflict is that lawyers perceive confidentiality to be a crucial element of promoting corporate compliance whereas for auditors it is the promoting of transparency that plays the key role in inducing compliance. The legal manifestation of the conflict is as follows. In 2002, the AICPA issued the "Statement on Auditing Standards No. 99" (SAS 99) "Consideration of Fraud in a Financial Statement Audit". SAS 99 obliges the auditor to conduct the audit of financial statements with scepticism in order to locate "red flags" which indicate potential fraud. In carrying out this role the auditor must pose questions to management and also to the auditing committee and when required - to any other personnel within the audited entity, including the company's legal counsel. Therefore, auditors are increasingly likely to ask for information that is supposed to be privileged under lawyer-client communications in order to alley fraud suspicions[365].

---

359 Hawkins, 486.
360 Hawkins, *id.*
361 Hawkins, 488; Ourednick, 175. The District of Columbia (DC) adopted Model Rules 5.4 in a version that allows MDPs. However, it appears that fee sharing is allowed only between lawyers working within DC.
362 Hawkins, 482-483.
363 Hawkins, 509.
364 Brodsky (2004).
365 Brodsky et al., 8.

The Securities Exchange Act §10A[366] requires auditors to plan procedures that will provide an assurance of detecting illegal acts that may affect financial statements. Section 10A requires that the auditor report "up the ladder" any suspect fraud or illegality and also report the information "outside" the company, to authorities if (1) the audit committee or the board are adequately informed of the act, (2) the illegal act has material effect on the financial statement, (3) no appropriate steps to remedy the illegal act have been taken and (4) the act will require the auditor to issue a qualified opinion or resign. SEC Regulation 13b2-2 from 2003 prohibits any misleading or false representations by the company to its auditor in relation to auditing financial statements[367]. The PCAOB (which succeeded the AICPA) issued two auditing standards that increase the possibility that auditors will seek privileged material to substantiate the audit[368]. Auditors are now seeking, for example, material indicating the reporting of lawyers "up the ladder" as a consequence of the SEC Regulations implementing §307 of the SOX Act[369]. But auditors may seek other legal advice material as well[370].

Tension between the two professions has not always been so high. In 1975, long before the notorious accounting and auditing scandals of the late 90s and early 2000s, the ABA and the AICPA struck a "treaty" detailing what auditors may require from lawyers and what information lawyers will reveal to auditors[371]. Under this agreement the lawyer may provide the auditor with information about an overtly threatened or pending litigation to which the lawyer has devoted work on behalf of the company and - with specific client consent - also regarding unasserted claims that the client plans to make. Evaluation of the potential result of the case would only be given by the lawyer in very rare situations[372].

Mostly, case law on attorney disclosure to auditors has arisen in conjunction with the disclosure of loss contingencies. These disclosures are systematically held to be waiver of the privilege, unless they occur in a state that has acknowledged an accountant-client privilege with such protection[373]. Most case law authorities in these states support the approach that disclosure by a lawyer to an auditor is not a waiver, but there is no uniformity in this area[374]. Post-SOX Act developments are discouraging for the supporters of the privilege. The PCAOB has succeeded the AICPA as the standard setting body. The AICPA Code of Professional Conduct Rule 301 prohibits disclosure of confidential client information without client consent. The PCAOB did not adopt this rule in its interim ethics standards[375]. This already contradicted the now historical "treaty" between the lawyers and the auditors.

The ABA-AICPA "treaty" stipulated that an auditor may not use a lawyer's confidential information in the financial statement produced, or in answers to governmental bodies or in subpoenas or other processes without the lawyers consent[376]. The SOX Act §105(b)(5)

---

366 15 U.S.C. §78j-1. Amended 1995.

367 17 C.F.R. §240. 13b2-2 "Representations and conduct in connection with the preparation of required reports and documents".

368 Auditing Standard No. 2: An Audit of Internal Control Over Financial Reporting Performed in Conjunction With an Audit of Financial Statements (PCAOB, 2004); Auditing Standard No. 3: Audit Documentation (PCAOB, 2004).

369 Brodsky et al., 9.

370 Brodsky et al., 10.

371 Brodsky et al., 15; The "Statement of Policy Regarding Lawyers' Responses to Auditors' requests for Information" (1975) referred to as "the treaty".

372 Brodsky et al., 15 at footnote 50.

373 Brodsky et al., 18.

374 Brodsky et al., 23.

375 Brodsky et al., 24.

376 Brodsky et al., *id.*

provides immunity and privilege to all materials provided to the PCAOB for the purpose of its investigations and processes. The PCAOB supervises the compliance of auditors with SOX and other regulations. However this procedure does not solve the waiver risk of providing the material to the auditor in the first place[377].

Therefore, the latest ABA "white paper" proposes to bridge the widening rift between the lawyers and the auditors by an amendment that would allow lawyers to provide information to auditors without this being considered a waiver of the privilege[378]. The proposal is still under discussion.

2.2 England

A UK survey presented in testimony before an ABA Committee noted that most corporations in the UK object to an "amalgamation" of lawyers with accountants[379]. England has an ingrained traditional separation between barristers who are trial lawyers and may not form partnership with anyone save for other barristers, and solicitors who are transactional lawyers and traditionally (although this is changing) may not represent the client in court[380]. Both barristers and solicitors are statutorily barred from forming MDPs[381]. For solicitors, the limitation is also self-imposed through the rules of practice[382]. Under these provisions solicitors may establish ancillary businesses that provide non-legal advice, but not legal advice[383].

In England, the government, through the Office of Fair Trade, was the driving force in support of legislative changes to allow the establishment of MDPs. The government viewed MDPs as an efficient tool in a competitive environment. However, until recently no significant action had been taken by solicitors to promote this agenda[384]. It seems, however, that the professional associations of solicitors in the UK are currently re-evaluating the prohibition, probably for a self-serving reason: they are facing strong competition. In England, solicitors have no monopoly on the business of providing legal advice and competing services are offered by other market participants (such as banks, accountants, etc.)[385]. The "Big Four" accounting firms are indeed acting as informal MDPs in the UK, already offering legal services (except representation in court). These market participants may drive the English solicitors to offer a wider variety of services in a "one-stop shop". Nevertheless, solicitors do have a monopoly on the professional title[386], and on the testimonial privileges attached to it.

---

377 Brodsky et al., 26-27.
378 Brodsky et al., 28.
379 Wolfman, Bernard, February 2000 Hearing Testimony on MDP at 2, available at http://www.abanet.org/cpr/wolfman4.html
380 Daly, 615-616.
381 Courts and Legal Services Act 1990, §66.
382 Daly, 616; Solicitors Practice Rule 7 (2002) forbids fee sharing with non-lawyers.
383 Daly, 617.
384 Daly, 620-621.
385 Daly, 616.
386 Nnona, 158.

2.3 Germany

MDPs have existed in Germany since the 1960s[387] and the law has specifically allowed them since 1973[388]. In 1982 the German constitutional court held that lawyers have a constitutional right to form MDPs. The court held that regulations limiting the ability of tax-advisors to join with non-tax advisors were unconstitutional and this decision applies to lawyers as well[389].

MDPs in Germany are either contractual or fully integrated[390]. Lawyers may form an MDP only with auditors, bookkeepers, tax advisors or patent lawyers[391]. Only individuals may be shareholders in such firms and no passive shareholding is allowed[392]. Most German MDPs are lawyer-controlled and when the rules do clash - the stronger ethical rule prevails[393]. ***Terry*** notes that MDP lawyers in Germany are satisfied with the rule according to which any non-lawyer working in an MDP is subject to lawyers' ethical obligations (§30 BRAO), but she also notes that in practice implementation of this rule in MDP organization is not observed, probably due to the lack of difference in the perceived ethical obligations of lawyers and auditors[394].

As is often observed in the literature, in Germany confidentiality differences between the professions are not the problem. As ***Daly*** writes, the "ethical gap" that exists in the Anglo-American system does not exist in Germany. Indeed, German accountants and auditors enjoy the same privilege as lawyers[395], and auditors have reduced disclosure obligations compared to their US counterparts[396]. However auditors in Germany perform a different role than that of their US colleagues. The historic role and purpose of auditors in Germany is securing the liquidity of the firm in the interests of creditors and debtors, rather than keeping tabs on management performance for the sake of an informed market. Therefore, the privilege and the reduced disclosure obligations may not have a detrimental effect on the role of German auditors in the German market as it is.

Still, though they may be less onerous compared to US obligations, German auditors do have an obligation to report irregularities in their capacity as gatekeepers, which lawyers do not share. While one scholar claims the reporting obligations of the auditor are not in conflict with the obligation to confidentiality to the client firm[397], there seems to be some opposition to this view. The opposing opinion is that a lawyer-auditor MDP is not desirable, unless the auditor is hired only to perform a "pre-audit" or a "test-audit" for intra-firm purposes[398].

Indeed, German MDPs are not without their own opponents. In the seventies, objectors claimed that partnerships between lawyers and auditors may cause the "economization" of the

---

387 BGH NJW 1968, 844; Hawkins, 495; Terry (2000), 1551-1552. The paper contains a good survey of the development and the laws regulating MDPs in Germany.

388 Terry, 1560.

389 Hawkins, 495.

390 Daly, 613.

391 Daly, *id.*

392 Daly, *id.*

393 Daly, 613-614.

394 Terry, 1595. This is true for the fully integrated MDPs. In the former big five ***Terry*** found some differences depending on the modfel of MDP they were using. See Terry, 1596-1598.

395 Michalski & Römermann, (1996).

396 Lucci, 168.

397 Lichtner, 87-88.

398 Heinicke, 27.

legal profession[399]. This point of view seems to focus on the risk that lawyers will be influenced by external considerations in their advice. However, no data was developed to support this case.

Terry's data from 1999 indicates a growing trend of forming "Lawyer Corporations" (Rechtsanwalt GmbH), which have only been allowed since 1999. The data also indicates that lawyers are leaders of approximately 10% (169) of the 1759 Wirtschaftsprüfer GmbH (Auditor Corporations). Notably, most German MDPs were small law firms, at least in the initial development of the MDP phenomenon[400]. These numbers are changing constantly and there are no current reliable data available. The development of the legal arms of the "Big Four" in Germany was rather slow at the outset, but their growth is now fast[401].

2.4 EU Law

The Council of the Bars and Law Societies of the European Union (CCBE) has traditionally opposed MDPs for reasons similar to the ABA and has published two objecting statements. Yet it seems to have been shifting its position, albeit very slowly[402].

In the EU, the member states are free to regulate the legal profession as long as equal treatment is maintained for lawyers not of the member state. Thus states are free to allow or disallow MDPs[403].

The lawyers' association in the Netherlands has prohibited accountant-lawyer MDPs and the ECJ has affirmed its right to do so after the decision was challenged in court[404]. The opinion of the Advocate General to the ECJ in the case of ***Wouters v NOVA***, discusses the assertion made by the plaintiff that restricting the ability of the two professions to combine their services amounts to a restriction of competition, and that integrating the two professions may provide an added value to consumers[405]. The Advocate General supported this position, but he also recognized that MDPs may compromise the independence of lawyers and their ability to maintain professional confidentiality[406]. ***Terry*** has observed that the opinion of the Advocate General, although mixed and inconclusive, was depicted in the ECJ's press release announcing the opinion as a victory for anti-MDP supporters. This depiction was in line with the US media losing interest with MDPs once the issue has been rejected by the ABA[407]. The ECJ's judgement adopted the Advocate General's view that a ban on MDPs does constitute a restriction on competition. This is despite Luxemburg's assertion that the ban prevents the concentration of legal services in a few large firms and thus promotes rather than hinders competition[408]. Yet the court decided that a member-state's bar can reasonably decide to protect the "proper practice" of the legal profession as it is established in the member-state

---

399 Michalski & Römermann, 3237.

400 Terry, 1570-1571.

401 Terry, 1576-1578.

402 Daly, 621-623.

403 Daly, 601.

404 ***Wouters v. Raad van der Nederlandse Orde van Advocaten („NOVA")***, C-309/99, 19 February 2002 (hereinafter – ***Wouters v. Nova***); Daly, 602-603.

405 Opinion of the Advocate General, 10 July 2001, C-309/99 ***Wouters v. NOVA*** §116-121 (hereinafter – Opinion of the AG in ***Wouters v. Nova***).

406 Opinion of the AG in ***Wouters v. NOVA***, §185-186.

407 Terry (2002).

408 ***Wouters v. NOVA***, §85.

(primarily the concern for independence and confidentiality by restricting MDPs)[409]. In sum, the ECJ's decision recognizes that restriction of the formation of MDPs is an impediment to competition in the market but also that the social loss from such an impediment may be justified by the need to protect – among other things – professional confidentiality. The correct balance between these two elements remains in the hands of the relevant institution in each member-state.

3. Summary

This part outlined the legal background for the MDP debate. The debate intensified in recent years in Anglo-American jurisdictions as professional consultants like lawyers, accountants and auditors are expected to perform an increasingly central role in ensuring the compliance of corporations with the law. The extant literature focused on whether MDPs increase or decrease compliance, but did not directly discuss the effect of professional testimonial privilege on the outcome.

As I explained in the first chapter of this work, when lawyers share information with accountants or auditors this results in the loss of the privilege due to the waiver doctrine unless the accountants and the auditors also enjoy a professional privilege. Therefore the lack of professional privilege for accountants and auditors is often an impediment for the formation of MDPs.

A survey of the legal situation with regard to the privilege for accountants and auditors unveils a stark difference between the Anglo-American and the German approach. Courts and legislators in the US and in England traditionally objected to the introduction of an accountant-client and an auditor-client privilege. In the case of the US, only after strong interest group activity a very limited accountant-client privilege was enacted on a federal level and some protection is also offered in state laws. Nevertheless, the privilege is highly limited. In England, the traditional objection to any such privilege remains. In contrast, German accountants enjoy a privilege that is almost identical to the privilege enjoyed by lawyers. Furthermore, auditors enjoy such a privilege as well. German legal literature claims that the reporting obligations of auditors are not in conflict with their obligation of confidentiality to the client-firm. Suggestions to curtail the privilege when the auditor is engaged in controlling the firm is criticized for the difficulty in separating these functions from others functions performed by auditors as well as due to the difficulty to determine whether information reached the auditor during the performance of one duty or another[410].

At least from a historical perspective, the difference between the Anglo-American and the German approaches to the accountant and the auditor privilege can be explained by the systemically different functions that these professionals fulfil in the capital market and the different approach to the role of financial reporting. The Anglo-American approach stresses the transparency of the corporate management, as a crucial element in a market of dispersed shareholders. Financial reporting and auditing are components of this transparency whereas the privilege is perceived to be in direct contradiction to transparency. Therefore it is rejected. In contrast, in Germany, transparency to the capital market had less importance historically since firms relied mainly on financing from the banking sector. Therefore,

409 ***Wouters v. NOVA***, §107.
410 Lichtner, 87-88.

financial reporting served different objectives, such as securing solvency for lenders. It follows that the recent attempts to strengthen the shareholder culture in the German capital market should not overlook the existence of a privilege for accountants and auditors, if indeed such a privilege affects the efficient performance of these professionals in the market.

In this part I went on to survey the legal approach to MDPs in the relevant jurisdictions. As shown, none of the jurisdictions discussed here regulates the formation of MDPs directly. The regulation of the matter is left to the professional groups themselves.

In the US, the lawyers prevent members of their professional group from collaborating in formal MDPs with other professions whereas accountants and auditors have no such ethical restriction. Of course, accountants and auditors do not risk losing a privilege by collaborating with lawyers. Nevertheless, informal MDPs where lawyers collaborate with accountants exist in the US. These informal MDPs are characterized by legal structures that attempt to increase the probability that a privilege will be recognized by the court even though information is shared by both lawyers and accountants. Even if some courts do recognize the privilege in such cases, this structure is less efficient than formal MDPs and therefore imposes higher costs on clients. Informal collaboration between lawyers and accountants is much more common than informal collaboration between lawyers and auditors. The reason for that is that lawyers and auditors often represent potentially conflicting interests and that in itself increases the risk that an exchange of information between the professionals would be considered a waiver of the lawyer's privilege.

The main difference between England and the US in this field is that in England barristers and solicitors do not have a monopoly on the offering of legal services, however, only holders of these titles enjoy the professional privilege. As in the US, English barristers and solicitors prevent members of their professional groups from collaborating in formal MDPs with other professions. However, other professionals in England offer "one stop shop" consulting services which include legal consulting, without a privilege. These MDPs compete with solicitor-firms. This market structure may have an interesting advantage: clients can self-select according to their preferences with regards to confidentiality. Firms that prefer to have a privilege should be willing to pay more and hire lawyers and accountants separately whilst firms that do not care for confidentiality should choose the cheaper yet unprivileged MDPs. If the market values transparency of firms as an indicator for good, or at least honest, managements, then the self-selection described above can be a good signal. This is because a management that uses the privilege in order to conceal wrongdoing will not be able to mimic the behaviour of an honest management by hiring unprivileged consultants.

Finally, in Germany, where all relevant professional groups enjoy the privilege, formal MDPs are both allowed by all groups and occur on a frequent basis.

On the EU level, the ECJ considered whether allowing professional groups to prevent their members from forming MDPs is a hindrance to competition. The court found that it is indeed so, but that interests of confidentiality and professional independence are also weighty and that it is for the relevant institution in each member-state to balance the competing elements.

II Modelling MDPs

In this chapter I explore the effects of systemic differences between the Anglo-American and the German legal systems on the social welfare implications granting of a privilege to MDPs. This is done by structuring a simple game which depicts the process of consultation regarding contemplated acts. The game is set up in section 1. I then introduce the legal and systemic background which should be further considered in the model in section 2. Following the discussion, modifications are introduced to the model and the comparative static results are discussed in sections 3, 4 and 5.

1. The Initial Model

The following model draws on the modelling of ex-ante legal advice and confidentiality by ***Shavell*** (1988) [411]. This model has three actors: a regulator, professional consultants (who act as one group) and the client, which is a firm. Since the focus here is on the social advantages and disadvantages of MDPs, with or without professional privilege, some simplifications on ***Shavell***'s model can be used in order to pinpoint the issues discussed here. Therefore the regulator's role will be reduced to a decision on whether to grant a privilege to formal MDPs or not. By that I mean that a regulator can decide to grant a privilege to professionals working within an MDP regardless of whether they enjoy a privilege when they work separately or not. The core interaction will be between the professional consultants and their client (the firm). It is the initial purpose of the game to examine whether there is a social welfare advantage in a regulatory decision to grant a privilege to consultation with MDPs when such a privilege does not exist for the same consultation when it is rendered by two separate consultants.

The Consultants. The consultants are lawyers, accountants and auditors. Assume that the type of advice sought from the consultants in this game is such that it can only be usefully obtained from consultation with two kinds of consultants. That is, for the advice to be useful the firm must hire both a lawyer and an accountant (or a lawyer and an auditor). Advice rendered by only one consultant is not an option in this game.

The consultants can choose to form MDPs in which lawyers and accountants (or lawyers and auditors) work together - or choose not to form MDPs. Assume that consultants work in a competitive market, both when they work separately and when they form MDPs. Hence, consultants can only earn the competitive market return on their services. This return is constant. When consultants act separately, the price they charge for their services is denoted by c. Since in this game the firm must consult with two consultants, the price for advice provided by two separate consultants is then 2c. When consultants form MDPs they save administrative costs and the client spends less time relating the information to the consultants since he only needs to relate the information once and not twice. Therefore the price for consultation services by an MDP is k, such that $c < k < 2c$.

The approach in common law is reflected by assuming that when a firm consults two consultants separately and one of the consultants is not privileged, then the privilege is lost. If only one profession is privileged, then consultation with both professionals is not privileged

411 See the discussion of the Shavell (1988) model on page 52, *supra*.

since communicating the same information to a non-privileged professional is considered a waiver of the privilege.

Initially, we assume that the role of the consultants is only to correct the firm's mistakes about the legality or illegality of the contemplated action. Most notably, the consultants do not point the firm in the direction of a superior choice even if such a choice exists. This restriction shall be relaxed later on.

The Firm (client). The firm in this game is an actor in the capital market that is considering pursuing some business activity. This activity can be pursued in a legal way or in an illegal way. Legal activities are socially desirable while illegal activities have an adverse effect on social welfare. The action contemplated by the firm is chosen randomly from the set of available actions given by a nature's move. A fundamental assumption is that the firm has an imperfect knowledge of the law. The quality of the firm's knowledge of the law shall be denoted by p. The firm is contemplating one action randomly selected from a variety of possible actions, which is normalized to 1 without loss of generality. When $p = 1$ and the firm contemplates a legal course of action and correctly identifies it as a legal course of action. Conversely, when an illegal course of action is contemplated it is also identified as illegal. When $p = 0$, the firm mistakes a legal course of action to be illegal and an illegal course of action to be legal. Assume the firm knows its own type and that p can take any value between 0 and 1.

The firm can observe whether the consultants offer their services separately or as MDPs, and whether they are privileged or not. The firm's decision in this game is whether to consult with the consultants, given their observed organizational form, or not. If the firm decides to consult, it is assumed that the consultants perfectly update the firm about the legality or illegality of the contemplated course of action. Hence, after consultation p always equals 1.

Modelling in this way fits many decisions with legal aspects faced by firms. For instance, in recent years several firms have ventured into the business of providing online gambling services. In many countries, gambling is illegal and the penalties are known. However, the provision of web-based online gambling services may or may not be illegal, depending on the formulation of the law and the intention of the lawmakers. Hence, the expected sanction - if the action is illegal - is known to the firm. However whether the action is legal or not, is uncertain[412]. Similar scenarios exist in civil litigation. For example, a firm may know the expected damages courts impose when victims of competition law violations sue the injurer. However, a firm may be uncertain as to whether a contemplated action is a breach of competition law or not.

The following assumptions are made with respect to the courses of action available for the firm. The proportion of legal and illegal potential courses of action is given by nature's move. As noted, illegal actions are also socially harmful, whereas legal actions enhance social welfare. Denote the proportion of legal (desirable) actions by θ and the proportion of illegal (undesirable) actions by $(1-\theta)$. The firm can observe the proportion of legal and illegal actions (hence, the firm knows θ), but not the legality or illegality of a specific contemplated action.

---

412 See for example, Wessel, David, "U.S. Law on online gambling is unlikely to rein in the Internet", Wall Street Journal Europe 5.10.2006. The article reports that laws are unclear about whether online horse racing bets are illegal in the US, or not. The uncertainty has a tremendous impact on a growing industry of online betting firms.

The firm expects to earn a low private return on legal actions, denoted by r_L. Illegal actions yield a higher return, denoted by r_H. The social value of the firm's action shall be denoted by v. For legal (and desirable) actions, v takes the positive value 1. For illegal (and socially detrimental) actions, $v = -1$.

The firm knows that an illegal action carries with it an expected sanction (denoted by s). When an unprivileged consultant knows that the firm has considered an illegal course of action then (assuming that the firm actually carried out the illegal action) the enforcement authorities or an opposing party in litigation may be able to obtain evidence from the consultant, thereby increasing the probability of being sanction by α, where $\alpha > 1$, such that the expected sanction for illegal actions after consulting with an unprivileged consultant is now $\alpha s > s$.

Several assumptions with respect to the firm's payoffs are required in order to motivate the interaction. First, assume $r_H - s > r_L$, but $r_H - \alpha s < 0$. This is a strong assumption: it means not only that the net gains from illegal actions are higher than the gains from legal actions but also *that expected sanctions are generally too low to deter illegal actions, unless consultants are not privileged and may implicate their clients.* The focus on only this sub-optimal level of sanctions follows from ***Shavell*** (1988). ***Shavell*** observed that the privilege has no effect on the client's behaviour when the sanction is sufficiently high because even if the privilege reduces the expected sanction it is still sufficiently high to deter the illegal action. Conversely, if the sanction is too low to deter, the illegal action will be preferred with or without a privilege. Hence, it is only interesting to focus on actions with some intermediate sanction, where the sanction is not high enough to deter the action, but in the absence of the privilege the probability of being punished increases to the effective level that deters the action.

It is important to note that in order to simplify the game, the signalling value of the return on the actions is disregarded. By that I mean that although the firm can perfectly observe that certain actions have a low return (r_L) and other actions have a high return (r_H), the firm does not infer from this fact that the low return actions are legal and the high return actions are illegal. The firm's ability to determine the legality of actions is given only by p. This allows the assumption, $r_L - s < 0$, which means that when a firm mistakes a legal action to be illegal, the perceived net payoff is negative. When firms face a perceived negative payoff, they can decide not take action at all, in which case their payoff is zero.

Notation	
r	the return on the firm's chosen action. $r \in \{r_H, r_L\}$. The return on socially desirable actions shall be denoted r_H, and the return on socially undesirable actions shall be r_L.
θ	the proportion of socially desirable (=legal) actions from the options available for the firm. Socially undesirable actions are thus $(1-\theta)$.
v	$\in \{1, -1\}$, the social value of the available actions.
p	the quality of the firm's knowledge of the law.
s	the expected sanction imposed on illegal/undesirable actions.
αs	the expected sanction on illegal/undesirable actions after consulting with an unprivileged consultant.
c	cost of consulting one consultant.
k	cost of consulting an MDP of two types of consultants. $2c > k > c$.

The Stages of the Game. The game progresses sequentially.

In stage 0, the regulator decides whether MDPs shall be privileged or not. This decision is observed by all actors. It should be clarified that a decision to privilege MDPs means that when consultants combine their services into an MDP they enjoy a privilege but when they provide the same advice "jointly but separately" (not as an MDP) - they are not privileged.

In stage 1 the interaction between the two main players starts. The first move is played by the consultants. After observing the decision of the regulator, the consultants decide whether to form an MDP or not. This decision is perfectly observed by the firm and denoted by the decision variable y.

Note that the regulator does not directly allow or forbid the formation of MDPs. This is a decision that is left to the consultants themselves. This is the case in the legal systems discussed here. The regulator can only indirectly affect the consultants' decision by influencing the firm's payoffs.

The first two stages of the game are depicted below.

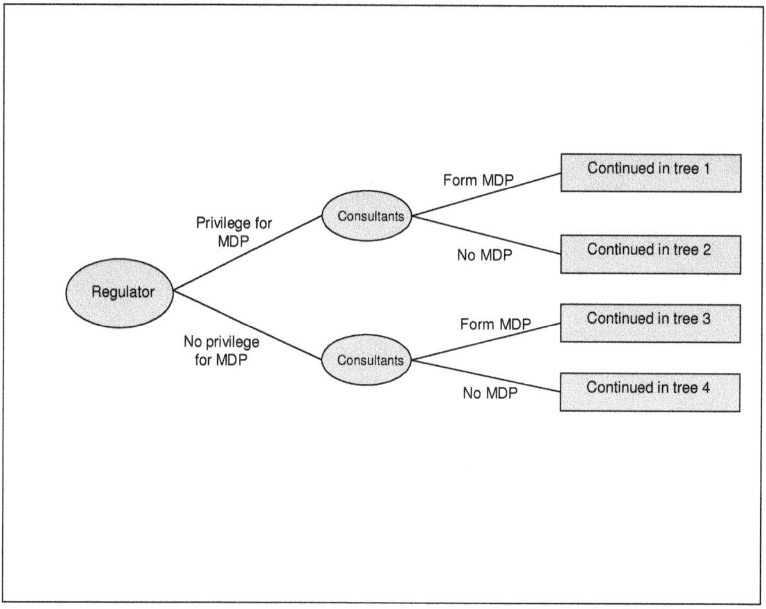

Figure 5: The Extensive Form of Stages 0 and 1

In stage 2, nature's move determines the proportion of legal (θ) and illegal ($1-\theta$) courses of action. Recall that this proportion is perfectly observable to the firm.

In stage 3, the firm learns its type (p) which represents the probability with which it can correctly ascertain the legality/illegality of a specifically contemplated course of action.

In stage 4, the firm decides whether to consult or not. This decision is denoted by the decision variable x. If the consultants formed an MDP, then the firm can only consult the MDP (at a price k). If the consultants did not form an MDP, then the firm can only consult with two consultants, which means the privilege will be lost (and consultation price will be 2c).

As shown above, once the consultants decide whether to form an MDP or not, there are four possible developments to the game: privilege/MDP (tree 1), privilege/no MDP (tree 2), no privilege/ MDP (tree 3) and no privilege/no MDP (tree 4).

The Firm's Decision

The firm decides whether to consult or not to consult. I analyze the payoffs under the four possible developments.

Tree 1. First the payoffs of the firm *as they are perceived by the firm* in all nodes of tree 1 are presented in the extensive form of stages 2, 3 and 4 of the game. For the sake of clarity, the payoffs of the other players are not presented here.

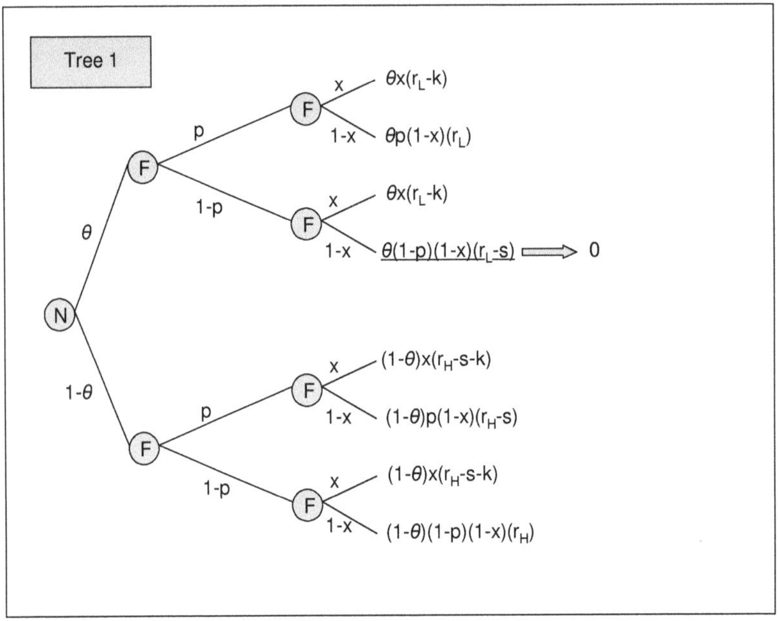

Figure 6: The Extensive Form of Stages 2-4 with the Firm's Payoffs for Tree 1

As described earlier, in stage 2 nature decides on the distribution of the proportion of legal (socially desirable) and illegal (socially detrimental) action alternatives. Then the firm learns its type (p) in stage 3 after which it decides whether to consult or not. In Tree 1, the consultants are working within a privileged MDP. Since the assumption is that the firm's contemplated action is drawn randomly from the set of possible actions given by nature's move, it will be a legal action with probability θ, and an illegal action with probability $(1-\theta)$. The firm correctly identifies the legality/illegality of the contemplated action with probability p, or makes a mistake with probability (1-p). Then the firm chooses to consult or not given its perceived expected payoffs. The payoffs that are perceived by the firm to be negative are underlined. This happens only when the firm contemplates a legal course of action but mistakes it to be illegal (which happens with probability $\theta(1-p)$) and decides not to consult with the MDP. In this case, the mistaken perception remains uncorrected and the firm - by assumption - chooses not to take any action, which results in the payoff 0.

All other payoffs in Tree 1 are positive. Starting from the top, if the firm correctly identifies a legal contemplated action yet still consults with the MDP, it expects a low positive return but pays the consultation fee, which for MDP is low (k). If the firm does not consult, as in the second payoff from the top, its return from the legal action is low but it saves the consultation fee. If the firm mistakes the legal action to be illegal but decides to consult (third payoff from the top) then the MDP perfectly corrects the firm's mistake and the firm expects a low return minus the consultation fee. The fourth payoff is perceived to be negative, as explained above.

In the lower part of Tree 1 the firm is contemplating an illegal action. If the firm correctly identifies that the action is illegal yet still consults, it expects the high return minus the expected sanction and the consultation fee. Note, that due to the fact that in Tree 1 the MDP has a privilege, the expected sanction does *not* increase after consultation. Since the expected payoff is positive, the firm will engage in the illegal action. If the firm decides not to consult, as in the sixth payoff from the top, it will still expect a positive payoff since it correctly perceives the action to be illegal but sub-optimally enforced. In the seventh payoff from the top, the firm mistakes the illegal action to be legal but decides to consult, in which case it learns that the action is actually illegal but that it is also sub-optimally enforced and therefore it engages in that action. In the last payoff the firm mistakes an illegal action to be legal but does not consult and therefore does not correct the mistaken belief. In that case the firm perceives the payoff to be high (recall, this was an assumption) and expects no sanction since it believes that the action is legal. Note again that the tree presents the subjectively perceived payoffs in this case and not the objective payoffs (although the latter would also be positive in this case).

Since the game is played sequentially, the firm can observe whether it has reached Tree 1 (which means the firm can see that the regulator has chosen to privilege MDPs and that the consultants have formed MDPs). Therefore, the firm will choose to consult when the following condition holds:

$$2\theta x(r_L\text{-}k) + 2(1\text{-}\theta)x(r_H\text{-}s\text{-}k) > \theta p(1\text{-}x)r_L + (1\text{-}\theta)p(1\text{-}x)(r_H\text{-}s) + (1\text{-}\theta)(1\text{-}p)(1\text{-}x)(r_H)$$

Since the legality of the contemplated action is uncertain, the firm's optimal solution would involve mixed strategies. The firm would choose to consult when:

$$x > \frac{\theta p r_L + (1\text{-}\theta)(r_H\text{-}ps)}{2[\theta(r_L\text{-}k) + (1\text{-}\theta)(r_H\text{-}s\text{-}k)] + \theta p r_L + (1\text{-}\theta)(r_H\text{-}ps)}$$

Note that the expression in the brackets, $[\theta(r_L\text{-}k) + (1\text{-}\theta)(r_H\text{-}s\text{-}k)]$, is always positive by our assumptions, regardless of nature's choice of θ. This means that the right hand side of the inequality is always smaller than 1. Hence, some rate of consulting will always be chosen since no consulting at all is not an optimal strategy. The rate of consulting will be set at:

$$x = 1 - \frac{\theta p r_L + (1\text{-}\theta)(r_H\text{-}ps)}{2[\theta(r_L\text{-}k) + (1\text{-}\theta)(r_H\text{-}s\text{-}k)] + \theta p r_L + (1\text{-}\theta)(r_H\text{-}ps)}$$

Examining the parameters shows that x increases as θ is higher. Looking at Tree 1 can clarify the intuition behind this result. The only perceived negative payoff occurs when the firm mistakenly believes a legal action to be illegal and then avoids acting in the absence of consultation. All other payoffs are positive. This is because sanctions are too low to deter illegal actions and because the existence of the privilege for MDPs ensures that even if the firm learns that an action is illegal it can still take the action since the sanction remains suboptimal. However, the firm pays for consultation even if it does not change the contemplated action. Paying for consultation is worthwhile only when the firm expects that it will alter its behaviour in a way that increases payoffs and that is more likely to happen the higher the proportion of legal alternatives.

The effect of the firm's knowledge of the law (p) is somewhat counterintuitive when θ is low (proportion of illegal actions is high). It seems that the more the firm is ignorant the less it would tend to consult. The reason for this is that the firm is motivated in its choice by the perceived payoffs and not by the real payoffs. When the firm mistakes a high-return illegal action to be legal, it assumes - wrongly - that no sanction will be imposed. In that case, due to ignorance, perceived payoffs are higher than they "really" are. The counterintuitive result is that the firm subjectively believes that consultation would only be costly and will not alter its course of action since it perceives that course to be both legal and profitable.

Tree 2/4. The following tree describes the payoffs when consultants decide not to form MDPs and the firm must consult two consultants separately, which in this game means that the consultation is not privileged.

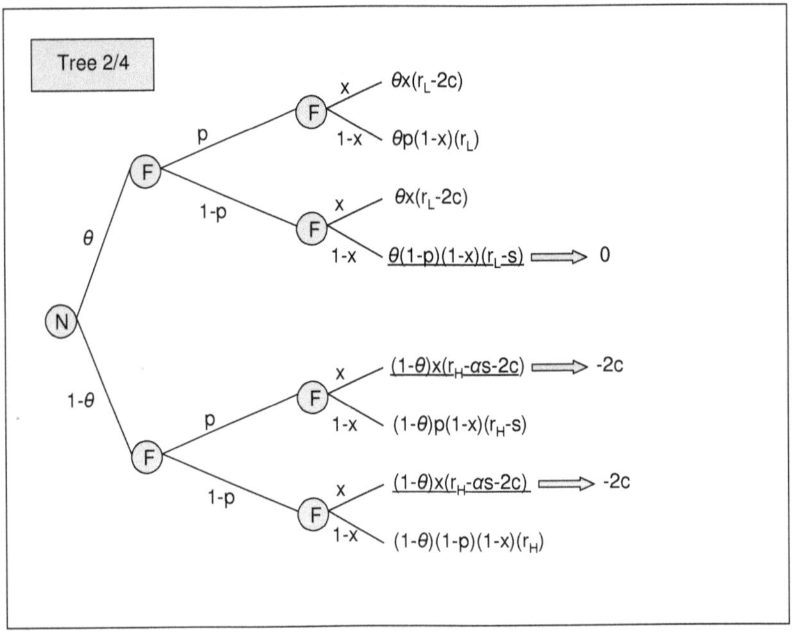

Figure 7: The Extensive Form of Stages 2-4 with the Firm's Payoffs for Tree 2/4

As in tree 1, when the firm mistakes a legal action to be illegal and decides not to consult, it perceives the payoff to be negative and therefore chooses not to act (payoff 0). In addition, when the contemplated action is illegal and the firm does consult, then the increase in the expected sanction as a result of the lack of privilege causes the payoff to be negative. In that case, shown in the fifth and the seventh payoffs from the top, the firm will again prefer not to take any action. The result is then that the firm pays only the consultation fee (2c).

Therefore the firm would choose to consult when the following condition holds:

$$2\theta x(r_L-2c) + 2(1-\theta)x(-2c) > \theta p(1-x)r_L + (1-\theta)p(1-x)(r_H-s) + (1-\theta)(1-p)(1-x)(r_H)$$

This translates to consulting in mixed strategies whenever:

$$x > \frac{\theta p r_L + (1-\theta)(r_H-ps)}{2(\theta r_L - 2c) + \theta p r_L + (1-\theta)(r_H-ps)}$$

The right hand side of the inequality is smaller than 1 whenever the expression (θr_L - 2c) is positive. This means that the proportion of legal actions (θ) plays an important role: when θ is very small, the right hand side of the inequality is greater than 1 and the firm's optimal strategy is never to consult. The condition can be rewritten as:

$$\theta > \frac{2c}{r_L}$$

When the proportion of legal available actions is sufficiently large, then the firm should consult the unprivileged consultants at least at some rate, since not consulting at all would not be an optimal strategy. This is since the loss from legal actions mistaken to be illegal and avoided outweighs the decrease in gains from illegal actions that will be deterred due to the absence of the privilege. Note that when θ is high the firm's knowledge of the law (p) becomes important as in Tree 1, and the lower p, the more valuable consultation becomes.

Tree 3. The following tree represents the payoffs when MDPs are formed even though the regulator grants no privilege for MDPs. The results in Tree 3 are essentially identical to the results in tree 2/4 with the difference that the consultation fee is lower. Therefore, the condition for consultation is whenever:

$$\theta > \frac{k}{r_L}$$

Comparing the conditions, it is immediately evident that since

$$\frac{k}{r_L} < \frac{2c}{r_L},$$

given the same proportion of legal actions (θ) the firm will choose consultation in Tree 3 at a higher rate than in Tree 2/4.

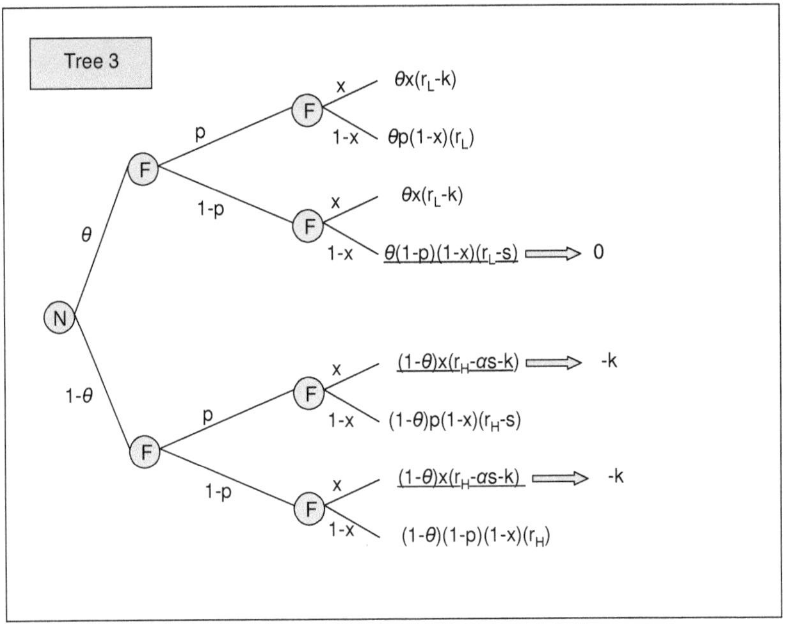

Figure 8: The Extensive Form of Stages 2-4 with the Firm's Payoffs for Tree 3

The reason for this is simple: though both in Tree 3 and in Trees 2/4 consulting means that the firm loses the opportunity to act on the contemplated more profitable, albeit illegal, course of action, the decision to consult in Tree 3 costs less (only k compared to 2c) and therefore can be chosen at a higher rate in mixed strategies. Summing up: the firm's optimal strategy is heavily dependant on θ. When the proportion of legal actions is high ($\theta \rightarrow 1$) the firm's payoffs are low (since actions yield only the low return, r_L) and the rate of consulting is influenced by p and increases when p is low because otherwise the profit from legal actions mistaken to be illegal is lost. Since most actions are legal, the presence or absence of a privilege has little or no effect on the firm's decision.

When the proportion of legal actions is very small ($\theta \rightarrow 0$) the presence of a privilege has a strong influence on the firm's strategy. In the presence of a privilege, the firm will be able to pursue illegal actions even after consultation. In that case, the rate of consulting depends on whether there is still a sufficiently high probability of legal actions that will be mistaken to be illegal and avoided. If the expected profit from such actions is low it might be outweighed by the cost of consultation and then the firm would rather avoid consultation altogether. Hence, decreasing consultation fees by forming MDPs will induce firms to increase consultation. In the absence of a privilege, the expected profit from illegal actions will be lost after consultation due to the increased expected sanction. If the proportion of illegal actions is sufficiently high, these lost profits cannot be outweighed by the benefits from legal actions that were mistaken to be illegal. In that case the firm would strictly avoid consultation.

To conclude, the firm's preference ranking is: Tree 1 > Tree 3 > Trees 2/4.

The Consultants' Decision

In the sequential game, the consultants can anticipate the firm's decision to consult or not given the previous moves. However, the consultants are not able to foresee nature's move with respect to the proportion of legal and illegal courses of action. This simulates the reality in which the legal issues faced by firms arise well after consultants have decided about the way they will structure the provision of consulting services. Due to this, the consultants' optimal strategy should be to always form MDPs since MDPs reduce consultation fees and therefore increase the probability of consultation, as shown in the comparison of Tree 3 to Trees 2/4.

Social Welfare

The social welfare planner decides whether to grant privilege to MDPs with the aim of maximizing social welfare. This decision is also taken prior to nature's move with respect to the proportion of legal and illegal actions.

The regulator anticipates the consultants' decision to form MDPs. This decision has a positive effect on social welfare when θ is high ($\theta \rightarrow 1$) since most of the actions are socially desirable and consultation ensures that the firm will pursue all desirable actions and not avoid them by mistake.

When θ is low, but not too low, the privilege can somewhat offset the social welfare loss from illegal actions by increasing the choice of legal actions that would have been mistaken to be illegal and avoided without consultation. If θ is very low ($\theta \rightarrow 0$) firms would rather not consult at all, in which case the privilege has no effect. This is the most undesirable social welfare result since firms will engage mostly in socially harmful actions and in addition avoid some (though admittedly very few) desirable actions due to legal ignorance. To sum it up, given the assumptions, the granting of a privilege for MDPs could either have a positive effect or no effect on social welfare.

2. Systemic Differences

In this section I briefly survey some relevant differences in the Anglo-American and German legal systems with respect to lawyers and accountants. The types of professional advice rendered by these consultants are considered here as well as the flexibility of the advice given a rule-based or a standards-based regime.

2.1 Lawyers

The differences between continental-European lawyers and their counterparts in the Anglo-American, and especially the American system, are well known by now. As one scholar put it: in the US the lawyer is a hired-gun, in Germany he is an aristocrat[413].

Legal professional culture plays a significant role: in the US, lawyers are a central part of the business and deal making, while in Continental legal systems lawyers are involved in routine business activities to a significantly reduced extent. The European legal profession is more divided into groups of specialized professionals who do not support or identify with each other[414]. European lawyers have always stressed their independence and distanced themselves from the business transactions of the client[415].

Continental lawyers are traditionally educated to refrain from offering non-legal advice[416]. This observation can explain the fast expansion of US auditing/consulting firms into Europe where the niche for pro-active consulting services has traditionally been left rather open, and thus promises a high yield.

In Europe, litigating lawyers rarely encourage the client to hire non-lawyers because continental law presentation of evidence minimizes the role of party-hired non-legal experts in the preparation of a case for litigation[417].

The manifestation of this professional and cultural difference in terms of the legal advice rendered by lawyers has to do with pro-activity and creativity. Lawyers that affiliate themselves strongly with the client may be willing to pro-actively direct the client to the most profitable action available to him, if they realize that the client is not aware or is not considering this option. Furthermore, lawyers have an incentive to develop creative profitable avenues of actions for their clients. The reasoning for this is clear: if firms wishing to raise capital face a budget constraint which includes the cost of hiring lawyers for the purpose of an initial public offering or raising debt capital, then the prospect of increasing the expected value of capital through creative legal advice with respect to such issues as tax structures, financial reporting etc., increases the number of firms that can enter the capital market, thereby increasing the revenue pool for the lawyers.

2.2 Accountants

The cultural differences in the accountancy profession between the Anglo-American and the Continental legal systems are, in fact, very similar to those of lawyers. However, they are often overlooked in normative discussions. I will examine the historical development of the profession, the approach to the role of the financial statements and the implications of the "rules versus standards" debate as well as the trend towards convergence on the field.

---

413 Daly, 646.
414 Daly, 628.
415 Daly, 629-631.
416 Daly, 594.
417 Daly, 594.

2.2.1 History

The practice of double-entry book keeping was invented in Europe. The earliest surviving examples date back to Florence in 1299. The first book which described the method that later spread as the "Italian method" was written by Luca Pacioli in the end of the fifteenth century[418]. The organization of the accountancy profession also originated in Europe; primarily in Scotland where the first association of accountants was established in 1853. The US accountancy profession spawned from Scottish immigrant roots[419].

The traditional role of the auditor in England was that of a trust servant in the English manorial household, hired by the owner to monitor the use of resources by other servants[420]. In fact, the auditing function in England is traced back, not to the accounting profession, but to the 13th century English practice of entrusting individuals with verifying the honesty of the execution of fiscal matters by other people[421]. Hence, in the English tradition, later enshrined in the Companies Act 1844, the shareholder (and not the manager) was in charge of hiring the auditor and the auditor could commission an accountant to help him review the report of the company director[422]. In the Companies Act 1900 engaging the services of an auditor became mandatory for all companies[423]. The Companies Act 1929 also added the mandatory audit of prospectuses[424], but the primary idea was always that the audit is a tool for the shareholders to control the management[425].

Modern accounting developed with the advent of the industrial revolution. As the corporate entity became the main business entity, accounting also shifted in the direction of accounting for outsiders, that is, those outside the corporate entity[426].

The development of the US accountancy profession was slower than in England, perhaps because of fewer financial scandals[427]. Towards the end of the 19th century US public accountants had no obligation to the public but only to the client and specifically mentioned third parties. At this time US public accountants were seeking to elevate their professional prestige beyond that of mere "bookkeepers". An opportunity to do so revealed itself when the steel and tobacco corporations that were facing increasing demand for public disclosure decided to pre-empt these requirements by disclosing internal audits that they had already prepared for shareholders as well as commissioning audits by external CPAs for the purpose of disclosure[428].

The traditional English auditor dealt with certifying that the accounts accurately reflected the state of the company. The US auditor grew as an accountant to a state where he could have been commissioned by management, or shareholders or creditors to evaluate more than that: namely, that the company is also properly managed. With the passing of the US Income Tax law of 1913, which had been promoted by the accountancy profession, accountants found a

418 Flower, 227.
419 Flower, 227-230.
420 O'Connor, 743-744.
421 O'Connor, 757-758.
422 O'Connor, 744 and 748. The Act stated that one of the auditors must be appointed by the shareholders directly.
423 O'Connor, 766. Previously mandatory only for banks.
424 O'Connor, 769.
425 O'Connor, 771.
426 O'Connor, 746, 750-751.
427 O'Connor, 751.
428 O'Connor, 778 and 780.

new wealth of prestige and income as planners and tax-advocates for their clients against the federal tax authorities[429]. As services and possibilities flourished, an editorial article in the Journal of Accountancy in 1912 called for legislation or court intervention to create a duty of care to induce conservatism in certification[430]. Meanwhile, until the stock market collapsed in 1929, accountants profited from "reputational intermediation". After that, courts introduced the requirement that auditors act without fraud and that their obligations also ran to the investors[431].

The 1929 crash ignited the question: who audits the auditors and who secures their independence. Meanwhile, legislation in 1933 and 1934 introduced obligatory audits for prospectuses and annual reports, but without maintaining the strong initial English concept that the shareholder is the retainer of the audit service[432]. This opened the door for future problems with regards to auditors being "captured" and influenced by the managers thathired them. The legislation delegated most of the rule making regarding the implementation of the obligations of auditors as well as the maintenance of their independence to the SEC[433]. The SEC's task was highly complex, particularly given the various services and relationships between accountants and their clients. The result was a huge set of rules[434]. The SOX Act 2002 is the latest addition.

2.2.2 The Purpose of Financial Statements

Financial statements can serve various purposes including[435]: (1) the maintenance of capital and regulation of dividends, (2) the monitoring of management, (3) information for investors, (4) information for the state, (5) information for employees, (6) information for the general public, (7) computation of tax.

Corporations in all the countries surveyed here are obliged to prepare financial statements. In Europe, these statements consist of a balance sheet and a profit and loss account (with notes) and often cash flow statements are also prepared. In Germany, corporations must submit individual statements and also consolidated group statements[436].

The maintenance of capital was the historical reason for the development of the balance sheet. As legal entities became popular, law makers wanted to ensure that owners did not reduce capital in a way that would have profited them and lead the firm to insolvency[437]. Financial reports were a method of assuring that owners maintain minimal capital requirements in order to pay debts. In Germany this was the main reasoning for the application of financial reporting rules after a wave of insolvencies followed the introduction of the AktienGesetz in 1870[438]. Hence, in Germany, prudence in the evaluation of assets and liabilities is a strong guiding principle for the prepaperers of financial statememts. Assets and income should not

429 O'Connor, 781-784.
430 Cited in O'Connor, 785-786.
431 ***Ultramares v. Touche***, 174 N.E 441 (N.Y., 1931).
432 O'Connor, 790-817.
433 O'Connor, 817.819.
434 O'Connor, 820-821.
435 Flower, 30.
436 Flower, 13.
437 Flower, 30.
438 Flower, 32.

be overstated and liabilities or expenses should not be understated[439]. The main critique of this principle is that it conflicts with the objective of supplying investors with an accurate picture about the firm's financial state. This is because a conservative and often historical picture is drawn rather than a current value picture, which often requires non-conservative estimations.

The balance sheet was developed also as a method of monitoring the management in corporate entities. However, historical value reporting complicates achieving this aim. This is because when only the historical value pof an asset is presented, it does not convey to external observers what should the correct treatment of this asset be[440].

In England, one can observe the seeds of a future collision between prudent accountants and creative lawyers in the debate over the distribution of profits as dividends. Courts have held that when fixed capital depreciates, the firm should not be barred from distributing profits as dividend, as long as the firm has sufficient funds to pay off debts. Professional accountants have abided by the traditional prudence requirement in their reports and therefore initially objected to such distributions[441].

Financial reports are a public good and are costly to supply. This supports the notion that they must be regulated in order to assure that firms actually provide them and do so in the proper way[442]. In England and Germany the stock exchanges play a relatively small role in regulating and influencing the development of rules and standards of financial accounting[443]. ***Flower*** points out that courts in England and Germany also play a relatively insignificant role in developing the rules of financial reporting and most of the development in both countries (regardless of the different legal tradition) is in the respective laws: The UK Companies Act and the German HGB[444].

In Germany, tax regulation strongly affects financial reporting, since financial statements are the basis for the tax calculation. As a result, the financial statements are increasingly tax-driven: preparers try to minimize profit by choosing the financial reporting rules that lead to the lowest reported profit[445].

In England however, an expense can be tax deductible without appearing in the financial statements and therefore statements are less tax-driven. However, it is cost effective to use the same financial statements for tax as well as other purposes.

EU regulation aims to promote a common market, to protect shareholders and investors and to create a "level playing field" for competition within the EU member states. To that effect the EU has taken on the task of harmonizing the financial reporting rules. Up until 2002, the EU enactments on the subject had been in the form of directives, which are not directly applicable and which still have to be adopted internally by each member state. In 2002 the EU finally

439 Flower, 32 citing IASB framework, Para. 37.
440 Flower, 34.
441 Flower, 33.
442 Flower, 46-57.
443 Flower, 86-87.
444 Flower, 77.
445 Flower, 73-74. This is referred to as the "reverse authoritative principle, "Umgekehrtes Massgeblichkeitsprinzip".

enacted regulations (effective since 2005) which have direct application to the member states without need for domestic legislation[446].

It is interesting to note how the directives reflected English and German perceptions of accounting. Article 31.1(c) of the Fourth Directive on individual account reporting deals with the issue of valuation and reads: "valuation must be made on a prudent basis...". This is an adoption of prudence and conservatism that signifies the German approach[447]. For example, all foreseeable risks and losses must be included in the financial reports according to §252(1)4 HGB while no such rule applies to foreseeable profits[448].

In the view of English accountants an important position is reflected in article 2 paragraph 3 of the Fourth Directive: "The annual accounts shall give a true and fair value of the company's assets, liabilities, financial position and profit or loss". Paragraph 5 allows departing from the directive when following the directive does not reflect the "true and fair" state of the company[449]. In England it is accepted that "true and fair" is a dynamic concept that embodies and reflects the current generally accepted accounting standards[450].

German law has adopted the "true and fair" requirement into §264(2) HGB which essentially implies that the annual reports should convey a picture of the company's wealth, financial position and results in accordance with the facts. When the reports do not provide such a picture, then additional remarks can be added in an annex[451].

As ***Flower*** explains, the incorporation of the "true and fair" clause into German law was carried out in such a way that it remains subjected to the German principles of bookkeeping (GoB) and therefore the Fourth Directive has had little impact in Germany. Unsurprisingly, the same end-result is true for England[452]. This can explain why in 2002 the EU had to resort to regulations – with direct applicability - in order to attempt once again to strengthen the convergence in this field.

In the US, according to the FASB (Financial Accounting Standards Board), the only purpose of the financial reports created by auditors is to serve investors. All other groups may be users as well but are secondary and are served by the reports as prepared for investment purposes[453]. The rules governing financial reporting are the US Generally Accepted Accounting Principles (US GAAP). The SEC delegated its authority to regulate the accounting rules of publicly traded corporations to the FASB, which is a private body. The

---

446 The Fourth Directive from 1978 deals with individual financial reporting and the Seventh Directive from 1983 deals with consolidated financial reporting. Also relevant are the Bank Accounts Directive (1986) and the Insurance Accounts Directive (1991).

447 Flower, 107-108.

448 Flower, 108.

449 Flower, 110-111.

450 Flower, 113.

451 The text is "(2) Der Jahresabschluß der Kapitalgesellschaft hat unter Beachtung der Grundsätze ordnungsmäßiger Buchführung ein den tatsächlichen Verhältnissen entsprechendes Bild der Vermögens-, Finanz- und Ertragslage der Kapitalgesellschaft zu vermitteln. Führen besondere Umstände dazu, daß der Jahresabschluß ein den tatsächlichen Verhältnissen entsprechendes Bild im Sinne des Satzes 1 nicht vermittelt, so sind im Anhang zusätzliche Angaben zu machen"

452 Flower, 118-120.

453 Flower, 44.

SEC has the right to veto any standard proposed by the FASB and so the US GAAP has developed in a very politicized process[454].

2.2.3 Rules versus Standards

The US GAAP are very detailed. More than 150 standards have been published so far. This high level of detail is explained by both the government's and the public's distrust of the accounting profession and also by the litigious nature of the US: complying with clear and detailed regulation allows auditors to escape liability when investors sue.

One lesson from Enron and related scandals is that, if given the opportunity, firms can aggressively use loopholes in the US GAAP and inflate earnings on their financial reports[455]. Rules are said to be formalistic and if they are not accompanied by backstop standards than they allow strategies of evasion because they cannot cover all contingencies[456].

In the beginning of this millennium, the SEC re-evaluated the GAAP in view of the "rules versus standards" debate. Its conclusion was that rules promote financial reporting that is more compliance-oriented and less communication oriented, whereas, standards allow higher level of discretion for managements which makes enforcement against "bad" managers more difficult[457].

It is common to claim that the US GAAP regime is a rule-based "check the box" system that overlooks the substance of the transactions and thereby allows strategic, but legal, evasion. On the other hand, ***Bratton*** suggests that a rule-based system helps disempowered professionals because it allows them to say "no" to their client. The demands of auditors to have more rules are only mimicking the behaviour of corporate lawyers, in his view. Therefore, rules decrease the risk for the client and for the lawyer – when things go wrong[458]. Indeed, US business law is shifting from broad standards (made concrete by case-law application) to rules[459].

In spite of this latter position and as a lesson from the Enron scandal, in order to better control auditors, the SOX reform established that the PCAOB will inspect audit firms and their compliance with auditing rules[460]. Hence, a rule-based regime per-se does not promise that professionals will not find ways for their clients to evade the law.

---

454 Flower, 152-153.

455 Flower, 206. Bratton, 1041. ***Bratton*** is one opponent of this position. He claims Enron acted illegally and its auditors failed. He criticizes the claims that Enron used legal strategic evasion of the deficient rule based GAAP.

456 Bratton, 1037.

457 Flower, 216.

458 Bratton, 1051.

459 Bratton, 1050-1051.

460 Flower, 210-213, 218. The PCAOB's scope of oversight also includes European auditors that audit European subsidiaries of US firms as well as EU firms that are traded in the US. This is obviously likely to cause conflicts between the German auditor's privilege and the US reporting obligations and compliance with PCAOB inspections and rules. Another element of SOX reform includes the prohibition of non-audit services. The provision of tax-advice is not precluded, leaving some place for contradicting interests.

European markets have also faced several cases of accountancy fraud in recent years, the most notable of which perhaps was Parmalat. This is in spite of the fact that in contrast to the US, the European professional accountancy bodies use vague standards and not detailed rules[461].

2.2.4 Convergence

The ownership structure differences between the Anglo-American systems and the Germanic system were discussed in the introductory chapter. In this context, the Germanic blockholder has control and access to information in the firm therefore he is less dependant on the auditor for financial information about the performance of the management. Auditing is more conservative because financial reports are important for creditors and the banking and lending markets. Hence, if an auditor fails to anticipate the default of the client on the loan his reputation will be severely damaged[462]. In the Anglo-American system, a quip by ***Flower*** sums up the differences: in British accountancy, the shareholder is king, in the US - even more so[463].

Some scholars contend that in practice things are not so clear cut. With respect to the US and England, two factors identified by ***O'Connor*** are relevant to our discussion: (1) the inherent separation between auditor and accountant roles in England was abandoned in the US, (2) the multi-party audience for audits in the US versus the sole use of audits by shareholders in England[464]. ***O'Connor*** also cites the centralised corporate legislation in England as opposed to the non-centralized US state laws as a reason for the race to the bottom in US corporate governance[465].

For reasons beyond the scope of this work, the convergence of corporate governance and of accounting standards has become almost synonymous in scholarly literature. This issue addresses the problems faced primarily by EU multinational firms that want to float their shares in the US: GAAP and EU standards do not converge[466]. In view of the needs of multinational companies the IASC (International Accounting Standards Committee) was set up in 1973 with the participation of accountants from 9 major industrial countries to formulate accounting standards that can be used worldwide.. Since the IASC faced many problems, mainly due to the fact that it was a private body, a reform was initiated which led to the formation of the IASB (International Accounting Standards Board) with similar objectives, yet with a stress being placed on enforceable, stock-market oriented and existing national-rule minded standards[467]. The EU has taken a step towards convergence in the 2002 regulation, by providing that all listed firms must present their consolidated financial statements according to IASB standards, and also have the option to apply IASB to individual financial statements and the statements of non-listed corporations[468]. However, the SEC does not yet recognize

461 Flower, 214-215.
462 Bratton, 1054.
463 Flower. 239.
464 O'Connor, 822-824.
465 O'Connor, 823.
466 Flower, 155-156.
467 Flower, 136-150 surveys the structure, staff and performance of the IASB noting the dominance of Anglo-Saxon and developed countries on rule-making.
468 Flower, 162.

the IASB standards as sufficient and the IASB and FASB are competing as to who will be the global rule-maker[469].

2.3 Abstraction

The systemic differences surveyed here will be abstracted for the sake of modelling in the following way:

(1) Lawyers in Continental legal systems are less pro-active and less creative in developing actions for the client. Lawyers from Anglo-American jurisdictions are more pro-active and creative.

(2) Accountants in Continental jurisdictions are less pro-active and creative (as a result of the conservatism) in comparison with their Anglo-American counterparts.

(3) Continental jurisdictions tend to have standard-based legislation. Anglo-American jurisdictions often use rule-based legislation.

3. Extension: Rules versus Standards

As a first step, and evidently the simplest step, comparative statics is used in order to simulate the "rules versus standards" debate in the context of the model developed here earlier. It is more difficult to foresee the way in which standards will be applied, since the they allow the court great discretion in application, whereas the application of rules is easier to foresee. Therefore, when the regulator chooses standard-based legislation, the firm faces more uncertainly regarding the legality of its actions, driving p down. When the regulator chooses rule-based legislation, the firm knows the law with a higher probability. The following table summarizes the effect of the choice on the variables:

Legislation	Effect on variable (p)
Standards	p_L
Rules	p_H

Table 3: Effects of Legislation on the Variables

The implications of the parameters on the results of the initial model are quite straightforward. The firm's knowledge of the law (p) is mainly influential when the proportion of legal actions (θ) is high. Then if p is low, as in the standard-based regime, the firm will avoid more legal (desirable) actions in the absence of consultation, compared to under a rule based regime. The introduction of a privilege for MDPs would have a desirable effect from a social welfare perspective: while privileged consultation would not decrease illegal activity, it will offset some of the social welfare loss. This happens because in the presence of the privilege firms know they can continue pursuing illegal actions but they also

469 Flower, 170.

correct their mistakes when legal actions are mistaken to be illegal. All other things being equal, a privilege is more likely to have a welfare enhancing effect in a standard-based regime than in a rule-based regime.

On the other hand, without a privilege, consultation results in a private loss of profits for firms deterred from pursuing illegal actions due to increased expected sanctions. Hence, if the proportion of legal actions is low and the proportion of illegal actions is high (low θ) firms may be privately better off not consulting in the absence of a privilege, since that will enable them to pursue the profitable illegal actions. The latter will occur regardless of the fact that most of the illegal actions will be pursued under the mistaken assumption that they are legal. In other words, when θ is low, the choice of rule or standard regimes makes less of a difference.

4. Extension: Pro-Activity

Consultants may, in addition to advising their clients about the legality or illegality of a specific contemplated action, suggest to their clients what alternative courses of action exist, both legal and illegal. By introducing pro-activity, we assume that consultants always divert clients to the privately optimal course of action. Given the assumptions in our model, the highest private return is strictly in the realm of socially undesirable actions ($1-\theta$).

In this extension of the model, the value of consultation for the firm increases whenever $(1-\theta) > 0$. Then, consultation will always be socially detrimental since whenever a firm avoids a legal action mistaken to be illegal, after consultation it would pursue the illegal course of action suggested by the consultant. Furthermore, whenever the firm contemplates a legal course of action which it correctly identified as a legal course of action but nevertheless decides to consult - it would then be diverted by the consultant from the legal and socially desirable action to the illegal and socially detrimental action which is privately more profitable. Note that this only holds when a privilege exists. In the absence of the privilege, even if the firm learns from the pro-active consultant about an alternative action with a higher return, the absence of the privilege means that the expected sanction increases in such a way that it is no longer rational to choose the illegal action. On the other hand, when illegal actions are no longer profitable, pro-active consultants will direct the firm to legal alternatives.

The changes in the payoffs are analyzed below as they are presented in the respective extensive forms of stages 2-4 of the game.

The Firm's Decision

Tree 1. This is the case of privileged MDPs. The significant change in the payoff scheme is the shifting of firms from legal actions to illegal actions.

Recall that in the initial model, mixed strategies were employed and there was no condition in Tree 1 in which it was optimal for the firm not to consult at all. This result does not change qualitatively as consultants become pro-active. However, now the rate of consultation will be set at:

$$x = 1 - \frac{\theta p r_L + (1-\theta)(r_H - ps)}{2(r_H - s - k) + \theta p r_L + (1-\theta)(r_H - ps)}$$

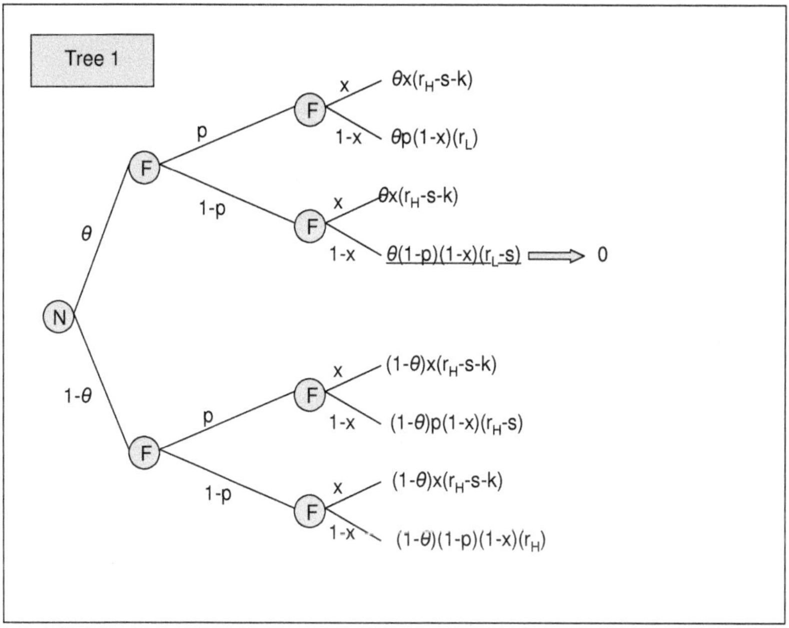

Figure 9: Extensive Form (Stages 2-4) with the Firm's Payoffs for Tree 1 Given Proactivity

All parameters being equal, this rate is lower than the rate of consultation without pro-activity found in the initial model. The rates in the two cases tend to converge as $\theta \rightarrow 0$ but there is no case in which the rate of consultation with pro-active consultants strictly surpasses the rate of consultation with "passive" consultants. The reason for this lies in the fact that illegal actions are not optimally sanctioned and therefore consultation does not alter firm behaviour when firms contemplate illegal actions. The firm's behaviour can be altered in a way that increases its payoff when it is contemplating legal action. However when the proportion of legal alternatives is low, the firm is more likely to contemplate illegal rather than legal actions in the first place, which means that costly consultation will have a very low probability of changing the firm's contemplated action in a meaningful way.

Tree 2/4. This is the case when no MDPs are formed (regardless of whether the regulator decides to grant privilege for MDPs) and therefore according to the common law waiver doctrine no privilege exists for consultation.

The main difference in this case with pro-activity concerns the payoffs on the "illegal nodes". In the initial model, after consultation firms would end up avoiding action (due to increased sanctions) but paying the consultation fee. With pro-activity however, consultants can still direct the firm to a legal course of action (as long as $\theta > 0$) and thereby secure a positive return for the firm after consultation.

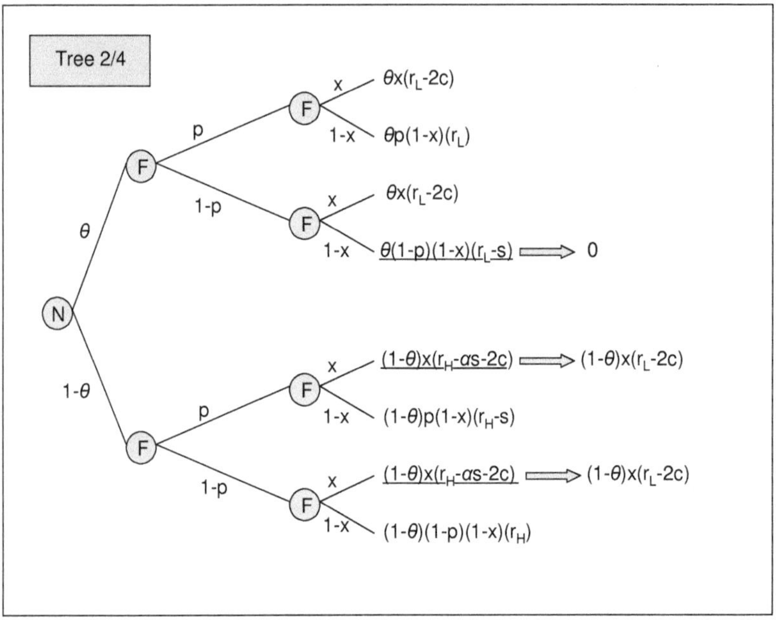

Figure 10: Extensive Form (Stages 2-4) with the Firm's Payoffs for Tree 2/4 Given Proactivity

The condition for consulting is now:

$$x > \frac{\theta p r_L + (1-\theta)(r_H - ps)}{2(r_L - 2c) + \theta p r_L + (1-\theta)(r_H - ps)}$$

Since the right hand side of the inequality is always smaller than 1, and taking the parameters into consideration, there is no case in which the firm would prefer no consultation at all. This finding differs from the initial model where for low θ the firm would have preferred setting $x = 0$ rather than setting some rate for consulting.

Tree 3. This is the case where consultants form MDPs even though the regulator does not grant them a privilege. There is no need to graphically present the extensive form of this tree since the payoffs are identical to Tree 2/4 with one exception - the cost of consultation is reduced from 2c to k. This means the condition for consultation is:

$$x > \frac{\theta p r_L + (1-\theta)(r_H - ps)}{2(r_L - k) + \theta p r_L + (1-\theta)(r_H - ps)}$$

The difference from Tree 2/4 of the game is that due to the lower consultation fee firms will be setting a higher rate of consultation in mixed strategies. To summarize, the firm's preferences remain: Tree 1 > Tree 3 > Trees 2/4.

The Consultants' Decision

Since the firm's strategy is never to strictly avoid consultation, the decision of the consultants on forming MDPs depends on the rate of consultation. Since the ranking Tree 1 > Tree 3 > Trees 2/4 reflects the rate of consultation as in the initial model it is clear that forming MDPs (Tree 1 and Tree 3) is the consultants dominant strategy.

Social Welfare

The social welfare planner anticipates the preferences of the firm and the decision of consultants to form MDPs. The anticipated social welfare outcome on the privileged MDPs node is the least desirable, since only socially detrimental actions are being taken. Therefore a social welfare planner would prefer not to grant the privilege to MDPs. The consultants will then form unprivileged MDPs on the equilibrium path and the firms will consult these MDPs at a lower consultation rate. Though some socially desirable actions will not be taken due to firm ignorance of the law, a substantial proportion of socially detrimental actions will be avoided as well. This is a consequence of (i) firm choosing legal actions and not being redirected to illegal actions due to the absence of a privilege, (ii) firms contemplating illegal actions but being redirected to choosing legal actions after consulting unprivileged MDPs.

5. Extension: Creativity

The initial assumption that the firm contemplates a randomly drawn action with its legality distributed over θ and $(1-\theta)$ such that $\theta + (1-\theta) = 1$, overlooks the fact that in reality the firm might be choosing its contemplated action from a smaller subset of actions: the set of actions of which existence it is *aware*. Let us assume that firms are aware of all legal avenues of action but not of all the illegal avenues of action. This is a sensible assumption since firms are often familiar with the legal avenues of action in their field of business, and they can also observe competitors and learn from their behaviour. However, creative consultants can develop new avenues of action for the firm which the firm was previously unaware of, as was the law maker. Further assume that the newly developed avenues of action are socially detrimental but not yet forbidden by law: they have high yield (r_H) but no sanction. Integrating the incompleteness of the subset from which the firm chooses its contemplated action is done by assuming that when an illegal action is contemplated it is selected from the subset $\beta(1-\theta)$ and that $0 < \beta < 1$. Only if firms decide to consult are they introduced by the consultants to the additional subset $(1-\beta)(1-\theta)$ which has a payoff $(r_H - k)$ in case of an MDP or $(r_H - 2c)$ when no MDPs exist. Since the new actions are not yet forbidden by the law maker there are no sanctions imposed on these actions.

Re-examining the case of privileged MDPs (Tree 1) when consultants are both creative and pro-active yields the following condition for consultation:

$$2x(r_H\text{-}k) > \theta p(1\text{-}x)r_L + \beta(1\text{-}\theta)p(1\text{-}x)(r_H\text{-}s) + \beta(1\text{-}\theta)(1\text{-}p)(1\text{-}x)(r_H)$$

The firm would set the rate of consultation at:

$$x = 1 - \frac{\theta pr_L + \beta(1\text{-}\theta)(r_H\text{-}ps)}{2(r_H\text{-}k) + \theta pr_L + \beta(1\text{-}\theta)(r_H\text{-}ps)}$$

Since $0 < \beta < 1$, the rate of consultation in this case will be greater than the rate of consultation without creative consultants when all other parameters are the same (and $\theta < 1$).

This extension has no effect on the qualitative decision of the consultants to form MDPs. Forming MDPs still makes consultation cheaper and therefore is mutually desirable for consultants and firms. However, since we assume that the creative actions developed and proposed to the firm by the consultants are neither forbidden nor sanctioned - the regulator is now indifferent with respect to the privilege decision. This would change if the newly developed (and hidden from the firm) actions were to fall within the scope of existing laws with sub-optimal sanctions as the rest of the illegal actions. In that case, without the privilege, consultants would have no incentives to develop these alternative actions since the absence of the privilege would prevent them from being pursued.

Considering the rules-versus-standards analysis, the common wisdom is that a rule-based regime enables consultants to develop more creative avenues of action which avoid the law. Therefore the proportion of hidden non-legal actions under a rule-based regime will be larger than the proportion under a standard-based regime. This indicates that under a rule-based regime, consultants have a stronger incentive to be creative and consequently, firms have a stronger incentive to consult, provided that they have the possibility of pursuing the non-legal actions.

Recall, the social welfare planner needs to determine whether to grant a privilege to MDPs or not. Given that consultants are creative and pro-active, the goal of the social welfare planner can only be to minimize welfare losses. This can be optimally achieved under a regime that minimizes the proportion of non-legal actions (a standard-based regime, in the abstract way it is employed here). Only when it is given that the creativity of consultants yields proposed actions that fall into sub-optimal sanction schemes, a privilege would enable firms to pursue socially detrimental courses of action. Hence, only then not granting a privilege would have a positive effect on social welfare.

Finally, in this section I have considered a case where creativity of professional consultants is only directed at the socially undesirable set of action $(1\text{-}\theta)$. It may very well be that firms are also not fully aware of the entire proportion of legal/desirable actions. One can assume the the firm can observe only the share $\beta\theta$ of legal actions and only learn of additional legal actions $(1-\beta)\theta$ after consulting with the consultants. This allows to detect the direction in which consultants will direct their creative efforts when they invest resources in developing new avenues of action for their clients.

So far I have assumed the rendering professional advice is costless. However, if developing new avenues of action for the clients is not costless, then consultants will prefer to invest development efforts only in the type of actions which increase the probability that clients choose to consult. When consultants are *not* pro-active, as in the initial model presented in part II.1., I have shown that increasing the expected payoff from legal actions increases the rate of client consultation with privileged MDPs. This was also a socially desirable result. Therefore, consultants that do not offer pro-active advice should choose to direct their development resources to legal avenues of action. In contrast, when consultants are pro-active and privileged, the higher benefit for the client lies in illegal actions and therefore pro-active consultants would better invest their resources in developing illegal courses of action. This is, of course, a socially detrimental outcome.

III Applications

1. Desirability of MDPs

Generally, accounting regulations in the US and England are assumed to be more rule-based whereas Germany's accounting regime is more standard-based. We employ this abstraction in order to evaluate the decision of these jurisdictions with respect to professional privileges and the effect it has on MDPs.

1.1 United States and England

Both lawyers and accountants in the US (and in England as well, but more mildly) offer creative and pro-active advice. This means that both types of consultants will direct the client to the most profitable action, which in our model is not legal. Additionally, both will try to develop avenues of action that create a higher value for clients. The main difference between the two professions in the US is that lawyers are protected by the testimonial privilege whereas accountants have a virtually non-existent privilege. Furthermore, when an MDP is formed, the lawyers lose the privilege whenever information is also shared with accountants. To sum it up, the decision of the US social welfare planner can be described as knowingly depriving MDPs of the privilege.

Clients are interested in hiring MDPs because they reduce consultation costs. Costs are reduced as a result of two factors: (1) some infrastructure savings result from the combination of legal and accounting services into a "one-stop shop", and (2) time is saved when the problem is presented and analyzed simultaneously by all relevant consultants rather than consecutively.

Entering the capital market is a costly process for a firm which requires hiring consultants such as lawyers and accountants. A firm enters the capital market when it believes that it can create profits from the additional capital, profits that would outweigh the costs involved in raising the capital. Since legal and accounting services are costs in the process of raising capital, reducing these costs increases the expected profit from capital and increases the incentives for firms to enter the capital market. In that respect, MDPs are mutually desired by both consultants and firms. Pro-active and creative consultants create value for their clients. This value is part and parcel of the expected profit from seeking to obtain capital in the market. If this value decreases, the incentives for firms to enter the capital market will decrease.

In the case of lawyer-accountant MDPs in the US, the loss of the privilege means that after consultation, the firm will be deterred from pursuing the actions described by $(1-\theta)$. Consequently, firms will find it less profitable to enter the capital market and fewer firms will do so. However, given that the deterred actions are presumed to be socially detrimental, the consequences are overall welfare enhancing.

In the US, lawyers have very few incentives to form formal MDPs with accountants. Instead, they opt for informal solutions that ensure the high return but do not reduce consultation costs significantly, such as using accountants as third-party advisers[470]. Another solution is the

470 Though the ability to do this has been narrowed in ***Kovel*** (US, 1961), *supra* note 250.

increased number of consultants that hold dual degrees in law and accounting. In order to practice law they must define themselves as lawyers but in practice they also offer the expertise of accountants. Dual degree consultants may charge higher fees for their advice, but reduce the cost of consultation for the firm since it needs to interact with only one consultant instead of two.

From a social welfare viewpoint, the objection to privileged MDPs in the US is correct only if we believe that the additional social loss that will be caused by more firms entering the market due to cheaper and privileged MDPs minus the savings in consultation cost (reduced from 2c to k, but increasing in quantity of firms), is higher than the social loss under separate consultation, with higher consultation costs. In a rule-based regime, there is ground to assume that privileged MDPs will encourage more firms to enter the market. Therefore, the increase in social losses due to non-legal actions will be significant. The increased market participation will likely countervail the reduction in consultation cost. I therefore conclude that in all likelihood, privilege for MDPs is not a socially desirable rule in the US.

1.2 Germany

As discussed earlier, lawyers and accountants in Germany are traditionally conservative with respect to pro-activity and creativity. The professional advice thus focuses on correcting mistakes rather than creating value through directing clients to harmful yet profitable alternative actions. Since laws and accounting rules are more standard-based, the expected profit from non-legal actions is also presumably lower compared to the US and England.

German lawyers and accountants are both privileged consultants. It is therefore rational for both consultants to form formal MDPs and reduce the cost of the services they provide, thereby increasing the number of clients willing to participate in the market.

From the viewpoint of the social welfare planner, granting the privilege to both professions has a relatively small effect in terms of increasing welfare loss. In fact, given the conservative nature of the professional advice and the standard-based regime, one cannot rule out the possibility that professional advice in Germany has a welfare enhancing effect, unlike the US and English structure. If so, MDPs only encourage more market participants to seek advice and are therefore desirable.

2. Lawyer & Auditor MDPs

Auditors are relational gate-keepers and as such they are obliged to report non-legal actions to shareholders, to the market as a whole or to authorities. Hence they disallow the firm's ability to choose a non-legal action even if the probability of being caught is very low. Auditors would presumably prevent firms from following illegal actions by threatening to report them and inducing enforcement. Auditors therefore render pro-activity and creativity on the part of lawyers worthless.

Lawyers in the US and England would be wary of MDPs with auditors. In Germany, another solution exists: auditors offer "pre-emptive auditing". This audit identifies the presumed results of real audits in advance, but the pre-emptive auditor is supposedly not bound by an obligation to report observations of wrongdoing, which means that the privilege is not disarmed. Such a solution is desirable from a social welfare perspective given the assumption that pre-emptive auditing provided in the framework of an MDP is less likely to lead firms to choose non-legal actions and more likely to induce ex-ante compliance.

There is, however, reason for concern in Germany, especially in auditing services. Concerns stem both from the global approximation of accounting standards, which may introduce a more rule-based regime and from the infiltration of the "big Four" US culture of consulting, which may threaten the traditional conservatism of German accountants and auditors. While these trends affect lawyers as well, they seem to have a stronger effect on the auditing profession in Germany and on German lawyer-accountant MDPs including the "Big Four" firms in Germany themselves. The risk is simply that "pre-emptive auditors" would not only advise their clients as to which accounting practices are legal and which are not but also pro-actively propose alternatively accounting practices that may be illegal but nevertheless sub-optimally enforced.

In Germany, the legal debate on this issue seems to revolve around the question which of the professionals shall control the MDP, or on a similar question: which ethical rule shall prevail in case of a conflict between the ethical rules of two professions in one MDP. The high court in Bavaria has noted that the lawyer's work is becoming specialized and internationalized in recent years[471], and that more lawyers are working as Syndikusanwälte (corporate in-house lawyers)[472]. The court held that lawyers can incorporate themselves in a corporate form but that since lawyer independence must be assured, a lawyer must be the manager of the firm and that the stocks of lawyer corporations may not be owned by external shareholders[473]. The shareholders in the lawyer GmbH are also forbidden from sharing profits with non-lawyers[474]. Finally, §59 BRAO allows lawyers to work in a partnership or corporation with certain other professionals including auditors. However, in a mixed corporation, only lawyers may be the managers of the corporation[475]. Auditor GmbH does not have these restrictions[476]. Section §44b.1 WiPrO allows auditors to work in a partnership with other free professions, as long as these professions are also privileged under §53 Abs. 1(1)(3) StPO. In the auditing firms, lawyers, auditors and tax advisors can be managers and majority voting shareholders. While the lawyer GmbH seems to be restricted to legal consulting, the auditor GmbH is not restricted to auditing[477].

Some scholars have criticized the limitations on lawyer GmbH and have called for an equalization of lawyers with auditors[478]. Our findings can justify the restrictive rule in the German mixed lawyer-auditor MDP. If indeed the German auditing profession is drifting towards pro-activity and creativity, while the legal profession remains more conservative, then placing the control in the hands of the profession that ensures a higher level of compliance makes sense, especially if Lawyer GmbHs that employ auditors provide primarily legal advice and the role of the auditors is essentially that of pre-emptive auditing.

---

471 BayObLG NJW 1995, 199, 201.
472 BayObLG NJW 1995, 199, 201.
473 BayObLG NJW 1995, 199, 201.
474 Pluskat, 60.
475 Michalski & Römermann, 3238.
476 §59 BRAO, §22 and §44b WPO; Pluskat, 60-61.
477 Pluskat, 62.
478 Pluskat, 60. Michalski & Römermann, 3238. ***Michalski*** questions the logic of this guideline, especially in cases where the majority of the firm consists of auditors.

As for auditing firms that employ lawyers, the question depends on the kind of services provided by these firms to their clients. If these MDPs provide ex-ante compliance advice, then they too must be controlled by the conservative culture (lawyers) rather than by pro-active consultants, if an abuse of the privilege which will lead to social welfare loss is to be avoided.

One possible solution that has been proposed in the literature with regards to ethical rules of conflict of interests in mixed firms is that in MDPs the stronger rule from the two professional rules should apply[479]. This solution might have a counterproductive effect if stronger confidentiality is applied when pro-activity and creativity are introduced. The ethical rule that should be followed in order to ensure optimal results is not confidentiality but the type of advice provided by the MDP. Namely, lawyers should be in control of the MDP if they can guarantee that clients are steered away from illegal actions better than auditors, not if they can guarantee better confidentiality.

479 Deckenbrock, 2458. Schramm, 1368.

IV Concluding Remarks

This chapter started out by outlining the debate on MDPs. The concern among regulators should be whether MDPs enhance or discourage corporate compliance. This chapter set out to fill a gap in the literature with regards to the effect of professional testimonial privilege on compliance given different systemic characteristics. I identified stark differences between the Anglo-American and the German systems – these were discussed in part I.

In the following parts I examined the performance of MDPs with and without a professional testimonial privilege as compared to the performance of unprivileged non-MDP (informal) collaboration between professional consultants. This was done by modelling the sequential interaction of the regulator, the consultants and the clients. The model simulated the decision of a client-firm to consult with an MDP or with a collaboration of consultants on a contemplated action. The game assumed that the firm chooses an action from a set of actions which are either legal or illegal yet sub-optimally sanctioned.

In analyzing the comparative Law & Economics effects of differences between the Anglo-American and the German legal systems on the social welfare implications of granting a privilege to MDPs this chapter focused on three systemic differences. I surveyed the manifestations of these differences in each of the legal jurisdictions.

- First, I have concluded that lawyers in the Anglo-American jurisdictions tend to be more pro-active in their professional advice whilst their counterparts in Germany tend to be more conservative. This means that German lawyers would traditionally tend to advise the client only with regards to the legality or illegality of a specific contemplated action brought up by the client whereas Anglo-American lawyers would propose alternative avenues of action if such alternatives have a higher expected benefit. Furthermore, Anglo-American lawyers tend to invest effort in the development of additional legal solutions for their clients – even if such solutions are in the "grey" legal zone. German lawyers traditionally demonstrated less creativity of that sort.
- Secondly, I suggested that the differences between Anglo-American and German accountants follow a similar line to the one described here for lawyers.
- Finally, for the sake of simplification, the Anglo-American legal system was abstracted as a rule-based system whereas the German legal system is described as one that tends to prefer standards.

Even before the analysis of the model, formalizing the MDP debate yields three interesting observations. The first insight is that the decision of professional consultants to collaborate in formal MDPs is taken prior to the decision of the firm to consult. Therefore, consultants anticipate the decision of the firm under uncertainty with regards to the legal options available to the firm. Secondly, the decision of the regulator to grant a privilege to MDPs is also taken given the same uncertainty with regards to the variety of legal and illegal avenues of action. And finally, the decision of consultants to form MDPs affects the cost of legal advice. It does not affect the ability of the client-firm to pursue more profitable yet illegal actions. The latter option is only affected by the existence of the privilege which is determined by the regulator.

Given these fundamental insights it is immediately clear that forming MDPs should always be the dominant strategy for professional consultants since reducing the cost of consultation should increase the demand for their services.

It then follows that the social welfare outcome depends largely on other factors: (1) the proportions of legal (=socially desirable) and illegal (=socially detrimental) avenues of action that the firm can contemplate, (2) the firm's own knowledge of the legality or illegality of the contemplated actions and (3) the conservatism or pro-activity of the consultants.

- When consultants are "conservative" (that is, they only advise about the legality of the contemplated action chosen by the firm and do not direct the firm to the most profitable action), the higher the proportion of legal avenues the more socially desirable it is to grant a privilege to MDPs. The reason is that granting a privilege in such a case will increase the probability that firms will consult with the MDP. Consequently, firms will pursue legal acts that were mistakenly perceived to be illegal. In other words, when consultants are conservative in their advice, the privilege enhances both social and private welfare.
- An extension of the former finding: given conservatism of consultants and considering the "rules versus standards" debate, I showed that granting a privilege to MDPs only matters when the proportion of legal avenues of action is high. If indeed there is a high proportion of legal actions available to firms, and all other things being equal, then granting a privilege to MDPs would have a higher impact on social welfare under a standards-regime than under a rules-regime. This is because under a standards-regime the client's knowledge of the law is more imperfect and therefore the social benefits obtained from correcting the client's mistakes are higher.
- Pro-activity of consultants changes the results dramatically. I show that given the assumption that sanctions are sub-optimal, privileged pro-active consultants will always direct their clients to illegal and socially detrimental avenues of action. MDPs, that reduce the cost of consultation, would therefore only increase the probability of undesirable actions being taken. I conclude that granting a privilege for MDPs would not be socially desirable in a system dominated by pro-active consultants.
- Finally, the creativity of consultants is taken into consideration. Creative consultants invent new avenues of action. Only two kinds of new avenues of action are relevant for this model: (1) actions that have not yet been forbidden by law and (2) actions that are forbidden by law but fall into the sub-optimal sanction group. If consultants focus on the first group of actions then granting a privilege to MDPs would have no impact at all. The reason is that the effect of the privilege is to reduce the expected sanction - but these actions are not sanctioned at all. On the hand, if creativity yields actions that fall into the second group, then granting a privilege to MDPs will increase the choice of such actions and is therefore not desirable.

Admittedly, the model does not take into account the fact that the regulator deciding on granting a privilege is often also the one that controls the proportion of legal and illegal avenues of action by investing in legislation and enforcement. However, incorporating into the model an additional step to account for the ability of the regulator to control this proportion complicates the game beyond tractability. Furthermore, it seems there is no need for the model to capture this step, for two reasons. First, the decision of legislative bodies to grant the privilege is often taken regardless of the level of investment in enforcement and sanctioning. Secondly, though I have used the term "sanction" in this chapter, recall that it refers also to civil actions. By that I mean that consultants can advise a firm to choose an action that is privately profitable but inflicts a socially undesirable harm on a third party that has the right to sue the firm. If the probability of a civil lawsuit is sufficiently decreased due to the existence of a privilege, the final outcome is detrimental to social welfare. Since the regulator does not control civil enforcement, the model's current structure reflects a realistic story.

In the final part of this chapter I applied the findings to the surveyed legal jurisdictions.

1. Given the pro-activity and creativity of Anglo-American lawyers and accountants it seems that the rejection of extending the privilege to accountants in Anglo-American jurisdictions, thereby decreasing the motivation of lawyers to collaborate with accountants in formal MDPs, is justified from a social welfare perspective.
2. On the other hand, accepting the assumptions that German professionals tend to be more conservative and that German law is standards-based, the traditional endorsement of MDPs in Germany is justified in light of the positive effects that it should have on client compliance.
3. The latter conclusion is also relevant for collaborations between "pre-emptive" auditors and lawyers in Germany, provided that the pre-emptive auditors also behave "conservatively".
4. As I have noted, there is a discussion in German legal literature on which of the professional groups should govern an MDP of lawyers and auditors. One answer that emerges from the analysis is that if one professional group is obliged to conservative consulting and the other is not, the group that subscribes to the conservative ethics should govern the MDP.

Chapter 3: The Reporter's Privilege

This part sets out to explore the professional privilege of reporters and how its application affects the efficient provision of information to the capital market. The reporter's privilege is often discussed in the context of information leaks about governmental and political actors. In these discussions it is hard to quantify the social welfare impact of the information provided as a result of unauthorized leaks. Leaks from within corporations, however, have an effect on the price of corporate stock. This effect can be measured. Therefore, the following analysis is directed primarily at leaks that emanate from inside a corporation and have an impact on the value of the corporation in the eyes of the capital market[480].

Part I presents the motivation for exploring the reporter's privilege given the importance of the media in a democratic society and the crucial role of confidential sources in the work of the media. Part II surveys the law of the reporter's privilege followed by a survey of the law of defamation in part III. In part IV the model of the privilege in defamation lawsuits is presented and analyzed. Part V applies the findings of the model to existing case law in the relevant jurisdictions. Part VI concludes.

I Introduction

Reporters claim that compelling disclosure of their confidential sources chills the flow of information to the press and thereby harms the democratic process. To protect confidential sources, all legal systems empower the press with a testimonial privilege, which allows a reporter to refuse to reveal his sources in court. Reporters often restrict themselves to the use of confidential sources very sparingly. There is a good reason for this: media consumers cannot evaluate the veracity of information based on anonymous sources. When veracity is doubted, the value of the information clearly decreases. Therefore, for the work of reporters to be meaningful, anonymous sources should not be used too extensively.

The reporter's testimonial privilege is most frequently raised in court in relation to government sources[481], but it also appears in connection with corporate leaks. In fact, examining the reporter's privilege in the corporate setting can be of unique value. If we assume that markets behave according to the semi-efficient market hypothesis, one can measure the value of information derived by the media from confidential corporate informants in terms of its effect on the price of shares.

In stark contrast to the right of the public to know, stands the interest of maintaining private reputation. In the corporate setting, reputation can be restrictively interpreted in financial, monetary, terms. Legal systems have consistently recognized that the freedom of the press must be limited by the right to reputation, and therefore that freedom of the press must also entail a duty to engage in responsible journalism.

---

480 The legal setting applied to such leaks in the jurisdiction surveyed here is almost identical to the one used in the political context. Hence, the analysis has possible implications also with respect to the political arena.

481 The most notable case is that of "Deep Throat", the source that guided journalists Bob Woodward and Carl Bernstein in the process of uncovering the Watergate scandal and eventually leading to the resignation of US President Richard Nixon. The identity of this source remained a secret for more than 30 years until former FBI second in command, Mark Felt, revealed himself to be the source. See: "FBI's number 2 was 'Deep Throat'", Washington Post, 1 June 2005.

The tort of defamation was developed in the English common law in order to protect reputation. Defamation is defined as communication that, among other things, lowers one's esteem in the eyes of others or injures one in his business[482]. In fact, defamation goes as far back as the Biblical Ten Commandments that forbad "false witness against thy neighbour". But in a free society the freedom of speech is highly esteemed as well thus reputation must be balanced against it, making this area of the law very confusing[483].

As will be discussed below, in England a media plaintiff sued for defamation bears the burden of proving that the allegedly defamatory information that he published is true. In Germany, a similar rule is applied but other remedies also exist. In the US however, the courts have switched the burden of proof: the plaintiff must first show that the information is false in order to proceed with the claim.

In balancing the right of the public to receive information, on the one hand, and the right to reputation, on the other hand, the legal systems surveyed here use the same legal mechanisms. Yet, these mechanisms are applied in fundamentally different ways. In this chapter, economic analysis is used in order to determine which of the applications is superior from a social welfare point of view and as such under which conditions a diversion from the socially superior application would be justified.

In this introductory note I proceed to discuss the importance of confidential sources in the work of the media. Part 1 provides some anecdotal evidence. In part 2 the role of the media in a democratic society is discussed along with the place of confidential source in promoting the functions that the media supposedly fills.

1. The Importance of Sources: Some Evidence

One need only skim through the daily financial press to realize how often confidential sources are used and what important information they provide. One US survey found that approximately 13% of 10,000 front-page articles relied at least in part on anonymous sources[484]. The Wall Street Journal's coverage of the Enron accounting scandal, uncovered two of the fictitious entities connected to Enron CFO Andrew Fastow through anonymous sources[485]. The corporation's stock crashed soon thereafter.

Enron is now commonly used as an example for every corporate scandal, but cases of insider supplying information to the press that leads to revealing wrongdoing arise on a daily basis. To mention just one: on the 27 December 2005 the New York Times reported about the allegedly corrupt conduct of the American copper and gold mining corporation, Freeport-McMoRan, in its mining activities in Papua[486]. The newspaper's investigative report about alleged illegal payments to military and police officials, along with ongoing environmental violations, relied heavily on confidential sources and the documents they provided. The paper

482 Teeter & Loving, 181.
483 Teeter & Loving, 182.
484 Cited in the testimony of Prof. Lee Levine before the US Senate Committee on the Judiciary, July 20, 2005.
485 Testimony of Prof. Lee Levine before the US Senate Committee on the Judiciary, July 20, 2005; Handman, at footnote 13.
486 Perlez, Jane and Raymond Bonner, "Below a Mountain of Wealth, a River of Waste", New York Times 27.12.2005.

reported on the ways in which - after stronger accounting requirements were introduced by the Sarbanes-Oxley Act - the corporation allegedly circumvented shareholders' requests for information and hid alleged illegal payments under general descriptions. It is doubtful if such a story could be substantiated without anonymous sources. Stock price for the corporation dropped about 3% on the day of the publication, after a concave shaped rise in the three days prior to the article's release.

A survey of the influence of defamation law on the media in England concluded that journalists understand that the purpose of defamation is primarily to encourage them to verify and confirm their information prior to publication[487]. However, the authors of the survey also found that due to the risk of exposing confidential sources, the media might "water down" or even avoid publication of information that is clearly in the public interest[488].

The use of confidential sources in news reporting is high[489]. However, over-use is a concern both for reporters and consequently to the consumers' perception of the news[490]. The more willing reporters are to report information from anonymous sources, the more sources demand to be confidential. As one commentator remarked: "Anonymity has become a commodity in which both journalists and their sources traffic"[491].

2. The Role of the Media

The role of the media in a democratic society, in the view of many scholars, is to further deliberative democracy. This point of view reflects the idea that only through information emanating from pluralistic and diverse media sources (or media outlets) can a citizen discern the truth and make optimal democratic choices[492]. Freedom of information is protected in Article 19 of the Universal Declaration of Human Rights as the right to seek, receive and impart information and ideas in all media[493]. Availability of information is crucial for the efficient performance of both political and economic markets[494]. The media is the intermediary that collects and transmits this information.

Where corporate players and capital markets play a significant social role, the media claims to fulfil informal gate-keeping functions[495]. Reporters claim that without the ability to promise

487 Barendt et al., 61-62.

488 Barendt et al., 62, 64 and 71. The authors cite one specific case in which they were told that information about prospectus fraud was "watered down" in order to avoid the disclosure of confidential sources that provided documentation of the fraud.

489 Kase, at footnote 22.

490 Kase, 569. Citing the 1981 case of reporter Janet Cooke that won a Pulitzer Prize for a story based on fabricated sources.

491 Kase, 571.

492 Freedom of the media and freedom of information can have various interpretations depending on the concepts of democracy utilized for their analysis. The most suitable for this discussion is that of a socially responsible media - a watchdog, aimed at uncovering hidden agendas and self-interested concerns. See generally, Baker, at 330, 333-4, 353.

493 The full text reads: "Everyone has the right to freedom of opinion and expression; this right includes freedom to hold opinions without interference and to seek, receive and impart information and ideas through any media and regardless of frontiers".

494 Note that it is the *availability* of full information that is important, not necessarily the actual consumption of full information.

495 Auditors focus on financial gate-keeping and rarely get involved in other issues. Media acts as a watchdog for a much wider span of moral and legal malfeasance.

corporate insiders the protection of confidentiality, those sources will be chilled from supplying the media with the information required for the performance of their "watchdog" role. While corporations cannot deter the activities of the investigative media with arrests, they have adopted another method, notoriously known as the SLAPP law-suit[496].

The codes of ethics of the journalistic profession permit reporters to promise confidentiality to their sources. Nevertheless, reporters are encouraged to make promises of confidentiality only when necessary. However, once such a promise has been made they are encouraged to protect confidential sources to the utmost[497]. In one of the very scarce discussions of reporters' privilege in the Law and Economics literature, ***Ronald Coase*** criticizes reporters for refusing to reveal their sources:

> "If we examine the actions and the views of the press, they are consistent in only one respect: they are always consistent with the self-interest of the press. Consider their argument that the press should not be forced to reveal the sources of its published material. This is termed a defense of the public's right to know – which is interpreted to mean that the public has no right to know the source of material published by the press. To desire to know the source of a story is not idle curiosity. It is difficult to know how much credence to give to information or to check on its accuracy if one is ignorant of the source.
>
> ...
>
> Of course, it would also impede the flow of information to reveal the sources of the material published in cases in which the transmission of the information involved a breach of trust or even the stealing of documents. To accept material in these circumstances is not consistent with the high moral standards and scrupulous observance of the law which the press expects of others."[498]

If ***Coase*** is right and protecting sources only serves the interests of the press, then the law should be very restrictive in its support of a privilege that allows reporter's to conceal their sources.

---

496 Jackson (2001). SLAPP stands for "Strategic Litigation against Public Participation".

497 Berger (2003), 1382; Article VI of the statement of principles of the American Society of Newspaper Editors (1996) states: "pledges of confidentiality to news sources must be honoured at all costs, and therefore should not be given lightly". The Code of Ethics of the Society of Professional Journalists states: "Identify sources whenever feasible. The public is entitled to as much information as possible on sources' reliability", but also allows promising confidentiality under the suggested caution: "Always question sources' motives before promising anonymity. Clarify conditions attached to any promise made in exchange for information. Keep promises". Available from: www.spj.org/ethics_code.asp. News-media often adopt or develop particular codes of ethics. One such newspaper with a clear treatment of the confidentiality issue is The San-Francisco Chronicle. Its code on the issue reads: "A reporter who pledges confidentiality to a source must not violate that pledge. If the reporter is asked by an editor for the identity of a source, the reporter should advise the source of the editor's request. If the source wishes to withhold his or her identity from the editor, then the reporter and editor must decide whether or not to use the information even though the source's identity remains known only to the reporter". See Steele, Robert and Jay Black, "Media Ethics Codes and Beyond" (April 2001), *Global Issues Media & Ethics*.

498 Coase, 386.

II The Reporter's Testimonial Privilege

In this part I survey the legal aspects of the reporter's privilege in the US, England and Germany. I show that the Anglo-American jurisdictions developed the privilege in case law which implied uncertainty in the application of the rule by the courts. The attempts to overcome this uncertainty by introducing legislation has only mildly improved the situation. In contrast, German privilege is very strongly formulated and enshrined in legislation. Courts seem to respect the strong protection of confidentiality. German privilege is absolure whereas the Anglo-American privilege is qualified.

1. United States

The reporter's testimonial privilege is governed by state law and varies from one state to the other. Therefore, one cannot discern one uniform set of rules that governs the reporter's privilege in the US.

Under the common law, traditionally, a "news-gatherer" did not have the privilege to refuse to testify about the identity of confidential sources of information[499]. In the first reported case, as early as 1848, the journalist John Nugent was arrested by order of the vice president of the US after refusing to reveal, in a Senate interrogation, the source that leaked secret information to him about a treaty between the US and Mexico[500]. Despite the occurrence of such earlier instances, the first discussion of the reporter's testimonial privilege by the US Supreme Court was not until 1972 in the criminal matter, ***Branzburg v. Hayes*** [501]. The Court held that a privilege does not exist in criminal grand jury proceedings, but it did recognize that the press is entitled to some protection under the constitutional First Amendment (the freedom of the press clause)[502]. ***Branzburg*** is a notoriously murky decision: some courts have used the test developed in the dissenting opinion of Justice Potter Stewart to develop a qualified reporter's privilege, yet other courts have interpreted ***Branzburg*** as rejecting the privilege altogether. Therefore, the result of the ***Branzburg*** decision is that uncertainty rules in the case law[503].

1.1 Shield Laws

The uncertain case law induced 31 states and the District of Columbia to enact, through the years, statutory "shield laws" allowing reporters to protect their sources[504]. These laws are

---

499 "Privilege of Newsgatherer Against Disclosure of Confidential Sources or Information", 99 **A.L.R.**3d 37 at §2. See for example: ***Branzburg v. Hayes*** 408 US 665 (1972); ***Garland v. Torre*** 259 F2d 545 (CA2 NY, 1958), Cert. denied 358 US 910.

500 ***Ex parte Nugent***, 18 F.cas 471 (May 1848).

501 ***Branzburg v. Hayes***, 408 U.S. 665 (1972) (hereinafter – ***Branzburg***).

502 The notoriety of the ***Branzburg*** decision stems from its divided opinions. Justice Byron White wrote a majority opinion rejecting the privilege claimed by three reporters in the case. He ruled that the first amendment protection of freedom of speech does not create a privilege and that the fear of "chilling" sources is unfounded. He was supported by 3 justices. The minority opinion of 4 other justices recognized a qualified privilege. The controversial opinion of Justice Powell is the problem. Powell weighed in for White's majority opinion. But he wrote a concurring opinion that actually supports the minority view. Bates, 5-6.

503 Dienes et al., §14.

504 Dienes et al., §15.

not, however, uniform and offer various degrees of protection[505]. About a quarter of the shield laws extend an absolute privilege to the source[506]. Some shield laws protect both confidential and non-confidential sources. For example, the New York shield law offers absolute privilege to confidential sources and qualified privilege to non-confidential sources[507]. About a third of the shield laws also protect the gathered information from disclosure (in addition to the name of the source), another third protects only unpublished information and the rest offer no protection to information in excess of the identity of the source. Only three jurisdictions with shield laws, Delaware, New Mexico and New York, expressly require that a confidentiality promise be explicitly given by the reporter for the privilege to be considered[508].

1.2 The Reporter's Privilege in Civil Defamation

In civil litigation, the qualified reporter's privilege protects confidential sources after taking into account the following considerations[509]: (1) the nature of the litigation, (2) relevance of the matter whose disclosure is sought to the lawsuit, (3) alternative sources, (4) importance of confidentiality, and (5) whether plaintiff has made *prima facie* showing that statement at issue is false.

Courts have held that disclosure may be compelled only upon a clear and specific showing that the information is highly material and relevant, necessary, or critical to maintenance of the claim, and not obtainable from other sources. This test applies in both civil and criminal contexts and applies to both confidential and non-confidential sources[510].

In defamation lawsuits, some state shield laws eliminate the privilege when the reporter bases his defence on the confidential source. One state shifts the burden of proof to the reporter, whilst, two other states eliminate the privilege after an initial showing by the plaintiff of sufficient need for the information. The majority of courts in the other states interpret the law's silence to mean that the confidentiality of the source should be protected[511].

According to ***Bruns***, in defamation cases, the reliance on shield laws is hardly ever successful, with the exception of the shield laws that assure absolute privilege[512]. Notably, once the plaintiff has been able to prove the remaining parts of the case, specifically the issues of falsity, courts are invariably willing to order the reporter to reveal the sources[513].

---

505 99 **A.L.R.**3d 37 at §2; Berger (2003), 1389; For a survey of American shield laws and the application of American qualified privilege see: *The Reporters Committee for Freedom of the Press*, In www.rcfp.org/privilege/item/cgi?I=intro.

506 Bruns, 301.

507 Bruns, 300.

508 Bruns, 300.

509 99 **A.L.R.**3d 37 at §4; See for example: ***Hopewell v. Midcontinent Broadcasting Corp.*** 538 NW2d 780 (SD, 1995).

510 99 **A.L.R.**3d 37 at §4; ***Gonzales v. Pierce***, 175 F.R.D. 57 (S.D.N.Y. 1997), order aff'd, 155 F.3d 618 (2d Cir. 1998).

511 Dienes et al., 784; Monk, 38-41.

512 Bruns, 302.

513 See for example: ***Cervantes v Time***, 464 F.2d 986, 994 (8th Cir. 1972).

2. England

Freedom of expression is highly regarded in the UK. This esteemed position is reflected in section 12(4) of the Human Rights Act (1998)[514] which incorporates the European Convention for the Protection of Human Rights into British law. Article 10 of the European Convention for the Protection of Human Rights specifically protects both freedom of information, and the concept of confidentially-provided information[515]. It has been interpreted by the European Court of Human Rights (ECHR) to give increasing weight to the social, cultural, political and democratic role of the media[516]. The privilege was first recognized by the ECHR in the ***Goodwin*** case[517].

The rule and the practice in the UK is not to compel a reporter to reveal his confidential sources. In conjunction with the protections offered under the Human Rights Act, Section 10 of The Contempt of Court Act 1981 reads:

> "No court may require a person to disclose nor is any person guilty of contempt of court for refusing to disclose, the source of information contained in that publication for which he is responsible, unless it be established to the satisfaction of the court that disclosure is necessary in the interest of justice or national security or for the prevention of disorder or crime".

Hence, the privilege is not absolute. It can be abrogated when stronger interests materialize in the opinion of the court. One such interest is "the interest of justice" which is an open term into which the court can call many unforeseeable situations.

514 The section reads: "(4) The court must have particular regard to the importance of the Convention right to freedom of expression and, where the proceedings relate to material which the respondent claims, or which appears to the court, to be journalistic, literary or artistic material (or to conduct connected with such material), to-
(a) the extent to which-
(i) the material has, or is about to, become available to the public; or
(ii) it is, or would be, in the public interest for the material to be published;
(b) any relevant privacy code."

515 Article 10 reads: "10. 1.Everyone has the right to freedom of expression. This right shall include the freedom to hold opinions and to receive and impart information and ideas without interference by public authority and regardless of frontiers. This article shall not prevent states from requiring thee licensing of broadcasting, television or cinema enterprises.
2. The exercise of these freedoms, since it carries duties and responsibilities may be subject to such formalities, conditions, restrictions or penalties as are prescribed by law and necessary in a democratic society, in the interests of national security, territorial integrity or public safety, for the prevention of disorder or crime, for the protection of health or morals, for the protection of the reputation or rights of others, for preventing the disclosure of information received in confidence, or for maintaining the authority and impartiality of the judiciary."

516 For a survey of recent judgements see "Media Diversity in Europe", Report prepared by the Advisory Panel on Media Diversity (APMD) on media concentrations, pluralism and diversity questions, Strasbourg, Dec. 2002, 5-6.

517 ***Goodwin v. United Kingdom***, (1996) 22 EHRR 123 (hereinafter – ***Goodwin***).

3. Germany

Freedom of speech is enshrined in the German basic laws (Grund Gesetze). §5 GG reads:

> "(1) Every person shall have the right freely to express and disseminate his opinions in speech, writing, and pictures and to inform himself without hindrance from generally accessible sources. Freedom of the press and freedom of reporting by means of broadcasts and films shall be guaranteed. There shall be no censorship.
>
> (2) These rights shall find their limits in the provisions of general laws, in provisions for the protection of young persons, and in the right to personal honour.
>
> (3) …"

In a 1966 opinion, the German constitutional court considered the legality of a search conducted by the German government in the offices of "Der Spiegel". The purpose of the search was revealing the source of a leak. In its decision, the constitutional court expressly attached the right to protect the confidentiality of sources to the freedom of press[518]. The court considered that the right of journalists to refuse to testify (Zeugnisverweigerungsrecht) is encapsulated within the constitutional protection[519]. The constitutional court stressed the role of the press in informing the public on political as well as economic issues. Therefore, as the "fourth estate", the press must have the independent powers to act as controller of the state and its social institutions[520].

A limited constitutional interpretation of the objective of the privilege would lead to only the protection of confidential sources. A wider interpretation however, stresses the need to ensure the flow of information to the public and the role this has in ensuring the democratic functioning of the state[521]. Indeed, it seems the press enjoys the constitutional freedom as part of its role as an instrument of providing information to the public[522], and therefore the sources of information are protected for that purpose. According to ***Bruns***, the constitutional protection is not given to the source personally (hence, his personality rights are not directly protected) but to the relationship between the reporter and the source[523].

German journalists have an ethical obligation to protect the confidentiality of their sources according to article 6 of the press code (Pressecodex, version 17.9.1997)[524]. Unlike lawyers, however, reporters can, but are not statutorily obliged to, privilege their sources[525]. The reporter's obligation is entirely ethical. Therefore, unlike the case for lawyers in Germany, there is no risk of criminal punishment for reporters who breach a promise of confidentiality.

---

518 Korthals Altes, 78-79; August 5, 1966 BVerfG 20, 162 (Der Spiegel). The case discussed the 1962 search of the editorial offices and private houses of Der Spiegel's owner and editors.

519 Freckman & Wegerich, 93.

520 Löffler-Ricker, 25.

521 BverfG 20, 162 (Der Spiegel case)

522 Mensching, 33; See for example BVerfG 66, 116 (Springer, the Wallraf affair).

523 Bruns (German), 89; BVerfG NJW 1997, 386, 387.

524 Prinz, 682.

525 Löffler/Ricker, 217.

However, at least theoretically, a court might read the ethical obligation as an implicit contractual obligation. I have not found cases considering this possibility.

The first recorded case of a journalist's refusal to reveal a confidential source occurred in 1850 when an editor for "Coburger Tagblatt" refused to disclose, during a police investigation, the source of a report about the "indiscretion" of a public official. The reporter held his stand in spite of several fines and the imposition of a six month imprisonment period. Other attempts to force source disclosure in other cases have also been mostly unsuccessful[526]. ***Löffler & Ricker*** observe that because the constitutional protection of sources emerged prior to the legislation of the privilege, therefore the press should be able to rely on a constitutional protection even when a statutory privilege fails[527]. Unlike the Anglo-American reporter's privilege, the German privilege belongs to the press and not to the source. Therefore, the press may also refuse to testify even when the source releases it from the obligation to secrecy[528].

A reporter, like any other individual, can be called to testify and give evidence. The obligation to give evidence can be enforced through §380 and §390 ZPO or §51 and §70 StPO. The right to refuse is an exception to the rule. In civil procedure the privilege is stronger since the interests of finding the truth are weaker[529]. In the criminal process finding the "material truth" is a matter of public and social interest. Therefore the possibility to assert the privilege may retreat as the crime under discussion becomes more serious[530].

The privilege was first introduced into the statutes during the Weimar Republic era in 1926 as §53.1(5) of the Criminal Procedure Ordinance (StPO). This provision was later also complemented by §97 5(1) StPO relating to protection in search and seizure. In 1953 it was amended into a more comprehensive version (including co-employees of the journalist)[531]. Due to the limited nature of the federal laws, states took the initiative and enacted the privilege in press laws between 1964 and 1966 (with the exception of Bavaria, which had already implemented the privilege since 1949).

After the constitutional court held in various 1973 and 1974 decisions that the states had no competence to enact laws in this area[532], a final reform was enacted on the federal level in 1975[533]. These modifications included incorporating the reporter's privilege in civil procedures to the ZPO as §383 1 (5)[534], thereby finally legislating the privilege (although it had been recognized in civil procedure even earlier)[535].

The ZPO privilege is given to:

> „Personen, die bei der Vorbereitung, Herstellung oder Verbreitung von periodischen Druckwerken oder Rundfunksendungen berufsmäßig mitwirken oder mitgewirkt haben, über die Person des Verfassers,

526 Himmelsbach, 7.
527 Löffler/Ricker, 206.
528 Löffler/Ricker, 217.
529 Mensching, 15, 158; Löffler, PresseRecht 4 Auf. §23, 130.
530 Mensching, 14; For example, BVerfG 20, 162; 56, 247.
531 Löffler/Ricker, 208; Mensching, 56.
532 BVerfG NJW 1974, 743; Mensching, 72-76; Himmelsbach, 11.
533 Löffler/Ricker, 209; Himmelsbach, 8.
534 Privilege can also be found in §102 Abs. 1 (4) AO (tax procedure).
535 Himmelsbach, 10.

Einsenders oder Gewährsmanns von Beiträgen und Unterlagen sowie über die ihnen im Hinblick auf ihre Tätigkeit gemachten Mitteilungen, soweit es sich um Beiträge, Unterlagen und Mitteilungen für den redaktionellen Teil handelt“[536].

As is shown by the wording of the text, the formulation of the privilege is absolute and no place is given to the consideration of countervailing interests. This was widely criticized when the government introduced the law, and since then attempts have been made to add some balance of interests criteria into the legislation (especially for the right to fair criminal process). However, these attempts have been rejected. In doing so the government asserted that a reform is unnecessary since there has never been a case where criminal justice has been obstructed due to the reporter's privilege[537].

In addition to the statutory privileges, the need to protect sources has been widely recognized by the German courts[538]. The reporter's privilege covers the disclosure of any information that could lead to the identity of the source[539]. When the reporter is not named, a journalist may also refuse to disclose whether or not he wrote the report himself[540]. Furthermore, the application of §383 1 (5) ZPO does not depend on an express promise of confidentiality the journalist[541] since its objective is to protect the institutional and public role of the press rather than the individual source[542]. Therefore, the press may also refuse to testify about already disclosed sources[543]. However, there seems to be a dispute as to whether a transaction of information must occur[544] for a privilege to be granted or if the privilege can also be granted to protect self-researched material[545]. There is no dispute that information obtained illegally may be privileged as well[546].

It is important to note that §383 1 (5) ZPO encompasses only periodic publications. It does not include leaflets and books. However, services with editorial components including online news services may benefit from the protection of the privilege[547].

Furthermore §383 1 (5) ZPO limits the privilege to reporting that is done "professionally" (Berufsmäßig). In practice this has not been a limitation, as reporters that are not regular employees, freelancers and part-time reporters have also been granted the privilege[548].

536 Translating liberally, the privilege applies to persons, who professionally participate or participated in the preparation, the production or dissemination of periodic printing or broadcasting, with regard to the identity of the author, the transmitter or origin of contributions and documents as well as regarding their activity concerning contributions, documents and reports for the editorial part.

537 Korthals Altes, 77.

538 BVerfG 20, 162; 36, 193; 64, 108.

539 BGH NJW 1990, 525.

540 Löffler/Ricker, 213; Himmelsbach, 32.

541 Bruns (German), 89, quoting the German journalistic code of ethics. This is also allowed by the court. OLG München NJW 1989, 1226.

542 Mensching, 160; OLG München NJW 1989, 1226.

543 This seems to be a disputed issue: BGHst 28, 240 (Terrorist Klein); Himmelsbach, 32. Here the reporter was forced to answer questions that were supposed to lead the police to the disclosed source in the story. The decision was criticized for not taking into consideration the interest in the publication.

544 March 4, 1981 BVerfGe 56, 247. A cameraman cannot refuse to testify about photos.

545 BGH NJW 1979, 1212, 1215 (Klein) – held no privilege for self-researched material. See also: Himmelsbach, 42-43. But for a different opinion see: OLG München NJW 1989, 1226; Löffler/Ricker, 206 and Mensching 172-173.

546 Himmelsbach, 45.

547 Himmelsbach, 23-29.

548 Himmelsbach, 29-31.

Whether a reporter that has published only once will be granted a privilege does however as yet remain unanswered.

Privilege can also be asserted through §383 1 (6) or §384 (3) ZPO[549]. However, an assertion under the first section, §383 1 (6) ZPO, will only hold as long as the source does not waive his right to confidentiality. A reporter may refuse to reveal a source under the latter section, §384 ZPO, if he believes that disclosure will place him in a difficult situation since it would prove he did not take due care. However, this is most likely to be used when a reporter is the defendant party. In that event, due to §385 ZPO (exceptions to the right of refusal) such a refusal will be counted to the party's detriment, which is exactly the result that the reporter's privilege is designed to prevent. However, in contrast to other sections, §383 1 (6) and §384 (3) ZPO also protect non-periodic media sources[550].

German press law is in significant parts judge made law[551]. This causes some differences in application from jurisdiction to jurisdiction. For example, it is in agreement in the literature that a journalist cannot rely on the civil law privilege when he is a party to the legal proceeding according to the laws in Baden-Württemberg, Nord-Rhein Westphalia and Berlin[552]. This fact can raise uncertainty concerns especially for national press that must consider the risk of facing lawsuits in different states.

As in England, article 10 of the European Convention on Human Rights is applicable to Germany. In England, the Convention has played a significant role in influencing the way courts treat the privilege. This is because the ECHR's interpretation of the Convention strikes a balance between the privilege and the principle of reputation that is more favorable to the privilege than the balance formerly used by the English courts. The Convention plays a lesser role in Germany however, since the German laws and especially the German Basic Laws (GG) already reflect a favorable appreciation of the reporter's privilege. This fact, in conjunction with a different approach to pre-trial discovery and the variety of defamation remedies availability, can serve to explain why it was England and not Germany that supplied the ECHR with its landmark case on the privilege[553].

4. EU Law

The issue of the reporter's privilege has reached the ECHR (as well as other EU level institutions) several times. It has been referred both from England and from continental countries. It is therefore interesting to inspect how the matter was handled on this level.

Voorhoof suggests that the structural commercial and economic circumstances of the media in the EU impede the development of strong investigative journalism. Therefore, at least legal protection for confidential sources should be assured[554].

In the case of ***De Haes and Gisjels v. Belgium*** (24 February 1997) the ECHR ruled that national courts may not refuse a reporter's request to mount his defence in a defamation

549 Himmelsbach, 47-48. Himmelsbach objects to the applicability of §383 1 (6) ZPO.
550 Mensching, 171.
551 Soehring, Jörg, Die neuere Rechtsprechung zum Presserecht NJW 1994, 16.
552 Himmelsbach, 68.
553 ***Goodwin***, *supra* note 517.
554 Voorhoof, at p. 2.

lawsuits by alternative means other than exposing their sources. By doing that, the ECHR ensured that the privilege will be subjected to the risk of removal only when there is no other alternative for the court to obtain sufficient information to reach a correct decision.

The ECHR's direct and most important recognition of the privilege dates to the ***Goodwin v. UK*** (27 March 1996) decision. In this case the ECHR held that the privilege stems from article 10 of the European Convention on Human Rights and that it is qualified. This was not a defamation case but it reflects the balance of interests as it is perceived by the ECHR. The ***Goodwin*** case concerned a demand by corporation to stop the publication of information regarding its financial difficulties which had clearly emanated from a confidential source within the firm. The English courts had not only accepted the firm's request to prevent the publication but also ordered that in the interest of justice the reporter should reveal his confidential source so that the firm could sanction him. The reporter Goodwin refused and was then himself sanctioned by the court. The ECHR held that the balance of interests in the English courts was wrong and that the interest of the freedom of the press should have prevailed in this case.

In ***Goodwin***, therefore, the ECHR affirmed the privilege in spite of the fact that the source had breached the confidence of the claimant-firm. But the ECHR also went further to protect the privilege when criminal violations may have occurred. In the case of ***Fressoz and Roire v. France*** (21 January 1999) the ECHR held that the editor and a reporter in "Le Canard Enchainè" could not be convicted of publishing the confidential tax file of the chief executive officer of the large car maker "Peugeot" obtained from confidential sources, although the information may have been obtained illegally (by theft). The court held that the reporters had a duty to report the information and that the public had an interest to know it[555].

On the institutional level, Recommendation R(2000) 7 of the Committee of Ministers of the Council of Europe to the member states recommended that they implement, into member state laws, principles that will protect the confidentiality of journalistic sources. Principle 4 reads: "In legal proceedings against a journalist on grounds of an alleged infringement of the honour or reputation of a person, authorities should consider, for the purpose of establishing the truth or otherwise of the allegation, all evidence that is available to them under national procedural law and may not require for that purpose the disclosure of information identifying a source by the journalist".

This broad provision, is however subject to principle 3 which contains guidelines for allowing disclosure, namely, the convincing proof that (1) no alternatives for disclosure exist, (2) there is a legitimate interest in disclosure outweighing the interest in non-disclosure, the overriding requirement has been proved, circumstances are sufficiently vital or serious, disclosure is necessary to respond to a pressing social need. Therefore, when taking the two provisions together, it seems member-states will have some latitude in the enforcement of the principles, subject to supervision by the ECHR, of course.

---

555 Voorhoof, 5.

III Defamation Law

Defamation lawsuits have a chilling effect on the media since they impose both litigation costs and potential liability payments. Furthermore, these lawsuits may lead to the revelation of confidential sources, thereby having a chilling effect on sources as well. Much depends on the distribution of the burden of proof. In addition, the amount of damages and the availability of alternative remedies also make a difference.

In this part I survey the legal situation on burden of proof in defamation, damages and other remedies as well as the status of corporations as claimants in defamation lawsuits in the relevant jurisdictions. I show that the main difference is that in US courts the burden of proof is shifted from the media defendants to the corporate plaintiffs whilst in England the traditional distribution of the burden of proof remains though some modifications were introduced recently. In Germany too, the burden of proof is on the reporter, as in England. However, in Germany a more complex set of remedies for defamation exists and the courts prefer non-monetary remedies when possible.

1. United States

The chilling effect that defamation lawsuits can have on the mass media has been widely discussed by the US Supreme Court[556]. The chill on sources comes from revealing them. The chill on the media stems from potential damage liability and from the cost of the legal process[557].

1.1 Burden of Proof

The rule in US common law prior to the landmark cases of ***New York Times v. Sullivan***[558] and ***Gertz v. Welch***[559] was - much like in England - that plaintiffs in defamation lawsuits had only to prove an initial showing that the statement in question was defamatory. Liability and damages were presumed and the defendant had the burden of proving the truthfulness of the statement (or other defences) in order to prevail[560]. This was the traditional English common law approach.

Departure from the English common law approach started with ***New York Times v. Sullivan***[561] in 1964. In one of the most famous decisions in US legal history, the court held that a "public official" must prove the defendant acted with "actual malice" in order to succeed in a defamation lawsuit. According to the court, "actual malice" means knowledge that the allegation was false or reckless disregard as to whether it was false or true[562]. Since it

556 Lidsky, at footnote 172 for an example citation of 20 cases dealing with the issue.

557 Lidsky, 890.

558 ***New York Times v. Sullivan***, 376 U.S. 254 (1964) (hereinafter – ***NYT v. Sullivan***).

559 ***Gertz v. Welch***, 418 U.S. 323 (1974).

560 Franklin & Bussel, 826.

561 ***NYT v. Sullivan***, 279-280. See also: Gilles, Susan M., "Taking First Amendment Procedures seriously: An Analysis of Process in Libel Litigation" (1998), 58 *Ohio State Law Journal*, 1753.

562 ***NYT v. Sullivan***, 279-280. The five elements required for a defamation suit are: (1) publication (2) identification (3) defamation (4) injury (5) fault. There are two levels of fault in the US defamation

is often very hard to prove that a media defendant had knowledge of falsity of the publication, courts usually rely on reckless disregard[563]. **Teeter & Loving** find that there are four general categories of reckless disregard: (1) reliance on a source that is not believable, (2) publishing an inherently improbable story, (3) failing to contact a necessary and proper source and (4) recognizing that the publisher has doubts about the truthfulness of the story and still publishing it[564]. The first of these categories is the focus of our attention.

Furthermore, the court in ***Sullivan*** required that a public official plaintiff will face a higher burden of proof in convincing that the defendant acted with actual malice. The court indicated that a standard of "convincing clarity" should be used[565].

Undoubtedly, the "actual malice" standard was designed to deter defamation lawsuits[566]. The court has purposefully aimed at protecting freedom of speech for constitutional reasons[567]. In ***Curtis v. Butts***[568] the rule was expanded to "public figures", and later extended to all matters involving "public concern"[569].

The test for determining who is a "public figure" was developed in ***Gertz v. Welch***[570]. According to this decision a public figure (1) enjoys greater access to the media and (2) has put itself voluntarily into the public domain. In addition, the ***Gertz v. Welch*** test requires that the plaintiff disprove the defamatory statement, i.e., prove that it is false. Switching the burden of proof meant a substantial change to the common law rule according to which statements that could not be proven true were actionable. The burden of proving falsehood of the defamatory statement was also shifted to public figure plaintiffs[571].

Offering an economic analysis of the actual malice standard, ***Bezanson & Cranberg*** propose that the requirement reflects a policy decision to externalise the cost of errors to the harmed party[572]. Truthful statements have an affirmative value for society[573]. However, errors can be negligent or deliberate and the "actual malice" requirement - undesirably - externalizes both of these as a result of the desire to encourage behaviour that will produce valuable information. Some false information is published by the media in spite of the fact that due care has been exerted to verify the truthfulness of this information. However, setting a higher burden of proof on claimants means that even when the reporters are negligent (and

---

jurisprudence: (1) negligence, and (2) "actual malice" which is the term of the trade for knowledge or reckless disregard to the probable falsity of the publication. See Teeter & Loving, 188, 244 and 270-271.

563 Teeter & Loving, 276.

564 Teeter & Loving, 276.

565 ***NYT v. Sullivan***, 285-286. Additionally, on appeals, the appeal court is instructed to decide on the evidence whether the "actual malice" has been proven rather than remanding the matter to the jury in the first instance. ***NYT v. Sullivan***, 285-286

566 Yannucci, 1193.

567 Gilles, 1758.

568 ***Curtis Publishing v. Butts***, 388 U.S. 130 (1967).

569 ***Rosenblum v. Metromedia***, 403 U.S. 29 (1971).

570 ***Gertz v. Welch***, 418 U.S. 323 (1974).

571 See also ***Philadelphia Newspapers v. Hepps***, 475 US 767 (1986); Franklin & Bussel, 855.

572 Bezanson & Cranberg, 925-927.

573 Franklin and Bussel, 852 quoting John Stuart Mill: "the same reasoning which provides that there should be perfect freedom of expressing opinions proves also that there should be perfect freedom of expressing true facts. It is obviously upon facts that all true opinions must be founded...". The authors explain that the shift in ***NYT v. Sullivan*** and ***Gertz*** was intended to prevent disseminators of information from facing liability without fault.

sometimes when they are malicious too) the plaintiff will not be able to prove his case. It therefore follows that this rule might weaken the deterrence against negligent journalism.

In ***Curtis Publishing v. Butts***[574], the court clarified that liability in defamation should be inflicted upon the defendant as a result of the non-professional conduct of the reporter, rather than the content of the defamatory allegation. The malpractice approach has since been adopted by the Restatement of Torts[575].

The legal literature in the US is aware and even sympathetic to the claim that plaintiffs face strong difficulties when they are required to produce negative proof to counteract a defamatory statement[576]. Nonetheless, The US Supreme Court held that in matters of public concern it would be unconstitutional to put the burden of proof on the media[577].

Since the requirement to prove actual malice imposes great difficulties on a plaintiff, the court has allowed plaintiffs to conduct extensive pre-trial discovery into the defendant's editorial process and state-of-mind[578]. In ***Herbert v. Lando***[579], the Supreme Court first allowed public figure plaintiffs to probe into the news-gathering and editorial processes[580]. The reasons such probes are required is that corporate claimants in the US try to attack the news gathering process by claiming that the sources were dubious, corroboration was lacking, sources and documents were not verified or not consulted. They argue that such questionable reporting techniques (or even the timing of publications, like "sweeps" timing in television) signals that the news gathering process was improper and indicates malice on the part of the media[581]. These pre-trial requests often clash with the reporter's privilege. It then follows that the way courts treat the privilege will have a strong effect on the resolution of such cases.

Much depends on whether the lawsuit takes place in a jurisdiction that enacted a shield law or not. In the latter, reporter's privilege is often found inapplicable in defamation cases or else is severely restricted[582]. The sanctions for refusing to reveal sources can include fines and

574 ***Curtis Publishing v. Butts***, 388 U.S. 130 (1967).

575 Restatement (second) of Torts §580B; Simon, 467. The applicable standard of care has been a matter of debate. Some courts applied the standard of a "reasonable person", but this caused criticism from media supporters. The latter claimed that a trained reporter is better equipped to determine if a news story is true or not than a "reasonable" layman. The debate is ongoing. ***Simon*** proposes that professional ethical journalistic codes be adopted as the national standard of due care, because they reflect the social responsibility of the media and will make the standard clearer for the purpose of following it and proving it. See on the issue: Simon, 471-477.

576 Teeter & Loving, 337.

577 The decision was a close vote of 5 to 4 in ***Philadelphia Newspapers v. Hepps***, 475 US 767, 777 (1986); See also Teeter & Loving, 337. For example, in ***McNabb v. Oregonian Publishing***, a police officer appealed the court's decision to grant summary judgement in favour of the newspaper and the court's refusal to order the reporter to reveal sources which claimed that plaintiff was a racist and used excessive force against blacks. Indeed how can one otherwise prove that he did not make racist remarks? The court rejected the appeal and held that the shield law privileges the reporter. The court acknowledged this may limit the ability of a plaintiff to prove his claim. The court ruled that the state has the right to limit the ability of public figures to sue in defamation and held: "to the extent that a state authorizes a claim for defamation, it may also limit a party's ability to prove the claim in order to promote other social purposes" (***McNabb v. Oregonian Publishing***, 685 P.2d 458, 463 (Or. App. 1984), cert. denied, 469 US 1216 (1985)).

578 ***Herbert v. Lando***, 441 U.S. 153, (1979).

579 *Id, id.*

580 *Id.*, at 175.

581 Kirtley, 1082-1083.

582 Kirtley, 1076.

imprisonment for contempt of court, but mostly it is the presumption that no source existed[583]. At least two cases clarify that when a state has decided not to enact a shield law, then this should be construed as a decision against the application of the reporter's privilege in that jurisdiction, and as a result that a refusal by the reporter to reveal the source should mean that no source existed[584]. The approach in these cases is based on the view that the burden of proof imposed on plaintiffs by ***New York Times v. Sullivan*** is so high that they cannot be denied the opportunity to prove their cases by probing into the sources of the reporter. Another often used sanction against reporters who refuse to reveal their sources is the exclusion of any evidence in connection with the source. In such cases, the reporter can only claim that he had a source and the jury then determines whether the reporter's testimony is truthful. Otherwise, the reporter is assumed to have had no source[585]. At the extreme, a court may simply enter a judgement against the reporter[586]. However in states where a shield law exists it has been held that a "no source" presumption cannot be inferred from a refusal to reveal the source[587].

1.2 Corporate Plaintiffs

It is not immediately evident that corporations should be able to sue for defamation, nor how they should be treated as claimants if they are allowed to do so.

Corporate defamation applies to statements which adversely impact the corporation's trade and business[588]. Although corporations do not have reputation in the personal sense, nevertheless they do enjoy some "personal" rights and business reputation[589]. The question of whether a corporate plaintiff should be treated as a "public figure" for the purpose of burdening it with the requirement of proving the "actual malice" burden has concerned US courts. The decision to treat a plaintiff as a public figure is a result of his fame, notoriety, power, influence or his status in connection with a public controversial issue[590].

583 Kirtley, 1076.

584 ***Downing v Monitor Publishing***, 415 A.2d 683 (1980); ***DeRoburt v Gannet Co.***, 507 F.supp 880 (D. Haw. 1981); See also Berger (1987), 613.

585 See for example: ***Desai v. Hersh***, 954 F.2d 1408 (7th Cir. 1992); ***Liberty Lobby, Inc. v. Rees***, 111 F.R.D. 19 (D.D.C. 1986); ***Sharon v. Time, Inc.***, 599 F. Supp. 538 (S.D.N.Y. 1984); ***Dowd v. Calabrese***, 577 F. Supp. 238 (D.D.C. 1983); ***Las Vegas Sun, Inc. v. Eighth Judicial Dist. Court***, 761 P.2d 849 (Nev. 1988); ***Sands v. News Am. Publishing Inc.***, 560 N.Y.S.2d 416 (App. Div. 1990).

586 ***Georgia Communications Co. v. Horne***, 294 S.E.2d 725, 726 (Ga. Ct. App. 1982); ***Sierra Life Ins. Co. v. Magic Valley Newspapers, Inc.***, 623 P.2d 103, 107-08 (1980). In one extreme case, a default judgement against the media defendant was granted without the plaintiff being required any proof of falsity or malice, after the defendant refused to reveal a source required by the plaintiff for another lawsuit. In the case, the Boston Globe was required to pay 2.1 million dollars following reports about deaths resulting from a new chemotherapy treatment by a leading cancer clinic. This was not a defamation case. See details in Handman, 581.

587 See Berger (1987), 620 and his discussion of ***Maressa v. New Jersey Monthly***, 445 A.2d 376, cert. denied, 459 US 907 (1982).

588 Jackson, 500-501, citing Restatement (First) of Torts §561 (1938) which suggests that defamation would be in this context allegations that deter third persons from dealing with the corporation. An example would be a false publication stating that a corporation is producing defective products.

589 Jackson, 502 and the case law cited therein..

590 Teeter & Loving, 301.

In ***Martin Marietta v. Evening Star Newspaper***[591], the corporation was treated as a public figure, but the reasoning seems to revolve around the public interest in the issue reported, namely the improper entertainment of government official by a defense corporation.

The fact that a corporation has used advertisements in order to put itself in the center of public focus in itself does not meet the second prong of the ***Gertz v. Welch*** test if the defamation does not concern a specifically advertised issue[592].

Widely held corporations are most likely to be treated as public figure claimants. However, as ***Jackson*** remarks, courts in the US have utilized different analyses in determining whether a corporation is a public figure and therefore have reached a variety of results, thereby creating some unpredictability for litigants[593]. He proposes to treat corporations as per-se public figures because this would deter SLAPP lawsuits and allow only the "most serious corporate criticism" to be challenged in court[594]. ***Jackson*** proposes that corporations, with their inherent role in the public arena and their power, require stronger scrutiny and therefore should face a higher burden[595].

The opposite opinion is that the press is actually overprotected. Therefore, corporate lawyers in the US oppose adding any additional burdens on corporate plaintiffs in defamation lawsuits. They claim that corporate plaintiffs are chilled from pursuing costly litigation with very low prospects of success and that any additional tilt in favour of the press is unwarranted[596]. The reasoning seems to be: if competition in the media increases the pressure on reporters to produce more news stories under ever increasing time pressure[597], it follows that the media needs more scrutiny rather than more freedom from lawsuits.

Only a few plaintiffs are able to overcome the hurdle of actual malice[598]. The reporter's privilege (with its uncertain application) is a barrier to successful litigation on the corporate

---

591 ***Martin Marietta v. Evening Star Newspaper***, 417 F.supp 947 (D.C. 1976).

592 Jackson, 504-505.

593 Jackson, 509.

594 Jackson, 510. This position seems to be based on the opinion that corporations deserve less first amendment protection and should be open to stricter legal and regulatory scrutiny compared to individuals. See Jackson, at footnote 184 for case law in that respect. Corporations, according to Jackson, also do not have the same reputation interests as individuals do and defamation tort was conceived for protecting personal and not corporate reputation.

595 Jackson, 516-517. In that context Jackson cites court opinions that emphasize that in a free market economy where allocation of resources is done also through private corporations, it is important to protect the free flow of commercial information. Jackson, at 520 citing in footnote 207 the case of ***Va. State Bd. Of Pharmacy v. Va. Citizens Consumer Council***, 425 U.S. 748 (1976).

596 Yannucci, 1189.

597 Yannucci, 1190.

598 Yannucci, 1194. The cases cited are: ***Harte-Hanks Communications, Inc. v. Connaughton***, 491 U.S. 657 (1989); ***Curtis v. Butts.***, at 130. These two cases upheld a finding of actual malice and emphasized the inadequacies of the media defendant's investigatory process in ruling for the plaintiff. In ***Curtis Publishing v. Butts***, for example, the Saturday Evening Post published an article which accused the athletic director of the University of Georgia of conspiring to "fix" a football game between the University of Georgia and the University of Alabama. Id. at 135. The Court upheld the jury verdict in favour of the plaintiff based on several factors, including the Saturday Evening Post's failure to investigate the credibility of its sources. Among the list of questionable reporting methods were (1) The Post knew that their only source had a criminal record, and did not seek to independently verify the story, (2) The Post did not utilize sports experts or game films that it knew existed to verify the story, (3) The Post was anxious to embark on a policy of "sophisticated muckraking," making libel more likely, and (4) there was no time pressure to publish the story. *Id.* at 156-58.

claimant's side[599]. ***Yannucci*** estimates that 10,000 stories are published about corporate entities every year and that the number of defamation cases is comparatively minuscule. In his view, any increase will only contribute to preventing undesirable and irresponsible behaviour by the media[600].

1.3 Data and Anecdotal Evidence

Evidence for cases where journalists were forced to reveal confidential sources in order to avoid liability is not highly pervasive, but such cases do exist. In one such case, the Los Angeles Daily News faced a default judgement in a $60 million defamation lawsuit after refusing to reveal confidential sources. After a summary judgement was given, the editors ordered the reporters to reveal their sources[601].

Perhaps the most notorious clash over source confidentiality and defamation in the US occurred between the ABC television network and tobacco corporation Phillip Morris[602]. In the investigative program "Day One", ABC charged Phillip Morris ("PM") with manipulating the ingredients of cigarettes. The corporation sued for 10 billion Dollars in defamation damages. As a public figure plaintiff, PM had to prove "actual malice" on the part of the ABC. The television company refused to reveal the identity of the main source, referred to as "deep cough", and who appeared on-camera in disguise. PM tried to trace the source through subpoenas for the reporters' phone bills and credit card bills. This was the main controversy in the pre-trial discovery process[603]. Judge Markow rejected PM's argument that the rationale of ***Herbert v. Lando*** justified seeking this information[604]. Nevertheless, Markow J, ordered ABC to disclose their source. His decision was based on the fact that "deep cough" was the primary source that shaped the state of mind of ABC's reporters, and that without knowing her identity the ability of PM to prove the "actual malice" would have been severely limited. The judge noted that there are no alternative means for PM to reveal the identity of the source other than by compelled disclosure. Following vehement protests from the ABC the judge agreed to stay his order and six months later admitted his error and reversed the order. Yet surprisingly, soon after this victory, ABC capitulated, publicly apologized and settled the case. ABC settled with PM only three weeks after its acquisition by Disney. This capitulation is presumed to have had primarily financial motivations[605]. An important observation that can be drawn from this case is that ABC was willing to incur significant costs in litigation in order to protect the source. Hence, it is safe to assume that revealing a source may cause a reputation loss to reporters and that this reputation loss can be significant. Another observation is that reporters may sometimes capitulate and withdraw a report rather than disclose the source. Hence, the reputation loss caused by capitulating is often smaller than the expected damages in defamation lawsuits or the risk of source disclosure and its repercussions.

---

599 Yannucci, 1094.

600 Yannuci, 1201-1202.

601 The case is described in Berger (1987).

602 ***Philip Morris Cos., Inc. v. ABC, Inc.***, 23 Media L. Rep. (BNA) 1434, 1439, vacated in part, 23 Media L. Rep. (BNA) 2438 (Va. Cir. Ct. 1995) (hereinafter - ***PM v. ABC***); Calvert (1996), 3 provides a detailed analysis of the case.

603 Calvert, 6-7.

604 ***PM v. ABC***, 23 Media L. Rep. (BNA) at 1435.

605 Calvert, 19-20. Calvert points to a series of capitulations and censorship cases in television networks owned by giants corporations. The "60 Minutes" Wigand interview and General Electric's control of NBC are the given examples.

Data about the effects of the procedural changes in defamation in the US (the shift of the burden of proof) on the results of litigation is impressive: approximately 80% of defamation lawsuits end with a summary judgement in favour of the defendant. This is a staggering result compared to other civil tort claims with a traditional burden of proof (no more than 2% of defence summary judgement requests granted). Interestingly, roughly 80% of summary judgement motions based on the claim that "actual malice" has not been shown were successful. When the motions were based on a no negligence ground, only 60% were granted. Other motions were only successful 53% of the time[606].

On the other hand, in trials, defendants' success rate drops to 28% and their losses are severe. Despite this, on appeal, 70% of defense appeals are upheld. Media defendants also tend to appeal unfavourable rulings rather frequently. Eventually, statistics points to a success rate of 5% to 10% for plaintiffs in defamation litigation[607].

Litigation costs in US defamation cases are extremely high. Parties conduct long pre-trial discovery procedures that include witness depositions and evidence collection. These processes generate enormous costs in legal fees for both parties[608]. The legal cost of a "routine" US defamation case can range from $100,000 to $150,000. Extreme cases reached $3 million and in one case $8 million were spent in pre-trial litigation and the lawsuit was then withdrawn by the plaintiff[609]. Litigation costs have a chilling effect on publication in and of themselves. These costs also motivate early settlements out of court.

One legal scholar quipped that a system that costs so much and is so inaccurate that almost all trials are turned on appeal must be viewed as a failure[610]. If the purpose of the defamation tort is to deter the publication of false information, then according to ***Dun & Bradstreet v. Greenmoss***, the ruling in ***New York Times v. Sullivan*** should be criticized, since it failed to achieve this goal[611]. What ***Sullivan*** supposedly achieved is the following: truth speakers will not be harmed at the cost of allowing some falsehood to go though to the public. This seems to have been the purpose of the decision, and was preferred over an approach that deters intentional liars but may also deter some truth speakers[612].

1.4 Damages

Damage awards in the US have been generally high. In 1996, for example, the average award was $3 million and median award was $2.3 million[613]. As a general trend, the amounts of damages awarded for defamation in the US are on the rise, although there are fluctuations.

---

606 The statistics refers to 1980-1994 and is reported in Gilles, 1774-1776 and footnotes 74 and 78.

607 Gilles, 1776-1779 and footnote 92.

608 Gilles, 1779-1780 and footnotes 94.and 95. The numbers cited are between $95,000 and $500,000 for a regular defamation case. Some cases reach six, nine or even ten million dollars.

609 Teeter & Loving, 185.

610 Gilles, 1783-1784 and 1790-1796. Gilles claims that in the interest of accuracy, the court has developed an inefficient and costly process – which does not work. Proof of the failure is the high appeal rate and the high rate of overturning decisions on appeal. Appeals are attributed to jury antipathy to the media but also (and a more favoured explanation by Gilles) to the complexity of the legal issue that creates a high probability of jury error.

611 ***Dun & Bradstreet v. Greenmoss Builders***, 472 US 749 (1985) at 769.

612 Gilles, 1787 and 1790-1796.

613 Gilles, 1776.

Plaintiffs often rely on the sympathy of the juries against big media firms. In one case, Judge Richard Posner remarked that the plaintiffs should prove their damage and not rely on jury generosity[614]. Jury awards in defamation cases often include high punitive damage awards. Wall Street Journal was once given a $222.7 million fine. As in most cases, appeal courts reduce fines significantly (The WSJ fine was reduced by $200 million and later overturned completely). But still, US awards are on the high end of the scale[615]. It is noteworthy that both in England and in the US there is no need to prove the actual monetary harm caused to the plaintiff[616]. Damages may be awarded even if it is clear that no monetary harm has occurred at all.

2. United Kingdom

In English common law, a statement adverse to a person's reputation gives rise to a defamation claim[617]. The tort of defamation was, historically, comprised of two torts: libel, which is written or televised and slander, which is spoken. The purpose of the tort is to vindicate the plaintiff's reputation and make reparation for damage done by wrongful publication of defamatory statements.

A possible defense against liability in defamation is that the publication was truthful[618]. The plaintiff does not need to prove that the statement is false - falsity is presumed. The burden of proof lies with the defendant to show that on the "balance of probabilities" the content of the publication is true[619]. This approach - starkly opposed to the US approach - has been recognized as having a chilling effect on freedom of speech[620].

In the press, the "repetition rule" applies. When the defendant publishes "X said that Y did α" and α is defamatory, it is not enough to show that X indeed made the allegation. Rather the media defendant must show that Y actually did commit act α in order to prevail in litigation[621]. English courts require that defamation is made with a degree of negligence that is equal to recklessness which is a higher degree than mere carelessness[622]. However, regardless of the effort a reporter has invested in verifying the information prior to

---

614 ***Douglas v. Hustler Magazine Inc.***, 769 F.2d 1128, 1144 cited by Teeter & Loving, 242.

615 Teeter & Loving, 237-242.

616 See ***Steel and Morris v. United Kingdom***, European Court of Human Rights Case number 68416/01. Judgement from 15.2.2005, paragraph D. Available at: http://cmiskp.echr.coe.int/tkp197/view.asp?action=html.&documentId=717965&portal=hbkm&source=externalbydocnumber&table=285953B33D3AF94893DC49EF6600CEBD49.

617 In the case of a company, a statement is defamatory when it is adverse to a company's reputation or goodwill. ***Jones v Jones*** [1916] 2 AC 481.

618 In fact, truth is not actionable as defamation. Gatley, 267.

619 Gatley, 269. See ***McVicar v. United Kingdom*** (ECHR) application 46311/99, Judgement 7 May 2002, p. 8.

620 ***Reynolds v Times Newspapers*** [2000] H.R.L.R., 134, 140 (hereinafter – ***Reynolds***). On the law of defamation in England Prof. Tony Weir noted: "(the plaintiff) can get damages (swingeng damages!) for a statement made to **other** without (is this really the direct quote? Because this doesn't make so much sense – check! Should be others or anothershowing that the statement was untrue, without showing that the statement did him the slightest harm, and without showing that the defendant was in any way wrong to make it (much less that the defendant owed him any duty of any kind)". And: "the courts could arguably have done more to prevent the law becoming as absurd, complex and unfair as it is, without resigning themselves to saying, as Diplock L.J. did, that the law of defamation "has passed beyond redemption by the courts". He concludes: "the law of England is certainly stricter than that of any free country... ". Weir, Tony , **A Casebook on Tort**, (8th ed., 1996) cited in ***Reynolds***, 158.

621 ***Galloway v. Telegraph Group***, [2005] E.M.L.R. 7, at §35.

622 Gatley, 249-250.

publication, if truth cannot be proven to be more likely than not, then the reporter will be liable[623]. Nevertheless, confidential sources may furnish the reporter with documents which cannot be disclosed since they reveal the identity of the provider but which could establish the truthfulness of the defamatory allegation[624]. In such a case, revealing the identity of the source may enable the reporter to protect himself if the source is reliable and the duty-interest privilege applies, as will be discussed here below.

2.1 The Duty-Interest Privilege

The Reynolds Decision. The House of Lords addressed the issue recently in the ***Reynolds*** case[625], which represented a direct clash of interests: freedom of the press on the one hand versus reputation on the other hand. It focused on a defamation lawsuit filed by the resigning Prime Minister of Ireland against the Sunday Times newspaper. The newspaper claimed that Reynolds deliberately lied and suppressed information from his cabinet colleagues. The information was attributed to an unnamed source who was uncovered during the trial. The source was the aide of one of Reynolds' political rivals. The trial court held that this person, clearly an interested source, was not a reliable source and the newspaper's defence was thus rejected[626]. The newspaper appealed to the House of Lords, which rejected the appeal. Writing for the majority, Lord Nicholls observed that case law has created privileged forms of speech when there is high public interest in uninhibited speech. According to Lord Nicholls his privilege was qualified: when the speech was used maliciously to further purposes other than those the public interest would have protected, the privilege was removed[627]. The qualified privilege defence was not traditionally available in defamation cases regarding dissemination of information to the general public[628]. The defense is based on the existence of a duty between the disseminator and the recipient of defamatory factual material to share this information. The courts have been unwilling to extend a duty to publish information to the media. One possible reason for not extending the qualified duty-interest privilege was the difficulty faced by a plaintiff in overcoming this defense. The plaintiff must prove "malice" on the defendant's part. This becomes difficult when sources are protected[629]. Lord Nicholls described the problem thus:

> "Those who read or hear [defamatory imputations of fact...] are unlikely to have any means of knowing whether they are true or not. In respect of such imputations, a plaintiff's ability to obtain a remedy if he can prove malice is not normally a sufficient safeguard. Malice is notoriously difficult to prove. If a newspaper is understandably unwilling to disclose its sources, a plaintiff can be deprived of the material necessary to prove, or even allege, that the newspaper acted recklessly in publishing as it did without further verification.

---

623 Williams, 115.

624 For example, in the ***Goodwin*** case, *supra* note 517 (although not a defamation case) the reporter based his report on a copy of a corporate business plan which was circulated in a very small number of numerated copies. Disclosing the copy would have revealed which of the copies had been leaked.

625 ***Reynolds v Times Newspapers*** [2000] H.R.L.R., 134.

626 ***Reynolds***, 175-176.

627 *Id*, 142.

628 Loveland, Ian, "The Ongoing Evolution of Reynolds Privilege in Domestic Libel Law" (2003) *Entertainment Law Review*, 14(7), 178.

629 *Id*, *id*.

> Thus, in the absence of any additional safeguard for reputation, a newspaper, anxious to be first with a 'scoop', would in practice free to publish seriously defamatory misstatements of fact based on the slenderest of materials. ...
>
> Some further protection for reputation is needed if this can be achieved without a disproportionate incursion into freedom of expression.
>
> This is a difficult problem. No answer is perfect. ... The appellant newspaper commends reliance upon the ethics of professional journalism. The decision should be left to the editor of the newspaper. Unfortunately, in the United Kingdom this would not generally be thought to provide a sufficient safeguard. In saying this I am referring to mistaken decisions. From time to time mistakes are bound to occur, even in the best regulated circles. ... the sad reality is that the overall handling of these matters by the national press, with its own commercial interests to serve, does not always command general confidence"[630].

Finally, despite his sceptical view of the media, Lord Nicholls extended the restricted approach[631]. Now, when information is such that "the public was entitled to know" it[632], a qualified privilege can be granted by the court, and the plaintiff would only be able to prevail after successfully proving malice on the defendant's part. Most importantly, the court held that unwillingness to reveal sources shall generally not be held against the press. Lord Nicholls' majority opinion included an illustrative ten point checklist for deciding if a particular story satisfied the "right to know" test[633].

Lord Nicholls observed that the suggested solution has the "disadvantage of unpredictability and uncertainty". Yet, he also noted that the degree of the "chilling effect" on the media resulting from this uncertainty should not be exaggerated[634]. The court rejected the proposal made by Lord Justice Lester to shift the burden of proof of truthfulness from the defendant to

630 ***Reynolds***, 159-150.

631 Loveland, 178.

632 ***Reynolds*** at 625, 622.

633 The 10 non-exhaustive points to be applied by the court in deciding whether the defendant's defamatory statement of fact should be granted a privilege were:
"1. The seriousness of the allegation. The more serious the charge, the more the public is misinformed and the individual harmed, if the allegation is not true.
2. The nature of the information, "and the extent to which the subject matter is a matter of public concern".
3. The source of the information. Some informants have no direct knowledge of the events. Some have their own axes to grind, or are being paid for their stories.
4. The steps taken to verify the information.
5. The status of the information. The allegation may have already been the subject of an investigation which commands respect.
6. The urgency of the matter. News is often a perishable commodity.
7. Whether comment was sought from the [claimant]. He may have information others do not possess or have not disclosed. An approach to [the claimant] will not always be necessary.
8. Whether the article contained the gist of the [claimant's] side of the story.
9. The tone of the article. A newspaper can raise queries or call for an investigation. It need not adopt allegations as statements of fact.
10. The circumstances of the publication, including the timing". ***Reynolds***, 153.

634 ***Reynolds***, 150.

the plaintiff, as done in the US. Lord Nicholls remarked that such a shift would indeed symbolize the importance of freedom of speech but cannot be justified[635]. Lord Justice Steyn, dissenting from Lord Nicholls' opinion, lamented the importation of a privilege that was developed in and for a different legal culture. He notes that given the rule of protecting the confidentiality of sources in England, adopting a "duty-interest privilege" for the information, removable only after proof of malice, in the absence of the ability to inquire into the sources of the reporter, places a plaintiff suing for defamation in England under substantial handicap[636]. This is in contrast to the plaintiff in the US which is entitled to a substantial pre-trial inquiry into the sources of the story and editorial decision-making[637].

While ***Reynolds*** itself does not refer to a negligence rule, its progeny have apparently adopted a negligence approach. Thus, defamatory "public interest" information is protected against defamation lawsuits only after proof that the reporter had reason to believe that the information is factually correct[638]. ***Loveland*** proposes that the 10 point ***Reynolds***-test can be used as indication of the level of precaution to be taken by the journalist with regards to the publication of information[639].

Gatley seems to explain the ruling as giving emphasis to the motive of the publication. Motive is important in defamation because of the perception that some speech - even in factual matters - is important even when it is false, if the motive for its publication was permissible[640]. However, applying the ***Reynolds*** defence requires the court to determine whether the reporter adhered to the principle of "responsible journalism". On that **Gatley** writes: "The principle is elastic and elasticity means a degree of uncertainty"[641]. It is therefore interesting to observe how the ***Reynolds*** "duty interest" defence has been applied so far in the case of confidential sources.

Application of the Reynolds Defence. The reliability of journalistic sources is often an important factor in deciding whether the ***Reynolds*** defence applies, yet English courts are cautious not to force reporters to reveal unnamed sources[642].

In ***G.K.R. Karate (U.K.) Ltd. v. Yorkshire Post Newspapers Ltd. and Others (No. 2)***[643] the source that confirmed the story was a named public official, thus the court could easily affirm the ***Reynolds*** privilege. In ***Al Misnad v. Azzaman Ltd***[644], the wife of the Emir of Qatar sued a newspaper that alleged that she had behaved improperly and illegally. The court declined the claimant's application for summary judgement holding that the reporters' level of verification may have been stifled by the difficult conditions of verifying information in the Middle East and that since the claimant would have been unlikely to respond to a request for comment, this would not be accepted as irresponsible journalism in this case.

---

635 ***Reynolds***, 151.
636 ***Reynolds***, 158.
637 Lord Steyn cites ***Herbert v. Lando*** (1979) 441 U.S. 153.
638 Loveland, 182.
639 *Id, id.*
640 Gatley, 21.
641 Gatley, 457.
642 Gatley, 459.
643 [2000] EMLR 410.
644 [2003] EWHC 1783, QB.

In another case where the sources were known, ***Galloway v. Telegraph Group***[645], a newspaper published allegations that a member of the English parliament (Galloway) who was in known opposition to the war in Iraq was "on the pay" of the Iraqi leader Saddam Hussein. Galloway sued. The sources were documents found by a reporter in a looted government building in Baghdad. The reporter testified as to the circumstances in which they were found and according to which he had no reason to believe they were forged[646]. The court ruled that the sources of the information - namely, the operatives in Saddam Hussein's regime that authored the documents - "could not be classified as inherently reliable"[647]. The information was not verified by other sources. The subject of the publication, Galloway, was given a very short time to comment on the upcoming publication and was not able to see the documents on which it was based.

The reason for haste, apparently, was the newspaper's desire to get a scoop (beat the competitors in publishing the information). The documents were in the sole possession of the newspaper and there was no real danger that the information would fall into the hands of competitors. The court ruled as a factual finding that the hastiness was self-imposed[648]. The defendant newspaper asserted the application of the ***Reynolds*** "duty-interest" privilege in this case: that no matter whether the information was true or false, the public had the right to know it[649]. The court rejected this justification[650].

In summary: the ***Galloway*** ruling found the defendant negligent due to the highly defamatory nature of the information, the relative uncertainty as to the reliability of the source and the fact that time could and should have been, but was not, used to verify the information to the appropriate level of care. The claimant was awarded 150,000 Pounds in compensation.

The most pertinent case for our issue was ***Jameel v. Wall Street Journal Europe***[651] and also drew the most interest in England. The plaintiffs were a Saudi businessman and his company, a Saudi trading company with no business in the UK. The defendant newspaper WSJE published an article reporting that the bank accounts of the claimants were monitored by Saudi authorities at the request of US authorities due to suspicion of them being tied to financing terrorist activities. When sued, the WSJE asserted the ***Reynolds*** privilege on the grounds that the public had the right to be informed about matters of public interest such as the terrorism.

The question of sources was a factual issue for the jury. The reporter, who wrote the story, James Dorsey, did not reveal the identity of his sources but testified that he relied on five confidential sources denoted by A to E. The reporter testified and was cross-examined about the sources. Dorsey testified that source A was a Saudi businessman whom he did not consider reliable enough. Source A was only treated as a "lead". Dorsey went on to testify about sources B to E who, he claimed, "firmed up" the story[652].

---

645 ***Galloway v. Telegraph Group***, [2005] E.M.L.R. 7.

646 *Id*, §99-§105.

647 *Id*, §161.

648 *Id*, §106.

649 *Id*, §24.

650 *Id*, §171.

651 ***Jameel v. Wall Street Journal Europe Sprl*** [2004] E.M.L.R. 11

652 With regard to sources, the defence claimed: "Mr Dorsey was informed by his sources in the banking community in early December 2001 of the existence of an "off the record" list of bank accounts being monitored at US request by the Saudi Arabian Monetary Authority in consequence of 11 September 2001. This list included at least one account associated with the Abdul Latif Group of companies of

An oddity of this case is that although English law has a presumption of falsehood, the plaintiffs insisted on presenting evidence to prove that the information was false[653] - hence, to prove what is already presumed to be proven. The trial judge allowed the request and admitted into evidence formal records confirming that the Jameel accounts were not being monitored. The WSJE defense resorted to convincing the jury that the reporter Dorsey was experienced and trustworthy. The plaintiffs counter-claimed that the reporter could not have been told by sources that their accounts were monitored when there is clear evidence that they were not[654] and therefore he cannot be trustworthy. Finally, the jury rejected the reporter's testimony and ruled that sources B to E had not confirmed the story[655].

Although the jury rejected the testimony of the defence in other matters of fact as well and preferred the evidence of the plaintiff, the judge, Eady J, pointed out that the case for the defence was not entirely forlorn[656]. According to ***Reynolds***, the court - and not the jury - should decide whether the ***Reynolds*** "duty-interest" privilege applies to the publication. In deciding whether the ***Reynolds*** privilege should apply the court went on to consider the 10 points set forth by Lord Nicholls in ***Reynolds***. On the first point, seriousness (or gravity) of the allegations, Eady J ruled that the information was on the higher end of the scale[657]. The court construed the gravity element as being positively correlated to the level of responsibility required from the journalist. The graver the allegation - the higher the potential damage to reputation or to the claimant's business activity and hence the higher need for responsible journalism[658]. In this respect, the court's hands were tied by the factual findings of the jury regarding sources. The court pointed out that the ***Reynolds*** privilege does not necessarily depend on reliability of sources. Even if the sources were "entirely impeccable" (which in this case they were found not to be), the information they convey is not *ipso facto* in the public interest. Nevertheless, reliability of the source is a factor in deciding whether the public has the right to know the information provided by the source[659]. The defendant's assertion of the ***Reynolds*** privilege case failed due to other reasons which the court construed to indicate negligent journalism[660].

---

which the Second Claimant alleges it is a part. This was confirmed by a highly placed Saudi banking source at the beginning of February 2002. The said account was subsequently confirmed as being on the list by a US diplomat who consulted an official file in the author's presence before providing this confirmation. The author, notwithstanding the authoritative status of this diplomatic source, made a further check prior to publications with a senior Saudi official, who independently confirmed that said account was on the list". See ***Jameel v Wall Street Journal Europe***, [2004] EWHC 37 (QB) (hereinafter – ***Jameel appeal***), §13.

653 ***Jameal appeal***, §35-§36. The plaintiffs insisted for three reasons: "First it would show that Mr Dorsey's account of what he had been told by his sources could not be correct, for the evidence would prove that no monitoring had been carried out. Secondly it would support the Jameels' claim to aggravated damages by proving conclusively that the central allegation in the article was false. Thirdly it would rebut Mr Simpson's evidence that he was convinced that the article was accurate".

654 ***Jameel appeal*** §41-§42.

655 ***Jameel***, §11-§13; ***Jameel appeal*** §40. The unnamed sources were described as a banker, a US diplomat, a US embassy official and a Saudi official.

656 ***Jameel***, §16.

657 ***Jameel***, §38.

658 ***Jameel***, §39.

659 ***Jameel***, §66.

660 For example, the court found that given the grave defamatory nature of the publication the reporter should have waited 24 hours for the company to get in touch with Mr Jameel who was away and was not available for an immediate and informed comment See ***Jameel***, §47-§48.

The ruling, which was considered a setback for the ***Reynolds*** privilege, was appealed by WSJE[661]. The appeal court held that truth is not a relevant issue when the jury is deciding on whether the reporter should have believed the sources. The jury should have no presumption of falsity when examining this factual matter. "What has to be considered is whether it was responsible to publish the article having regard to the risk that the defamatory imputation in the article might prove to be untrue. Relevant to that question may be the information given to the publishers by the sources of the article, the nature of the sources, and the extent to which they backed that information"[662]. The presumption of falsity is required only for the determination of liability and damages.

The appeal court stated that in order to prove "responsible journalism" which provides the basis for the ***Reynolds*** privilege, the defendant may need to prove why he believed the information to be true[663]. The appeal court agreed with Eady J that the ***Reynolds*** privilege should be interpreted as setting a two-stage test. First, the defendant must prove they have engaged in "responsible journalism" which means the degree of care increases with the gravity of the information. Secondly, the court must be convinced that there is a public interest in the information being published[664]. The appeal court upheld the high court's ruling that responsible journalism had not been carried out regardless of the issue of whether the corroborating sources were reliable or not and therefore rejected the appeal.

The WSJE appealed to the House of Lords. The much awaited decision was handed down in October 2006[665]. The lords focused on two main issues: (1) whether a trading corporation with reputation but no actual business in England needs to prove actual monetary harm in order to sue for defamation and (2) whether the rejection of the "Reynolds defence" by the lower courts was correct.

On the first issue, the need to prove harm, the majority of the judges opined that corporate reputation has positive value and is hard to prove. The court held that according to English law corporations may sue in defamation and be awarded damages without need to prove the actual harm. Lord Scott noted that the purpose of defamation damages is not compensation but "vindication of reputation"[666] whereas Baroness Hale in a minority opinion on this point suggested that such an approach would chill the media from criticizing corporations[667].

However, the latter issue was subsided due to the fact that the House of Lords unanimously allowed the appeal and rejected the imposition of damages on the newspaper. First of all, the lords criticized the misdirection given to the jury by Eady J. The lords ruled that the jury was directed to consider whether the sources denoted B to E confirmed the story of the reporter. But Eady J had instructed the jury to make their decision on the assumption that sources B to E knew that the story is false. The lords concluded that this tainted the chance of the jury reaching a correct conclusion[668].

---

661 ***Jameel appeal*** §55. One prong of the appeal was the claim that the presumption of falsity in English defamation law runs contrary to the European Convention on Human Rights.

662 ***Jameel appeal***, §60-§61.

663 ***Jameel appeal***, §27.

664 ***Jameel appeal***, §87.

665 ***Jameel and Others v. Wall Street Journal Europe Sprl***, [2006] UKHL 44 (hereinafter - Jameel HL)

666 ***Jameel HL***, §123.

667 ***Jameel HL***, §157. Baroness Hale proposed to require corporations to show some probability that they were harmed by the defamatory statement.

668 ***Jameel HL***, opinions of Lord Hoffman, §§60-61, Lord Scott, §140.

The lords further criticized Eady J for his rigid and strict application of the 10 point test developed in the ***Reynolds*** case. The House of Lords held that the ten points should be applied with flexibility and not turned into ten "hurdles"[669]. The lords then re-evaluated the lower courts decision that WSJE did not act with "responsible journalism" because it did not delay the publication for 24 hours waiting for Mr. Jameel's comment on the story. The lords concluded that any comment that would have been given after 24 hours would not have changed the story and therefore that the absence of delay cannot be considered negligent journalism in the given circumstances[670]. Hence, the newspaper's appeal was allowed and the award of damages was cancelled. Nevertheless, the discussion of the ***Jameel*** case in the House of Lords only stresses the uncertainty of the English Rule in defamation lawsuits. This uncertainty stems from the fact that the attempt to protect investigative journalism in defamation lawsuits through the ***Reynolds*** defence is stifled by the vagueness of the test. It was Lord Hope that remarked that the article in ***Jameel*** was a hallmark of "responsible journalism"[671]. Yet his colleague Lord Hoffman observed that a judge can interpret the 10 point ***Reynolds*** test in such a way that it will become ten impassable hurdles and that Eady J's rigidity in ***Jameel*** did exactly that[672].

2.2 Challenging the English Distribution of the Burden of Proof

The European Court of Human Rights has addressed the burden of proof in defamation in the UK. The case of ***McVicar v. UK*** (ECHR judgement 7 May 2002) concerned the reporter McVicar claiming that athlete Linford Christie had used banned drugs. Christie brought a defamation lawsuit in England. The jury held that the reporter was not able to prove the claim. Christie did not seek damages but was awarded trial costs. McVicar appealed to the ECHR. One prong of the appeal concerned the unavailability of legal aid to defendants in defamation lawsuits. The other concerned the burden of proof.

The UK argued that it is correct to place the burden of proof on the person that made a positive accusation rather than on the party that denies the accusation, given the difficulty of proving negative facts, and that this burden encourages journalists to act responsibly and check their sources to ensure their allegations have an objective basis prior to publication. The government indicated that this allocation of the burden of proof is typical in civil procedural law[673]. The ECHR ruling stressed the right of the press to report on public interest issues and the right of the public to receive such information, yet noted the "duties and responsibilities" that the press must assume in reporting this information[674]. The ECHR notes that the sources of the reporter are not known and therefore the court cannot determine whether the reporter could have reasonably relied on them. Yet there are indications that the reporter based his allegations on circumstantial evidence and only started verifying them to a high standard once defamation proceedings against him commenced[675]. The ECHR therefore rejected the appeal with respect to all its prongs, including the allocation of burden of proof. **Gatley** remarks that the rejection may have been context dependant[676]. Notably, **Franklin &**

---

669 ***Jameel HL***, Lord Hoffman §§56-57.
670 ***Jameel HL***, Lord Bingham §35, Lord Hoffman, §83.
671 ***Jameel HL***, §111.
672 ***Jameel HL***, §§56-57.
673 ***McVicar***, at §41-42.
674 ***McVicar***, §72-73.
675 ***McVicar***, §86.
676 Gatley, 270.

Bussel reject the view that proving negative facts is necessarily harder than proving the positive. They show that in many cases the plaintiff is required to prove negative facts as part of his claim[677]. They contend that this saves discovery costs since cases that cannot be proven false on their initial merit can be summarily dismissed.

2.3 Compelled Disclosure

In non-defamation cases concerning clashes between corporations and the press, English courts have been willing to compel reporters to disclose their sources. In the ***Goodwin***[678] case, the courts consistently held that a reporter must reveal the source who leaked a secret corporate business plan in alleged breach of his confidential obligation to the corporation. The courts both prevented the publication of the information by issuing an injunction and also held that the corporation had a right to take legal action against the informant and therefore have the right to reveal his identity. To the relief of the reporter Goodwin, the European Court of Human Rights overturned the national courts decision and indicated that freedom of the press should be given a stronger weight in the future.

Nevertheless, English courts have compelled the Financial Times and other newspapers to disclose confidential sources of reports about a contemplated takeover by Interbrew (a Belgian brewery) of SAB (a South-African brewery) at the request of Interbrew[679], after the court learned that the sources provided partially forged documents. The court held that while the media may not be required to guarantee the veracity of all its reports, it cannot expect to protect false sources with the same strength afforded to truthful sources. However, the court held that disclosure should be allowed when it is clear to the reporter at the outset that the documents which the source had provided are not authentic and may have been forged[680].

2.4 Damages

In England, a plaintiff in a defamation lawsuit does not have to prove actual damage. Once defamation has been proved, damage is presumed since it is perceived to be extremely hard to prove the actual harm to reputation[681]. Attempts to require that corporations - that cannot be damaged in feelings but only in pocket - be required to prove damages as a preliminary requirement for claiming defamation has been rejected by the courts. The reasoning was that proving actual monetary damage to business reputation from a defamatory statement might be very difficult and prevent a defamed corporation from vindicating their reputation[682].

---

677 Franklin & Bussel, footnote 140. For example, in a misrepresentation lawsuit in the US, the plaintiff must prove that the representation was false. Many tax laws in the US require negative proof. For example – a taxpayer claiming deduction for travel expenses must prove that the expenses were not personal in nature. In a claim for breach of contract due to non-performance, the plaintiff must prove that the defendant did not perform the obligation. Some of the examples are arguable. For instance, proving that expenses were not personal for the purpose of tax deductions is often done by positively proving that the expenses were for business purposes.

678 ***Goodwin***, *supra* note 517.

679 ***Financial Times LTD & Others v. Interbrew SA***, [2002] EWCA Civ 274.

680 ***Financial Times LTD & Others v. Interbrew SA***, opinion of LJ Sedley, para. 56.

681 Gatley, 231.

682 Gatley, 208. See for example the discussion in ***Jameel appeal***, §103-§113.

Damages are in the domain of the jury and are "at large" in the sense that there is no objective arithmetic for them[683]. In England, monetary compensation is almost the only remedy for defamation[684]. English courts may not order the defendant to apologize or publish a correction. An exception to that is the summary procedure introduced in the Defamation Act 1996, which allows a maximum compensation of 10,000 pounds but the court may also order an apology or a correction and if the parties cannot agree on the timing, content and size of the correction the court can order the publication of its verdict instead[685].

3. Germany

Similarly to Anglo-American jurisdictions, German law is no stranger to the possible collisions between freedom of speech, freedom of the press and the public's right to information on the one hand, and personality rights on the other hand[686].

Protection against defamation exists both in criminal and civil law in Germany. In the criminal process, §186 StGB (Üble Nachrede) and §187 StGB (Verleumdung) deal with factual defamatory statements while §185 (Beleidigung) concerns opinion (Werturteil)[687].

Defamation torts are derived from the BGB which protects any intentional and negligent violation of personality rights. The tort protects corporate entities since personality rights are applicable to legal entities to the extent that they are relevant[688]. The corporate entity has a right to a sphere of secrecy, a sphere of privacy (but not intimacy) and to informational self-determination[689]. Public law entities such as government corporations are an exception and do not have personality right protection for defamation[690].

A corporation can sue through §823 BGB, and also through §826 BGB for damages from business criticism when the publisher knew or should have known the statements were incorrect[691]. The injured corporation must prove that the publication had caused business damage, such as a loss of business contracts[692].

Section §824 BGB and the related literature discuss defamatory statements by competitors and their compensation. While I only briefly discuss §824 BGB in this analysis, note that a factual critique targeted at one specific corporation which harms its competitive stand in a market can also give rise to a claim under §824 BGB[693]. Through §252 BGB the firm can

683 Gatley, 233.
684 Gatley, 228.
685 Gatley, 229.
686 Fechner, 46-47.
687 Fechner, 78.
688 **Planadt Kommentar zum BGB** Buch 2 Ab. 8, §823; Prinz, 123-124; For example, BGH NJW 1986, 2951 (BMW); BGH NJW1994, 1281 (Jahresabschluss) – the last case concerned the further dissemination of the publicly-open annual reports of a building company as an example in training classes to bankers and auditors without erasing the name of the company. The court held that the company has the right to prevent further dissemination of its reports even when they are open to the public.
689 Prinz, 124-125.
690 BVerfG NJW 1967, 1411.
691 Münchener Kommentar, 195.
692 Münchener Kommentar, 195; BGHZ NJW 1984, 1607, 1608 (Deutsche Bahn case).
693 Münchener Kommentar, 197.

also sue for lost profits - which can be calculated on the basis of average prior earnings. Corporations cannot sue for compensation of pain and suffering (Schmertzgeld).

Initially, the BGH required that critique of corporations, protected under the right to free expression, be objectively justified, in form as well as in content[694]. The BGH later changed this position following the constitutional court's opinion about the balancing of constitutional rights versus general civil law rights[695]. The ***Münchener Kommentar*** now suggests that the right to free expression allows too wide a freedom to criticize corporate entities, as the BGH ruled that freedom of expression in matters of public importance may outweigh commercial interests, as protected by the BGB[696].

German law differs from its Anglo-American counterparts by the variety of civil remedies that are prescribed by law. An injury of a personality right by the press can be remedied by the following civil remedies[697]:

1. Right of reply (Gegendarstellung)[698] – the right of the injured party to reply to a publication is also based on the protection of personality rights[699]. It exists in all German state press laws. It is perceived to be a weaker right compared to the right to a correction or retraction (which will be discussed below) since the press may distance itself from the reply by adding that the reply is printed under the order of the court. The demand for a reply must be made within three months of the publication. Remarkably, the question whether the content of the reply is true or false is insignificant. However, in court, a legal action in demand for the right of reply can be rejected only if the reporter can prove that the allegedly defamatory statement is true or - conversely - if the reporter can prove that the reply is false[700].

2. Correction & retraction (Widerruf)[701] – this is a strong remedy which requires the reporter to retract or correct the factual publication. This action was developed in the civil law (§1004 1 BGB with §823 BGB) and applies to factual information. Since this action has serious consequences for the injuring party, the burden of proving the falsity of the information is on the plaintiff, and the factual falsity must be proven with high probability. Widerruf does not rule out the possibility of suing for monetary compensation. The reason is that the initial impact of the false publication might never be entirely erased by the correction

---

694 Münchener Kommentar , 196; BGHZ NJW 1952, 660, 661- (Constanze case) – the case acknowledged the possibility of protecting corporations through the constitutional personal right to reputation, but noted that the protection to reputation (honour, in fact) must be balanced against the justification of the publication.

695 BVerfGE 7, 198, in NJW 1958, 257 (Lüth case) – balancing the right to freedom of expression under §5 of the basic laws (a call to boycott a film) against a tort claim under §826 BGB.

696 Münchener Kommentar, 196; BGHZ NJW 1966, 1617 (Höllenfeuer case), 1618; BGHZ NJW 1962, 32, 34 (Waffenhändler case).

697 The following is based on Fechner, 84-103.

698 Fechner, 87-90.

699 BVerfG, 63, 131.

700 The rule applies only to factual statements which can be proven. For example, the statement "the manager is incapable of understanding the balance sheet" might not be a provable factual statement. However, the statement "the manager has not done a thing to promote the deal" has been interpreted by the constitutional court to be a factual statement which requires proof that the manager did "too little" or "not enough". See Fechner, 89; BVerfG decision 825/99 from 17.9.2003 (Fussballverein case).

701 Fechner, 91-95.

and the correction may not reach all the readers (in fact, some readers may hear about the initial publication only by reading the correction)[702].

In the event that the plaintiff has proven that the statement was false, the court can order a complete retraction. If the plaintiff has only proven on the balance of probabilities that the information is false and the defendant cannot prove that the statement is true - the court can order a partial retraction, where the defendant must announce that he does not uphold the defamatory claim[703]. The relative ease with which German courts shift the burden of proof applies here too: when negative facts are hard to prove, the burden is shifted to the press to prove the truthfulness of the claim. When the press does not meet the burden, the plaintiff prevails (§138 3 ZPO).

3. Damage compensation[704].

(1) Defamation damages can be sued for through §823 1 BGB[705] and §823 2 BGB with §186 StPO (restricted to factual statements). The burden of proving truthfulness is on the defendant. The defendant can avoid liability even when untrue information is published when the publication served "justified public interests" (according to §193 StGB) and a due level of journalistic care can be proven.

Section §823 1 BGB protects any injury to the value of the firm, including reputation injuries to the name of the firm or other spill-over effects[706]. Although this is a "basket" norm, it is interpreted strictly. For example, it requires that the injury would be to the specific business that the firm is pursuing, concrete damage must be shown and so on[707]. A general critique of a product that is manufactured by several companies will be protected from tort liability. Similarly, a comparative critique of branches will not create liability[708].

Section §823 1 BGB can also protect the corporation when true information is published, such as the publication of a frivolous bankruptcy proceeding[709]. The statement must directly apply to a business interest of the specific corporation[710].

(2) Defamation lawsuits can also be filed via §824 BGB (Kreditgefährdung, credit endangerment) which excludes the use of §823 1 BGB but not the claim through breach of personality right. Section §824 BGB protects financial reputation from factually untrue statements that harms or disadvantages the value of the business. The injurious statement can also be a rumour, a speculation or a question[711]. The damage should be specifically proven[712]. The plaintiff bears the burden of proving falsity[713]. The purpose of this section is not to privilege negligent publishers. If the plaintiff has proven that the information was false, the defendant can only protect himself by proving that he has taken the due level of care. This

702 Fechner, 93. A correction does mitigate the damage.
703 Bruns, 289-290.
704 Fechner, 95-101.
705 Prinz, 163.
706 Löffler/Ricker, 354.
707 Löffler/Ricker, 355.
708 OLG Hamburg NJW 1988, 3211 (a consumer organisation's publication about the comparative usage of sugar by producers was allowed) and OLG Köln NJW 1985, 1613 cited in Löffler/Ricker, 353.
709 Prinz, 167.
710 Prinz, 168.
711 Löffler/Ricker, 352.
712 Löffler/Ricker, 353-354.
713 Prinz, 146.

will allow him to avoid monetary liability, but does not necessarily imply that correction cannot be required[714].

(3) Another option is §826 BGB which protects against deliberate immoral damage. This is interpreted dynamically and therefore may apply as a "basket" norm as well[715]. An example would be when the press joins a campaign to boycott a specific firm[716].

(4) The law governing fair competition (UWG) can be used when the statement is attributed to a person who, in accordance with this law, harmed the fair competition in the market by the statement[717].

Monetary remedies through §§823 1, 2 BGB (with §186 and §187 StGB), §824 BGB, §826 BGB, require damage and causal relation[718]. It seems that the BGH prefers that monetary liability be the last resort in defamation cases, in the absence of other means of resolution. When inflicting monetary liability on the media the need to maintain the freedom of the press is also taken into consideration by the BGH[719]. Since the monetary sanction is correctly perceived by the BGH to have a deterrence effect on publications, the BGH tries to apply this sanction only where it supposes that such an aim is clearly desirable[720].

German law also contains prior restraint norms which are beyond the scope of this discussion. Omission (Unterlassung) is possible when a potentially injured party learns about a future publication. The plaintiff must prove the future statement is false. If the statement is too general and proving the negative is too difficult, the burden of proof is shifted to the reporter. Revealing confidential sources is not required (§1004 abs, 1 BGB with §823 BGB)[721].

3.1 The Burden of Proof

The focus here will be on the burden of proof in lawsuits where the requested remedy is monetary compensation for defamation. In this area, German law and English law are similar. The burden of proof in criminal law (§186 StGB) is on the reporter to show that the information is true[722], since false factual statements do not contribute to public discussion, but rather hamper it[723]. In civil defamation, the burden of proof has also been shifted through §823 2 BGB to the defendant (the reporter) to prove that the kernel of his statement is true.

In 1998 the BGH introduced an innovative ruling, based on §193 StGB, concerning publications that are in matters of public discussion and deal with a public figure plaintiff which has himself put the matter in the public discussion[724]. In such cases, the plaintiff must prove falsity and the defendant can escape liability - even if the factual information was false - if the publication concerned "justified interests" (Wahrnehmung berichtigter Interessen) and

714 Prinz, 152; BGH NJW 1989, 1923 (Warentest).
715 Löffler/Ricker, 359.
716 Example given in Löffler/Ricker, 360.
717 Prinz, 188-221.
718 Prinz, 479-482.
719 Prinz, 492; BGH NJW 1995, 861 (Carolin von Monaco 1).
720 For example, the protection of privacy rights: BGH NJW 1996, 284 (Carolin von Monaco 2).
721 Fechner, 85-86.
722 Münchener Kommentar, 135. BGH NJW 1996, 1131, 1133 (Lohnkiller case).
723 Münchener Kommentar, 197, citing a list of constitutional court decisions.
724 Kübler, 1287; BGH NJW 1998, 3047, 3049.

due care has been observed in the process of verifying the information[725]. This is only available for injuries under §823 2 BGB and §186 StPO concerning factual information and not to injuries of personality rights through §823 1 BGB[726].

The court has recognized some justified interests, for example: organised crime[727], environmental protection[728], illegal fur imports[729] and so on. It seems that the standard of care required from the reporters is the professional ethical standard. Reporters must abide by their ethical standards when disseminating information, check their information, especially when taking a one-sided position, and not rely on sources without verification[730]. Sources have no obligation to verify the information they provide to the press (but they may be liable for providing knowingly false or misrepresented information)[731].

The courts try to take into consideration the press's role in collecting information and promoting freedom of expression when dealing with the press' standard of due care[732]. The media's professional duty of care is to ensure that reported facts are true[733]. This need not reach the level of search for truth employed by judges[734]. However, the level of due care in verification increases with the value of the information[735]. For the injured: the more important the information is to the public the less weight is attached to any personality right breach that has occurred. The converse also applies: the less important the interests of the public in the information the more weight attached to the harmed interest of the injured plaintiff[736]. The standard of care may be reduced if there is a public interest in an immediate publication and when the subject of the publication has put themselves into the public discussion[737]. Since the media is also liable for the act of dissemination, the media will be liable also for statements by third persons that it has not verified and not distanced or qualified[738]. The duty of care is comprised of the scope of research[739] which increases with the harshness of the injury, the effort to find the truth, and the reliability of the sources[740]. The level of care can take into consideration the fact that the press might work under time

725 Münchener Kommentar, 136 and 197; Prinz, 138, 227, 233; BGH NJW 1987, 2225; BGH NJW 1985, 1621 (Türkol); BGHZ NJW 1984, 1607,1610 (Deutsche Bahn case). This seems to include the evaluation of the source of information and the validity of the content of the information itself - BGH NJW 1993, 525 (Mafia case) – concerning the leak of an internal letter within a bank describing a client firm as involved in illegal activities (the case concerned the obligation of the bank to verify the information when the letter was primarily intended for internal use).

726 Prinz, 228.

727 BGH NJW 1996, 1311 (Lohnkiller).

728 BGH NJW1987, 2225.

729 BGH NJW 1993, 930.

730 Bamberger/Roth, 33.

731 Bamberger/Roth, 36; BGH NJW 1973, 1460; BGH NJW 1964, 1181 – the cases concern liability of the press and its sources for information about products of business competitors. In this case, the legal action is based on §824 BGB and the burden of proof is on the injured party to prove that the information is false, unlike the burden in §823 BGB and §186 StGB. See Bamberger/Roth, 48.

732 Bamberger/Roth, 34.

733 Fechner, 219.

734 Prinz, 251; BGH NJW 1987, 2225.

735 Prinz, 231. BVerfg decision from 23.8.2003 (concerning a stylist's comment in a press agency interview about Kanzler Gerhard Schröder's hair color).

736 Prinz, 230; BGH NJW 1996, 1311 (Lohnkiller).

737 Münchener Kommentar, 136; BGH NJW 1998, 3047, 3049 (Stolpe case); NJW 1993, 525, 527 (Mafia case).

738 Prinz, 251.

739 Prinz, 252; BGH NJW 1996, 1311 (Lohnkiller) – one source which was not confirmed – not sufficient.

740 Prinz, 254.

pressures[741]. However, when a report that might injure a personality right is not satisfactorily proven, the press is advised to avoid publishing identifying facts about the subject so as to not endanger its chances of receiving protection in court[742]. Time pressures may not excuse the need to conduct the research - unverified publications should be postponed[743].

As in England, reporters are not compelled to disclose sources in order to prove the truth of their statement. However, they may need to explain in the publication to what extent the confidential sources are reliable, or they may be required to so in court in a general way[744]. If the explanation is insufficient, a reporter may eventually be obliged to choose between disclosure or liability.

3.2 Damages

The use of monetary sanctions distinguishes the US and England from the German system which prefers a wide palette of remedies and rejects excessively high monetary fines. Monetary liability is almost the exclusive sanction in the US and highly prevalent in the UK.

German law has always been careful not to introduce excessive (and punitive) damages in defamation as a deterrence mechanism[745]. Damages focus on restitution and can be mitigated by such measures as the right of reply or retraction[746]. The level of damages awarded in Germany is significantly lower than that awarded in the US, although it is increasing[747]. ***Prinz*** shows that German courts have recently opened the door for deterrence justifications in the calculation of damages for strong breaches of the sphere of intimacy and personality rights of individuals. This is especially true in sensational publications which create profit to the publishers through higher sales[748].

Generally, the determinants of the level of damages include the solvency of the plaintiff, the solvency of the media defendant, the strength and extent of the injury, the level of blame on the part of the defendant, the type of medium used and the subsequent effect on public opinion[749]. Data is scarce. The upper limit of monetary sanctions for private claimants has been around 100,000 Euro[750]. Corporations, unlike individuals, cannot sue for pain and suffering, but may suffer deeper financial damages than individuals. Courts are instructed that damages should not lead to the insolvency of the media-defendant - a consideration unique to the German legal system. However, courts acknowledge that financial difficulty cannot be an excuse to completely exempt the injurer from financial liability[751].

---

741 Fechner, 220.

742 Fechner, 220; BVerfG NJW 1963, 904.

743 Prinz, 258; BGH NJW 1997, 1148.

744 Münchener Kommentar, 134.

745 Prinz (1996), 954.

746 Prinz (1996), 955.

747 ***Bruns*** reports that until 2000 the highest damage award in Germany was DM100,000, equivalent roughly to €50,000. This is much lower than the million Dollar awards in the US. Bruns, 287.

748 Prinz (1996), 955, referring to decisions concerning Princess Carolin of Monaco. In one case the court specifically noted that the damages should inhibit future injurious publications. BGH NJW 1996, 984.

749 Prinz (1996), 954.

750 Prinz, 507-508.

751 Prinz (1996), 955. On consequence may be that media corporations would prefer to form a separate corporate entity for each medium.

4. Interim Summary

The previous parts have outlined the legal situations with regards to the reporter's privilege and the law of defamation in the US, England and Germany.

The privilege in Anglo-American law is qualified, and very uncertain, as a result of mixed interpretations by the courts. In the US an attempt to improve the situation by introducing shield laws in state legislation has done little to reduce uncertainty. In England, the privilege has been legislated, but the implementation of the statute remained in the hands of the courts.

The de-centralized nature of US state law makes it impossible to draw a clear picture of the law of the privilege in the US. In England, courts traditionally ruled against the media when balancing interests of freedom of the press against other interests of justice. However, the balance has been shifting in favour of the media since the incorporation of the European Convention on Human Rights into English law, and since the ECHR has intervened in the matter.

In contrast to the Anglo-American uncertainty, the German reporter's privilege is absolute and it is strongly supported by the courts since it is perceived to be supported by a constitutional foundation.

This chapter intends to focus on the role of the media in informing the public about wrongdoing in corporations. This kind of information is one of the tools that enable market players to monitor corporate compliance with the law. However, the publication of such information will oftentimes be countered by defamation lawsuits filed by the corporation that is the subject of the publication.

Defamation is a tort designed to protect reputation. All the jurisdictions surveyed here recognize the right of corporations to sue in order to vindicate their business reputation. Anglo-American jurisdictions do not require the plaintiff-corporation to prove that it had suffered monetary damage by the publication. Monetary compensation is the main remedy in Anglo-American law and the amount of compensation is determined by a jury. Damage awards are often high, especially in the US.

In Germany, non-monetary remedies like retractions and corrections are preferred by the courts. However, the choice of the remedy is initially in the hands of the plaintiff. The firm can choose to claim monetary compensation or a non-monetary redress. If the plaintiff pursues the monetary remedy, then unlike in the Anglo-American systems, it must prove the monetary harm caused by the publication.

As shall be shown in detail below, the value of the reporter's privilege in defamation lawsuits depends on the distribution of the burden of proof in trial. On this issue, American and English laws are pitted against each other. In England, the defendant (the reporter) must initially prove that the publication is true for the trial to proceed, or else he would be found liable. Since this distribution of the burden of proof is cumbersome for the media defendants, recent developments in case law have been introduced in order to encourage publication of public interest information: the reporter can prove that the publication concerned a matter of public interest and that the information was collected through the use of due care ("responsible journalism") and thereby escape liability. Nevertheless, sometimes proving either one of the defences will require the reporter to disclose his confidential sources. Hence, in English law the reporter faces the dilemma: revealing the source or being found liable.

In the US, the burden of proof has been reversed. The plaintiff (the firm) must first prove that the publication for which it is claiming compensation is false in order for the lawsuit to proceed. Only if the court is convinced by the firm's initial showing, then the reporter faces the source revelation dilemma mentioned above.

In German law, the distribution of the burden of proof depends on the remedy sought by the plaintiff. If the firm sues for monetary compensation – the traditional English Rule applies. If the firm sues for non-monetary remedies – the American Rule applies.

Notably, in Germany, when the English Rule is applied, the courts have also developed an easier alternative for the defendant. As in the English alternative, the reporter is asked to prove that the information was of public interest and that responsible journalism was employed.

The conflict between the English Rule and the American Rule does not remain in the realm of pure theory. In fact, it generates legal hostility between the US and England. In at least one case, a US court refused to recognize an English defamation judgement in favour of a plaintiff, and held that recognizing it would be unconstitutional. The court said: "It is true the England and the United States share many common law principles of law. Nevertheless, a significant difference between these two jurisdictions lies in England's lack of an equivalent to the First Amendment to the United States Constitution. The protection of free speech and the press embodied in the amendment would be seriously jeopardized by the entry of foreign libel judgements granted pursuant to standards deemed appropriate in England but considered antithetical to the protection afforded the press by the U.S. Constitution"[752].

Since the American and the English Rules are strictly opposed to each other, the question which if the two rules is more efficient could be answered by modelling the interaction of the court players under the two rules. This will be done in the next part.

---

752 ***Bachchan v. India Abroad Publications Inc.***, 154 Misc.2d 228, 235 (N.Y., 1992).

IV Modelling Reporter's Privilege in Defamation Lawsuits[753]

In defamation lawsuits, what the privilege means in reality turns significantly on the burden of proof.

We consider the case of claims for monetary compensation. In many cases, it will be difficult to prove whether a published statement is correct or not without questioning the source which has provided the information. Furthermore, it will be difficult for the reporter to prove that he has taken due care without revealing his source. Hence, under the English (and German) Rule[754], the reporter will often risk being found liable and paying damages if he refuses to reveal his source. By contrast, under the American Rule, the plaintiff will often find it difficult to prove that a statement is false, so that the reporter might escape liability without revealing his source.

As discussed earlier, a more comprehensive comparative examination of the law shows that the two systems are somewhat closer to each other than it initially seems. The reasons are first, because plaintiffs in the US are entitled to substantial pre-trial discovery. Secondly, court decisions vary considerably between the different state jurisdictions in the US. Nevertheless, the allocation of the burden of proof is an important difference between the two systems and the level of abstraction used for the purpose of this model captures the essential difference between the two contradicting approaches.

The model considers information relevant for capital markets and the assumption is that the information is about some wrongdoing within a firm. Social costs arise whenever true stories are either not published at all, or if the court mistakenly rules to withdraw or compensate for the correct information, or if the court (and hence the capital market) takes some false information to be correct. The court can choose between applying the American Rule or the English Rule. The court also decides about damages to award under either rule. Courts face some uncertainty about the private benefits and costs of the source which means that courts need to apply the same liability rule to different cases. This uncertainty is required since if courts were able to design a liability rule on a case by case basis and face no uncertainty, there would be no problem at all. Then, a source decides about leaking information. Assume that the source knows perfectly whether the story is true or not. If the story is leaked, the reporter publishes the story, and the firm concerned sues for defamation.

In the following stage, the allocation of the burden proof becomes important. This is modelled in the simplest feasible way by assuming that, under the English Rule, the court never believes the reporter if he does not reveal his source. Revealing the source is thus the only way to avoid liability, but the reporter might nevertheless keep his secret because of the reputational consequences of divulging the source. Conversely, under the American Rule, the firm needs to move first, and if it does not offer satisfying evidence about the falsity of the information, then the court believes the reporter even though he does not reveal his source. Afterwards, the firm (under the English Rule) or the reporter (under the American Rule) may present additional evidence to make the court change its mind.

---

753 This model has been developed jointly with Prof. Dr. Eberhard Feess and Dr. Ansgar Wohlschlegel, both from RWTH (Aachen).

754 The English rule is also the German rule in defamation lawsuits seeking monetary compensation. Since the issue in legal literature has focused on the difference between English and American rules, we abide by the traditional names.

The focus is on the source's incentives to leak and on the reporter's incentives to reveal the source in a defamation suit. If the court induces the reporter to reveal his source, this has two advantages: (1) the court gets additional information which increases its probability of reaching a correct decision, and (2) sources having false stories may be deterred from leaking. In fact, a separating equilibrium where only true stories are leaked requires that sources be revealed in the courtroom with positive probability as otherwise all sources can leak at no risk. On the other hand, revelation may also discourage sources with true stories.

Though the basic trade-off always exists, the way it operates is quite different under the two rules. Since the English Rule imposes the burden of proof on the reporter, it bears a higher risk that true stories are not published at all or withdrawn in the courtroom (type I error). By contrast, the American Rule is *ceteris paribus* more likely to uphold even wrong stories (type II errors). The two rules are analyzed and compared in three respects:

(1) First, the impact of different parameters on the optimality of damages is considered. The finding then is that, under the American Rule, high damages which induce the reporter to reveal all sources are optimal if the (ex ante) number of true stories is high and the quality of the court (defined as the capability to distinguish between true and false stories for a given degree of information) is low. The opposite holds under the English Rule - high damages should be awarded if the number of true stories is low and if the court's quality is high.

(2) Secondly, the rules for given separating or pooling equilibria are compared. In a separating equilibrium where only true stories are leaked under both rules, the American Rule is superior. The reason is that only type I errors matter in a separating equilibrium, and these are more likely under the English Rule. In a pooling equilibrium with revelation, the American Rule is superior if and only if the ex-ante probability for true stories is high because, the higher this probability, the more important are type I errors compared to type II errors. Finally, in a pooling equilibrium without revelation of sources, the American Rule is again superior if the ex-ante probability for a true stories is high, and if the court's quality is high.

(3) Then, a comparison is made with respect to the optimality of the two rules for different realizations of the source's private benefits and costs when damages are ex-ante optimally chosen under both rules. The most clear-cut result is then that the American Rule is weakly superior, regardless of the ex-ante probability that the story is true, whenever the source's private benefit from leaking is sufficiently small. If the private benefits from leaking are high, the American Rule may still be superior if the ex-ante probability for true stories is neither too high nor too low.

1. The Model

The model consists of four players: a court designing and enforcing a liability rule for defamation, a source who may either possess a true or a false story, a reporter who publishes the story and decides whether to protect the source or not, and a firm which may sue the reporter for defamation. The information structure and the decisions are as follows.

Source. By a source, we mean someone deciding about whether to leak a true or a false story. With prior probability θ, the source has a true story, and with $(1-\theta)$ the content of story is false. θ is common knowledge, but whether the particular story is true is the private information of the source and the firm. The source's benefit from leakage is α. If the source is disclosed in the courtroom, and if the court rules that the reporter has to withdraw a published story (and pay damages), then the source has private costs S regardless of whether the story is true or not. One may think of S as the formal or informal sanction of the firm against the source. For example, S could represent the cost of losing a job or a promotion opportunity.

Define $x = (\alpha/S)$ as the ratio between the source's private benefits and (expected) costs. Assume that x is known by all players except the court who only knows that $x \in (\hat{x}, \check{x})$ is distributed with $f(x)$. This assumption is required to exclude that the court can perfectly tailor a liability rule to each particular case at hand[755].

Reporter. In order to focus on the right to confidentiality, assume that all leaked stories are published. Thus, the reporter's only decision is whether to reveal the source in the courtroom. Revealing the source causes reputation loss L, but it may reduce the probability of being held liable. Damages are denoted *d*.

Firm. The firm knows whether the story is true or not. Assume that the firm always sues, even if the information is true[756]. Social costs of $(v = 1)$ arise whenever the capital market gets wrong information. This is the case if a true story is not published at all or mistakenly considered to be false by the court, and if a wrong story is upheld in the courtroom. When designing the liability rule, the court's objective is to maximize the probability that the market gets correct information[757].

Court. The objective of the court is to set the damages in a way that maximizes the probability that correct information will be leaked. However, the court has imperfect information with respect to the facts of the case. Assume that when only *one* party (the firm or the reporter) presents evidence in court, then the court will reach the correct decision with probability q. If the opposing party also presents evidence then the assumption is that the court will never change a correct decision, but if the court had reached a wrong decision in the previous stage then after observing the additional evidence it will reach a correct decision, again, with probability q. Hence, the probability q is a measure for the court's quality[758]. Note that the only way in which a reporter can present evidence is by revealing the identity of the source.

Under the American Rule, the burden of proof is imposed on the firm which moves first and presents its evidence. The court then comes to a correct decision with probability $q > ½$ and errs with probability $(1 - q)$. If the court does not believe the firm, the game ends. If the court believes the firm, the reporter may present his own evidence to make the court change

755 The assumption is crucial for the knowledge of the court. It creates a realistic uncertainty with respect to what the court knows about the expected gains and sanctions of the confidential source. Since the court can observe the corporation from which the information was leaked and the nature of the information that was leaked it might have some general idea of the gains that s ource might expect to have and of the sanctions that will be imposed on him in case he is revealed. But these parameters are not observed with perfect certainty and this is captured in the assumptions about x.

756 Since there is always a probability that the court will believe the firm and not the reporter, when the cost of filing a lawsuit is sufficiently low such that expected damages are higher than the the cost of suing, it makes sense for the firm to sue regardless of whether the information is true or false.

757 Taking L and x into account does not yield interesting insights.

758 The court's quality is the ability of the court to reach a correct decision.

its mind[759]. The assumption is that the reporter can only do so by revealing the source. The court will then change a wrong decision with probability q, if the publication is true.

Under the English Rule, the burden of proof is allocated to the reporter. Thus, he will be held liable if he refuses to reveal the source and the game ends there. If the reporter reveals, the court again comes to a correct decision with probability $q > ½$. If the court does not believe the reporter or if the court believes a true story, the game ends. If the court has mistakenly believed the reporter (the story is false), the firm discloses, and the court will revise the wrong decision with probability q.

A type I error occurs if, in the end, a court takes a correct story for a wrong one, and a type II error occurs if the court mistakenly believes a wrong story.

Timing under the two legal rules. At stage 1, players learn their private information as described above. At stage 2, the source decides upon leaking, which - in this model - implies that the story is published. From then on, the timing depends on the legal rule.

Under the American Rule, the firm moves first and discloses (stage 3). At stage 4, the court comes to a correct conclusion with probability q. If the court believes the firm, the reporter decides about revelation (stage 5). If so, the court will revise a wrong decision with probability q (stage 6), and enforce the liability rule. Under the English Rule, the revelation decisions of the firm and the reporter are reversed with the difference that the reporter will not always reveal (while the firm always discloses).

759 There is an implicit assumption here that the reporter knows the decision of the court after the firm has presented its evidence. This is not unrealistic. First of all, judges in common law often make comments from which parties can infer the court's impression on the case. But mainly, the second mover can ask the court to rule that the plaintiff did not substantiate its case and that it should be rejected on the merits. If the court rejects such a motion, the second mover knows that he must present contradicting evidence in order to prevail. This is essentially the procedure called "request for summary judgement". In German civil procedure things are simpler since the judge will often indicate to a party that it has not presented sufficient evidence to support its case before handing down the decision.

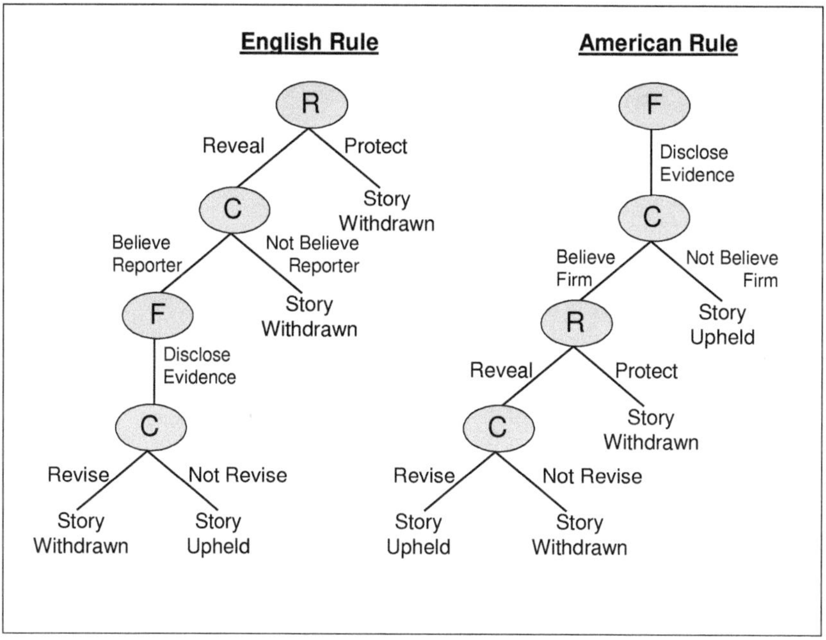

Figure 11: Extensive Form of Stages 3-5. Timing under the American and English Rules

The game is now solved by backwards induction and a Perfect Bayesian Equilibrium (PBE) is applied as the solution concept. As an equilibrium selection concept, assume that a separating equilibrium will be played whenever it exists.

1.1 The American Rule

1.1.1 Judicial Errors

The firm moves first under the American Rule. If the story is true and the firm sues for defamation, the court will mistakenly believe that the story is wrong with probability (1–q). If the reporter then decides to protect the source the court makes a type I error. If the reporter reveals the source, the court revises its wrong decision with probability q, so that the overall probability for a type I error in this case is $(1-q)^2$. Hence, a type I error occurs with probability (1–q) if the reporter protects the source, and with probability $(1-q)^2$ if he reveals the source. Therefore, the difference between (1–q) and $(1-q)^2$ represents the social welfare benefit of revealing the source if a true story has been published.

If the story is false, the court will mistakenly not believe the evidence presented by the firm with probability (1–q). Then, the reporter never reveals, as the court already believes him, and a type II error thus always occurs with probability (1–q). It is important to understand that under the American Rule, if the court errs and mistakenly believes the firm that the story is wrong, then the reporter can still correct the decision by revealing the source and a type I error can be avoided. However, if the court mistakenly does not believe the firm that the story is wrong then the game ends. This is not an artefact of the model - this is a result of the American Rule on the allocation of the burden of proof.

1.1.2 The Reporter's Revelation Decision

If the court believes the firm, the reporter will always be liable if he protects the source. If he reveals the source, he incurs the reputation loss L, but escapes liability with probability q if the story is true, and with (1–q) if it is false. In a PBE, the reporter's beliefs on whether the story is true are consistent with the source's equilibrium play. Hence, in a separating equilibrium, the reporter knows that he will escape liability with probability q and thus reveals if and only if[760]:

$$d^A > \frac{L}{q}$$

In a pooling equilibrium, where all stories are leaked regardless of whether they are true or false, the fact that the court believes the firm is used by the reporter to update the prior probability of having a true story θ. This yields a conditional probability for true stories of

$$\tilde{\theta} = \frac{(1-q)\theta}{(1-q)\theta + q(1-\theta)}$$

so that the reporter reveals the source in a pooling equilibrium if and only if

$$d^A > \frac{L[(1-q)\theta + q(1-\theta)]}{q\theta(1-q)}. \qquad \textbf{Inequality [1]}$$

Since

$$\frac{L[(1-q)\theta + q(1-\theta)]}{q\theta(1-q)} > \frac{L}{q},$$

the reporter's incentive to reveal the source is higher in a separating equilibrium because the probability that the court believes him is higher if only true stories are leaked and published.

---

760 The liability payments will be denoted by d^i with $i \in \{A,E\}$. The superscripts A and E represent the American and English Rules.

1.1.3 The Source's Decision

If the reporter protects the source in equilibrium, then the source will always choose to leak. Note that sources having a true story are sanctioned if the reporter reveals and the court makes a type I error, while sources having wrong stories are sanctioned if the reporter reveals and the court does not make a type II error. This means that the probability of the source being sanctioned if the story is true is $(1-q)^2$ and if the story is false, the probability of being sanctioned is q. Therefore, true stories are leaked if and only if $x > (1-q)^2$ and wrong stories are leaked if and only if $x > q$.

1.1.4 Equilibria

Depending on various parameters and the court's choice of damages d^A, there are four possible equilibria:

1. **No Publication (NP)**: if the reporter reveals the source at least in a separating equilibrium ($d^A > (L/q)$) and the source's benefit from leaking is too small compared to the expected sanction ($x \leq (1-q)^2$), then the source will not leak at all. In this case there will be no damage in the capital market from false stories, but true stories will not be published either. Expected social costs are then θ.

2. **Separating Equilibrium (SE)**: the reporter will reveal the source only when the court believes the firm and $d^A > (L/q)$. A source would want to tell true stories but not false ones, which means $(1-q)^2 < x \leq q$. In that case, a separating equilibrium arises where only true stories are published and the reporter always reveals the source if the court believes the firm. Again, there are no social costs from false stories. Given that the story is true, social costs arise if the court makes a type I error, which happens with probability $(1-q)^2$. Hence, expected social costs are $\theta(1-q)^2$.

3. **Pooling with Revelation (PR)**: for pooling with revelation to occur, the reporter must benefit from revealing the source even if the reporter does not know if the story is true. This happens when **inequality [1]** holds. This equilibrium also requires that the private benefits of the source are high ($x > q$) to ensure that sources leak both true and false stories regardless of the fact that they expect to be revealed with a high probability.

Since all stories are published, true stories impose social costs if the court makes a type I error (probability $(1-q)^2$), and false stories impose social costs if a type II error occurs (probability $(1-q)$). Hence, expected social costs are $\theta(1-q)^2 + (1-\theta)(1-q)$.

4. **Pooling with Protection (PP)**: this equilibrium requires that damages are so low that the reporter never reveals the source. This requires that **Inequality [1]** does *not* hold. Since the reporter will never reveal the source, all stories are leaked. Since the court only receives evidence from the firm, the probability of a judicial error is $(1-q)$ for both true and false stories. Hence, expected social costs are $\theta(1-q) + (1-\theta)(1-q) = (1-q)$.

The occurrence of equilibria and the associated social costs is summarized in the following table. For expositional clarity, we denote high levels of damage in the American Rule

$$d^A > \frac{L[(1-q)\theta + q(1-\theta)]}{q\theta(1-q)} \text{ by } d^{A(H)}.$$

Intermediate damages in the American Rule are denoted

$$\frac{L[(1-q)\theta + q(1-\theta)]}{q\theta(1-q)} \geq d^A > \frac{L}{q} \text{ by } d^{A(M)}$$

and low damages $d^A \leq (L/q)$ are denoted by $d^{A(L)}$.

	$x \leq (1-q)^2$	$(1-q)^2 < x \leq q$	$x > q$
$d^{A(H)}$	NP: θ	SE: $\theta(1-q)^2$	PR: $\theta(1-q)^2+(1-\theta)(1-q)$
$d^{A(M)}$	PP: $1-q$	SE: $\theta(1-q)^2$	PP: $1-q$
$d^{A(L)}$	PP: $1-q$	PP: $1-q$	PP: $1-q$

Table 4: Equilibria and Social Costs under the American Rule

Observe for example, the second column in the table above, where the benefits of the source from leaking are intermediate ($(1-q)^2 < x \leq q$). This means that *if* the reporter will reveal the source on the equilibrium path, then only sources having true stories will be willing to leak in the first place. This happens when the damages imposed on the reporter are high or intermediate (first and second rows). Therefore, a separating equilibrium is created in the first and second rows of the second column. In the third row, $d^{A(L)}$, damages are so low that the reporter will be willing to pay the liability payment and not reveal the source even when he knows that the story is true and that revealing the source will increase the probability of avoiding the payment. In such a case pooling with protection occurs since all sources are protected and therefore all are willing to leak.

Note that the claimed occurrence of a separating equilibrium for intermediate $d^{A(M)}$ and x is due to the assumption that a separating equilibrium will be played whenever it exists.

1.1.5 Optimal Damage Levels

The social costs in Table 4 are minimal for separating equilibria. Social costs for pooling with revelation are lower than pooling with protection. The social costs of other equilibria depend on the parameters.

Now observe, in Table 4, that low damages are weakly dominated by intermediate damage levels: when damages are low, the reporter always protects the source and therefore pooling with protection occurs under all variations of the source's benefit ratio x. When damages are intermediate, pooling with protection occurs whenever the private benefits of the sources induce them to behave in the same way. If x is high ($x > q$), both types of sources will leak, even the reporter will reveal the source. If x is low, $x < (1-q)^2$, both types of sources will *not* leak if the reporter reveals the source. Since by definition under intermediate damages the reporter does not reveal the source, pooling with protection is the equilibrium in these two cases. The only difference between $d^{A(L)}$ and $d^{A(M)}$ occurs when only true stories are leaked given that the reporter reveals the source (pooling with revelation) which occurs only for intermediate range of x under $d^{A(M)}$. Hence, intermediate damages, $d^{A(M)}$, weakly dominate low damages, $d^{A(L)}$ [761].

For the comparison of intermediate damages, $d^{A(M)}$, and high damages, $d^{A(H)}$, the court will decide based on expected social costs, as it only knows the probability distribution of x when deciding on the damage level. Denote the probabilities that x is high, intermediate and low by $p^{A(H)}$, $p^{A(M)}$ and $1-p^{A(H)}-p^{A(M)}$. Expected social costs for high damage levels are

$$SC^{A(H)} = p^{A(H)}\theta + p^{A(M)}\theta(1-q)^2 + (1-p^{A(H)}-p^{A(M)})(\theta(1-q)^2 + (1-\theta)(1-q)),$$

and for intermediate damage levels

$$SC^{A(M)} = p^{A(H)}(1-q) + p^{A(M)}\theta(1-q)^2 + (1-p^{A(H)}-p^{A(M)})(1-q).$$

High and intermediate damage levels are equivalent for intermediate levels of x, since in both cases we get a separating equilibrium.

For high x, high damages are superior: in both cases we have a pooling equilibrium where sources leak true and false information. However, whereas under intermediate damages the reporter never reveals the source and we get pooling with protection, under high damages the court gets more information because - given that sources leak - the reporter reveals the source. Under pooling with revelation the court receives more information and court errors decrease.

For low x, either rule may be superior: for high damages, even true stories are not leaked (leading to social costs of θ), whereas all stories are leaked for intermediate damages (leading to social costs whenever the court errs, hence to $(1-q)$).

To sum, when deciding on the damage level, the court trades-off getting more information in the pooling equilibrium with revelation under $d^{A(H)}$ for high x against the risk of discouraging the source from leaking in the first place for low x. Considering the impact of the relevant parameters, our results reinforce economic intuition that liability payments should be so high that the reporter always reveals his source after the court believes the firm's evidence (hence, $d^{A(H)}$) if:

(i) the probability for low private benefits from leakage is low compared to the firm's sanctioning potential (the $x = \alpha/S$ ratio). High damages are then optimal because only a few stories are discouraged.

(ii) the probability for true stories (θ) is low. High damages are then optimal because there are not many true stories that can be discouraged anyway.

(iii) the court's quality is low. High damages are then optimal because publishing true stories creates little gain for the capital market if the court errs very often.

---

761 And recall, intermediate damages imply that the probability of a one-step correct decision (q) times the liability should always be above the reporter's reputational loss ($qd^{A(M)} \geq L$) to induce that sources - where the reporter certainly knows that the story is true - are revealed.

If intermediate damages $d^{A(M)}$ are ever optimal, this will be when $\theta > (1-q)$ and $p^{A(H)}$ is sufficiently high.

1.2 The English Rule

1.2.1 Judicial Errors

If the reporter decides not to reveal the source, the court will always believe that the story is false, leading to a type I error with probability 1 and to a type II error with probability 0. If the reporter reveals his source, true stories are considered wrong then we have a type I error with probability (1–q) and the game ends. If the court is convinced that a false story is true then we have a type II error and the firm will disclose its evidence and the court revises its incorrect judgement with probability q. Hence, with revelation a type II error occurs with probability $(1-q)^2$.

1.2.2 The Reporter's Revelation Decision

In a separating equilibrium, the reporter knows that the story is true. If he reveals, he is only liable if the court makes a type I error, i.e. with probability (1–q). Hence, he reveals if

$$d^E > (L/q).$$

Since the reporter moves first, he cannot update his prior in a pooling equilibrium: his belief that the story is true remains θ. He will be liable if the story is true and the court makes a type I error, which happens with probability $\theta(1-q)$, or if the story is false and the court does not make a type II error, which happens with probability $(1-\theta)(1-(1-q)^2)$. To sum, the reporter reveals the source if and only if:

$$d^E > \frac{L}{1-\theta(1-q) - (1-\theta)(1-(1-q)^2)} > \frac{L}{q} \qquad \textbf{Inequality [2]}$$

1.2.3 The Source's Decision

The source will always leak if the reporter protects him. If the reporter reveals, the source will be sanctioned after telling a true story if the court makes a type I error. Hence, a source will tell a true story if and only if $x > (1-q)$. If the story is false, the source will be sanctioned if the court believes the reporter and then still believes the reporter even after the firm presents its evidence, hence, when the court does not make a type II error *twice*. Therefore, the source leaks if and only if $x > 1-(1-q)^2$.

1.2.4 Equilibria

As in the American Rule, there are four possible equilibria under the English Rule:

1. **No Publication** (**NP**): if the reporter reveals the source at least under a separating equilibrium, $d^E > (L/q)$, and the private benefits of the source are low compared to the probability of a type I error, $x \leq (1-q)$, no story will be published. As under the American Rule, social costs are θ.

2. **Separating Equilibrium** (**SE**): a separating equilibrium requires that the reporter reveals the source when he knows that the story is true, $d^E > (L/q)$, and that the private benefits of the source are such that only true stories are leaked, $(1-q) < x \leq 1-(1-q)^2$. Social costs arise if the story is true and the court makes a type I error, and are thus $\theta(1-q)$.

3. **Pooling with Revelation** (**PR**): if **inequality [2]** holds, the reporter reveals the source in a pooling equilibrium. Pooling requires that false stories are also leaked, so $x > 1-(1-q)^2$. Social costs arise when the story is true but the court does not believe the reporter (type I error). If the opposite is true and the court believes a false story, there is a possibility of correcting this mistake after the firm introduces its evidence. Hence, the risk of a type I error is higher than the risk of a type II error. This is the gist of the difference between the American and the English Rules, as discussed below. Social costs are the total probability of judicial errors, $\theta(1-q) + (1-\theta)(1-q)^2$.

4. **Pooling with Protection** (**PP**): if damages are so low (**inequality [2]** does not hold) that the reporter always protect the source, sources will always leak. The court will never believe the reporter, so that social costs are θ. This represents a unique aspect of the English Rule: since neither the firm nor the reporter ever discloses their evidence, if damages are low, a high number of stories will be published but their informational value will be negligible.

The following table summarizes:

	$x \leq (1-q)$	$(1-q) < x \leq 1-(1-q)^2$	$x > 1-(1-q)^2$
$d^{E(H)}$	NP: θ	SE: $\theta(1-q)$	PR: $\theta(1-q) + (1-\theta)(1-q)^2$
$d^{E(M)}$	PP: θ	SE: $\theta(1-q)$	PP: θ
$d^{E(L)}$	PP: θ	PP: θ	PP: θ

Table 5: Equilibria and Social Costs under the English Rule

1.2.5 Optimal Damage Levels

According to the same reasoning as the American Rule, low damage levels are dominated by intermediate ones. However now, intermediate and high damage levels are equivalent unless the private benefit of leakage is high, $x > 1-(1-q)^2$ (hence, in the first and second column). The reason is that under the English Rule it makes no difference if there are no publications (when x is low), or when there is pooling with protection, where both true and false stories are published but none of them is believed. Inspecting high levels of x (the third column), it follows that high and intermediate damage levels differ under the English Rule. High damages are now optimal if and only if:

$$\theta > \frac{(1-q)^2}{q + (1-q)^2} \quad . \qquad \textbf{Inequality [3]}$$

It is now possible to compare these findings to those obtained in the American Rule. Some important differences can be observed:

(i) In contrast to the American Rule, the decision between intermediate and high damage levels under the English Rule does not depend on the probabilities p^E that x is in a certain range. In other words, the private benefit and the firm's sanctioning potential have no impact on the optimal damages. The reason is that high and intermediate damages matter only for high x. For low and intermediate x the high and intermediate damage levels matter as to whether a story is published or not, but yield the same social welfare result.

(ii) High damages $d^{E(H)}$ tend to be superior if the ex-ante probability for true stories (θ) is high. This is in stark contrast to the American Rule. Under the English Rule, high damage levels with high x result in pooling with revelation (PR). Intermediate damages with high x result in pooling with protection (PP). Pooling with revelation is better if the story is true as otherwise the court never believes the reporter. However, if stories tend to be false, pooling without revelation (PP) is better, since then the court is more likely to reach the correct conclusion (i.e., that the story is false).

(iii) Again, contrary to the American Rule, high damages level $d^{E(H)}$ tends to be superior if the court's quality (q) is high. To see this, note that the right-hand side of the condition in **inequality [3]** is decreasing in q. Hence, the value of additional information in a pooling with revelation (which requires $d^{E(H)}$) increases with the court's ability to make use of the information.

In short, intermediate damages are desirable if the story is probably false (if θ is low) and the court's quality is low (q is low).

1.3 Comparison of Equilibria

Sections 1.1 and 1.2, showed that damages should be high under the American Rule if there are many false stories and if the court's capability to distinguish between true and false stories is low, while exactly the opposite holds under the English Rule. Furthermore, the private benefits and costs of leaking influence the optimal damage levels only under the American Rule. And furthermore, damages so low that sources are always protected should never be imposed under either one of the rules.

In this part, the two rules are further compared by looking at social costs given that particular equilibria are played[762]. Inspecting tables 1 and 2 shows:

762 However, it should be borne in mind that the different equilibria occur under different parameter constellations.

6. **No Publication** (NP): in this case social costs are identical under both rules since, $SC^{E(NP)} - SC^{A(NP)} = 0$.
7. **Separating Equilibrium** (SE): the American Rule strictly outperforms the English rule since $SC^{E(SE)} - SC^{A(SE)} = q\theta(1 - q) > 0$. The reason is that only type I errors matter since under SE wrong stories are not leaked and there are no type II errors. As shown, type I errors happen more often under the English Rule.
8. **Pooling Equilibrium with Revelation** (PR): $SC^{E(PR)} - SC^{A(PR)} = (1 - q)q(2\theta - 1)$. Hence, the American Rule is superior if and only if $\theta > ½$. Given revelation, the only difference between the two rules is that the firm moves first under the American Rule while the reporter moves first under the English Rule. Since the game ends whenever the court's first assessment is in favour of the second mover, the situation is symmetric. Under the American Rule, the court makes less type I errors and under the English Rule the court makes less type II errors. Therefore, the American Rule is superior if the ex ante probability for true stories is high.
9. **Pooling Equilibrium with Protection** (PP): $SC^{E(PP)} - SC^{A(PP)} = \theta - (1 - q)$. The American Rule is superior if (θ) and court quality (q) are high. Under the English Rule, only type I errors are made as all defamation suits are successful. Hence, if θ is high, the English Rule tends to be inferior. Under the American Rule, the court decides only on the basis of the firm's evidence. Hence (q) is important and (θ) has no impact.

These results support the overall impression that the American Rule is weak and the English Rule is tough. Whenever the number of true stories published is high (in a separating equilibrium because only those stories are leaked and in a pooling equilibrium when θ is high) the American Rule tends to outperform the English Rule. But if θ is low, the main concern is to deter and detect false publications by setting up a tough rule, and this is achieved by the English Rule. Finally, the court's quality is more important under the American Rule (see the pooling with protection) because the firm's evidence matters more often.

1.4 The Optimal Rule

The former parts discussed under which circumstances high liability payments should be set by the court, and the rules were compared equilibrium by equilibrium. However, this comparison is incomplete, first of all because the court can only alter the *probabilities* that different equilibria are played as it does not know x with certainty. Secondly, there will be different probabilities for the equilibria under the American Rule and the English Rule depending on the court's choice of low ($d^{E(L)}$) or high ($d^{E(H)}$) damages. This is now taken into account.

As found in parts 1.1 and 1.2, damage levels in which sources are never revealed ($d^{A(L)}$ and $d^{E(L)}$) are dominated. Furthermore, intermediate damage levels can never be optimal under both rules at the same time. Under the American Rule intermediate damages can only be optimal when $\theta > 1 - q$ which contradicts **inequality [3]** which is the optimality condition for intermediate damages under the English Rule.

This given, we now rank the two rules when optimal damages are chosen under either rule in such a way that different equilibria arises for identical private costs and benefits of the source, as expressed by x.

First, it proves useful to rank the different cases with respect to the proportion of true stories:

- If θ is low, then $d^{E(M)}$ and $d^{A(H)}$ are optimal.
- If θ is intermediate (or if θ is high, but $p^{A(H)}$ is very low, then $d^{E(H)}$ and $d^{A(H)}$ are optimal.
- If θ and at the same time $p^{A(H)}$ are high, then $d^{E(H)}$ and $d^{A(M)}$ are optimal.

Given this, we can rank the ex-post optimality of the rules as a function of x (the results are derived from the appendix):

	$d^{E(M)} / d^{A(H)}$	$d^{E(H)} / d^{A(H)}$	$d^{E(H)} / d^{A(M)}$
$x < (1-q)^2$	Equivalent	Equivalent	American
$x \in [(1-q)^2, (1-q)]$	American	American	American
$x \in [(1-q), q]$	American	American	American
$x \in [q, 1-(1-q)^2]$	English	Undecided	English
$x \geq 1-(1-q)^2$	English	Undecided	English

Table 6: Optimal Rules for Different Parameter Values

It should be emphasized that whether intermediate or high damages are optimal depends on θ and the probability distribution over x, so it is more convenient to consider directly the optimal damages in the columns. This means that the different entries in Table 6 reflect the optimal rule for different realizations of x, given that optimal damages are chosen under each rule. Results for the overall optimality of a rule could only be derived for specific distribution functions over x. This would be arbitrary and does not yield additional insights. Note also that the borders of the relevant ranges of x differ across rules, but they can be ordered as in Table 6 because of the ranking $(1-q)^2 < 1-q < q < 1-(1-q)^2$. Employing this ranking yields the following conclusions:

1) A striking result is that the American Rule is weakly superior for all θ if $x < q$ (see the first three rows in Table 6). Thus, the realization of the source's utility from leaking in relation to the firm's sanctioning potential ($x = \alpha/S$) is more important in determining the optimal rule than the ex-ante probability that a story is true (θ). The reason for this is the following: if $x < (1-q)^2$, the rules are only different if θ is high. But then, intermediate damages are chosen under the American Rule which leads to a pooling equilibrium with protection. By contrast, high damages are optimal under the English Rule which prevents all stories from being published. But high θ and $x < (1-q)^2$ then ensures that the American Rule is superior. And if $x \in [(1-q)^2, q)]$ (rows 2 and 3), we get a separating equilibrium under the American Rule which is the best outcome. Note that this implies that the American Rule should be chosen whenever the probability that x is small is sufficiently high.

2) There are no values for x where the English Rule weakly outperforms the American Rule regardless of the optimal damages. Even for high x (where one would expect that discouraging sources from leaking is most important) the American Rule may be superior if high damages are optimal under both rules (e.g., for intermediate values of θ). Then, we

know from the previous sections that in the relevant case of $x \geq q$, there is always a pooling with revelation under the American Rule, while a separating equilibrium is played for $x \in [q, 1-(1-q)^2]$, and a pooling with revelation for $x \geq 1-(1-q)^2$ under the English Rule. However even a separating equilibrium under the English Rule may be inferior to a pooling equilibrium with revelation under the American Rule due to the high risk of type I errors.

3) The expected difference in social costs between the American and the English Rule is strictly decreasing in θ. The higher θ, the more important is it to encourage publication, a result which can be reached by the "weak" American Rule.

4) Since the conditions expressed via x could alternatively be expressed via q (for a given x), it follows immediately that the choice of the optimal rule depends heavily on the quality of the legal system. If q increases, we move upwards in Table 6 which implies that the American Rule is more likely to be superior. The advantage of the English Rule is that the court gets more information as sources are more frequently revealed, albeit at the cost of discouraging publication. However, if the court comes to (almost) perfect decisions even with little information, the relative advantage of the English Rule decreases.

Finally, note again that for any distribution function of x given, we can uniquely derive the overall optimal liability rule as a function of θ.

1.5 Conclusions

The model yields three kinds of results. First, under the American Rule, high damages that induce the reporter to reveal the source are optimal if the number of true stories is high and the quality of the court is low, while the opposite holds under the English Rule. Secondly, the American Rule is superior in a separating equilibrium, while the ranking of the two rules in pooling equilibria depends on the parameters. These parameters can be clearly and intuitively interpreted. Thirdly, the American Rule is weakly superior regardless of the ex-ante probability that the story is true whenever the source's private benefit from leakage is sufficiently small[763].

These findings are very much in favor of the American Rule. It is therefore worth discussing which of the assumptions are crucial for this result. In fact, these results are driven by the inherent asymmetry difference between the firm and the reporter with respect to their willingness to disclose evidence: the assumption was that firms disclose whenever the court believes the reporter (under the English Rule) or whenever the burden of proof is reversed (under the American rule). In contrast, reporters disclose their sources only when damages are sufficiently high. The reason is that the reporters' reputational loss stems from the decision to reveal, whereas the firm's loss stems from the publication and the court's decision, but not from the revealing of its own evidence. Modelling the firm as a strategic player, which means treating the decision to sue for defamation as a signal to the market, creates a significantly more complicated game with only mixed equilibria.

---

763 However, anecdotal evidence indicates that private benefits from leakage in the US are likely to be higher than elsewhere as whistle-blowers often become popular. For instance, Sharon Watkins (the whistleblower in the Enron case) is highly demanded as a public lecturer. Then, the ranking of the Rules depends on the cases at hand.

Furthermore, another assumption was that the court (and the capital market) never believe the reporter if he does not reveal his sources under the English Rule and also that he will always be held liable if he refuses to disclose. With respect to the first assumption, it is made without a loss of generality since introducing some parameter β which represents the court's and the capital market's prior belief, if the reporter does not disclose the source under both rules, does not alter the qualitative findings. Along the same lines, note that under the English law the burden of proof is slightly more complicated since the reporter can escape liability by proving he has engaged in "responsible journalism" and then the firm must prove that the reporter acted with malice in order to prevail. Since the first threshold for the reporter remains, our initial assumptions are not invalidated.

The assumption that the reporter always publishes is more problematic. However, adding new information whereby a second signalling stage is created for the reporter before the decision to publish complicates the game in a way that does not produce interpretable results.

Appendix: Proof of Table 6

For the proof of Table 6, subtract the social costs under the English Rule from the social costs under the American Rule for each of the cases. This yields the following results:

	$dE(M) / dA(H)$	$dE(H) / dA(H)$	$dE(H) / dA(M)$
$x < (1-q)^2$	0	0	$1 - q - \theta$
$x \in [(1-q)^2, (1-q)]$	$-\theta q(2 - q)$	$-\theta q(2 - q)$	$-\theta q(2 - q)$
$x \in [(1-q), q]$	$-\theta q(1 - q)$	$-\theta q(1 - q)$	$-\theta q(1 - q)$
$x \in [q, 1-(1-q)^2]$	$(1 - q)(1 - \theta(1 + q))$	$(1 - q)(1 - \theta(1 + q))$	$(1 - q)(1 - \theta)$
$x \geq 1-(1-q)^2$	$1 - q - \theta - \theta q(1 - q)$	$Q(1 - q)(1 - 2\theta)$	$q(1 - q)(1 - \theta)$

Table 7: Differences in Social Costs

The signs of most table entries are self explanatory except for the last entry in the first row and the first two entries in the last two rows. In some of these entries, the definition of the columns can be used in order to derive the sign.

In the last cell of the first row $(1 - q - \theta)$, the column indicates that intermediate damages are optimal under the American Rule. This can only happen when $\theta > 1 - q$. Hence, the sign must be negative, $1 - q - \theta < 0$ which implies that the American Rule is superior.

In the first column, intermediate damages are optimal under the English Rule. Recall that this implies:

$$\theta < \frac{(1-q)^2}{q + (1-q)^2} \quad . \qquad \textbf{Inequality [4]}$$

This implies that:

$$(1-q)(1-\theta(1+q)) > (1-q)\,\frac{q+(1-q)^2-(1-q)^2(1+q)}{q+(1-q)^2}$$

$$=\frac{q(1-q)}{q+(1-q)^2}\,(1-(1-q)^2)$$

This latter expression is strictly positive and therefore implies that the English Rule is superior in the first entry in the row before last.

Correspondingly,

$$1-q-\theta-\theta q(1-q) > \frac{q(1-q)+(1-q)^3-(1-q)^2-q(1-q)^3}{q+(1-q)^2}$$

$$=\frac{1-q}{q+(1-q)^2}\,(2q-1+(1-q)^3)$$

The latter expression is also strictly positive given the initial assumption that $q > ½$. Hence, the English Rule is superior also in the first cell of the last row.

Finally, to see how the differences in Table 7 change when the probability for true stories (θ) increases observe the derivatives of the entries with respect to θ:

	$dE(M) / dA(H)$	$dE(H) / dA(H)$	$dE(H) / dA(M)$
$x < (1-q)^2$	0	0	–1
$x \in [(1-q)^2, (1-q)]$	$-q(2-q)$	$-q(2-q)$	$-q(2-q)$
$x \in [(1-q), q]$	$-q(1-q)$	$-q(1-q)$	$-q(1-q)$
$x \in [q, 1-(1-q)^2]$	$(1 \quad q^2)$	$-(1-q^2)$	$-(1-q)$
$x \geq 1-(1-q)^2$	$-1-q(1-q)$	$-2q(1-q)$	$-q(1-q)$

Table 8: Changes in Differences in Social Costs

All the entries in Table 8 are weakly negative.

Results under Alternative Equilibrium Selection

Changing the equilibrium assumption and assuming that the Pooling Equilibrium with Revelation (PR) is chosen whenever it coexists with a Separating Equilibrium (SE) yields the following changes in Table 4:

- The first cell in the third row now reads $\theta((1 - q)^2 - 1) > 0$. The American Rule is still superior.
- The first cell in the fourth row now reads $1 - q - \theta - \theta q(1 - q)$. Since the optimality of the English Rule still implies that **Inequality [4]** is true (although the equivalence no longer holds), with the analysis given above, it follows that the English Rule is still superior.
- The last entry in the second row now reads $1 - q - \theta$. This entry must be negative if intermediate damages are optimal under the American Rule since selecting a pooling equilibrium has made high damages superior to intermediate damages for intermediate values of x (under the selection of SE they are equivalent in this case). Hence the American Rule remains superior.
- The last entry in the third row now reads $(1 - q)(1 - \theta)$ which is strictly positive and implies that in this case the result changes and the English Rule is better.

Hence, the only change in Table 1.4 when switching the choice of equilibrium assumption from PR to SE is that the English Rule would become superior in the last entry of the third row. Deriving the entries with respect to θ shows that monotonicity is always conserved since all the entries are weakly decreasing in θ.

V Applications

1. Case Law: Political and Business Defamation in US and England

Although modelling the reporter's privilege in this case stemmed from the corporate defamation case, it yields insights that can be carried over to political defamation cases, which are more common.

In competitive situations, one might observe systematically high x ratios. By that I mean that sources expect a high benefit and a low expected sanction. For example, this systematic phenomenon can be presumed in political campaigns or business competition, where information regarding a plaintiff in a defamation lawsuit may be traced to a source affiliated with the political or business opponent. Sources affiliated with an opponent of a defamed person, or a defamed firm, stand to gain from the decline in the value of the defamed party and will likely not be punished if they are revealed. Hence, the source expects to garner a high value from the publication of the information compared to the sanction that may be imposed on him in the event that his identity is revealed.

There are various examples for this in the case law:

Revisiting the English case of ***Reynolds***[764]: the resigning Prime Minister of Ireland, Albert Reynolds, sued the newspaper for claiming that he had knowingly lied to members of his coalition government. The publication followed the collapse of the government after the head of a rival party in the coalition announced the party's withdrawal from the government. The reporters based the allegations in the report on an anonymous source related to the head of the rival coalition party. During the trial, the source's identity was voluntarily revealed as of the top advisors of the said rival. The court held that the information was false and that reliance on one obviously interested source for such a serious allegation was insufficient. The court also refused an appeal by the newspaper to set more lenient proof requirements for political information.

In the specific parameters of the ***Reynolds*** case, the English Rule seems to be justified, as the source was clearly an interested person, his party stood to gain from the downfall of the subject of the defamatory information and he was unlikely to be sanctioned by his own party for leaking the information (high α, low S, hence high x ratio).

The ***Jameel*** case provides an interesting example of an evaluation of a source without its revelation. In this case, the newspaper relied on 5 unnamed sources in its publication. The newspaper claimed that the bank accounts of the plaintiff, a Saudi corporation, were monitored for suspected connection to terror funding. The reporter testified that he received the initial information from a Saudi businessman (denoted in the decision as source A), which the reporter did not perceive to be a sufficiently reliable source. However, the story was then firmed up by four other sources (denoted B to E).

Sources B-E were mainly diplomatic and government officials. In the decision of the House of Lords, Lord Hoffman quotes the newspaper reporters on how one of these sources, an unnamed official in the US Treasury department, confirmed the story[765]. The official merely stated that the US treasury "has no objection to the story" and this was supposedly a

764 *Supra* in footnote 141.

765 ***Jameel HL***, opinion of Lord Hoffman §§64-78.

"Washington code" between reporters and their sources that meant that the source confirms the story. The fact that the newspaper required such confirmations from *four* sources indicates that each source provided very little information. I propose that the reason for that is that these were all government sources. They stood to make little or no personal gain from leaking the information (low α, in terms of our model) but they would have faced punishment for leaking (high S). Therefore all the sources were in the *low x ratio range*. This justifies the application of the ***Reynolds*** defence in this case. Without the ***Reynolds*** defence, the English Rule would have meant that the reporter must reveal the sources in order to prove the reliability of the information and escape liability or remain silent and pay the damages. Revealing sources with low x ratio, according to our model, would have discouraged such sources from leaking. By introducing the ***Reynolds*** defence, when it is applied correctly (that is, flexibly) the court can reach the correct conclusion without the revelation of the sources. The final outcome in the ***Jameel*** case: the firm presented evidence which convinced the court that the publication was false. The newspaper convinced the House of Lords that it acted with "responsible journalism". Therefore, the court accepted that the publication was false, but exempted the newspaper from liability.

In US cases involving political figures, some courts shift the burden of proof to the reporter after an initial *prima-facie* showing by the plaintiff that there is an issue of fact regarding whether the defamatory allegation is correct or not (which is a lower level of proof compared to proving the falsity of the statement). For example, in ***DeRoburt v. Gannett***[766], the plaintiff was the president of Nauru and the publication claimed he financially supported a separatist movement in the Marshall Islands which was both an illegal action and also caused a political backlash against the plaintiff in his state. After an initial showing regarding the factual accuracy of the allegations the court ordered the reporters to disclose their sources or else a presumption would be drawn that the report had no source. The latter is the strongest sanction applied by courts in such circumstances.

Similarly, in ***Woodcock v. Journal Pub. Co., Inc.***[767] the plaintiff was a member of a zoning committee and sued for defamation following a publication that alleged she had treated an application favourably ahead of schedule. The plaintiff claimed the publication was timed to damage the re-election campaign of her husband to the state legislature. She had asked for a disclosure of sources prior to having to prove the falsity of the publication. The court agreed.

Both cases can be justified within the framework of our model, given the assumption that in political contexts, sources have an interest to leak information about opponents, and expect a relatively low sanction (or none at all) if they are revealed. In fact, sources in such circumstances may not be concerned about sanctions at all, but act in order to conceal their identity because their affiliation decreases the value of the information for the market. If the marker trusts the reputation of the reporter as an intermediary of information, it would attribute positive value to information from anonymous sources whereas it would otherwise attribute no value or negative value when the interested source is known. Under such circumstances, the shift of the burden of proof by US courts in the cases cited above, which effectively means the *de-facto* adoption of an English Rule, is correct.

In ***Maressa v. New Jersey Monthly***[768], as opposed to the cases cited earlier, the court held that sources will be absolutely protected from disclosure and that no presumption against the

766 ***DeRoburt v. Gannett***, 507 F. Supp. 880 (D. Haw. 1981.

767 ***Woodcock v. Journal Pub. Co., Inc.***, Not Reported, 1990 WL 283989 (Conn. Super., 1990).

768 ***Maressa v. New Jersey Monthly***, 445 A.2d 376 (N.J. May 06, 1982).

journalists will be drawn following their refusal to reveal their sources. The underlying report concerned criticism of the performance of a senator, but was not connected to an ongoing election campaign and relied on several sources.

In this case, of course, sources may also have had a political interest in defaming the senator. However, the publication did not concern an immediate election and was initiated by the newspaper rather than the sources (they were approached by the newspaper seeking the information). Given these circumstances, the sources can be presumed to be in a lower x ratio compared to the previous examples, which would justify applying the "weaker" American Rule. However, a sweeping rule of no revelation at all, as the court adopted, is not advisable.

Looking at cases applying the rule in the business setting: in ***Howard v. Antilla***[769], a reporter was sued for publishing an article about the plaintiff, a businessman. The article discussed the performance of Howard's corporation and SEC investigations related to it. The reporter cited information according to which Howard was in fact operating under an assumed identity masking a person formerly convicted of securities fraud. Howard sued for defamation. In spite of the fact that the allegations regarding his former identity were proven to be false, the court refused to order the disclosure of the confidential sources in order to assist Howard in establishing "actual malice" which was a precondition for an award of damages[770]. The decision is especially interesting since the report regarding the assumed identity was based on anonymous rumours which supposedly emanated from short-sellers of Howard's corporation.

Given our findings, the decision in this case seems mistaken. The court had indications that the sources of the information were short-sellers of the stock, which evidently stood to gain a profit from the fall of the share price due to the negative implication of the information. This corresponds to high (α) in our model and probably a very high x ratio. The party behind the rumours only attempted to boost the effect of the information on the market by hiding its interests behind the veil of the privilege and using the reputation of the reporter. Therefore, a court order to disclose the identity of the sources would have been a better strategy from a social welfare perspective.

2. Case Law: Germany

German defamation lawsuits for monetary compensation follow the English Rule. Liability materializes when the reporter knew about the falsity of the information, or was negligent. The burden of proof lies with the defendant. However, if the reporter can prove that he took due care and that the information was of public interest, he will prevail even if the information was false[771]. If the reporter cannot prove that due care has been taken because he does not want to disclose the source - this is counted to his detriment[772]. Nevertheless, as is discussed below, there are cases that diverge from this approach.

---

769 ***Howard v. Antilla***, 2000 WL 144387 (D.N.H. Nov 17, 1999).
770 ***Howard v. Antilla***, 191 F.R.D. 39, 42 (D.N.H. Oct 22, 1999).
771 Löffler/Ricker, 353.
772 Mensching, 158.

Cases that adhere to the rule:

In a case from 1974[773], the BGH failed to refer to the privilege and found the publisher of a flyer (head of the local labour union) concerning work conditions in a records production firm was liable due to a failure to prove the truthfulness of the factual claims. The flyer claimed that the firm imposed hard work on women yet the defendant did not show supporting evidence, although the lower court asked him to substantiate the claim. The defendant did not reveal the source of information out of concern of reprisal. The court noted this fact, but did not change the ruling. According to §138 ZPO, the parties have the burden of substantiating their claim. The court held that the defendant knowingly withheld evidence from the court and that this must be taken into account[774].

This decision is clearly problematic given the findings in the model. The source, apparently a person within the firm, expected a high sanction. Even if the source was a woman and she may have gained an improvement in working conditions through leaking, this benefit would have been small, and she would have been unable to internalize the benefit enjoyed by the other women in the firm. As described here, the rule employed by the court discourages the publication of such information, when it is most likely true.

In a case from the OLG Hamburg[775], a former Minister of Interior, who was also in charge of the security services in former German Democratic Republiuc (GDR), sued a magazine claiming falsity of the reports concerning his actions during the GDR era and demanding a retraction. The court held that when the defendant relies on information that emanated from confidential sources, the burden of proving why this information should be relied upon (§138 ZPO) is not changed or relieved. If the defendant refuses to reveal the source for this matter he will bear the procedural consequences. The court restated an earlier case from 1974 for this purpose[776].

To a certain extent, after the reunification of Germany, accusing former GDR political figures of wrongdoing in their past functions during the GDR era was an easy method for defaming political opponents (though the information might of course also have been true). If indeed this case was the purpose of the defamation, then, as suggested earlier, the English Rule, which was applied in this case, is justified.

One should be careful in the case of political defamation not to be confused by the circumstances of the defamation. Note, for example, the ***Stolpe*** case, where the head of the federal state of Brandenburg, formerly a high ranking official in the Evangelist church of Brandenburg in the former GDR, sued the investigative program "Frontal" aired by the German second television channel (ZDF) for alleging he had previous contacts to the Stasi[777]. The allegation was made during a live discussion on the program and not as part of a serious journalistic research into the past of the plaintiff. The court noted that §823 2 BGB together with §186 StGB shift the burden of proof to the defendant to show that his statement is true[778]. The court found that the factual evidence brought by the defendants did not confirm nor disprove the allegation in question. Obviously, since no significant journalistic research had been undertaken to confirm the information at the outset. Although the defendants did

---

773 BGH NJW 1974, 1710; Reported in Himmelsbach, 59-60.
774 BGH NJW 1974, 1710, 1710.
775 OLG Hamburg NJW-RR 1992, 1378.
776 BGH NJW 1974, 1710.
777 BGH NJW 1998, 3047 (Stolpe).
778 BGH NJW 1998, 3047, 3048-3049.

not meet their burden of proof, the court rejected the claim, primarily because the plaintiff was a political persona who voluntarily engaged in the political arena, and on the basis of the circumstances in which the statement was made i.e., a live televised discussion[779]

The court was correct in setting the burden of proof as in the English Rule, assuming that the core of the dispute was a matter of political defamation. Note that the case did not involve a matter of source disclosure, primarily because the defendants did not really have one. By absolving the defendants due to the nature of the televised discussion, the court acknowledged a problematic reality in the value of political televised discussions: when statements are made, they need not be checked, nor do the makers of the statement bear any liability if they are wrong. Under such circumstances, the value of political statements depends entirely on thee reputation of the speaker.

Another case where the German court applied the English Rule is ***Lohnkiller***: a civil defamation action by the local head of a city police force, which was named in a book alleging he was involved in contacts between the police and the "Red Light District milieu"[780]. The plaintiff focused on a defamatory allegation attributed to an unnamed source, referred to as "O", alleging ties between the plaintiff and the owner of a prostitution establishment. The BGH held that "O" was not in itself a reliable source and that the author did not take the required actions to verify the truth of the statement[781]. The identity of "O" was not revealed. The court in this case made a point of the fact that the defendant did not "distance" himself from the statement of the source. Thus the defendant had made the reader understand that he believed the factual statement to be true.

The reporter decided not to disclose the source "O". This could have been due to several reasons: (1) the expected damages were not sufficiently high, (2) the reputational loss from disclosure provided deterrence or (3) even if reputational loss from disclosure was low, if the source was not reliable, the disclosure would not have prevented liability damages but would have produced a reputational loss and thus it was better to protect the source.

Earlier we have observed that defamation damages in Germany are lower in comparison to US and English damages[782]. The model suggests that in order to effectively induce revelation, damages must be higher than the reputation loss. In Germany, another factor should be considered. On top of any reputation loss, reporters are exposed to liability for a breach of personality rights action by the source if a source is revealed against his will. This right for sources can be drawn from the decision of OLG Bremen. The case concerned a memoir book written by a former director of the security services. The book identified a former informer, who then filed a civil claim for breach of his personality rights – the court accepted the assertion that such a right can be the basis for a lawsuit[783]. Since the model indicates that low damages are always dominated by intermediate and high damages, the ability of the source to increase the expected loss from revelation, (L), means that a socially efficient can be obtained through such a measure.

With respect to the rule from ***Lohnkiller***, according to which liability can be avoided if the reporter distances himself from the content of the statement: this is a well established rule in

779 BGH NJW 1998, 3047, 3049.

780 BGH NJW 1996, 1131 (Lohnkiller case).

781 BGH NJW 1996, 1131, 1132.

782 See section III.3.2.

783 OLG Bremen, VersR 1997, 500. See also a similar result in a case of breach of confidentiality by an auditor LG Berlin. 8.5.1998 cited in Lichtner, 122.

German defamation law. The press can avoid liability by distancing itself from a statement of a third person, even an anonymous one, by remarking that this statement is not supported by the reporter[784]. When this rule is applied to anonymous statements, the result is that media consumers have no means of evaluating the truthfulness of the statement. This is exactly the criticism mentioned by ***Coase***. Hence, the value of the information is zero.

There are exceptional German cases where the refusal of reporters to reveal their sources has not counted to the defendant's detriment.

In the ***Metzler*** case[785] the plaintiff, a company, sued the newspaper "Die Welt" over a line in a report claiming that certain ministries would only support additional streaming of capital to the firm under certain circumstances. The newspaper refused to reveal its sources. The BGH held - unlike the previous case - that the newspaper is freed from the obligation to substantiate the truth of its statement according to §138 ZPO if this requires the revelation of sources. The BGH conducted a weighing of the balance of interest between the burden of substantiating the defence in §138 ZPO, and the freedom of the press which is protected by §5 GG and manifested in this case through the privilege in §23 LandPresseRecht Baden-Württemberg. The BGH held that if it is definitely required to protect the source, the defendant should not reveal his sources to counter the plaintiff's claim that the information was untrue. The lawsuit was rejected.

This decision was criticized in the literature for making defamation lawsuits almost impossible for plaintiffs to maintain. Instead, it is proposed that the court should employ §446 ZPO which allows the court to decide upon its own convictions whether a party should be viewed as if it met its burden of proof after calling upon the privilege and given all the circumstances of the case[786].

As derived in our model, the decision in ***Metzler*** is problematic only if one assumes that leaked information is mostly false, in which case it would be optimal to force revelation.

In the case of the magic stick water company[787], the plaintiff, a company that conducted searches for underground water reservoirs by using a special "search stick" sued for retraction against a newspaper and an official in another firm that claimed the plaintiff was a fraud and that the firm had abused the ignorance of the community that hired the plaintiff-firm. The court held that the statements referring to the use of a special water-searching stick as simple magic tricks and fraud and the general contract of the firm as "abuse of the ignorance of the community" were factual statements[788]. The BGH held - reversing the decision of the lower court - that the plaintiff must prove that the factual statement are wrong (and that he did not defraud the community) in order to prevail in the claim for retraction and monetary damages (sued under §823 and §824 BGB)[789].

---

784 Bamberger/Roth, §824, 30; BGH NJW 1997, 1148, 1149 (Chefarzt), dealing with a program on "Stern TV" alleging malpractice by a gynaecologist quoting other medical doctors. The court held that the program did not distance the statements but rather made the viewers think that the statements are supported by the program

785 BGH AfP 1975, 801, reported by Himmelsbach, 60-62.

786 Himmelsbach, 67-68 citing Löffler, Presserecht, (3. Auf. 1983) and Wenzel, Das Recht des Wort und Bild Berichterstattung (4. Auf., 1994).

787 BGH NJW 1989, 1958.

788 BGH NJW 1989, 1958, 1959.

789 BGH NJW 1989, 1958, 1960.

This decision fits into the competitive defamation pattern discussed above. However, it seems that the decision of the BGH to use the American Rule was motivated by the unusual nature of the firm in question and the common knowledge with regard to the scientific nature of searching for water with sticks. In other words, the court's quality in this case was high as a matter of basic judicial knowledge. Shifting the burden of proof was the only method for the court to ensure that the party that should prevail - indeed did prevail. In the US or England, such a claim would have most likely been rejected immediately, for lack of merit. The German court had to switch the burden of proof to obtain the same result.

Note that the legal literature on defamation in Germany is of the opinion that , as discussed in the previous section, in financial and economic reporting, the reporter must take a high level of care to check the veracity of sources from the business arena (in view of competitors interested in defaming) whereas government and official sources are more trustworthy[790].

3. Special Remedies in German Law: Retraction and Right of Reply

The preference in German law, where possible, is to solve defamation disputes with non-monetary remedies. The two common remedies are retraction (Widerruf) and the right of reply (Gegendarstellung). The right of reply does not exist as a *per-se* remedy in Anglo-American law, although it may be used to mitigate damages.

The right of reply is well established in all the press laws of the German federal states[791]. Additionally, it has a constitutional foundation through §2 GG[792]. The right of reply stems from personality rights designed to protect reputation. These rights have been extended to corporations as well[793]. Free speech is encouraged so long as the right of reply is also kept[794].

According to the right of reply, the publisher of a defamatory statement must publish the reply of the injured party, which must be a factual response, with prominence comparable to the initial publication[795]. In the Hamburg Press law, for example, the right is granted at no cost, to any person (also legal entity) who is affected by a statement[796]. The reply must be published in the same section and the same size of the original statement[797]. The reply may only concern factual matters, which are matters that are subject to proof. The publisher may refuse to publish the reply if it is untrue, yet he must be able to prove in court that the original statement is true, or that the reply is false[798]. This is the procedure for all laws concerning the right of reply in Germany. If the publisher refuses to publish the reply, the injured can file

790 Löffler/Ricker, 310; BGH NJW 1966, 2011.

791 Hesse (1994).

792 Freckman & Wegerich, 89; Hesse, 98; BVerfG 63, 131; BVerfG 72, 118.

793 Kübler, 1284.

794 Kübler, 1284; The exception is government corporations which are not protected by personality rights. The reasoning is that government and political institutions should be open to stronger criticism in a democratic society. See: Wenzel, Karl Egbert, **Das Recht der Wort und Bild Berichtstattung: Handbuch des Äußerungsrecht** (4Auf. Köln 1994), 5.106.

795 Bruns, 291.

796 Hamburgisches Pressegesetz §11 Gegendarstellung.

797 Hamburgisches Pressegesetz §11(3).

798 Hesse, 100.

suit in a civil court. If the court finds the rejection without merit, the court can order the publisher to publish the reply[799].

The reply procedure is fast and almost costless, as long as the media does not object[800]. The reply is restricted to factual matters and the principle of "all or nothing" applies: the media must publish all the reply or none of it[801]. The press has the right to add a comment (Redaktionsschwantz) to a reply that is perceived to be untrue, when the falsity is not evident from the reply. The comment can clarify why the reporter believes the reply is untrue, yet it must be restricted to facts[802].

In the opinion of ***Prinz***, the right of reply serves the concept that media consumers should hear both sides of a story and can then discern the truth by themselves[803]. In contrast, the German constitutional court observed that facts promote the formation of public opinion when they are true. Factual statements are constitutionally protected only insofar as they promote the public's right to freedom of opinion. Since evidently false information does not promote freedom of opinion[804], it is not protected. The court was aware, nonetheless, that when too stringent limitations are imposed in order to prevent the publication of false information, some truthful information may also be lost. To that effect, the court held that the requirement for factual statements to be true cannot be such that it will eventually hinder freedom of opinion[805].

Some courts and scholars have expressed the notion that the truthful content of the reply is immaterial to the obligation to publish the reply[806]. This is a misconception. Only when the reply is clearly a lie can the reporter reject it[807]. Since the burden of proof is then on the reporter, truth may be costly to prove and legal proceedings are also costly, the publication of the reply might be the cheapest solution[808].

Unlike the right of reply, the legal action for retraction (Widerruf) puts the burden on the injured party to show that the information was false in order to prevail[809]. If the plaintiff is able to prove falsity, the defendant must retract the publication entirely.

---

799 Hesse, 101. In three cases the burden of proof is shifted to the plaintiff: (1) the plaintiff has no entitled/protected interest, Löffler/Ricker, 191 (The rule does not exist in the state laws of Hamburg, Bavaria, Mecklenburg-Vorpommern, Niedersachsen, Saarland and Sachsen-Anhalt), (2) inadequate extent of the requested correction and (3) the requested correction is an advertisement that serves the plaintiff's business interests. Löffler/Ricker, 190-191.

800 Prinz. 340.

801 Prinz, 341.

802 Hesse, 101.

803 Prinz, 339.

804 Löffler/Ricker, 191. BVerfG NJW 1998, 1383.

805 BVerfG NJW 1992, 1439, 1440 (Bayer).

806 Prinz, 346; Hesse, 98; BVerfG NJW 1998, 1381.

807 Prinz, 398; OLG Hamburg, NJW-RR 1994, 1179.

808 The defendant bears the cost of the reply. Löffler/Ricker, 196. Even if a newspaper could prove after a reply had been published that the content of that reply was false, it would be very hard for the newspaper to impose a legal sanction on the party that sent the reply. The only material loss that the newspaper can claim is the benefit from an advertisement that could have been published instead of the reply. The medium would then have to prove that an advertisement had been specifically rejected for the same spot. Prinz, 440.

809 Münchener Kommentar, 54; Hesse, 102. See BGHZ 37, 187, 189 f. NJW 1962, 1438f.; BGHZ 69, 181, 183f. NJW 1977, 1681, 1683; OLG Düsseldorf NJW-RR 2002, 1427.

In short, retraction follows the American Rule and the right of reply follows the English Rule. When a firm sues following a defamatory publication under German law and it does not seek monetary damages, or is not able to show monetary damage, it must resort to one of these two remedies. However, unlike our model, the choice of the remedy has a signalling value from the perspective of the reporter.

Since under the American Rule, the firm must reveal its version first, and the court with quality $q > ½$ is more likely than not to detect and reject a false defamation claim by the firm, then firms having non-meritorious defamation lawsuits would rather demand a right of reply. If they do so, the reporter must either publish the reply or exert costs in court. If the reporter chooses the latter (fighting) the English Rule, which is tougher on the reporter, is played.. Analyzing the consequences of the operation of this combined mechanism is intractable since one must also take into account that the court also observes the signal of the remedy chosen by the firm, and therefore should update its position with respect to the truthfulness of the statement in dispute, which in turn influences the decision of other players.

Nevertheless, given that: (i) the English Rule is more favourable to plaintiffs, (ii) the American Rule is more favourable to defendants, the following observations can be drawn. German plaintiffs are therefore more likely to choose the remedy that is favourable to them, right of reply, which employs the English Rule. Consequently, the probability that a reporter will be forced to publish factual replies that are false, is higher. From that it follows that the market will place a lower value on the reply. This also means that when a reporter decides to fight a demand for the right of reply in court, the court should place a higher probability on the truthfulness of the publication.

Conversely, the probability that the court will order a false retraction is lower, since the American Rule is used (the firm must prove the falsity of the publication); therefore the market places a higher belief on the truthfulness of retractions.

Note that under both remedies reporters are not likely to reveal their sources, since monetary damages are not imposed. Hence, neither remedy will affect the willingness of sources to leak. However, the market attributes a higher valuation (attaches higher accuracy) to published information about a firm if the firm's reaction is to demand a right of reply than to published information that evokes a demand for retraction. Retracted information does not necessarily have zero value since court quality is not perfect. Since reporters will never expose the source in a retraction lawsuit and courts do make mistakes, some small share of retracted information should also be assumed to be true.

VI Concluding Remarks and Comparative Notes

The reporter's privilege is a mechanism that is designed to increase the flow of information from insiders within organizations to the media. The public dissemination of such information is one of the components of enforcing corporate compliance, since it enables the market to evaluate the true value of the firm. The privilege, however, does not ensure in and of itself, that the information provided by the sources that it protects is truthful or accurate.

In this chapter I have shown that the reporter's privilege does not operate in a legal vacuum. The law of defamation gives the subjects of publication a tool that is designed to protect their reputation. In the legal survey presented in the first parts of this chapter I have shown that all the legal systems discussed here offer some degree of protection to confidential sources and that all of them also allow firms to protect their reputation by the civil tort of defamation. Hence, the conflict between the interest in reputation and the interest in the flow of information to the public through the media is inherent to all jurisdictions.

It is important to bear in mind that the conflicting interests should eventually contribute to the following goal: the publication of as much *truthful* information as possible and the suppression of as much *false* information as possible. As shown, there are two fundamentally contrasting procedural mechanisms of trial in which the conflict is solved in the surveyed jurisdictions. In both solutions, the distribution of the burden of proof plays a key role. In the English Rule, the first onus in a defamation lawsuit is on the defendant-reporter to show that the information that he published is true (or that he had taken due care to ensure that it is true), whereas, in the American Rule the first burden is shifted to the plaintiff-firm to show that the story is false.

Note that the English Rule is also the rule applied by German courts when adjudicating defamation lawsuits for monetary compensation.

The interaction between the source, the reporter, the firm and the court has been modelled in part IV. The model yields several results, the most interesting of which is that the American Rule is weakly superior to the English Rule in achieving the objective of maximizing true stories and minimizing false stories regardless of whether sources leak more true stories or more false stories, provided that the source's utility from leaking is small.

The English Rule, which is tough towards the media, is optimal when the ratio of benefits/sanction faced by confidential sources is high. In that case setting intermediate or high damages on the reporter is also optimal. The reason is that sources have a high motivation for leaking both true and false stories and the tougher English Rule thus deters more false stories. As the benefits/sanctions ratio of confidential sources decreases, the American Rule encourages more sources to leak. Then, high damages in defamation lawsuits are still optimal because they will induce the reporter to disclose the source in order to avoid liability and thereby deter sources with false stories.

The model assumes courts cannot perfectly observe the utility of sources from leaking (described by the benefits/sanction ratio x). In the application of the model, I suggest that the courts can, however, expect that in some situations the x ratio will be systematically high, or systematically low. In the political setting, for example, an anonymous source that is known to be a member of one party and provides information regarding an opponent in another party will often times expect a high benefit from leaking and only a small sanction if he is exposed. Hence, the use of the English Rule in such cases should be preferred.

In the business arena, a similar systematically high ratio may be attributed to short-sellers that disseminate false negative rumours about a firm. Since short-sellers stand to gain from the decline in the firm's value and can expect only a small sanction for disseminating rumours, the English Rule would be optimal in deterring the publication of such information.

Finally, I discussed the unique German solution: allowing the plaintiff-firm to choose between monetary compensation (where the English Rule procedure applies in court) and non-monetary remedies (where the American Rule applies). It is difficult to foresee whether this solution is optimal since the firm's choice could be interpreted as a signal as to the firm's ability to prove its claim. However, the value of this signal would be dampened in reality by the fact, for example, that in Germany the firm must prove the monetary harm in order to sue for compensation.

Two comparative observations should be made, in conclusion, with respect to the German solution. The first remark concerns the information that eventually reaches the public. The use of monetary damage awards in the Anglo-American jurisdictions - if applied optimally - means that truthful information is published and false information is suppressed. In contrast, the use of non-monetary remedies, as in Germany, means that *all* information is published, however, if the information is deemed to be false, an additional publication (correction or retraction) is published in order to correct the false impression. Hence, the German solution provides more information to the public.

There are advantages and disadvantages to the German approach. One possible disadvantage is that the public might not be able to absorb all the conflicting pieces of information and end up confused. Another possible disadvantage is the creation of undesirable predispositions. For example, if the public is informed several times that the products of a certain company are defective and then each of these publications is retracted, the consumers might still develop a negative predisposition towards the company (as the saying goes, "where there is smoke there is fire"). On the other hand, the advantage of the German solution is that the managers of this company now learn that there are disgruntled disloyal employees within the firm that have leaked this negative information. In the Anglo-American systems, this information may not have been published at all and in this case the management would not learn of this internal problem. Hence, the publication of false information can be valuable even if the content of the information is not.

The second remark concerns an attempt in English law to adopt the non-monetary German solution. The English Defamation Act 1996 was amended in 2000 to include the possibility of an offer of amends. This procedure is designated for use in situations where defendants who were not aware of the falsity or defamatory nature of the statement wish to make amends to the claimant. The law prescribes the procedure of an offer of amends (which must be detailed, express and in writing, according to sec. 2 of the statute). The offer can be monetary or other. If the offer is accepted, the defamation lawsuit is discontinued. If the offer is rejected - the defendant will be able to use it as a defence against a defamation suit, unless the defendant knew or had reason to believe that the statement is false and defamatory[810]. In the latter case, the burden of proof shifts to the claimant to show that the defendant knew or had

[810] Gatley, 551-552.

reason to know the falsity and defamatory nature of the statement (sec. 3(3) of the Defamation Act 1996)[811].

The similarity between this amendment and the German Rule is that the English law now allows the parties to settle (in or out of court) by choosing a non-monetary remedy. The difference is that this is only possible (1) if the defendant did not know that the information was false, and (2) if the defendant initiates an "offer of amends". In other words, whilst in Germany the plaintiff decides on the remedy, in England it is the defendant that gets to choose.

This choice of clearly contradicting rules can be explained by the different overall approaches in English and German laws. In Germany, the protection of the media is highly regarded by the courts and imposing monetary sanctions on the media is not encouraged, hence defamation lawsuits for monetary compensation are set up as a costly option. In such a setting it is desirable to enable the plaintiff a cheap alternative, such as retraction or correction, which does not deter the initial publication. In England, the courts' approach towards the media is tougher. The media often pays high damages for defamation, even if the defamation is the result of an honest mistake. Such a harsh rule might dissuade the media from publishing any negative information. By allowing the media to offer "amends" and correct its honest mistakes, the harm of "journalistic accidents" is internalized and the social loss from over-precaution is avoided.

811 Gatley, 552, notes that the standard of proof must be higher than mere negligence because otherwise a journalist reporting on a controversy with two opposing factual versions will already be found liable. Thus, for media defendants the standard should be exercising all due professional care.

Conclusion

Our voyage here has encompassed three countries, related to two starkly different legal systems (common law and civil law), and three professions that collaborate with each other at times, but oftentimes find themselves in conflicting roles in both the legal and social arenas. This voyage has maneuvered the oceans of three classical fields of law - corporate law, civil procedure and evidence law - and also sailed the sea of a relatively newer field, media law. In this concluding note I shall summarize the main observations and conclusions, and remark on the interaction between the professional privileges of the professions that have been discussed.

The objective of this work has been to evaluate the role of professional testimonial privileges of attorneys, accountants and journalists in promoting corporate compliance with the law. These professionals are often mentioned as important gatekeepers and monitors against wrongdoing in corporations and against the socially detrimental behaviour of corporate actors.

At least some of these professionals recognize that gatekeeping and monitoring is one of their key market functions, namely, auditors and reporters. Others, especially lawyers, accept the role with little enthusiasm. However, all professionals claim that the professional testimonial privilege is crucial for the efficient performance of their work.

In examining the comparative Law & Economics of the professional privilege I realized that certain background systemic differences between the legal jurisdictions should be taken into account. These differences are located mainly in corporate law and in the law of civil procedure.

Continental law systems (e.g. German law) emphasize the protection of the privacy of litigants. Compelling the production of evidence is discouraged and procedures for exploring evidence held by opponents are rare. In contrast, Anglo-American courts interpret evidentiary privileges restrictively since they are perceived to be detrimental to accurate adjudication. Additionally, parties are encouraged to collect evidence from the opponent prior to the trial.

Corporate ownership tends to be dispersed among many shareholders in the Anglo-American legal system, and concentrated in one significant block-holder in the German system. Anglo-American capital markets face problems regarding the monitoring and control of management, presumably due to this characteristic. Consequently, Anglo-American law contains well developed mechanisms for the provision of information, both to the market and for takeovers. In contrast, German law allows better control of the management, but is said to provide weak protection for minority investors in corporations.

The Corporate Lawyer-Client Privilege

Bearing these systemic differences in mind, I have analyzed the lawyer-client privilege in the corporate setting. The operation of this privilege enables lawyers not to disclose confidential lawyer-client communications in court.

As shown in the Law & Economics literature, the existing justifications for the privilege either fail to consider the social objective that the privilege claims to promote, or build on dubious assumptions. In Anglo-American systems, the prevalent justifications for the privilege are the utilitarian and neo-utilitarian rationales. The utilitarian rationale claims that the privilege promotes social welfare, even if it deprives the courts of some evidence. Law &

Economics literature has shown that the benefits of the lawyer-client privilege depend on the optimality of enforcement and the accuracy of sanctions. The neo-utilitarian rationale advances compliance as the primary social good that is gained from the privilege. However, this rationale is founded on the misperception that lawyers can enforce compliant behavior on their clients.

The extension of the lawyer-client privilege to corporate clients is entrenched in years of precedents despite the constant criticism from legal scholars. It seems that in jurisdictions surveyed here, the privilege was extended to the corporate lawyer-client relationship without due consideration of the nature of the corporate client, as compared to the individual client. In the meanwhile, path-dependence has evolved: courts now believe that turning the wheel back and revoking the corporate privilege is no longer feasible.

I then turned to examine three aspects of the corporate lawyer-client privilege in which a Law & Economic perspective could advance the current understanding of the rule. Furthermore, comparative legal implications can be drawn in these issues.

The principal-agent problem. The Anglo-American and the German legal systems apply the privilege to the corporate entity but not to the agents of the corporation. I observed that this can distort the alignment of interests between the principals and the agents in the firm.

In the Anglo-American jurisdictions this problem may sometimes be resolved by imposing direct liability on managers. However, this is not always possible. In Germany, the problem is solved by concentrated ownership that ensures better monitoring of the management. By way of a policy recommendation, however, as the German market strives to increase shareholder culture, and given the strong German corporate lawyer-client privilege, the introduction of more personal liability for managers should be considered.

Who represents the corporation? The second aspect discussed here was, the rules applied by courts in order to determine which agents can communicate with the corporate lawyer on behalf of the firm, under the protection of the privilege. In the US, two main rules are used: (1) the "control group" test, which protects only the top echelon that can influence corporate decisions or (2) the "subject matter" test which protects not only the top management, but also whomever they authorize to act on their behalf. By modeling the decision making process in firms I concluded that the choice of a restrictive rule, such as the control group test, has a socially detrimental effect on the structure of corporate managements. Furthermore, if the objective of restrictive rules is to reduce the risk that corporate privilege is used as a cover for illegal or tortuous actions, then these rules fail to achieve this goal.

It was shown that the control group test motivates some corporations to inefficiently increase their management circle in order to "squeeze" into the criteria of the test. In the wake of this, it then follows that the altered firm would be able to pursue undesirable actions as a result of the privilege, thereby reducing social welfare. Furthermore, in control group jurisdictions, corporations have an incentive to assert the privilege, even when the assertion is false. This is because it is costly for plaintiffs to expose mimicking by defendants. Hence, even corporations that do not meet the criteria of the privilege may pursue non-compliant behaviour.

This analysis supports the decline of the control group test in the US, and provides food for thought to the English courts where the test has been recently proposed and applied by litigating parties with the court's silent agreement. Notably, in Germany, all agents of the corporation are protected in their communications with the corporate lawyer. However, in the absence of pre-trial discovery, this lenient rule is of little consequence in civil litigation.

Inadvertent waiver - an accident. The final section analyzed the doctrine of inadvertent waiver by applying the analytical framework from the economic analysis of accidents. It observed that in cases of accidental waiver, the court decides whether to declare that a private harm has materialized whereas, in the case of a "regular" accident the existence of harm is taken as given.

A survey of the representative case law from the US and England indicated that courts have not given sufficient attention to a consistent analysis of the theoretical foundation of the inadvertent waiver doctrine. This is illustrated by the fact that courts use inconsistent standards of care to determine whether accidental disclosure has occurred, and apply inconsistent levels of harm (i.e., how much of the privileged information will be "outed" following the accidental waiver).

In the corporate setting, the more information is shared with the lawyer, the higher the risk of inadvertent waiver. Therefore, waiver liability and harm rules influence the amount of information exchanged between the corporate client and the lawyer. It follows that the quality of legal advice depends on the toughness of the inadvertent waiver doctrine.

If corporations believe that the privilege can be used to conceal illegal or tortuous activities they will have an incentive to reduce the risk of inadvertent waiver. Finally, I showed that corporations can circumvent tough inadvertent waiver regimes by shifting from non-durable to durable precautions.

Multi-Disciplinary Practices

The second chapter discussed the MDP debate. Professionals such as lawyers, accountants and auditors debate the desirability and feasibility of collaborating in MDPs, and the risks that MDPs pose towards their ethical obligations to confidentiality. However, little has been said on whether MDPs enhance or discourage corporate compliance. This chapter therefore concerns the effect of professional privileges in the context of MDPs, given the different comparative law characteristics. The systemic differences on which I focused concerned the behaviour of professionals and the institutional setting. These three differences are captured by (1) pro-activity versus passivity, (2) creativity versus conservatism and (3) the rules versus standards debate.

This chapter analyzed the performance of MDPs, with and without a professional privilege, in comparison to the performance of unprivileged non-MDP (informal) collaborations between professional consultants. This was done by modelling the sequential interaction of the regulator, the consultants and the clients.

The decision of consultants to form MDPs affects the cost of legal advice. It does not in itself affect the ability of the client-firm to pursue more profitable yet illegal actions. This latter option is only affected by the existence of the privilege, which is determined by the regulator.

Building on this fundamental understanding I concluded that forming MDPs should always be the dominant strategy for professional consultants. I then proceeded to examine when a regulator should grant a privilege to MDPs. I found that this depends largely on the proportions of legal and illegal avenues of action available to the firm, the firm's knowledge of the law, and the conservatism or pro-activity of the consultants.

I concluded that when consultants only advise about the legality of the contemplated action chosen by the firm and do not direct the firm to the most profitable action, then the higher the proportion of legal avenues, the more socially desirable it is to grant a privilege to MDPs. Furthermore, granting a privilege to MDPs will have a higher impact on social welfare under a standards-regime than under a rules-regime. Allowing for the pro-activity of consultants however, changes the results dramatically. I showed that granting a privilege to MDPs would not be socially desirable in a system dominated by pro-active consultants.

The model fortifies the institutional approach of the surveyed legal jurisdictions. For example, given the pro-activity and creativity of Anglo-American lawyers and accountants, the refusal of regulators to extend a privilege to accountants decreases the willingness of lawyers to form MDPs with them, which is the socially preferred outcome. In contrast, if German professionals tend to be more conservative, and given that German law is standards-based, the traditional endorsement of MDPs in Germany is justified and produces a positive effect on compliance.

Finally, there is a discussion in the German legal literature as to which of the professional groups should govern an MDP of lawyers and auditors. As a policy recommendation, the answer that emerges from this analysis is that if one professional group is obliged to render conservative consulting services and the other is not, the group that subscribes to the conservative ethics should be placed in charge of the MDP.

The Reporter's Privilege

The reporter's privilege in the corporate context aims to facilitate the flow of information from corporate insiders to the media. Insiders may hold valuable information that can enable the market actors to monitor the firm or to exert their "exit" rights. However, insiders may disseminate false information, either intentionally or due to carelessness. The law of defamation is designed to protect the reputation of the firms in such a case. The conflict between reputation and the flow of information to the public is inherent to all jurisdictions. The objective of the legal system should be to ensure the flow of as much *truthful* information as possible about corporate wrongdoing and the suppression of as much *false* information as possible.

In the jurisdictions surveyed here two fundamentally contrasting legal mechanisms are used in order to solve this conflict. Under the English Rule, the onus in a defamation lawsuit is on the defendant-reporter to show that the information that he published is true (or that he had taken due care to ensure that it is true). In contrast, the American Rule puts the burden on the plaintiff-firm to show that the story is false.

Modelling the interaction in court results in the conclusion that the American Rule is weakly superior to the English Rule in achieving the objective of maximizing true stories and minimizing false stories, regardless of whether sources leak more true stories or more false stories, provided that the source's utility from leaking is small. The English Rule, which is tough towards the media, is optimal when sources expect to obtain high gains and suffer small sanctions from leaking.

The applications of the model run beyond the corporate setting. Whenever the court can identify that confidential sources face a systematically high, or low, ratio of benefits to sanctions from leaking, the English Rule, or the American Rule, should be applied, respectively. In the business arena, for example, a similar systematically high ratio may be attributed to short-sellers that disseminate false negative rumours about a firm. Since short-sellers stand to gain from the decline in the firm's value and can expect only a small sanction for disseminating rumours, the English Rule would be optimal in deterring the publication of such information.

The discussion of comparative law also reviews the unique German solution: allowing the plaintiff-firm to choose between monetary compensation (where the English Rule applies in court) and non-monetary remedies (where the American Rule applies). I conclude that the German Rule, though more complex than its Anglo-American counterparts, has one significant advantage: the use of non-monetary remedies means that *all* information is published, however, if the information is deemed to be false, an additional publication (correction or retraction) is published in order to correct the false impression. Hence, the German solution provides more information to the public, since the knowledge that false information has been leaked could be valuable in itself.

Final Note: Looking at the Big Picture

After analyzing the professional testimonial privileges of the three market actors, something can be remarked on the interaction between the privileges.

The professional testimonial privilege is a mechanism that trades off ex-post efficiency for ex-ante efficiency. By trading off the accuracy of adjudication (thereby decreasing ex-post efficiency), the professional privilege presumably increases the ability of professional consultants, like lawyers and accountants, to furnish their clients with advice that will direct the clients to socially desirable, legally compliant, avenues of actions (thereby enhancing ex-ante efficiency). The professional privilege is therefore desirable when the ex-ante increase in social welfare gained as a result of more corporate clients opting for compliant behavior is greater than the welfare loss suffered by private litigants and by society as a whole (due to inaccurate precedents) as a result of inaccurate judgments.

Whilst the reporter's privilege also trades off ex-post and ex-ante efficiency, that is, the suppression ex-post of the identity of confidential sources in order to encourage ex-ante information flow from sources, through the reporters, to the market, it is different from the privileges of lawyers and accountants. First of all, it lacks the attribute of being an agency relationship which is often cited as the basis for the privilege of free professions ("Freie Berüfe"). The reporter is not the agent of the confidential source.

Secondly, the function promoted by the reporter's privilege in the market differs from that of the privilege of relational gatekeepers. Relational gatekeepers monitor firms in order to prevent wrongdoing from taking place, thereby enhancing ex-ante compliance. The professional privilege of these consultants (if and when it is welfare enhancing) increases the probability that wrongdoing is prevented at the cost of inaccurate adjudication. In contrast, the reporter's work is done ex-post. It exposes the wrongdoing after it has occurred. Therefore, the reporter's product is valuable as a deterrent, (only?) if the market can efficiently deter wrongdoing. If the latter condition holds, then the media can complement the work of enforcement authorities in detecting wrongdoing.

The media can also ensure that corporations comply with moral, non-legal, norms. Since public "shaming" (i.e., reputation loss) can be an effective tool, even behavior that does not violate legal norms but affects the reputation of firms in the eyes of consumers, can be deterred by the media. For example, consumers may boycott a fashion company if they learn though confidential sources that the firm buys fabrics from "sweat shops" in developing countries. When occupying this role, the media complements relational gatekeepers whose functions are usually restricted to monitoring legal compliance.

To a certain degree, media and relational gatekeepers may also be substitutes. If relational gatekeepers fail to optimally prevent wrongdoing ex-ante, then it is possible to use the media as a mechanism of ex-post deterrence. Therefore, ensuring a strong securities market requires the social welfare planner to consider the efficiency implications of the professional privileges on the production of compliance. The implications are as follows:

- If the systemic legal structure produces only a weakly welfare enhancing professional privilege for relational gatekeepers (lawyers, accountants, auditors or MDPs), then the regulator should guarantee a high level of deterrence by setting up the optimal application of the reporter's privilege in order to increase the transparency of corporations.
- If the systemic legal structure is such that the professional privilege of relational gatekeepers is only socially detrimental, then the regulator should take steps to narrow the scope of this privilege, and simultaneously enhance the reporter's privilege.

From the legal systems surveyed here, it seems that the Anglo-American jurisdictions present the most disconcerting signs with regards to the weakness, or possibly detrimental affects, of the privileges of relational gatekeepers. These jurisdictions also rely heavily on information and transparency for monitoring and control of the capital markets. It is therefore proposed that the reporter's privilege should be strengthened in these jurisdictions, in accordance with the application developed here.

In Germany, the importation of Anglo-American shareholder culture and the expansion of Anglo-American legal services into Europe should raise attention to the changes that may follow. The strong privileges that enhance welfare in the hands of "conservative" consultants may become disadvantageous if those consultants turn into pro-active rent-seeking relational gatekeepers.

Bibliography

ABA Committee on Multidisciplinary Practice, Report to the House of Delegates (1999). Available from: www.abanet.org/cpr/mdpreport.html (last visited: February 7, 2006)

Akerlof, George A., "The Market for 'Lemons': Quality Uncertainty and the Market Mechanism" (1970) 84(3) *The Quarterly Journal of Economics*, 488.

Alexander, Lawrence B., "Looking Out for the Watchdogs: A Legislative Proposal Limiting the Newsgathering Privilege to Journalists in the Greatest Need of Protection for Sources or Information" (2002) 20 *Yale Law & Policy Review*, 97.

Alexander, Vincent A., "The Corporate Attorney Client Privilege: A Study of the Participants" (1989) 63 *St. John's L. Rev.*, 191.

Alfes, Holger, **Das Anwaltsgeheimnis des Syndikusanwalts und des fest angestellten Unternehmensjuristen** (Diss., Verlag Recht und Wirtschaft, Heidelberg, 1998).

Allen, Ronald J. et al, "A Positive Theory of the Attorney-Client Privilege and the Work Product Doctrine" (1990) 19(2) *Jour. of Legal Studies*, 359.

Arlen, Jennifer, "The Potentially Perverse Effects of Corporate Criminal Liability" (1994) 23 *Jour. of Legal Studies*, 833.

Arlen, Jennifer and William J. Carney, "Vicarious Liability for Fraud on Securities Markets: Theory and Evidence" 1992 *U. of Illinois L. Rev.* 691.

Arlen, Jennifer and Renier Kraakman, "Controlling Corporate Misconduct: An Analysis of Corporate Liability regimes" (1997) 72 *New York University Law Review*, 687.

"Attorney Client Privilege: Perceptions and Implications in the Corporate Setting", A Survey of Personnel, Evidence Project, American University, April 1998.

Auburn, Jonathan, **Legal Professional Privilege – Law & Theory** (Hart Publishing, Oxford, 2000).

Baetzgen, Eberhard, **Das Berufsgeheimnis des Rechts- und Steuerberatenden sowie den Wirtschaftsprüfenden Berufe gegenüber den Steuerbehörden** (Köln, 1970).

Baker, Edwin, "The Media That Citizens Need" (1998) 147 *U. of Pennsylvania L. Rev.*, 317.

Bates, Stephen, "The Reporter's Privilege Then and Now" (2000) The Joan Shorenstein Center, Harvard University, *Research Paper R-23*.

Barton, Benjamin H., "Why Do We Regulate Lawyers?: An Economic Analysis of the Justifications for Entry and Conduct Regulation" (2001) 33 *Arizona State Law Journal*, 429.

Baum, Harald, "Change of Governance in Historic Perspective: The German Experience" (2005) ECGI Law Working Paper 28/2005, 4.

Baums, Theodor and Kenneth E. Scott, "Taking Shareholder Protection Seriously? Corporate Governance in the United States and Germany" (2003) Insitut für Bankrecht, Johann Wolfgang Goethe University (Frankfurt am Main), working paper 119.

Becht Marco and Ekkehart Boehmer, "Voting Control in German Corporations" (2003) 23 *International Review of Law and Economics*, 1, 7.

Becker, Gary S., "A Theory of Competition among Pressure Groups for Political Influence" (1983) *The Quarterly Jour. of Economics*, 371.

Bell, Martin, **Anwaltshaftung gegenüber Dritten** (Deutscher Anwalt Verlag, Bonn, 1996),

Ben Basat, Caryl and Julian D. Nihill, "International Legal Developments in Review: Corporate Counsel" (1997), 31 *International Lawyer* 245.

Bentham , Jeremy, **A treatise on Judicial Evidence**, 1825 (Rothman & Co, 1981).

Berger, Linda, "Shielding the Unmedia: Using the Process of Journalism to Protect the Journalist's Privilege in an Infinite Universe of Publication" (2003) 39 *Houston L. Rev.*, 1371 (hereinafter – Berger (2003)).

Berger, Robert G., "The 'No Source' Presumption: The Harshest Remedy" (1987) 36 *American University Law Review*, 603, 613 (hereinafter – Berger (1987)).

Bezanson, Randall P., "The Developing Law of Editorial Judgement" (1999), 78 *Nebraska L. Rev.*, 754.

Bezanson Randall P. and Gilbert Cranberg, "Institutional Reckless Disregard for Truth in Public Defamation Actions Against the Press" (2005) 90 *Iowa Law Review*, 887.

Black, Bernard S., "The Legal and Institutional Preconditions for Strong Securities Markets" (2001) 48 *UCLA Law Review*, 781.

Bok, Sisela, **Secrets – On the Ethics of Concealment and Revelation** (Vintage Books, NY, 1983).

Boudreaux, Donald, "Per Se Rules" in **The New Palgrave Dictionary of Economics and the Law**, Peter Newman, ed. (UK, 1998) Vol. III, 31.

Bovitz, Gregory L., James N. Druckman & Arthur Lupia, "When Can a News Organization Lead Public Opinion? Ideology versus Market Forces in Decisions to Make News" (2002) *Public Choice*, 113.

Bratton, William W., "Enron, Sarbanes-Oxley and Accounting: Rules versus Principles versus Rents" (2003) 48 *Villanova Law Review*, 1023.

Brodsky, David M. et al., "The Auditor's Need for the Client's Detailed Information vs. The Client's Need to Preserve the Attorney Client Privilege and Work Product Protection: The Debate, the Problems and Proposed Solutions" (2004) available from: www.abanet.org/buslaw/attorneyclient/publichearing20050211/testimony/brodsky2.pdf (last visited: February 20, 2006).

Brown, George H., "Financial Institution Lawyers as Quasi-public Enforcers" (1994) 7 *Georgetown J. of Legal Ethics*, 637.

Brown, J.P., "Toward an Economic Theory of Liability" (1973) 2 *Journal of Legal Studies*, 323.

Browne, Desmond, "Libel and Publication in the Public Interest", *Law for Journalists Conference* (December 2005) available from: www.5rb.com (last visited: July 10, 2006).

Bruns, Alexander, **Informationsansprüche gegen Medien** (Tübingen, 1997) (hereinafter – Bruns (German))

Bruns, Alexander, "Access to Media Sources in Defamation Litigation in The United States and Germany" (2000) 10 *Duke Journal of International and Comparative Law*, 283.

Buhart, Jacques, "Confidentiality of Advice Given by In-House Legal Counsel Practicing in the European Union", 2 (available from www.acca.com. Last viewed: 25.11.2005).

Bundy, Stephan and Einer E. Elhauge, "Do Lawyers Improve the Adversary System? A General Theory of Litigation Advice and its Regulation" (1991) 79 *Cal. L. Rev.*, 313.

Calvert, Clay, "The Reporter's Privilege v. The Corporate Interest Muzzle: Phillip Morris Cos Inc., v. ABC Inc." (1996) 22 *University of Dayton Law Review*, 1.

Causey, Denzil and Frances McNair, "An Analysis of State Accountant-Client Privilege Statutes and Public Policy Implications for the Accountant-Client Relationship" (1990) 27 *American Business L. Jour.*, 535.

Choi, Stephen, "Market Lessons for Gatekeepers" (1998) 92 *Northwestern U. L. Rev.*, 916.

Clermont, Kevin M. and Emily Sherwin, "A Comparative View of Standards of Proof" (2002) 50 *American Journal of Comparative Law*, 243.

Coase, Ronald H., "The Nature of the Firm" (1937) *Economica*, 392.

Coase, Ronald H., "The Market for Goods and the Market for Ideas" (1974) 64 *The American Economic review*, 384.

Coffee, John C., "What Caused Enron? A Capsule Social and Economic History of the 1990's" (2003) Columbia Law School, Working Paper 219.

Cooter, Robert D. and Daniel L. Rubinfeld, "An Economic Model of Legal Discovery", (1994) 23 *Jour. Of Legal Studies*, 435.

Cramton, Roger C., "Enron and the Corporate Lawyer: A Primer on Legal and Ethical Issues" (2002), 58 *Business Lawyer*, 143.

Croson, Rachel and Robert H. Mnookin, "Does Disputing through Agents Enhance Cooperation? Experimental Evidence" (1997) 26 *Jour. Of Legal Studies*, 331.

Cross On Evidence – Eighth New Zealand Edition, (Wellington, Lexisnexis NZ Limited, 2005).

Cunningham, Lawrence A., "Sharing Accounting's Burden: Business Lawyers in Enron's Dark Shadows" (2002) 57 Business Lawyer, 1421.

Curran, Christopher, "Regulation of the Professions" in **The New Palgrave Dictionary of Economics and the Law**, Peter Newman, ed. (UK, 1998) Vol. III, 247.

Daly, Mary C., "The Cultural, Ethical and Legal Challenges in Lawyering for a Global Organization: The Role of the General Counsel" (1997) 46 *Emory Law Journal*, 1057 (Hereinafter - Daly (1997)).

Daly, Mary C., "Monopolist, Aristocrat, or Entrepreneur?: A Comparative Perspective on the Future of Multidisciplinary Partnerships in the United States, France, Germany, and the England after the Disintegration of Andersen Legal" (2002) 80 *Washingron University Law Quarterly*, 589.

Daly, Mary C., "The Dichotomy between Standards and Rules: A New Way of Understanding the Differences in Perceptions of Lawyer Codes of Conduct by U.S. and Foreign Lawyers" (1999) 32 *Vanderbilt Journal of Transnational Law*, 1117 (hereinafter - Daly (1999)).

Damaska, Mirjan, "The Uncertain Fate of Evidentiary Transplants: Anglo-American and Continental Experiments" (1997) 45 *American Journal of Comparative Law*, 839.

Day, Robert G., "Administrative Watchdogs or Zealous Advocates? Implications for Legal Ethics in the Fact of Expanded Attorney Liability" (1993) 45 *Stanford L. Rev.*, 645.

Deckenbrock, Christian, Interessenkonflikte bei Wirtschaftsprüfern und Rechtsanwälten unter dem besonderen Aspekt der beruflichen Verschwiegenheitspflicht, BB 2002, 2453.

DeMott, Deborah A., "The Discrete Roles of General Counsel" (2005) 74 *Fordham Law Review*, 955.

Demougin, Dominique and Claude Fluet, "Preponderance of Evidence" (May 2002). CESifo Working Paper Series No. 725. Available at SSRN: http://ssrn.com/abstract=316767

Dewatripont, Mathias and Jean Tirole, "Advocacy" (1999) 107(1) *The Journal of Political Economy*, 1.

Dienes, C. Thomas, Lee Levine & Robert C. Lind, **Newsgathering and the Law**, (2nd Ed., Lexis Law Publishing, 1999).

Docherty, Bonnie, "Defamation Law: Positive Jurisprudence" (2000) 13 *Harvard Human Rights Journal*, 263.

Dyck, Alexander, Adair Morse and Luigi Zingales, "Who Blows the Whistle on Corporate Fraud?" (2007) University of Chicago Working Papers. The paper can be obtained from: www.ssrn.com/abstract=959410.

Dyck, Alexander and Luigi Zingales, "The Corporate Governance Role of the Media" (2002) *NBER Working Paper* 9309, available from: www.nber.org/papers/w9309.

Easterbrook, Frank, "Insider Trading, Secret Agents, Evidentiary Privileges, and the Production of Information" (1981) *Supreme Court Review*, 309.

Ede, Roger, "Study of the Laws of Evidence in Criminal Proceedings Throughout the European Union" (Oct. 2004) The Law Society of England & Wales.

Fechner, Frank, **Medienrecht** (6. Auf., Mohr Siebek, 2005):

Fischel, Daniel R., "Lawyers and Confidentiality" (1998) 65 *U. Chicago L. Rev.*, 1.

Flower, John, **European Financial Reporting – Adapting to a Changing World** (New York, Palgrave MacMillan, 2004)

Fox, Loren, **Enron – The Rise and Fall** (New Jersey, 2003).

Franklin, Marc A. and Daniel J. Bussel, "The Plaintiff's Burden in Defamation: Awareness and Falsity" (1984) 25 *William and Mary Law Review*, 825.

Franks, Julian and Colin Mayer, "Ownership and Control in Europe" in **The New Palgrave Dictionary of Economics and the Law**, Peter Newman, ed. (UK, 1998) Vol. II, 722.

Franks, Julian and Colin Mayer, "Ownership and Control of German Corporations" (2001) 14(4) *The Review of Financial Studies*, 943 (hereinafter – franks & Mayer, (2001)).

Freckmann, Anke and Thomas Wegerich, **The German Legal System** (Sweet & Maxwell, London, 1999).

Furman, Joshua, "Cybersmear or CyberSlapp: Analysing Defamation Suits against Online John Does as Strategic Law Suits against Public Participation" (2001) 25 *Seattle University Law Review*, 213.

Furse, Mark, **Competition Law of the UK and the EC**, (3rd Ed., Oxford University Press, New York, 2002).

Furubotn, Eirik E. and Rudolf Richter, **Institutional and Economic Theory** (The University of Michigan Press, Ann Arbor, 1998).

Garfield, Alan E., "Promises of Silence: Contract Law and Freedom of Speech" (1998) 83 *Cornell Law Review*, 261.

Gatley on Libel and Slander, (10th Ed., Milmo et al, ed.)(Sweet & Maxwell, London, 2004).

Gergacz, John W., **Attorney Corporate Client Privilege**, (2nd Ed., Garland Law Publishing, NY, 1990).

Gibbons, Robert, **A Primer in Game Theory** (Prentice Hall, 1992)

Gilles, Susan M., "Taking First Amendment Procedures seriously: An Analysis of Process in Libel Litigation" (1998) 58 *Ohio State Law Journal*, 1753.

Gillet, Phillip w., "The Federal Tax-Practitioner Client Privilege (I.R.C. section 7525): A Shield to Cloak Confidential Communication or a Dagger for both the Practitioner and the Client?" (2000) 44 *UMKC*, 33.

Gilson, Ronald J., "The Devolution of the Legal Profession: A Demand Side Perspective" (1990) 49 *Maryland L. Rev.*, 769.

Goergen, Marc and Luc Renneboog, "Why Are the level of Control (So) Different in German and UK Companies? Evidence From Initial Public Offering" (2003) *ECGI Finance Working Paper* 07/2003 (hereinafter – Goergen & Renneboog).

Goergen, Marc et al., "Recent Developments in German Corporate Governance" (2004) ECGI Finance Working Paper 41/2004, 1.

Gordon, Jeffrey N., "Pathways to Corporate Convergence? Two Steps on the Road to Shareholder Capitalism in Germany: Deutsche Telekom and DaimlerChrysler" (2000) *Columbia Law School, The Center for Law & Economics Studies*, Working Paper 161.

Handman, Laura R., "Protection of Confidential Sources: A Moral, Legal and Civic Duty" (2005) 19 *Notre Dame Journal of Legal Ethics and Public Policy*, 573.

Hawkins, Rees M., "Not 'If' but 'When' and 'How': A Look at Existing De Facto Multidisciplinary Practices and What They Can Teach Us About the Ongoing Debate" (2005) 83 *N. Carolina Law Review*, 481.

Heinicke, Petra, "Multidisciplinary Partnerships" in: **Ethics of Lawyers**, Council of Europe (2000).

Henssler, Martin, Das Anwaltliche Berufsgeheimnis, NJW 1994, 1817.

Hesse, Karina, "The Right of Reply under German Press Law" in Holznagel, Bernd & Catja Möller (Eds.) **Media Law in Europe - Conference Proceedings** (Hamburg, Baden-Baden, 1994).

Himmelsbach, Gero, **Der Schutz des Medieninformanten im Zivilprozess** (Diss. München, 1998).

Hirst, D. Eric, "Auditors' Sensitivity to Source Reliability" (1994) 32(1) *Jour. Of Accounting Reaserch*, 113.

Hopt, Klaus J., "Takeovers, Secrecy and Conflicts of Interest: Problems for Boards and Banks" (2002) *ECGI Law Working Paper* 03/2002, www.ssrn.com/abstract_id=343520.

Hopt, Klaus J. and Patrick C. Leyens, "Board Models in Europe: Recent Developments of Internal Corporate Governance Structures in Germany, The United Kingdom, France and Italy" (2004) *ECGI Law Working Paper* 18/2004.

Jackson, D. Mark, "The Corporate Defamation Plaintiff in the Era of SLAPP: Revisiting New York Times v. Sullivan" (2001) 9 *William & Mary Bill of Rights Journal*, 491.

Jensen, Michael C. and William H. Meckling, "Theory of the Firm: Managerial Behavior, Agency Costs and Ownership Structure" (1976), 3(4) *Journal of Financial Economics*.

Johnson, Martin, "Rationalizing Betrayal: Incentives, Institutions and the Willingness of Journalists to Burn their Sources" (2003) 7 available from: faculty.ucr.edu/~**martin**j/research/RationalizingBetrayal.pdf (last visited: 22.12.2005).

Johnson, Simon, Rafael La Porta, Florencio Lopez de Silanes, and Andrei Schleifer, "Tunneling" (2000) 90 *American Economic Review*, 22.

Kaplan et al., "Phases of German Civil Procedure" (1958) 71 *Harvard Law Review* 1193.

Kaplow, Louis, "The Value of Accuracy in Adjudication: An Economic Analysis" (1994) 23 *Journal of Legal Studies*, 307.

Kaplow, Lewis and Steven Shavell, "Legal Advice About Information to Present in Litigation: Its Effects and Social Desirability" (1989) 102 *Harvard L. Rev.*, 565 (hereinafter - Kaplow & Shavell (1989)).

Kaplow, Lewis and Steven Shavell, "Legal Advice About Acts Already Committed" (1990) 10 *Intl. Rev. of Law and Econ.*, 149 (hereinafter - Kaplow & Shavell (1990)).

Kaplow, Lewis and Steven Shavell, "The Private Versus Socially Optimal Provision of Ex-Ante Legal Advice" (1992) 8(2) *The Jour. Of Law Econ. & Org.*, 306 (hereinafter Kaplow & Shavell (1992)).

Kase, Kathryn M., "When a Promise Is not a Promise: The Legal Consequences for Journalists Who Break Promises of Confidentiality to Sources" (1990) 12 *Hastings Communications & Entertainment Law Journal*, 565.

Kirtley, Jane E., "Vanity and Vexation: Shifting the Focus to Media Conduct" (1996) 4 William & Mary Bill of Rights Journal 1069.

Kleine-Cosack, Michael, Neuordnung des anwaltlichen Berufsrechts, NJW 1994, 2249.

Kornhauser, Lewis A., "An Economic Analysis of the Choice between Enterprise and Personal Liability for Accidents" (1982) 70 *California Law Review*, 1345.

Korthals Altes, Willem F., "The Journalistic Privilege: A Dutch Proposal for Legislation", (1992) *Public Law* 73.

Kostant, Peter C., "Paradigm Regained: How Competition from Accounting Firms May Help Corporate Attorneys to Recapture the Ethical High Ground" (1999) 20 *Pace L. Rev.* 43.

Kostant, Peter C., "Breading Better Watchdogs: Multidisciplinary Partnerships in Corporate Legal Practice" (2001) 84 *Minnesota Law Review*, 1213.

Kötz, Hein, "Civil Justice Systems in Europe and the United States" (2000) 13 *Duke Law Journal of Comparative and International Law* 62.

Kraakman, Renier, "Gatekeepers: The Anatomy of a Third-Party Enforcement Strategy" (1986) 2 Jour. Of Law, Econ. & Org. 53.

Kübler, Friedrich, "Ehrenschutz, Selbstbestimmung und Demokratie" (1999) NJW 1999, 1281.

La Porta, Rafael et al., "Law and Finance" (1998) 106(6) *The Journal of Political Economy*, 1113.

La Porta, Rafael, et al., "Ownership Around the World" (1999) 54 *Journal of Finance*, 471.

Langevoort, Donald C., "Where Were the Lawyers? A Behavioral Inquiry into Lawyers' Responsibility for Clients' Fraud" (1993) 46 *Vanderbilt L. Rev.*, 75.

Langevoort, Donald C., "Ego, Human Behavior, and Law" (1995) 81 *Virginia L. Rev.*, 853.

Langevoort, Donald C. and Robert K. Rasmusen, "Skewing the Results: The Role of Lawyers in Transmitting Legal Rules" (1997) 5 *Sou. Cal. Interdisciplinary L. Jour.*, 375.

Langevoort, Donald C., "Organized Illusions: A Behavioral Theory of Why Corporations Mislead Stock Market Investors and Cause Other Social Harms" (1997) 146 *U. of Pennsylvania L. Rev.*, 141.

Larsen, Kara A., "The Demise of the First Amendment Based Reporter's Privilege: Why This Current Trend Should Not Surprise the Media" (2005) 37 *Conn. Law Rev.*, 1235.

Levinson, Sanford, "Testimonial Privileges and the Preferences of Friendship" (1984) *Duke L. Jour.*, 631.

Louis, Henock et al., "Managers' and Investors' Responses to Media Exposure of Board Ineffectiveness" (University of Southern California, 2004).

Lex Mundi, "In House Counsel and the Attorney Client Privilege – A Multi Jurisdictional Survey" (September 2005), 33. Available from www.LexMundi.com (last viewed: 22.12.2005). (Hereinafter - "Lex Mundi Survey").

Lichtner, Rolf, **Die Verschwiegenheitspflicht des Wirtschaftsprüfers im Vergleich mit dem sonstigen Rechts und Steuerberatenden Berufen** (Osnabrück, 1999).

Lidsky, Lyrissa Barnett, "Silencing John Doe: Defamation & Discourse in Cyberspace" (2000) 49 *Duke Law Journal*, 855.

Lindenberg, Frank, **Wahrheitspflicht und Dritthaftung des Rechtsanwalts im Zivilverfahren** (Deutscher Anwalt Verlag, Diss. Köln, 2001).

Lindberg, Marian E., "Source Protection in Libel Suits After Herbert v Lando" (1981) 81 *Columbia Law Review*, 338.

Löffler, Martin, **PresseRecht**, (4. Auf., Beck, 1997).

Löffler, Martin and Reinhardt Ricker, **Handbuch des Presserecht** (4. Auf., Beck, 2000).

Loudenslager, Michael W., "Cover Me: The Effects of Attorney Accountant Multidisciplinary Practices on the Protection of the Attorney-Client Privilege" (2001) 53 *Baylor Law Review*, 33.

Lucci, John P., "New York Revises Ethics Rules to Permit Limited MDPS: A Critical Analysis of the New York Approach, the Future of the MDP Debate after Enron and Recommendations for other Jurisdictions" (2003) 8 *Fordham Journal of Corporate and Financial Law*, 151.

Loveland, Ian, "The Ongoing Evolution of Reynolds Privilege in Domestic Libel Law" (2003) *Entertainment Law Review*, 14(7), 178.

Mattei, Ugo and Alberto Monti, "Comparative Law and Economics: Borrowing and Resistance" (2001) 1(2) *Global Jurist Frontiers*, Article 5, 1.

Matthews, Paul and Hodge M. Malek, **Disclosure** (2nd Ed., Sweet & Maxwell, London, 2000).

Media Diversity in Europe, Report prepared by the Advisory Panel on Media Diversity (APMD) on media concentrations, pluralism and diversity questions, Strasbourg, Dec. 2002.

Mensching, Michael, **Das Zeugnisverweigerungsrecht der Medien** (Bonn, 2000).

Michalski, Lutz und Volker Römermann, Interprofessionelle Zusammenarbeit von Rechtsanwälten, NJW 1996, 3233.

Milgrom, Paul and John Roberts, "Relying on the Information of Interested Parties" (1986) 17 *The RAND Journal of Economics*, 18.

Miller, Gregory S., "The Press as a Watchdog for Accounting Fraud" (2003) *Harvard Business School Working Paper.*

Möllers, Thomas M. J., "The Progress of German Information Disclosure Requirements: A Comparative Law Prospective in Light of Recent Developments in European Capital Markets Law" (2005) 30 *N.C. Journal of Int'l Law & Com*, 279.

Monk, Carl C., "Evidentiary Privilege for Journalists' Sources: Theory and Statutory Protection" (1986) 51 *Missouri L. Rev.*, 1.

Münchener Kommentar zum BGB, (Heermann, 5. Auf., 2005)

Nestler, Jeffrey S., "The Underprivileged Profession: The Case for Supreme Court Recognition of the Journalist's Privilege" (2005) 154 *University of Pennsylvania Law Review*, 201.

Newman, Joel S., "Tax Practice and Privilege: A Tale of Two Countries" (2003) *Wake Forest University School of Law, Public Law and Legal Theory*, Research Paper 03-04.

Nnona, George C., "Multidisciplinary Practice in the International Context: Realigning the Perspective on the European Union's Regulatory Regime" (2004) 37 *Cornell International Law Journal*, 115.

O'Connor, Sean M., "Be Careful What You Wish For: How Accountants and Congress Created the Problem of Auditor Independence" (2004) 45 *Boston College Law Review*, 741.

Oliva, Robert R., "The CPA Client Privilege under I.R.C. §7525: Does it Protect Client Confidentiality?" (2003) at p. 4. (available at www.cba.uri.edu).

Ourednick, Karel, "Multidisciplinary Practice and Professional Responsibility after Enron" (2003) 4 *Florida Coastal Law Journal*, 167.

Painter, Richard W., "Toward a Market for Lawyer Disclosure Services: In Search of Optimal Whistle-blowing Rules" (1995) 63 *George Washington L. Rev.*, 221.

Painter, Richard W., "Lawyers' Rules, Auditors' Rules and the Psychology of Concealment" (2000) 84 *Minnesota L. Rev.*, 1399.

Painter, Richard W., "Convergence and Competition in Rules Governing Lawyers and Auditors" (2004) University of Illinois College of Law, *Law and Economics Working Paper* 5, available from www.bepress.com.

Parker, Richard, "Journalism and Economics: The Tangled Webs of Profession, Narrative, and Responsibility in a Modern Democracy" (1997) *Discussion paper D-25*, The Joan Shorenstein center on press, politics and public policy.

Palandt Kommentar zum BGB (Auflage 63, 2004) Buch 2 Ab. 8.

Phillips, Richard M., "Client Fraud and the Securities Lawyer's Duty of Confidentiality" (1992) 49 *Washington & Lee L. Rev.*, 823.

Pietsch, Christa, **Berufliche Privilegien und Zeugnisverweigerungsrechte im Englischen und Deutschen Zivilprozess** (Diss. Göttingen 1974).

Pluskat, Sorika, Chancen für eine Interprofessionelle GmbH von Rechtsanwälten, Steuerberatern und Wirtschaftsprüfern mit gleichberechtigten Gesellschaftern - Diskussionsanstoß und Reformvorschlag, DStR 2004, 58.

Posner, Eric, "The Regulation of Groups: The Influence of Legal and Non-Legal Sanctions on Collective Action" (1996) 63 *University of Chicago Law Review*, 133.

Posner, Richard A., "Free Speech in an Economic Perspective" (1986) 20 *Suffolk University Law Review*, 1.

Posner, Richard A., "Privacy" in **The New Palgrave Dictionary of Economics and the Law**, Peter Newman, ed. (UK, 1998) Vol. III, 103.

Prentice, Robert A., "The Case of the Irrational Auditor: A Behavioral Insight into Securities Fraud Litigation" (2000) 95 *Northwestern U. L. Rev.*, 133.

Prinz, Matthias, Geldentschädigung bei Persönlichkeitsrechtsverletzungen durch Medien, NJW 1996, 953 (hereinafter – Prinz (1996)).

Prinz, Matthias und Butz Peters, **Medienrecht** (Beck, München, 1999) (hereinafter – Prinz).

"The Professional Secret, Confidentiality and Legal Professional secret in Europe" (The Edward's Report Update 2003) CCBE Council of the Bars and Law Societies of the European Union. Available from: www.ccbe.org/doc/En/update_edwards_report_en.pdf (last visited 14.7.2005).

Reitz, John C., "Why We Probably Cannot Adopt the German Advantage in Civil Procedure" (1990) 75 *Iowa Law Review*, 987, 990.

Roe, Marc J., "Chaos and Evolution in Law and Economics" (1996) 109 *Harvard Law Review*, 641.

Rhode, Deborah L., "Ethical Perspectives on Legal Practice" (1985) 37 *Stanford L. Rev.*, 589.

Rotunda, Ronald D., "The Notice of Withdrawal and the New Model Rules of Professional Conduct: Blowing the Whistle and Waiving the Red Flag" (1984) 63 *Oregon Law Review* 455 (hereinafter – Rotunda (1984)).

Rotunda, Ronald D., **Professional Responsibility** (6th ed., West Group, 2002).

Rühl, Giesela, "Preparing Germany for the 21st Century: The Reform of the Code of Civil Procedure" (2005) 6(6) *German Law Journal*, 909.

Ryan, Patrick S., "Understanding Director & Officer Liability in Germany for Dissemination of False Information: Perspectives from an Outsider" (2003) 4(5) *German Law Journal*, 439.

Savage, Joseph and J. Luster, "Getting the Help You Need: Privileges Protecting Non-legal Professionals", *White Collar Crime Reporter* (May 2005).

Schäfer, Hans-Bernd and Andreas Schoenenberger, "Strict Liability versus Negligence" (1999) in Bouckaert, Boudewijn and De Geest, Gerrit (eds.), **Encyclopedia of Law and Economics, Volume I. The History and Methodology of Law and Economics**, (Cheltenham, Edward Elgar), 597.

Schäfer, Hans-Bernd and Claus Ott, "Begruendung und Bemessung des Schadenserzatzes wegen entgangener Sachnutzung" (1986) 7 *Zeitschrift fuer Wirtschaftsrecht*, 613.

Schmidt, Matthias, "'Whistle-blowing' Regulation and Accounting Standards Enforcement in Germany and Europe – an Economic Perspective" (2004) (manuscript to be published in the Intl. Rev. of Law and Econ.)

Schramm, Wibke, Interessenkonflikte bei Wirtschaftsprüfern, Steuerberatern und Rechtsanwälten unter dem besonderen Aspekt der beruflichen Verschwiegenheit, DStR 2003, 1316.

Shavell, Steven, "Legal Advice About Contemplated Acts: The Decision to Obtain Advice, Its Social Desirability, and Protection of Confidentiality" (1988) 17 *Jour. of Legal Studies*, 123, 130 (hereinafter Shavell (1988)).

Shavell, Steven, "Legal Advice" in **The New Palgrave Dictionary of Economics and the Law**, Peter Newman, ed. (UK, 1998) Vol. II, 516.

Simon, Todd F., "Libel as Malpractice: News Media Ethics and the Standard of Care" (1984) 53 *Fordham Law Review*, 449.

Simpson, Brian A.W., "English Common Law" in **The New Palgrave Dictionary of Economics and the Law**, Peter Newman, ed. (UK, 1998).

Skeel, David A., "Shaming in Corporate Law" (2001) 149 *University of Pennsylvania Law Review*, 1843.

Skinner, Douglas J., "Why Firms Voluntarily Disclose Bad News" (1994) 32(1) *Jour. Of Accounting research*, 38.

Soehring, Jörg, Die neuere Rechtsprechung zum Presserecht, NJW 1994, 16.

Spindler, **Bamberger/Roth Kommentar zum BGB** (2004).

Steele, Robert and Jay Black, "Media Ethics Codes and Beyond" (April 2001) *Global Issues Media & Ethics*. The paper is available from the US Department of State website at usinfo.state.gov/journals/itgic/0401/ijge/ijge0401.htm.

Stein, Alex and Daniel J. Seidmann, "The Right to Silence Helps the Innocent: A Game-Theoretic Analysis of the Fifth Amendment Privilege" (2000) 114 *Harvard Law Rev.*, 430.

Strong, J.W. et al. (Eds.), **McCormick on Evidence** (4th ed., St. Paul, Minn., 1992).

Subin, Harry I., "The Lawyer as Superego: Disclosure of Client Confidences to Prevent Harm" (1985) 70 *Iowa L. Rev.*, 1091.

Taupitz, Jochen, **Die Standesordnungen der Freien Berufe** (Walter de Gruyter, Berlin, 1991).

Teeter, Dwight L. and Bill Loving, **Law of Mass Communications** (11th Ed., Foundation Press, New York, 2004).

Terry, Laurel S., "German MDPs: Lessons to Learn" (2000) 84 *Minnesota Law Review*, 1547.

Terry, Laurel S., "MDPs, 'Spinning' and Wouters v NOVA" (2002) 52 *Case Western Reserve Law Review*, 867.

Thornburg, Elizabeth G., "Sanctifying Secrecy: The Mythology of the Corporate Attorney Client Privilege" (1993) 69 *Notre Dame L. Rev.*, 157.

Tullock, Gordon, **Trials on Trial** (Columbia University Press, NY, 1980).

Voorhoof, Dirk, "The Protection of Journalistic Sources Under Fire" (March 2005) available from: www.ifj-europe.org/docs/POS-Voorhoof2005.doc (last visited: 11.8.2005).

Weaver, Russel L. and David F. Partlett, "Defamation, The Media and Free Speech: Australia's Experiment with Expanded Qualified Privilege" (2004) 36 *George Washington International Law Review* 377.

Weinberg, Steve, "ABC, Phillip Morris and the Infamous Apology" (Nov.-Dec. 1995) *Columbia Journalism Review.*

Wenzel, Karl Egbert, **Das Recht der Wort und Bild Berichtstattung: Handbuch des Äußerungsrecht** (4 Auf. Köln 1994).

Wichmann, Herman, **Das Berufsgeheimnis als Grenze des Zeugenbeweises** (Peter Lang Verlag, Frankfurt 2000).

Wigmore J.H. and J.T. McNaughton, **Evidence in Trials at Common Law** (Boston, 1961).

Williams, Alan, Chapter on England and Wales, in Campbell, Christian (ed.) **International Media Liability** (Wiley & Sons, 1997).

Yannucci, Thomas D., "Debunking 'The Big Chill' – Why Defamation Suits by Corporations Are Consistent with the First Amendment" (1995) 39 *St. Louis U. Law Journal*, 1187.

Zacharias, Fred C., "Rethinking Confidentiality" (1989) 74 *Iowa L. Rev.*, 351.

Zampa, Julie M., "Journalist's Privilege: When Deprivation is a Benefit" (1999) 108 *Yale Law Journal*, 1449.

Zöller, Richard, **ZivilProzessOrdnung Kommentar** (25. Auf., Köln, 2005).

Kolibri 360 GmbH
Ferdinand-Jühlke-Straße 7
99095 Erfurt, Deutschland
produktsicherheit@kolibri360.de